inconed

Dodson

McCall's
SEWING BOOK

McCall's
SEWING BOOK

Random House / McCall's

CONTENTS

INTRODUCTION

This is a book for the woman who sews—and for the woman who wants to. It explores the art of sewing in all its facets to show you how to transform a piece of fabric into a lovely gown, how to change a dowdy appearance into an attractive, individual one. For just knowing how to sew is not enough. You must know how to select the right pattern for your figure, your personality, your way of life, and then fit it and finish it to give the clothes you make the smart look of good ready-to-wear ones.

This book has been planned to help you do just that. It takes you step by step through the selection of a becoming and appropriate style, the choice of a flattering fabric, and then into construction. Beginning sewers will find outlined the simple construction methods that will let the merest novice turn out a professional-looking garment. And more experienced sewers will welcome details on advanced construction techniques, as well as the fact-filled chapters on tailoring and home decoration.

Even the woman who seldom sews will find helpful the information on how to choose the most becoming styles, the instructions for mending and remodeling, the wealth of data on selection and care of fabrics valuable, not only for home sewing, but in choosing ready-mades as well.

Sewing can be fun, and easy to do if you take it one detail at a time. You can make it a pleasant, satisfying hobby with the added and long-lasting enjoyment of being able to wear the results of your creativity with pride.

CHAPTER 1

BUILDING A NEW YOU

YOUR GOAL— FASHION PERFECTION

The look of fashion is an intangible thing, difficult to analyze, but easier than you think to achieve. There are several ways to earn a place in the list of "best-dressed" women in your town. You can put yourself in the hands of a top couturier and expect for the price you pay to get dresses made just for you, properly fitted, in the right size, in styles which are most becoming to your face and figure, and in colors and fabrics which are flattering. Or, if you are one of the lucky few who is a "perfect" size 10, 12 or 14, you can find, if you search diligently, ready-made garments that you can wear right off the rack.

Realistically, of course, few women have the money it takes to be a full-time patron of the *haute couture*. Even fewer are so perfectly proportioned that any ready-to-wear garment will fit perfectly without some adjustment to individual measurements. They are subject, too, to the curse of mass production—thousands of copies of their dress—any of which is just waiting to be met at a party, a PTA meeting or at the home of a friend.

Thousands of women are finding that there is a practical answer to their desire for clothes that look right, fit right and have the touch of individuality that a ready-made can never give them. They are becoming their own couturiers, are making their own clothes and at a fraction of what even ready-to-wear would cost. Like them, you too can always be sure of having the right dress in the right color. You can free yourself from the whims of manufacturers, from the dictates of fashion whose current decrees may not be the most becoming styles or hues for you. You can create a new you with a wardrobe tailored to fit *your* specifications.

Personal Analysis

Like the beauty of a work of art, which is dependent upon an artist's ability to create pleasing line composition and use color attractively, fashion perfection is also achieved by correct application of line and color. However, in the case of a fashion design, you are the canvas. And you are a great deal more complex than a flat cloth surface. So the first step in creating the appearance you want is to analyze yourself and decide exactly how you want to look.

Because it is difficult to see oneself as one really is, don't rely on a mirror. A snapshot or two (one full-face, the other side view), preferably in a bathing suit, will give you a better answer. Flaws never seem quite so realistic in a mirror as they do in a picture. And don't be disheartened. Once you know what's wrong, there's a great deal you can do to correct it.

FIGURE CHECK. First study the general effect you present to the world. Are you short or tall, fat or thin, average in weight and height? How is your posture? Are your shoulders squared and straight, or do they have a tired droop? How about your tummy? Is it flat and tucked in? Is your head held confidently high? Is your waistline clearly defined? Are you well proportioned, or do you bulge in the wrong places? Are you tall enough for your width?

Your body measurements can also be revealing, so make a record of them. Measure around chest, bust, waist, abdomen, upper hip, lower hip, thigh, knee, calf, ankle, upper arm and wrist. And measure your height accurately, without shoes and with the height heel you normally wear. Because the appearance of clothes is improved when placed on a well-proportioned figure, now's the time to begin correcting any irregularities. But whether you try to change your proportions or not, measurements have a disconcerting habit of changing, so keep your record up to date.

FACIAL CHECK. Push back your hair and look into the mirror. The ideal facial shape is an oval. Decide whether your face is oval, round, oblong, square or triangular. By choosing the correct neckline you can often make the shape of the face seem to change.

COLOR CHECK. Decide which colors are most flattering to your skin, hair and eye colors. Drape fabrics of different colors over your shoulders and see which bring out the highlights in your hair, emphasize the color of your eyes, make your skin look its glowing best. These are the colors you should stress in your wardrobe planning.

THE EFFECT OF LINE

Since line is a major factor in developing a pleasing appearance, line and the things you can do with it deserve first place in your choice of a style. The total appearance you present to the world contains a profusion of line—not only in the clothes your wear, but in the contours of your face and figure. Notice how lines define the basic body outline, how they separate the form into various areas. Necklines, sleevelines, waistlines and hemlines act as dividers which form shapes and spaces. They make the design interesting and pleasing to the eye. If the direction and spacing of each line is not carefully plotted, the result can be one of confusion.

Line Analysis

In order to use line correctly, it is important to understand that lines have both functional and emotional significance. Although there are only two types of line, straight and curved, they offer infinite variety. Straight lines may follow a vertical, horizontal or diagonal direction; they can be continuous or broken and combined into angles. Curved lines can be round as a full moon or flattened until they appear almost straight. No matter what form a line takes, it has an inherent power to create strong impressions.

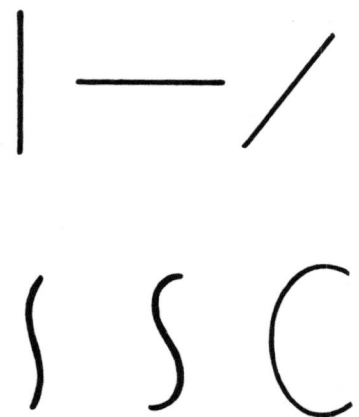

STRAIGHT LINES. The straight line seems stiff and unrelenting to the point of seriousness or sternness. However, the direction it takes can influence the mood of a design. Vertical lines give a feeling of dignity and sophistication, while horizontal lines are calm and gentle. Diagonal lines are a satisfying combination of both. They modify the vertical qualities of dignity and sophistication to give a more relaxed feeling.

CURVED LINES. The curved line, on the other hand, creates an entirely different mood, and is considered to be more graceful than a straight line. However, curved lines must be controlled if they are to be completely lovely. A full circle can become monotonous. The most graceful curved line is one which takes a diagonal direction. Curved lines can be merry half moons, large luxurious graceful curves, or gay little restless round circles.

DOMINANT LINES. When several lines appear simultaneously, as they do in most dress designs, the eye will follow the strongest line. It is this reaction that makes it possible to emphasize figure assets and minimize faults by attracting the eye to a certain area. If you can keep attention focused on a pretty face, a badly proportioned figure may go unnoticed.

The drawings shown here illustrate various dominant line patterns. Notice the strong horizontal line in each case. A large collar draws attention to a pretty face; pockets and waistline interest emphasize a tiny waist, and a decorative motif attracts the eye to lovely legs.

Tricks with Line

Sometimes it is hard to believe that your eyes don't always tell the **truth**, but because they don't, you can employ fallacies of vision to create a more attractive appearance. To do so, it's important to understand optical illusion and understand how this magic can be put to work to produce the kind of effect you want. Here are some simple examples:

Take the first group of lines, *A*. You can see immediately that one looks longer than the other although, when you measure them, they are identical in length. Now notice how the vertical lines in *B* seem to curve. Actually, they are straight. And while the circles superimposed on the pentagon *C* may seem to flatten out, they are really perfectly round.

Now look at the rectangles in *D*. Certainly the one divided by the vertical line looks narrower than the one divided by the horizontal line, yet they are identical. The rectangle in *E* with the narrow panel appears much narrower than the one with the wide panel; they too are alike. As a final example, in *F*, the rectangle divided by a diagonal which starts at the top line looks narrower than the same rectangle with a diagonal which starts at the side.

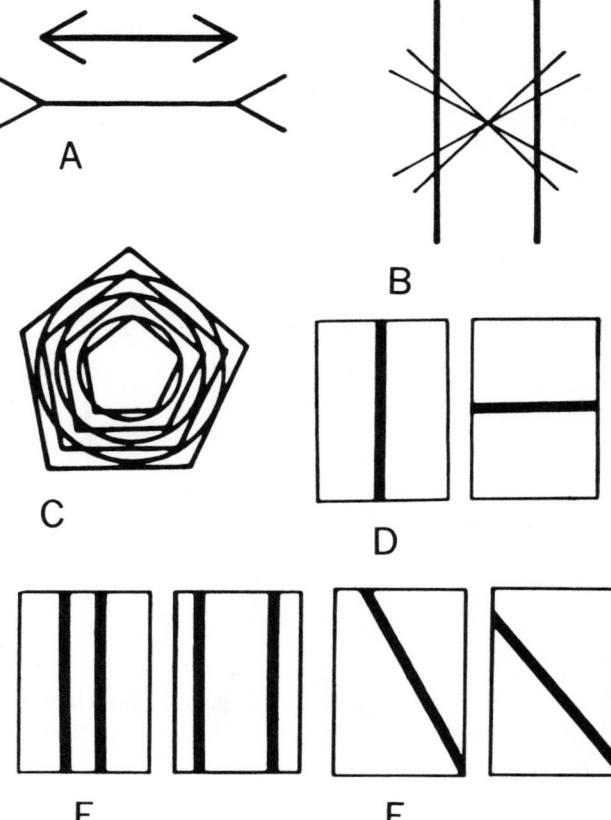

You may wonder how these geometric shapes can apply to dress design. By applying these same principles to your clothes, you can make yourself look taller and thinner, or shorter and wider.

Notice how the diagrams shown here illustrate this.

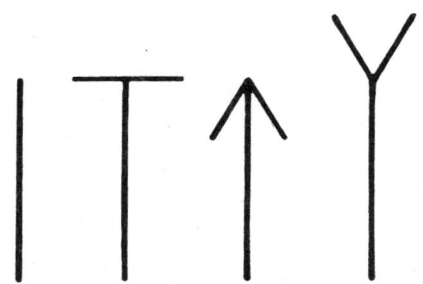

In the first line, there is no opposing force. Therefore the eye continues upward to the end of the line, and an illusion of height is created. Going up the second line, the eye meets the opposing horizontal and starts to travel from side to side, making the vertical line seem shorter. In the third line, the eye is forced downward by the diagonal lines and so this line seems even shorter than the second; in the fourth line, the diagonal lines carry the eye upward so that the vertical line seems even longer than it did in the first diagram.

By analyzing line direction in the design when you select a pattern, you can often achieve the effect you wish.

Remember: lines which carry the eye in a vertical direction will make you look taller; those which move in a horizontal direction will give an effect of width; while those that travel diagonally will create an effect of tallness or wideness depending on whether their emphasis is vertical or horizontal.

Tricks with Space

Line is not the only factor to use in creating illusions. Spaces can play tricks too. The manner in which a design is divided into areas by lines influences the appearance. Remember how much wider the rectangle looked when it was divided by a horizontal line? In

dress design the same principle can be followed. A straight hip-length jacket presents the same illusion as the rectangle divided by a horizontal. Conversely, a simple sheath dress with a straight front closing can create the same effect as the rectangle divided by a vertical line. In dividing an area into smaller sections, the reaction of the eye must always be considered. For instance, study again the rectangles divided into panels. The narrow center panel makes the rectangle appear narrower because the eye travels upward between the lines with little attention to the rest of the design. When the wider panel is used, however, the eye moves back and forth between the lines giving an impression of width.

Thus, although the general principle of line is that verticals make an object appear taller while horizontal lines widen, there is always the exception that proves the rule. A reverse effect may occur when pleats, tucks or striped fabrics are used. Notice in this drawing how

much wider the vertical lines make the area look than the horizontal lines do. This is due to the spacing between the stripes, so in planning an arrangement which gives a striped effect, it is important to study the reaction of the eye so that the effect is the one you want to achieve.

Vertical Illusions

One of the best ways to produce a tall slender illusion is to use the tubular silhouette, unbroken by horizontal lines. A straight princess-line sheath is an excellent example of this line. The garment should fit the figure gently, being neither too tight nor too loose. A narrow center panel, often seen in a princess-line dress, will add height if it is correctly proportioned to the figure. The long lines of surplice openings and full-length coats, or a short bolero jacket with the corresponding long line of a straight skirt, will emphasize the tall

illusion. Tuxedo collars which extend the entire length of a coat can produce the same effect.

If you wish to make your face and throat appear more slender, wear a V-line at the neck. The U-line, particularly a deep U, can produce this effect too, but it will be less pronounced than the V-line. Fairly narrow collars that produce a V-shape, or a coat collar worn open at the throat and high at the back of the neck will keep the eye moving upward and add length to the face.

Your choice of accessories, too, can help to maintain a vertical illusion. Scarves and hats can add to the upward look. Belts should be narrow with unobtrusive closings and in the same fabric as the dress so that the eye will not be stopped in its vertical movement.

Horizontal Illusions

Generally the bouffant or bell-shaped silhouette will produce a horizontal illusion. However, the impression it creates will depend on the width of the skirt. Wide

or full sleeves, or sleeves with cuffs that end at the bustline or hipline will carry the eye across the figure, making it seem wider especially at that spot. Pockets can produce the same effect. Wide belts make the waistline seem broader, and suits, two-piece dresses, short capes, or short jackets which cut the figure in half, or three-quarter-length coats will tend to shorten the figure. Tunics and peplums, particularly if they flare, will have the same effect.

In order to make a thin face seem broader, round, bateau and square necklines can add width. High, close necklines, and round collars such as a Peter Pan, can

create the same illusion of width. Collars with wide revers extending almost to the armhole with the points falling below the shoulder line, or a scarf tied so that the ends extend horizontally will also keep the eye moving from side to side.

THE EFFECT OF FABRIC DESIGNS

The optical illusions that are accomplished by proper use of line can often be achieved or heightened through the use of patterned fabrics such as stripes or prints. These effects may often be more difficult to accomplish than the ones in which you depend upon line alone, but the figure flattery you can achieve may be well worth the effort.

Tricks with Stripes

Stripes are a perennial favorite, and variations in widths, colors and arrangement give them a new look each year. Not only do stripes produce interesting effects, they can also create flattering illusions. Usually stripes running in a vertical direction will make a person look taller and thinner, but this is not a hard-and-fast rule. There are times when stripes can make the figure appear much wider. The same principle holds true when using stripes horizontally. Although usually stripes moving from side to side make the figure seem stouter and shorter, it is also possible for this direction to make the figure look taller. It all depends on how your eye reacts to the width of the stripes and the distance between them.

If this is hard to believe, notice how the different arrangements of lines shown here seem to create varying illusions. In *A* the vertical lines do keep the eye moving upward, creating a feeling of height, but in *B* the vertical lines carry the eye from side to side, increasing the apparent width of the area. If you can't quite believe what your eyes are telling you, measure each of the areas to be sure. When the spaces between the stripes are proportioned so that the eye moves easily from one line to the other without stopping, a sideways illusion is created.

Using stripes in a diagonal direction can also create optical illusions. Notice how the diagonals converging at one spot can make two parallel lines seem to bulge.

Therefore, it's very important to analyze a striped fabric before you buy it. Always keep your dress pattern in mind and visualize the direction the stripes will take. Will this have the effect on your figure you desire? Usually, a simple design will give the most pleasing results.

Tricks with Prints

Like stripes, prints also can be used to create desirable effects. However, you should remember that prints

usually make the figure look larger than a plain fabric in the same color. Usually designs of medium size with close color contrasts will prove the most flattering to any figure type. Light and bright colors, sharp contrasts and large motifs will tend to increase the apparent size of the wearer; while darker, blurred, all-over patterns will act to decrease size.

Motifs arranged to give a vertical movement to the design seem to add height. When this kind of design is made up of colors that are close in value and the motifs are closely spaced, the print will be flattering to a short figure. Widely spaced, sharply contrasted motifs will call attention to the wearer's size even though the background may be subdued. Circular motifs give an illusion of roundness and will have a flattering effect if you are thin.

Border prints used at the hemline will have a tendency to attract the eye, particularly if the border is dark and wide. Such a border is ideal if you wish to call attention to pretty legs. However, the strong horizontal illusion makes it impossible to create a feeling of height at the same time, so this type of print is more becoming on a tall slender figure than a short one.

There is one way to create a lengthening effect with a border print, and that is to use it as the central panel running up and down the dress. Thus the panel creates a path for the eye to follow. This is most successful if the border is a narrow one.

THE EFFECTS OF FABRIC

Fabrics, like lines, can also influence your apparent size. Often a person can select just the right style and lines for figure flattery and then ruin the effect by selecting the wrong fabric. Whether a fabric reflects or absorbs light, is rough or smooth, stiff or clinging will account to some degree for its effect on your appearance.

Light Reflection

Shiny fabrics which reflect a great deal of light will make the figure appear larger, while dull surfaces will tend to minimize size. The illusion created is the same as when an object is placed in a bright clear light, then in a dim diffused light. Naturally, the more light it receives and reflects, the larger the body appears. So, the heavy person who selects a design with long, tall vertical lines and then makes the dress in a very shiny satin is defeating her own purpose. She may wonder why she looks so large, yet if she had used a dull silk broadcloth, the gown would have been just as dressy and vastly more flattering.

Some fabrics both reflect and absorb light. Velvet is a good example of this type in which the pile catches light and also casts shadows. As long as the fabric is not a bulky one, it will not noticeably affect the apparent size of the figure.

Rough and Smooth Textures

Rough-textured fabrics tend to appear bulkier than they are, and will increase the size of the figure in proportion to their roughness and bulkiness. Naturally, a pebbly crepe will not noticeably add pounds, but a very rough, nubby wool tweed may have a decided effect. Smooth textures will not affect the appearance of the figure as long as they are not shiny.

Transparent Textures

Although see-through materials can often be draped in soft, graceful folds, they also reveal the outline of the figure. It is not wise to use transparent fabric if you wish to hide extra folds of flesh or a too thin bony structure.

THE EFFECT OF COLOR

Stiff Textures

Stiff materials tend to conceal the outline of the figure because they do not follow it. However, although they can hide some figure faults, they usually make the body seem somewhat larger. For example, a person with heavy hips, but with a waistline and bustline in proportion to her height, could wear a stiff fabric to advantage, whereas a person who is heavy all over should avoid it.

Clinging Textures

Fabrics of this type have a double personality. When used for straight, tubular designs, clinging materials outline the figure so completely that they often make it seem larger or thinner than it actually is. However, when they are draped into soft silhouettes, they can be very flattering.

Lines and textures do not offer the only "bag of tricks" at your disposal for creating optical illusions and enhancing the effects you wish to achieve. Colors can produce illusions, too.

Although there are hundreds and hundreds of different hues, they all come from three basic colors—red, yellow and blue—which are called primary colors. When two primary colors are combined in equal parts,

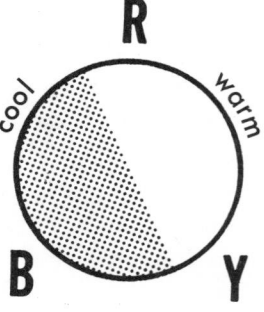

secondary colors—orange, green and purple—are created. This type of combination can continue indefinitely to give us the infinite variety of colors we see all around us.

Colors may vary in other ways, too. Depending upon whether they are mixed with white or black, they have qualities of lightness and darkness which are known as

values. Colors also have brightness or dullness, which is described as their *intensity*. All of these factors can affect the way your eye will react to a color, so it is important to know just what tricks color can play.

Tricks with Color

Colors can make you feel warmer or cooler; they can make you look larger or smaller. Some hues will cause your skin to seem clear and lovely; others may tinge it with unpleasant red or yellow tones.

In terms of comfort, red and orange seem to give an impression of warmth; blue and blue-violet of coolness. Dark colors and black which absorb light also make you feel warmer, while white and light colors which reflect light actually make you feel cooler. Keep these ideas in mind when selecting colors to wear at various times of the year.

As far as size is concerned, hues containing red and yellow are called advancing colors; they make an object seem closer and in turn larger. On the other hand, colors containing blue are receding; they make an

object seem farther away and of course smaller. However, value and intensity also influence the size, so you cannot say that every red dress will make you look larger than every blue dress. A bright crimson may increase size, but dark, grayed red will probably not affect the size of your figure at all. A good way to test this is to look at your feet in white and in black shoes; in shiny patent leather and in suede.

Facial Flattery

Tones of the skin, hair and eyes vary so widely that it is impossible to give definite rules for color selection that will be flattering to everyone. Probably the best results are obtained by actually testing colors against your face, to find out which hues give the best effect with your individual combination of skin, hair and eyes.

Generally, the skin is considered first when selecting a color for a costume. Skin tones are composed of varying amounts of red and yellow, and naturally you will want to subdue any predominance of either of these tones. By remembering that color will be emphasized both by repetition and contrast, you will avoid using complementary colors such as green if your skin is ruddy, or purple if your skin is sallow. You won't choose yellow if there is a predominance of yellow in your skin tone, or red if there is too much red. Usually, dark colors grayed in tone are becoming to a person with a florid complexion but should be avoided if the skin is yellow.

The power of white to reflect light and black to absorb it should be considered when choosing colors to be worn next to your face. Black seems to remove the color from your skin. This is the reason for wearing a light collar on a dark dress. Although a dark color can create a dramatic effect if worn by a person with a clear white skin, it is usually better for a person with a pale complexion to avoid it. Large amounts of bright color will have the same effect. To emphasize the pink tones in your cheeks, wear greens and blue-greens.

If your skin is dark in tone, you will find the blue-greens especially becoming. Grayed medium colors will be more pleasing than the very bright, light or dark.

To emphasize the color of the hair, you will find that light colors make black and dark brown hair seem darker, whereas dark colors will emphasize the golden lights in blond hair.

Sometimes, a person with lovely eyes wants to enhance their beauty. This can be done by repeating the color of the eyes in small amounts of a bright color, large amounts of a grayed one, or by using complementary colors.

Figure Flattery

Although colors are usually chosen to enhance the beauty of the face, their effect on the figure should not be forgotten. Remember how dark, grayed and receding colors make the figure appear smaller, whereas light, bright and advancing colors make it seem larger? Although black makes the figure look smaller, it does clearly define the outline. If you want to camouflage a figure irregularity, such as heavy hips, you will want to avoid the use of black and use instead medium or grayed colors that blend with the background.

The possessor of a tall and well-proportioned figure is fortunate. She can wear all types of colors. She can even introduce strong color contrasts in her outfit, dividing the costume into definite parts.

The tall, angular figure can also use color in many ways. Two-color costumes will be good. They give an illusion of soft roundness, which she needs.

The tall, heavy figure should wear color carefully. She should avoid colors which will add bulk to her large figure. Grayed medium colors that make the outline indefinite will be best. Sometimes a front panel

of a lighter color will create a slimming illusion.

The short, slender figure will find one-color costumes most flattering. Designs using two colors, such as a light blouse and dark skirt, should be avoided.

The short, stout figure should also wear one-color costumes. Dark- or medium-value colors will make the heavy figure appear taller and thinner. Light and bright colors, as well as costumes that have a definite contrast in color, should be avoided.

When the figure is out of proportion in certain areas, it is best to wear medium grayed colors. Light and bright colors, as well as sharp contrasts, will only emphasize the imperfection.

BECOMING LINES, FABRICS AND COLORS

All of the factors just outlined have to be put together to get results that will be right for you. As a guide, here are the most important points to remember in relation to your figure type:

Tall and Slender

You're a natural for high fashion and may as well enjoy it. Lines or color values and intensities shouldn't offer many problems for you. Do avoid lines and colors that make you appear too tall and slender for fear of looking gaunt. Maintain the slenderness without too much height by selecting soft, curved vertical lines. Use bright, vivid colors if they suit your coloring and personality; make good use of striking color contrasts. Avoid very coarse or heavy fabrics which may overpower the delicacy of your figure.

Tall, Too Thin

The flat, angular look may be right on the pages of fashion magazines, but in real life you're apt to look scrawny. A rounded feminine figure is more pleasing to the eye. Use restrained and slightly full curves in your clothes. Wear bouffant skirts, wide collars, full sleeves. Divide your rectangular figure into spaces to produce a widening effect. Peplums, tunics, hip-length jackets, tiered skirts will do this. If possible, wear bright colors that add a bit of fullness to the figure. Color contrasts at waist and hip will make your figure seem shorter and fuller. Select medium-weight fabrics which drape nicely and add roundness, stiff fabrics which add fullness, and fairly heavy-weight fabrics with smooth surfaces. Avoid clinging fabrics which reveal the thinness of the figure and too coarse or too heavy fabrics.

Tall, Heavy

Lines for the "viking" type are a problem. You'll want those which slenderize without adding height. Diagonal lines are the answer; they have the power to be both horizontal and vertical at the same time. Surplice closings, draped effects, gentle flares will be flattering, as long as they are kept simple in design. Softness is what you want, rather than severely tailored or very frilly designs. Grayed colors or those of medium intensity will be more flattering than very light or very dark ones. Select medium-weight fabrics which drape nicely, dull fabrics which have slightly uneven textures, and smooth textures for tailored garments. Avoid large patterns, very crisp and shiny fabrics.

Short and Slender

Usually the short person wants to appear taller, and seeks vertical illusions in her clothes. Coat dresses, princess lines, narrow front panels, surplice closings will all create the tall illusion. Be careful when selecting suits or jackets; keep them fairly short, usually waist-length. A long expanse of skirt will make the figure appear taller. Keep costumes in one color, matching belts; if contrast is used, keep it high. Select soft fabrics in light or medium weights and small patterned fabrics. Avoid coarse and heavy fabrics which may overpower the figure.

Short and Plump

Vertical is again the general direction for the short and plump figure—not perfectly straight lines, but carefully controlled diagonals and verticals which slenderize. Actually, many of the same lines used for the tall, heavy person can be used here, but in a slightly different manner. The diagonals should be almost vertical in direction. Surplice closings, princess lines, coat dresses with a slight flare will be good choices. Jackets that cut the figure in half are best avoided. One-color

costumes in medium grayed tones will make the outline of the figure indefinite and will be more flattering. Select dull, soft fabrics, blurry indistinct patterns. Avoid heavy, crisp, coarse and shiny fabrics.

You may be happy with the height of your figure and its size, but have a particular problem which you'd like to camouflage; or maybe you have a lovely feature you would like to emphasize. Line and color illusion can be used equally effectively for these purposes.

Hip-Heavy

This is the most common problem of all, since women are naturally full-hipped. Keep bodices trim; avoid very straight skirts. Select flattering flares instead and keep skirts smooth fitting over the hips. Place interest high on the costume, using neckline interest to draw attention away from the hipline. Avoid jackets, overblouses and peplums which cut across the hip. Do not use color contrasts at hipline. However, if you have a tiny waist and well-proportioned bustline, a dark skirt and a light bodice will de-emphasize hips.

Small Bust

If you have a small waist and bust, then look for set-in midriff styles, gathers beneath the bust, slightly bloused bodices. For a large-waisted figure, yokes, soft fullness at the neckline and draped bodices will be more flattering. You can use overblouses if your hips are fairly narrow.

Low, Full Bust

Start with the proper foundation garments, and if possible, have them fitted by a professional. Then select softly draped bodices, with not too much fullness but just a little. Keep interest high on the figure. Avoid very high or low necklines. Do not use bodice colors that are light, bright or shiny, or fabrics that cling.

Thick Rib Cage

Center the interest away from the rib cage, at neckline or hemline, depending on your best feature. Boxy jackets, bloused bodices, soft draping, overblouses will help de-emphasize this area.

Short-Waisted

Make the waist look longer through low-waisted designs, hip-length jackets, overblouses. Wear one-color costumes with smooth, uninterrupted lines. Avoid contrasting belts, very full skirts or very slim ones.

Long-Waisted

Wide sashes, contrasting belts, set-in midriffs will give a lift to the waistline. Tunics, peplums and long jackets are equally effective. This figure must be careful, when short, short skirts are the fashion, to avoid looking top-heavy.

Round Shoulders

Bloused bodices will help conceal the curved line, as will necklines with angular rather than curved collars. Try using shoulder pads to raise the shoulder line at the right spot, and placing the shoulder line of a garment back of its normal position will help.

Narrow Shoulders

Set-in sleeves with a small amount of padding to build up the shoulder will best conceal too-narrow shoulders. Avoid kimono sleeves, dolman and raglan styles which only emphasize the narrow line.

Short Neck

Choose necklines no higher than a jewel neckline. Stand-away collars, collarless styles and V- or U-shaped necklines will make the neck seem longer.

Long Neck

The swanlike throat can be enviable, but it can also look plain scrawny. Shorten it with high turtle and mandarin necklines, or large collars and high chokers.

Prominent Abdomen

Start with a good foundation garment and check your posture. Pleats or shirring at sides of the skirt with a straight front panel will be the best camouflage. Wear boxy hip-length jackets. Strive for vertical lines to carry the eye up the figure, skimming over the problem area.

Prominent Derrière

Look for flowing lines, particularly those which flow in back. Hip-length boxy jackets will help; box-pleated skirts, flared skirts and shirred waistlines are effective. Fill in the hollow above the derrière with blousing such as a sash or a flying panel.

WARDROBE NEEDS

With the tricks of optical illusion at your disposal and a definite idea of what you want to do to change your appearance, you should consider your wardrobe needs. No matter how carefully you have chosen your design, the effect will be spoiled unless the garment is right for the occasion at which it is worn. This doesn't mean that you need lots and lots of clothes. A few costumes which can be used for different occasions are a wise choice. Usually every woman needs a simple coat, a classic suit, several basic dresses which may be dressed up or down by the use of accessories, a casual dress, skirt, blouse, sweater, sports ensemble and after-five dress. However, when to wear them may be confusing. A few general suggestions are given here for you to consider in planning your wardrobe.

At Home

The homemaker often makes the big mistake of thinking she does not have to look her best when doing her daily chores. Actually, ill-fitting clothes lower her morale and make her less able to cope with everyday trials. This doesn't mean she has to dress up, but it does mean that she should look neat and trim.

If you look well and feel comfortable in slacks or shorts, wear them when working in the home. But be sure you look well in them and that they fit properly.

A simple shirtwaist dress or wrap-around with flared or pleated skirt will often present a much more attractive appearance and be just as comfortable as pants.

For evenings at home a simple dress is always in good taste. But dress up a little bit if you wish. It adds a touch of gaiety or elegance to a family gathering. However, the degree of dressing-up depends on your situation. Fancy pants or long skirts may look ludicrous in one place, marvelous in another.

On the Job

A simple dress, suit, skirt, jacket, and blouse that can be mixed and matched form the basis of this wardrobe. Keep the clothes tailored, uncluttered and easy to care for. Usually a career girl's wardrobe is largely

selected in dark and basic colors, but don't be afraid to include some brighter colors just to add a little pep.

Clothes that are too tight or too revealing are taboo in an office. Dressy, low-cut clothes should be avoided. Casual clothes that look wonderful on the campus are out of place in a more sophisticated business atmosphere.

For School

Separates are the answer to the schoolgirl's needs. Skirts, sweaters, jackets and blouses that can mix and match are perfect. A few basic dresses for social occasions such as church, teas, informal gatherings, and a party dress or dressy separates for formal functions will complete the schoolgirl's wardrobe. Of course, a good cover-everything coat is a necessity.

For Sports

Sportswear in our modern sense covers both clothes for sports events and casual clothes in general. Naturally, participating in special sports requires special costumes. What you need for golf is wrong for tennis. And as a spectator at sports events, choose comfortable, sturdy-looking clothes. Separates, simple dresses and classic suits are always appropriate.

For Shopping

By this, we mean shopping in a city department store. Slacks and shorts are taboo. Again, simple dresses and suits are best. A comfortable topcoat which can be worn over suit or dress is most useful.

For Evening Parties

Evening clothes depend entirely on the type of social life you lead. For informal parties, an afternoon or cocktail dress or suit can be used. For formal dances, long or short evening gowns can be worn. The formality of your evening clothes will depend upon the community you live in.

For Traveling

Tailored clothes are always best. Flared skirts are more comfortable to sit in, and give a more pleasing look as well. When you reach your destination, the clothes you need will depend on the locale. Resorts require rather gay, festive clothes; cities more conservative businesslike costumes, while rough country life demands casual, comfortable garments.

For Club Activities

Dressmaker suits, simple dresses, such as the sheath, shirtwaist and coat dress are always appropriate. They may have soft touches, but avoid fussy styles.

CHAPTER 2

KEYSTONE TO FASHION— A PERFECT PATTERN

Naturally, not every pattern style will look equally well on everyone, just as no ready-made garment is the answer for every woman. But unlike ready-to-wear, the garment you plan to make at home cannot be tried on in advance. You have to take a chance, but if you know how to pick the right pattern, your risk can be a very small one. This is not just a matter of flipping through the pages of a pattern catalog and selecting an appropriate style. It involves finding your correct figure type and size.

Choosing a pattern in the correct figure type and size seems to be a difficult thing for many women to do. They prefer to choose a style and then worry about how to make it fit, whereas if they chose the correct pattern in the first place, it would solve a great many of their problems. It may also make the difference between a smooth, professional look and an amateurish one. Pattern companies divide their catalogs into sections depending upon figure types, so that once you have determined your type, you can turn directly to the section you need.

NEW SIZING

Pattern sizing has been changed to correspond more closely to standard ready-to-wear sizing. Measurements for the new sizing were developed and approved by the Measurement Standard Committee of the Pattern Fashion Industry. All major pattern companies have adopted the new standard of body measurements. Patterns issued after November 1, 1967 have the new sizing. The patterns using the new standard body measurements are indicated with this symbol NEW Sizing .

The figure types remain the same except for a new Young Junior/Teen figure type which replaced the Teen and Pre-Teen types. All patterns within this new figure type are marked with this symbol NEW SIZE Range . The size ranges within the different figure types have been extended to correspond more closely to sizes available to ready-to-wear.

The sizing for Toddlers', Children's and Girls' patterns have minor changes in the measurements, but these changes do not affect pattern size. No changes have been made in the Men's and Boys' sizing.

To see the differences between the former and the new sizing or revised standard measurements, compare the body measurement charts on page 17. As a general rule, you may be buying one size smaller in the new

sizing than you do in the former sizing. However, this may not always be true, so be sure to check the new measurement charts. Your bust measurement is the key to your correct size. The waistline in the new sizing is slightly smaller in proportion to the bust and hips than in the former sizing.

Figure Types

Because of varying human shapes, patterns are designed to fit seven different groups of figures with differences in height and contour; Misses', Women's, Half-Sizes, Junior Petite, Junior, Young Junior/Teen and Girls. Your lengthwise or vertical measurements determine figure type. Age is not a factor.

Pattern Sizes

Patterns are made not only for seven different figure types but also for different sizes within each figure type. Your size is determined by your measurements taken horizontally around the body. Numbers indicate sizes. Even numbers are used for Misses' 6-18 and Women's 38-50; odd, for Junior 5-15 and Junior Petite 3-13; half, for Half-Sizes 10½-24½. A combination of odd and even numbers are used for Young Junior/Teen ⅚-15⁄16 and Girls 7-14.

Body Measurements

It is important for you to know your measurements to obtain a pattern correct for you in size and figure type. Your measurements determine the pattern which fits you best. Essential body measurements are the actual measurements in inches of your height, bust, waist, hip and back waist length taken over foundation garments you will wear with your fashions.

Have someone take the measurements for you. Tie a cord around your natural waistline. Then stand in stocking feet in a normal posture with your feet together and have person doing measuring stand in back of you. Measure *height* by standing flat against a wall, lightly marking the position of the top of your head on the wall. Then measure from the floor up and record the actual feet and inches. To measure the *bust*, place the tape over the fullest part of the bust and measure around the body, high under the arm, and straight across the back. For *waist* measurement, place the tape snugly around the natural waistline. For *hip*, measure around the fullest part of the body, 9 inches below the natural waistline for Misses', Women and Junior; 7 inches below the natural waistline for Half-Sizes, Junior Petite and Young Junior/Teen. *Back waist length* is measured from the top of the most prominent bone at the base of the neck to the cord tied at the natural waistline.

Record these measurements and the date they were taken. Be sure to check measurements frequently. It is surprising how they can change in a matter of a few weeks.

Selecting Figure Type and Size

Determine your figure type first by comparing your height, back waist length and bust position with figure type and measurement chart. If you are short with a young figure, consider Young Junior/Teen; if you are short-waisted, Junior and Half-Sizes; in case you are very short, Junior Petite; if average-waisted, Misses'. A Women's figure type is actually a large version of the Misses'.

To determine your size, compare your measurements with the ones for your figure type. Find the size with the measurements closest to yours. If you fall between two sizes, select the smaller size if you are small boned; the larger size if your bone structure is large.

Buy the same size pattern for a suit and coat as you would for a dress. Slim skirts are selected by waist measurement unless hip is 2 inches larger than the hip measurement of pattern. Full skirts are bought by waist measurement. In purchasing a pattern for slacks, shorts and pants the hip measurement, rather than the waist measurement, should be given first consideration.

MISSES' is considered the "average" figure type, 5'5" to 5'6" tall, with "average" waist length and bust position. All other figure types will be compared to Misses'.

WOMEN'S patterns are made for the larger figure 5'5" to 5'6" tall with average bust position.

HALF-SIZE patterns are designed for the figure 5'2" to 5'3", shorter-waisted and with a lower bustline than the Misses'. Waist and hip are larger in proportion to bust than other figure types.

JUNIOR PETITE patterns are for the small, mature figure 5' to 5'1" tall, shorter-waisted than the Misses' but with average bustline position.

JUNIOR patterns are designed for the figure 5'4" to 5'5" tall, shorter-waisted and with higher bustline than the Misses'.

YOUNG JUNIOR/TEEN is the new size range designed for the developing pre-teen and teen figures, about 5'1" to 5'3" tall.

GIRLS patterns are made for the very young figure about 5' tall. Notice that she has no defined bustline and is shorter-waisted than the Misses' figure.

Comparison of Body Measurement Charts

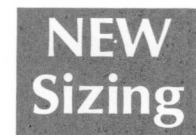 **NEW Sizing**

FORMER SIZING

MISSES'

Size	6	8	10	12	14	16	18
Bust	30½	31½	32½	34	36	38	40
Waist	22	23	24	25½	27	29	31
Hip	32½	33½	34½	36	38	40	42
Back Waist Length	15½	15¾	16	16¼	16½	16¾	17

Size	8	10	12	14	16	18	20
Bust	30	31	32	34	36	38	40
Waist	23	24	25	26	28	30	32
Hip	32	33	34	36	38	40	42
Back Waist Length	15½	15¾	16	16¼	16½	16¾	17

WOMEN'S

Size	38	40	42	44	46	48	50
Bust	42	44	46	48	50	52	54
Waist	34	36	38	40½	43	45½	48
Hip	44	46	48	50	52	54	56
Back Waist Length	17¼	17⅜	17½	17⅝	17¾	17⅞	18

Size	40	42	44	46	48	50
Bust	42	44	46	48	50	52
Waist	34	36	38½	41	43½	46
Hip	44	46	48	50	52	54
Back Waist Length	17⅛	17¼	17⅜	17½	17⅝	17¾

HALF-SIZES

Size	10½	12½	14½	16½	18½	20½	22½	24½
Bust	33	35	37	39	41	43	45	47
Waist	26	28	30	32	34	36½	39	41½
Hip	35	37	39	41	43	45½	48	50½
Back Waist Length	15	15¼	15½	15¾	15⅞	16	16⅛	16¼

Size	12½	14½	16½	18½	20½	22½	24½
Bust	33	35	37	39	41	43	45
Waist	27	29	31	33	35	37½	40
Hip	37	39	41	43	45	47	49
Back Waist Length	15¼	15½	15¾	16	16¼	16½	16¾

JUNIOR PETITE

Size	3JP	5JP	7JP	9JP	11JP	13JP
Bust	30½	31	32	33	34	35
Waist	22	22½	23½	24½	25½	26½
Hip	31½	32	33	34	35	36
Back Waist Length	14	14¼	14½	14¾	15	15¼

Size	3JP	5JP	7JP	9JP	11JP	13JP
Bust	31	31½	32	32½	33	33½
Waist	22½	23	23½	24	24½	25
Hip	32½	33	33½	34	34½	35
Back Waist Length	14	14¼	14½	14¾	15	15¼

JUNIOR

Size	5	7	9	11	13	15
Bust	30	31	32	33½	35	37
Waist	21½	22½	23½	24½	26	28
Hip	32	33	34	35½	37	39
Back Waist Length	15	15¼	15½	15¾	16	16¼

Size	9	11	13	15
Bust	30½	31½	33	35
Waist	23½	24½	25½	27
Hip	32½	33½	35	37
Back Waist Length	15	15¼	15½	15¾

YOUNG JUNIOR/TEEN

Size	5/6	7/8	9/10	11/12	13/14	15/16
Bust	28	29	30½	32	33½	35
Waist	22	23	24	25	26	27
Hip	31	32	33½	35	36½	38
Back Waist Length	13½	14	14½	15	15⅜	15¾

TEEN   PRE-TEEN

Size	10T	12T	14T	16T	8PT	10PT	12PT	14PT
Bust	30	32	34	36	28	29	31	33
Waist	24	25	26	27	23	24	25	26
Hip	32	34	36	38	31	32	34	36
Back Waist Length	14¾	15	15¼	15½	13½	13¾	14	14¼

GIRLS

Size	7	8	10	12	14
Breast	26	27	28½	30	32
Waist	23	23½	24½	25½	26½
Hip	27	28	30	32	34
Back Waist Length	11½	12	12¾	13½	14¼

Size	7	8	10	12	14
Breast	25	26	28	30	32
Waist	22½	23	24	25	26
Hip	27	28	30	32½	35
Back Waist Length	11	11½	12¼	13	13¾

Generally, dresses, suits and coats are selected according to bust measurements. Skirts are selected by waist measurement unless the hip is two inches larger than the standard hip measurement given for the size. If this is the case, then select skirts for the hip measurement and alter the waist to fit. Full skirts can be bought according to waist measurement, since there is usually enough fullness to take care of the larger hip. Slacks are selected by hip measurement.

Ease Allowance

There is one important thing to keep in mind when determining your size in a pattern. The measurements given for each size are *standard body measurements,* not actual measurements of the pattern pieces. If garment measurements were the same as the figure, the fabric would pull across the figure and probably split with every movement of the body. To assure that a garment will fit comfortably and smoothly, there has to be a certain amount of ease. McCall's Patterns provides this ease in every pattern.

Generally, the ease allowance in McCall's Patterns is:

Bust: 3 inches over the standard bust measurement, in most dresses. Evening bodices which are designed to fit very tightly in the bodice may have less.

Waist: ½ inch.

Hip: Approximately 2 inches on slim skirts.

Back Waist Length: ¼ to ⅜ inch.

Proportioned Patterns

Many women find that they have normal body proportions for a Misses' or Junior size but the over-all height in the figure type does not correspond to their own. McCall's has a special pattern to meet this need, the proportioned-to-height patterns in the Misses' and Junior figure types. These patterns are designed to fit tall (5′ 8″ to 5′ 10″), average (5′ 6″ to 5′ 7″) or short (5′ 3″ to 5′ 5″) figures. All construction markings and proportioning details such as darts, crotch lengths, pleats and hemlines are printed on the pattern for tall, medium and short figures.

If none of the pattern types and sizes have back waist length measurements to suit your figure, don't despair. Select the type and size which is closest to your measurements and general contours. You will be

able to adjust the pattern using the Easy-Rule Guide for the short- or long-waisted figure, which is another special feature of McCall's Patterns.

Once you have determined your figure type, please don't be tempted to try a different type simply because you like a particular style. And insist on buying the size that fits you best. If the store doesn't have it, ask them to order it. It will be better to wait a few days for it than to struggle through the great amount of adjusting that is necessary to alter the wrong size.

Sizes for Children

Once you've developed your sewing skill, undoubtedly you'll want to make garments for your family.

Children's, Toddlers', Boys' and Girls' pattern sizes are based on waist and chest measurements. They should never be selected according to the age, height or weight of the child. Compare the child's measurements with the standard body measurements for each size shown here. It is easy to lengthen or shorten bodices, skirts or sleeves by using the printed Easy-Rule Guide.

Children's Sizes:

Size	1	2	3	4	5	6	6X
Breast	20	21	22	23	23½	24	25
Waist	19½	20	20½	21	21½	22	22½
Hip					25	26	27
Back Waist Length	8⅛	8½	9	9½	10	10½	11

Toddlers' Sizes:

Size	6 Mos.	1	2	3
Breast	19	20	21	22
Waist	19	19½	20	20½

Children need lots of room in their garments, since they are more active than adults. Patterns provide this ease at the waistline of dress patterns, generally two to three inches over the standard body waist measurement. Skirts, slacks and shorts which must fit snugly at the waist do not have this additional ease allowance.

On many dress patterns, the design features a raised waistline located above the child's normal or natural waistline. When the design does feature this type of waist, you will find the words "high-waisted" in the description of the style on the back of the pattern envelope. If you want a dress which fits the natural waistline, you should select another style.

There is often some confusion about the differences between Toddlers' and Children's sizes. Toddlers' sizes are designed for the non-walking child and are two inches shorter than children's sizes, with the same chest and waist measurements.

Sizes for Men

When sewing for the men in your life, select their shirt patterns according to the neck size, no matter what the chest measurement is. It is almost impossible to alter the neckline of a shirt, but with the pattern's full eight inches of ease through the chest, there is ample allowance for chest girth variations. If you find there is too much ease to suit him, the pattern may be easily altered according to the instructions given in Chapter 6.

Men's shorts, pants and slacks are sized according to waist measurements; sport coats and vests by chest measurements.

Men's Sizes:

Chest	32	34	36	38	40	42	44	46	48
Waist	28	30	32	34	36	38	40	42	44
Neck Base Girth	13½	14	14½	15	15½	16	16½	17	17½
Shirt Sleeve Length	33	33	33	33	34	34	34	35	35

PATTERNS AND SKILL

When you choose a pattern, remember not every seamstress is an expert. Your own prowess should be a determining factor in pattern selection. Don't choose a pattern that is too difficult. It is much better to select something simple and construct it in a professional way than to do an unprofessional job on a more difficult design. As you become more proficient, you can proceed from the easy to the more difficult constructions.

Slim or flared skirts make excellent beginning projects. A blouse with an unmounted sleeve such as kimono and raglan also can be made by the novice. Graduate from blouses and skirts to jumpers and dresses before you attempt a coat or suit.

THE LANGUAGE OF PATTERNS

A beginning seamstress may feel that Einstein's theories are as easy to understand as the intricacies of a first pattern. Here again is a place where first steps should be taken slowly. Once you have the basic information that will allow you to read the easy-to-follow directions, when you can decipher the symbols and follow the charts that come with your pattern, you will find using a pattern no more difficult than using a recipe. And, whether you are a beginner or an experienced home-sewer, every pattern should be carefully studied before you lay out your pattern and start to cut.

Each pattern company differs to some extent in the symbols used to mark its patterns and in the sewing methods it recommends. Be sure to choose a pattern from a firm that marks them clearly and accurately and provides adequate directions presented in an easily understandable manner. A McCall's pattern, for example, not only gives complete instructions for constructing the garment, but also suggests the proper fabrics to use and provides basic information on preparing fabric, adjusting the pattern, cutting, marking and sewing techniques. Vital directions are clearly printed on the pattern tissue, and each pattern has an Easy Sewing Guide to lead you through the construction step by step. Once you know how to interpret each symbol and direction correctly, working with a pattern is easy.

The Pattern Envelope

Your study should begin with the pattern envelope before you buy the pattern. The envelope is a storehouse of valuable information. It provides enough data to help you judge how the garment will look and fit your figure, and whether you can easily handle the construction of it. Remember, patterns cannot be returned.

THE FRONT DESIGN. No doubt the sketch of the design on the front of the envelope will catch your eye first. Study it. Be sure the silhouette and design lines are right for you. Check the different views and versions of the design. Decide which one will be most suitable for your needs. Note the fabric and trims illustrated. If the design is a good one for plaids, prints, checks or stripes, the illustration will feature these fabrics. If the designer feels that certain trims will enhance the design, these are also illustrated.

TYPE AND SIZE. Double-check the figure type and size of the pattern. Be sure it is the right one for you. Do not accept another size or type even if the one you wish is not readily available. The figure type is listed under the large pattern number, preceding a very brief description of the type of garment. Size is noted below the large pattern number.

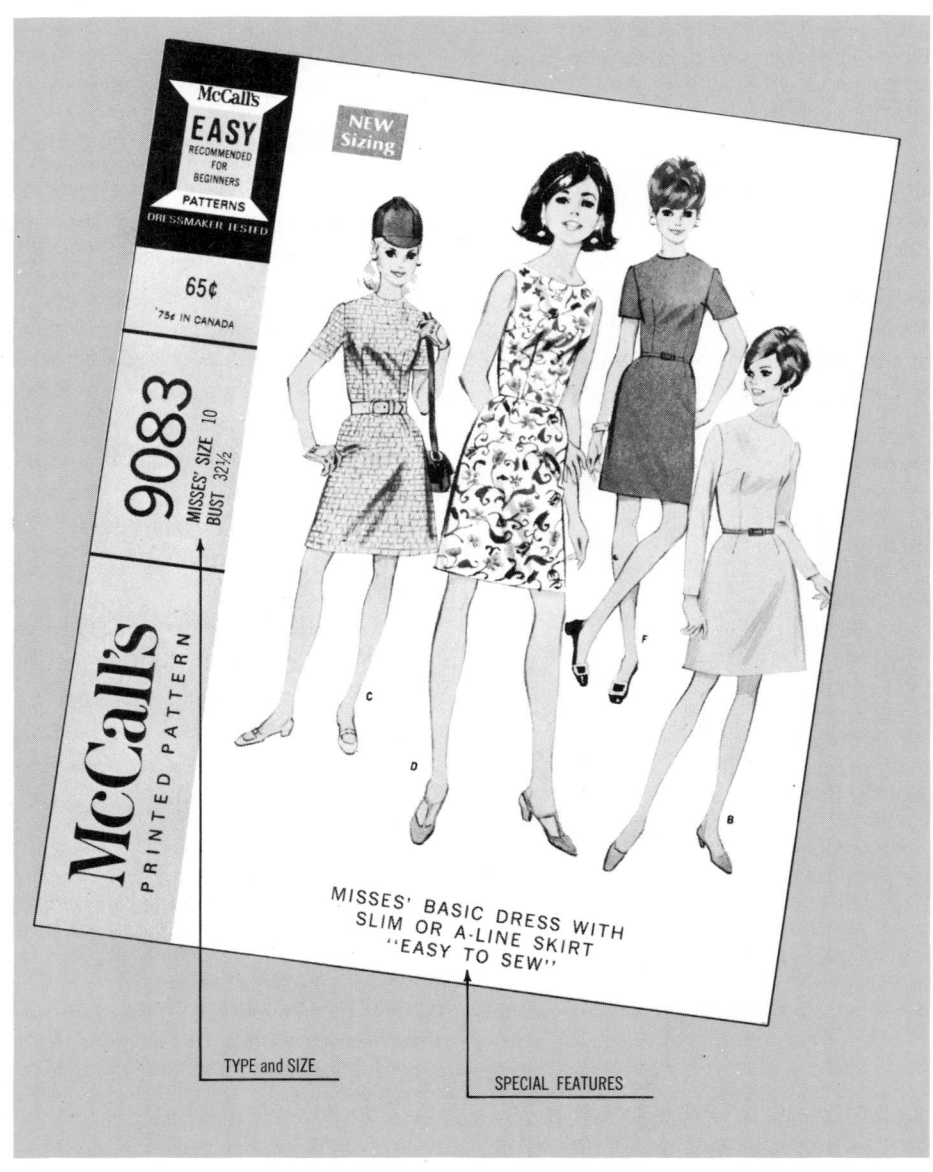

SPECIAL FEATURES. Special pattern features such as EASY, INSTANT and Proportioned will be clearly marked on the front of the envelope. The EASY and INSTANT patterns are identified in big red letters which can't be missed. The Proportioned patterns have the word "proportioned" preceding the figure type. Look for these names and use them for quick, easy sewing. Detailed instructions for handling these special patterns are given in Chapter 8.

THE BACK SKETCHES. On the back of the pattern envelope there is quite a bit of information to digest. First check the sketch of the back view of the design to see if it will be flattering. Read the detailed description of the design above the sketch, noting the type of sleeve, collar, skirt and closings used. Decide whether the design features the details you want. Beginners may wish to avoid certain design features such as gussets, long button-front closings, complicated collars, intricate darting. These features may not be clearly shown in the sketch, but they will be noted in the description. Use this information to judge whether the construction of the garment is within your level of skill.

The sketch of each pattern piece which appears on the back of the envelope is mainly to help you sort the pattern before cutting. Here each piece is sketched to scale and identified as to section. The experienced seamstress can tell a great deal about the construction

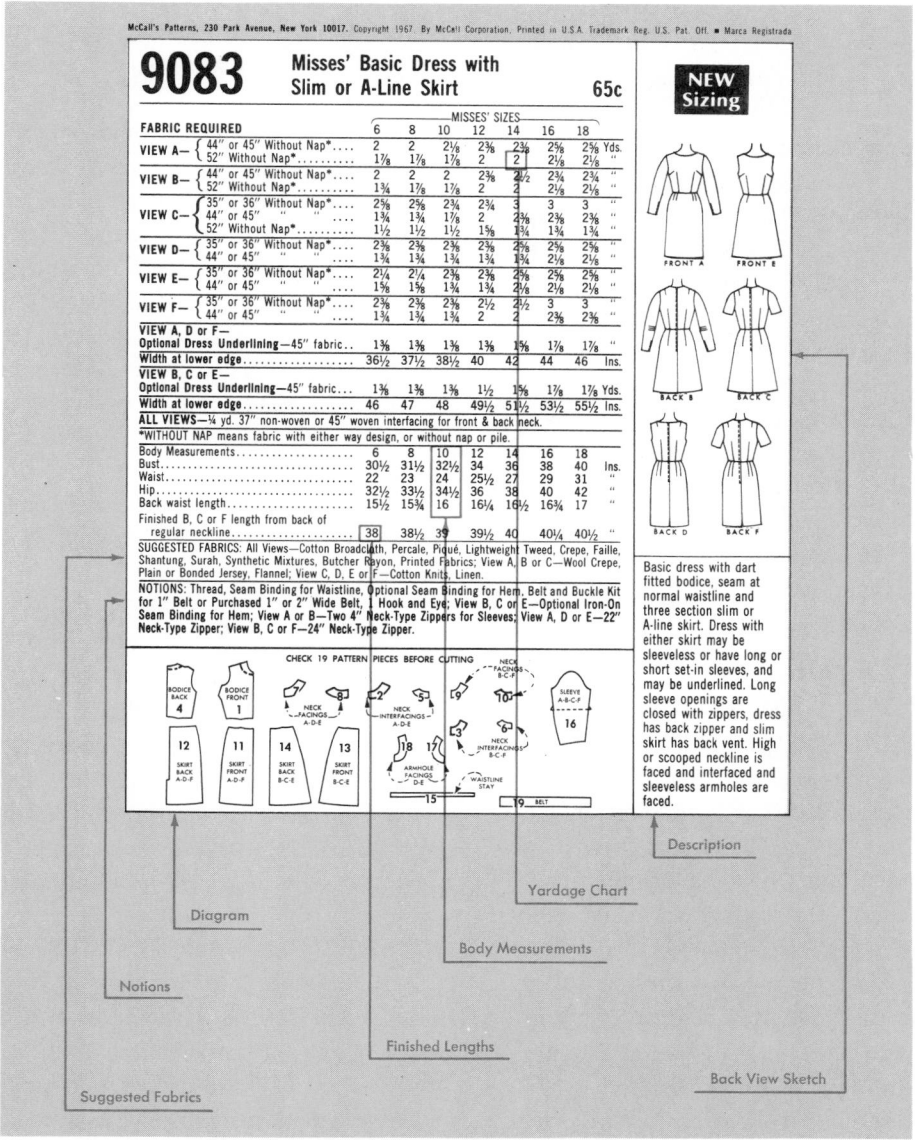

Notions
Diagram
Suggested Fabrics
Finished Lengths
Body Measurements
Yardage Chart
Description
Back View Sketch

of the garment from studying the pieces sketched, and can judge approximately how much time it will take to construct the garment. The beginner should avoid designs made with a great many pieces, since these are usually more time-consuming and more difficult to handle than the simpler styles.

SUGGESTED FABRICS. Perhaps the most important and most neglected section on the back of the pattern envelope is the "Suggested Fabrics" listing. Here the designer notes the fabrics he knows have the proper weight and draping quality for the design. Remember that in discussing fabric for a design in Chapter 1, the importance was stressed of finding a fabric which naturally drapes or falls into the general silhouette and line of the pattern. If you neglect to follow the suggestions given, your fabric may create a silhouette which is entirely different from the one intended.

Here is a sample "Suggested Fabrics" list found on one pattern. All the fabrics indicated are medium-weight materials that have firmness and body. Any of these can be successfully used, or one of comparable weight and body such as a waffle piqué, firm rayon similar to linen, brocade, denim or cotton tweed. A sheer voile, a soft batiste or a heavy-weight fleece would completely alter the look of the design.

If you plan to use a diagonal print or weave or stripes, checks or plaids, read the "Suggested Fabrics" section very carefully. If the design is cut so that these fabrics are unsuitable, a notation "Not Suitable for Diagonal Prints or Diagonal Weaves" will appear in the section. The same notation will be made for stripes, checks and plaids.

YARDAGE CHART. Once you have the type of fabric in mind, refer to the yardage chart to find out how much material you will need for the garment in your size. The yardage chart has been carefully tested to give the exact yardage needed for each size, view and width of fabric when using the layouts given in the pattern instructions. By reading down the column from the size and across from the widths of fabric listed, the exact yardage for size and width of fabric is noted. On proportioned patterns, yardage is given for height as well as size and width of fabric. Be sure to note whether the fabric is listed as "Without Nap" or "With Nap." "Without Nap" refers to any fabric which can be cut with the pattern pieces laid in op-posite directions, up and down. "With Nap" means that all pattern pieces must be cut in one direction on the fabric. Among "With Nap" fabrics are one-way designs, prints or weaves; those which reflect light in different ways depending on the up-and-down direction of the weave (satin); all the pile or napped fabrics such as velveteen, velvet, fleece, fake furs; and some flannels and bouclés.

If you do plan to use a napped fabric and the yardage chart doesn't indicate "With Nap" yardage, examine the design sketch carefully to be sure a napped fabric can be used successfully. You'll have to devise your own cutting layout because there will not be one in the pattern instructions, so try a sample layout before purchasing fabric. Lay the pattern pieces out, all going in the same direction, on brown paper folded to the width of the fabric you plan to use. Measure the length needed to lay out the pattern and buy that length of fabric.

When interfacings or other shaping materials are essential to the design, the yardages will be listed. Since shaping materials are becoming increasingly important in garment construction, many patterns are now suggesting linings and underlinings which are optional. You should use them whenever you feel they will help the look and wear of the garment. If you do plan to use a lining or underlining and yardage is not given, figure the proper yardage by laying out the pieces to be lined in a sample layout, and measure the length of fabric needed.

Yardages for belting for fabric belts and for special trims suggested for a design will also be noted in this section.

NOTIONS. While making a list of fabrics and trims needed, check the "Notions" section to see what notions are required. You will save time by buying everything at one time, and it's easier to match color of thread, zipper, buttons and trims if they are all purchased at once. Be sure to buy all the notions listed. It's frustrating to have to interrupt a sewing session just to run out and pick up a forgotten item.

BODY MEASUREMENTS. For your convenience, the body measurements of the figure types and sizes available in a particular pattern are listed on the back of the pattern envelope. Although you should be fully aware of your proper type and size before you request a pattern, you may wish to refer to this for a double-check.

FINISHED LENGTHS. When you become familiar with pattern alterations, and know generally whether you need to shorten or lengthen a pattern to suit your figure, you will want to check the finished lengths listed on the pattern envelope. As you sew, become familiar with the length jacket, skirt, blouse, dress you prefer. Compare these to the finished length indicated on the pattern you plan to purchase. You can estimate whether you'll have to shorten or lengthen, and this may affect the yardage needed. Become familiar with the width skirt you find most flattering, and also compare this to the notation on the pattern envelope.

Certainly, with all this information right at your fingertips, it should be an easy decision whether to purchase the pattern or not. If one pattern doesn't suit your specific needs, look for another. The large collection of McCall's Patterns most certainly will include more than one pattern that is a perfect choice for you.

Sewing Guide

A special sheet of instructions is placed in every pattern. Each pattern company prepares this guide in a different manner. McCall's has given the preparation of its Easy Sewing Guide a great deal of thought, making it simple to understand and follow. Directions are presented in step-by-step form. Illustrations are clearly drawn and profusely shown.

Before any work is done with your pattern, read the sewing guide carefully. This is important even for the experienced seamstress. Study each step of the construction process. If any part is not clear, find out how it should be handled before you begin to sew. This sewing book has been written for just that purpose, to provide reference material which will amplify and clarify sewing instructions. Beginners may find that the printed instructions are not as detailed as they might be, because instruction sheets are printed to fit a certain space and sometimes do not include minute details. The pattern company must assume that the customer has certain basic sewing knowledge and understands the sewing language.

In addition to the basic construction information, the Easy Sewing Guide contains helpful suggestions for altering the pattern by the Easy-Rule Guide, preparing the fabric, and general tips on cutting, marking, sewing and pressing. Even the experienced seamstress will find this worthwhile reading. McCall's staff

sketch of the pieces found on the back of the pattern envelope to make sure the right pieces are included in

9083   **VIEW A**

44 or 45" FABRIC

NECK FACINGS — FOLD
BELT — SLEEVE — BODICE FRONT — SKIRT FRONT — BODICE BACK — SKIRT BACK — SELVAGES
SIZES 6-8-10

NECK FACINGS — FOLD
SLEEVE — BODICE FRONT — SKIRT FRONT — BELT — SKIRT BACK — BODICE BACK — SELVAGES
SIZES 12-14

NECK FACINGS — FOLD
SLEEVE — SELVAGES
SIZES 16-18
FOLD HERE — BODICE BACK — BODICE FRONT — SKIRT FRONT — SKIRT BACK — BELT — SELVAGE

52" FABRIC

NECK FACINGS — FOLD
SKIRT FRONT — BODICE FRONT — SKIRT BACK — SLEEVE — BELT — BODICE BACK — SELVAGES
SIZES 6-8-10-12-14

NECK FACINGS — FOLD
BELT — SKIRT FRONT — BODICE FRONT — SKIRT BACK — SLEEVE — BODICE BACK — SELVAGES
SIZES 16-18

INTERFACING

37" NON WOVEN or
45" WOVEN INTERFACING

NECK INTERFACINGS — FOLD HERE
SELVAGE
ALL SIZES

A

of experts constantly experiments to find new and easy methods of sewing. When they do discover better ways of doing things, their findings are included in the Easy Sewing Guide.

One of the most important features of the Easy Sewing Guide is the section which provides pattern layouts for various sizes and widths of fabric. Circle the one for your view, size, and width of fabric. You'll be referring to it often when you begin laying the pattern on the fabric. If you plan to use a napped fabric, check to see if a napped layout is provided.

The Pattern

Sort the pattern pieces carefully, selecting only those needed for the version of the garment you're making. Use the layout as a guide for sorting as well as the

the pattern. As you sort, check each piece to see that the correct pattern number and size are printed on it. Patterns are packed by hand, and once in a great while a wrong piece is inserted in the envelope, or a piece is omitted. It rarely occurs, but it's best to double-check. If you do find a mistake in packaging, return the pattern to the pattern company, and they will replace it with the correct pattern.

Each pattern company provides various markings on the printed pattern pieces which help you construct the garment. McCall's prints all markings on the patterns, making construction as easy, accurate and quick as possible. There are markings which aid in quick sorting of the pieces, markings for pattern alterations, markings for proper layout, and the actual construction markings. Outlined here are the various types of markings, and a brief description of each.

Markings for Sorting Pattern Pieces

☐ Pattern number, figure type and size printed in center of each pattern piece.

☐ Pattern view lettered by an identifying *A, B, C, D.* Select only those pieces with the letter symbol for the view you plan to make.

Markings for Pattern Alteration

☐ Easy-Rule Guide, a solid and dotted line marking, divided like a ruler, is printed on bodice, sleeve, shoulder and skirt to make shortening and lengthening the pattern piece an easy task.

☐ Lines on Proportioned patterns indicating where height adjustments are to be made.

Markings for Correct Layout

☐ Arrow line indicates fabric grain line and should be placed along a single yarn of the fabric. Printed along arrow line will be the words "lengthwise [or crosswise] of goods," indicating the direction in which the piece should be laid.

☐ Single line at edge of pattern will have "place this line on fold of fabric" printed along the line. This appears at center back or center front of a garment.

☐ "Cut 1," "Cut 2" or the words "to be faced" printed on the pattern piece indicates the number of fabric pieces to be cut from the one pattern piece.

When "to be faced" appears, a second piece of fabric or facing material is cut from the pattern piece.

Markings for Accurate Cutting

☐ Double cutting lines, an exclusive feature of McCall's Patterns, make cutting more accurate and easier. Cutting is done directly between the two lines.

☐ Direction arrows along the seam line indicate the direction to cut and stitch the fabric in order to maintain proper grain direction. This will prevent stretching the fabric, reduce raveling of cut edges and prevent any grain distortion.

☐ Notches are used to match seams quickly and accurately and are indicated by diamond shapes along the seamline. Cut notches out from, never into, seam allowance which may be needed for alteration. Cut along the solid line across the top of double or triple notches; it is much easier to cut and as easy to match as separately cut notches. Notches are numbered in the order in which they are to be joined.

Markings for Accurate Sewing and Fitting

☐ Printed name of each pattern piece appears in the center of the piece. Skirt front, bodice front, sleeve, facing are quickly identified by simply looking for the name on the pieces.

☐ Darts and tucks are marked by short broken lines indicating the stitching line. Stitching lines must be accurately matched; the solid line in the center of dart and tuck markings is used as a fold line, making matching of stitching lines easier and more accurate.

☐ Circle markings may appear along stitching lines of darts and tucks indicating points to match for accurate stitching. Circles along seam lines may also indicate the beginning and ending of an opening. Stitch the seam only as far as the marked circle.

☐ Seam line stitching lines are long broken lines along the edge of pattern piece, normally ⅝ inch from the cutting line which is the standard seam allowance.

☐ Pieces for set-in sleeves have large circles at the top of a sleeve-cap seam line to indicate the point on the sleeve that should be matched to the shoulder seam line of the bodice. Notches and small circles on the seam line of the sleeve cap and bodice armhole are matched so fullness or ease may be evenly distributed.

☐ Buttonholes are marked by solid lines with small circles at outer edge which indicate the termination of buttonhole. These markings will be the correct length for the size buttons suggested in the "Notions" section on the pattern envelope. They are also in proper position for the design, unless the pattern piece must be shortened or lengthened.

☐ "Clip" or "slash" will be printed along a solid line on the pattern piece, meaning the piece must be clipped or slashed along that line. Study the guide sheet before clipping or slashing. Sometimes the seam is stitched, then clipped; at other times a slash has to be reinforced before it is cut. Be sure to read the instructions to find which method is required for each particular design.

Markings for Correct Fit

☐ Center front and back are marked along the fold or stitching line except when button closings are used. On buttoned closings, there will be a separate solid line with the words "center front" or "center back" printed along it. Mark these clearly on the garment section with basting. These markings indicate width of lap and emphasize proper grain line, which help in checking the grain and fit of the garment.

☐ Natural waistline for the standard figure in each pattern size is marked by a short straight line, and the words "natural waistline." Check waist length measurement from this point and shorten or lengthen according to your needs.

GLOSSARY OF SEWING TERMS

Following directions of any kind requires a pretty thorough knowledge of the terminology. By using this glossary you can check your own sewing vocabulary and add new terms. Keep it handy for quick reference and browse through it when you have time. The larger your knowledge of terms, the easier sewing becomes.

A

Allowance Extra fabric outside the seam line, or within the garment, to accommodate gathers, tucks, shirrings or bloused effects.

Appliqué Small piece(s) of fabric applied as decorative trimming by hand or machine.

Armscye or Armhole The opening in a garment for the arm. It is faced or bound, or a sleeve is set into the opening.

Arrowhead Tack A small, hand-embroidered, triangular trim detail used on tailored garments as a reinforcement stay at the ends of pleats, vents, pockets.

B

Back-Stitch A small hand-stitch that looks like machine-stitching on the right side but with stitches overlapping on the wrong side.

Bands Strips of fabric, ribbon or bias applied to edges or set into garments to finish or decorate. They may be cut on the bias or straight of grain.

Bar Fagoting Decorative trim used between seams and created by wrapping your needle with thread and making parallel bars from edge to edge.

Bar Tack Hand-worked decorative trim used across ends of pockets, buttonholes, etc., to reinforce the ends.

Basic Pattern A pattern printed on non-woven fabric, fabric, or paper assembled and altered for correct garment fit. Used then as a guide to compare with other patterns to make correct pattern alterations.

Basting A loose, long, temporary stitch made by hand or machine. Usually made with a contrasting colored thread.

Beading A narrow open-work insertion through which ribbon can be run. It is usually placed between fabric edges but can also be used with lace edges.

Belt Carrier A thread or fabric loop used to hold belt in place.

Belting A stiff ribbonlike banding used inside a waistline as a stay, or covered with fabric and used outside as a belt.

Beveling *See* Grading.

Bias The 45-degree diagonal of a fabric. It is used when you need "give" in your material.

Bias Band A strip of bias used to finish edges or decorate a garment.

Bias Facing A strip of bias-cut fabric used to finish curved edges.

Bias Seam Binding A bias rayon, silk or nylon binding used to finish curved raw edges.

Bias Tape A bias cotton binding used to bind, face or pipe curved edges. Comes in double or single fold.

Bishop Sleeve A long sleeve, wide at the bottom and gathered into a band.

Blanket Stitch A decorative edge finish formed by looped, interlocking stitches.

Blend A mixture of different fibers in one yarn, or different yarns in one fabric, each lending its own characteristics to the fabric.

Blind-Stitch A form of hemming made by catching only one thread of the outer fabric.

Bodkin A blunt needle with an eye or a pin on the end used for threading tape, elastic or ribbon through beading or casing.

Body Measurements Actual measurements of the body—bust, waistline, hip, back waist length—used to purchase the correct pattern. Also, measurements given on the back of the pattern envelope that are correct for the size and figure type of a specific pattern.

Boning Stiff piece of bone, plastic or metal used within a seam or along a dart to give added support or fit in a bodice or hip area.

Box Pleat Two side pleats which turn away from each other.

Braid A woven novelty trim finished on both edges. Comes in cotton, wool, rayon and nylon in a variety of widths and weights and can be applied by hand or machine.

Breakline The roll line of a lapel when it turns back from the garment.

Bridle A strip of pre-shrunk tape that is applied behind the breakline of a lapel to prevent stretching.

C

Canvas Firmly woven fabric used for coat interfacing. Can be of linen, cotton, wool or hair fabric.

Cartridge Pleats Unpressed, rounded pleats used decoratively.

Casing A hem with an opening so that ribbon or elastic can be drawn through.

Catch-Stitch A cross-stitch used to hold raw edge in place securely.

Chain-Stitch A decorative stitch formed by interlocking loops.

Chalk Tailor's chalk is a firm grade of chalk used for marking pattern lines and fitting marks. French chalk is a powder that can be dusted on your hands to keep them fresh and your garment unstained.

Clean Finish An edge finish for facings, hems or seams in non-bulky fabrics that ravel. Turn under raw edges ¼ inch and machine-stitch close to turned edge.

Clip A short cut into the seam allowance of a garment which allows a corner or a curved area to turn and lie flat.

Cording A cord which is encased in bias fabric and used to finish and decorate edges, waistlines, buttonholes.

Couching An embroidery stitch in which a long, heavy double thread or cord is laid along a design and caught in place by another thread at equal intervals.

Crease A folded line pressed into the material.

Crosswise Grain The grain of the fabric that runs from selvage to selvage at right angles to the lengthwise grain.

Crow's Foot A triangular-shaped thread design used as an end stay for pleats and pockets.

Custom Finish Professionally perfect in its fit and construction.

D

Dart A stitched fold of fabric tapering to a point at one or both ends, used to shape a garment to fit the curves of the body.

Design Allowance Extra ease in a garment to permit blousing, tucking or shirring.

Diagonal Basting A temporary stitch used to hold two layers of fabric together without slipping.

Directional Cutting, Stay-Stitching, Stitching, and Pressing Working with the grain of the fabric to retain the original shape. The pattern is marked with small arrows on each seam indicating the direction in which to work.

Drape Soft folds of fabric controlled by pleats or gathers.

Dress Form A duplicate of the human figure made of padded fabric, wire, paper or plastic. Helpful for fitting or draping a garment.

Dressmaker's Carbon Carbon of many colors used with a tracing wheel to mark construction lines.

E

Ease When one section of a seam is slightly fuller than the section to which it is joined, the fullness is distributed evenly without gathers or puckers and pressed so that the threads within the fabric are crowded closer together. This ease allows shaping for curved areas such as the bust in princess line, set-in sleeves, etc.

Ease Allowance An allowance in measurement over and above the given body measurements of a pattern. This ease allowance gives needed room in a garment for it to be comfortable and allow for movement.

Edge Finish Any finish applied to the raw or cut edge of fabric, such as hemming, binding, stitching, fringing, overcasting, zigzagging or pinking.

Edging Any lace, tatting or novelty trim with one straight edge and one decorative edge.

Edge-Stitch A line of stitching placed close to a finished edge of a garment.

Elastic Thread Thread made with a rubber core that gathers fabric as you stitch. Can be applied by machine as well as by hand.

Embroidery Machine- or hand-stitching worked for decorative effect.

Emery Bag A small bag filled with an abrasive powder used to sharpen and remove rust from pins and needles.

Entre-Deux Another term for beading or veining; it is an open-work strip that can be inserted between fabric edges and run through with ribbon.

Even Basting Large stitches equally sized and spaced, used for temporary joining.

Extension Any additional fabric jutting out beyond a seam or a center marking.

Eyelet A small hole in a garment, finished by hand-stitches or a metal ring to hold the prong of a buckle. Also used to give lacing effect with ribbon, yarn or cording.

F

Facing A piece of fabric, fitted or bias, applied to finish the edges of neckline, armhole and openings in a garment.

Fagoting A trim placed between seams. It is either handmade or commercially purchased as tape.

Fashion Stitches Decorative stitches used for trimming. Made by hand or with sewing machine.

Fastenings Hooks, eyes, snaps, buttons, etc., used to close garments.

Featherboning Light-weight, fabric-covered boning that is used for support of seams in strapless bodices, wide belts, etc.

Feather Stitch Blanket stitches that are slanted to create a decorative pattern.

Felling A slanted hemming stitch used in tailoring to attach undercollar to coat.

Fibers Natural or man-made substances used to form the yarns of fabrics.

Figure Type The classification for various figures according to height and body proportions. Within each figure type are various size ranges.

Filling The yarns interlaced at right angles to the warp yarns to produce fabrics. These run across the fabric from selvage to selvage.

Findings *See* Notions.

Fish Dart A dart that tapers at both ends, generally used at waistline.

Fitting Adjusting pattern or garment to fit your individual figure.

Flap A piece of fabric that hangs loose and is attached at one edge only. Found on pockets.

Flat-Fell Seam used on shirts, slacks and other tailored garments in which one seam is trimmed and the other stitched over it. Gives a flat, finished seam on both sides of the garment.

Flounce Circular, gathered or pleated length of fabric that is applied to the bottom of skirts, curtains or furniture.

Fly Front Closing that conceals buttons or zipper, usually associated with men's pants, topcoats and Chesterfield-type coats.

French Chalk See Chalk.

French Knot Decorative hand-stitch in which the thread is twisted around the needle and brought down through the fabric at almost the same spot to form a small dot.

French Seam A double-stitched seam that looks like a plain seam on the right side and a small neat tuck on the wrong side. Used on straight seams and as a finish for sheer fabrics or infants' clothes.

French Tack A thread bar fastening used to hold two pieces of a garment together loosely. Used to attach lining to coat at hemline.

Fringe Decorative edge finish purchased by the yard or formed by raveling the edge of fabric.

Frog Decorative closing formed by looping braid, bias binding, or cording. Usually associated with Oriental style garments.

G

Gathering One or two rows of stitching, either hand or machine, that are drawn up to form even fullness.

Gauging Fullness drawn up in uniform-sized deep folds of fabric where a long length of fabric is to be gathered into a small space. This produces a decorative effect.

Gimp A heavy thread that is often used on worked buttonholes.

Glove Stitch Decorative top-stitching made by taking the same size stitch on both sides of the work.

Godet Triangular or shaped piece that is set into skirts, curtains, etc., for added width at the bottom.

Gore Tapered or flared section of fabric that is narrow at the top and wide at the bottom. Usually refers to a skirt section.

Gorge Line Part of the seam line that joins the collar and the facing. It extends from the crease or roll line to the notch.

Grading Trimming all the seam allowances within a seam to different widths to eliminate bulk. The interfacing seam allowance is always trimmed close to the seam.

Grain The direction of fabric threads. The yarns running parallel to the selvages form the lengthwise grain; the yarns running from selvage to selvage form the crosswise grain.

Grain-Line Arrow The arrow line printed on a pattern indicating the exact grain-line for each garment piece. Place this printed line along one yarn of the fabric, lengthwise or crosswise, as indicated on the pattern.

Guide Sheet Printed instruction sheet included with each pattern giving specific detailed instructions for the complete construction of each pattern view in that particular pattern.

Gusset A small triangular or shaped piece of matching fabric set into a slash or seam to give added ease and shaping. Usually placed at underarm.

H

Ham A ham-shaped cushion that is used for pressing or molding shaped areas and curves.

Hand-Pricking A variation of the back-stitch used for applying zippers by hand or as an edge finish on a tailored garment.

Hand-Rolled Hem A fine edge finish for sheer fabrics or for a scarf, sash or ruffle formed by rolling raw edge between fingers and hemming by hand.

Heading Area above the pleating or gathering line of a casing, flounce or ruffle.

Heavy-Duty Thread Heavy-weight thread used for sewing on buttons or sewing on heavy fabric such as sailcloth, drapery or upholstery fabric.

Hem An edge finish formed by folding back the raw edge and stitching it by hand or machine. The depth of the hem and the method of stitching depend on the garment and type of fabric.

Hemline The marked line at the bottom of a garment where the hem is turned.

Hemstitch A decorative open-work stitch made by drawing lengthwise threads of the fabric and fastening the crosswise threads in clusters.

Honeycomb Stitch A basic smocking stitch worked alternately on two rows at a time. Fits smoothly over curved areas since it tends to spread and close like an accordion.

I

Insertion A piece of lace or decorative banding (straight on both edges) set into a garment for trimming.

Inset   A piece of fabric inserted in a garment for fitting or decorative purposes.

Interfacing   A suitable fabric sewn between the garment and facing to give added body, shaping and support to the garment. Usually used along edges, in collars, cuffs, pockets, waistbands.

Interlining   A suitable fabric sewn and shaped the same as the garment, placed between the garment and lining to give added warmth.

Inverted Pleat   Two side pleats which turn toward each other.

Invisible Stitch   Used for hems and attaching facings and interfacings in tailoring.

K

Key   To match pattern markings or seam edges on the sections to be joined.

Kick Pleat   A short pleat at the lower edge of a skirt. It is formed by an extension cut on the center or side seam and is top-stitched across the upper edge to hold it in place.

Kimono Sleeve   Bodice and sleeve cut in one piece with or without a shoulder seam.

Knife Pleats   Series of pleats that turn in the same direction, are usually equal in width and are pressed straight to the hem.

Knot-Stitch   *See* Lock-Stitch.

L

Lap   To place one piece of fabric over another.

Lapel   Upper edge of a coat front that turns back.

Lapped Seam   A seam used for yokes and applied pieces such as gussets. One seam allowance is lapped over the other seam allowance and top-stitched.

Layering   Another term for grading, staggering or beveling; trimming one seam allowance narrower than the other to eliminate bulk.

Layout   The way the pattern pieces are placed on the fabric for cutting. The pattern guide sheet has diagrams showing the easiest and most economical way to place the pattern pieces on the fabric for each width of fabric, pattern size, and pattern view.

Lazy Daisy Stitch   Embroidery stitch that is a long chain stitch arranged to form a flower.

Lengthwise Grain   The yarns in the fabric that run parallel to the selvage. It usually has a greater number of yarns to the inch, is stronger and will stretch less than the crosswise grain.

Lingerie Hem   A rolled hem that is caught with two overcast stitches at intervals of ⅛ to ⅜ inch gathering it in puffs.

Lingerie Seam   Supposedly "rip-proof"; made by pressing both edges of a seam to one side and top-stitching with a zigzag stitch along the edge.

Lining   A suitable fabric constructed in the shape of a garment to cover and finish the inside of the entire garment or a section of it. It can also give shaping and prevent stretching.

Link Buttons   Two flat buttons held together with several threads covered with blanket stitches. Used as cuff links.

Lock-Stitch   Stitch used to secure thread at beginning and end of stitching, made by releasing presser foot and stitching in one place several times.

Loop   A fastening, which extends beyond the finished edge, used on closings with no lap. Can be made of thread, cording or fabric.

M

Machine-Basting   A long machine-stitch used in place of hand-basting. Can be pulled out easily.

Machine-Gather   One or two rows of long machine-stitches pulled up to hold fullness evenly.

Machine Hem   A hem stitched in by machine. Usually found in sportswear, curtains or slip covers.

Marking   Transferring all necessary pattern symbols to the wrong side of the fabric by one of the various methods best suited to the fabric.

Matching   Joining construction markings.

Military Braid   A flat rayon or metallic braid used as a trim.

Miter   Diagonal joining of two pieces of fabric or lace that meet at a corner.

N

Nap   The short fibers on the surface of the fabric that have been drawn out from the yarns of the fabric and brushed in one direction.

Needle Board   A board covered with fine steel wires set vertically for use in pressing velvet and other nap or pile fabrics.

Notch   A small diamond-shaped printed marking or group of markings on the cutting edge of the pattern that indicate where fabric edges match corresponding edges.

Notions   All dressmaking supplies that are used in the construction of a garment: thread, zippers, tape, buttons, etc.

Nylon Closure Tape Nylon tape with a fleece side and burr side which adhere firmly to each other, used for fastening openings, belts, etc.

O

Open-Work Decorative insertions of open designs and patterns; can be made by hand or machine.

Outline Stitch An embroidery stitch made with a short back-stitch worked from left to right.

Overcasting A small, slanting stitch placed over the raw edge of fabric to finish the edge and keep it from raveling.

Overhanding A straight stitch used to hold finished edges together when a strong, flat, invisible seam is needed, as in table linen, undergarments, sewing on lace or patching.

Overlap Part of a garment that extends or laps over another part.

P

Padding Stitch Tiny, diagonal hand-stitches used to hold interfacing to the fabric securely on tailored garments. The stitches do not show on the right side of the garment.

Permanent Basting Any type of basting with matching thread that remains in the finished garment.

Pickup Line The center fold line of a dart or tuck.

Picot An edge finish made by cutting through a line of machine hemstitching.

Piecing Sewing two pieces of fabric together when more width is needed as in a circular skirt; should always be done on grain.

Pile Fabric woven with a third set of yarns forming tufts or loops on the surface of the fabric. Loops may be cut or uncut. Velvet, velveteen, corduroy, terry cloth are examples.

Pin-Basting A method of joining seams before stitching them. Place pins at right angles to edge and an even distance from the edge.

Pin-Fit To pin and adjust the garment to your figure before permanent stitching.

Pin Tucks Tucks pressed on a thread of the goods and stitched close to the edge.

Pinch Pleats Cluster of pleats used in drapery headings. Made by dividing one pleat into several smaller ones.

Pinking A notched seam finish cut with pinking shears. Can only be used on fabrics that do not ravel badly.

Pins Dressmaker or silk pins—rustproof and sharp— used to hold pattern and fabrics together and to hold pieces of fabric together.

Piping A fold of bias fabric, ribbon or braid inserted in a seam.

Pivot Refers to way of stitching a sharp corner. Leave the needle in the fabric, lift the presser foot, turn the fabric to the desired angle, lower the presser foot and continue stitching.

Placket Opening in a garment that allows for ease in dressing. Plackets are closed by means of snaps, hooks and eyes or zippers.

Plain Seam The stitching together of two pieces of fabric placed right sides together. Most common seam used in sewing.

Pleats Folds of fabric used to control fullness in a garment.

Pocket Stay A strip of interfacing sewn to the wrong side of a pocket opening for reinforcement.

Pre-Shrink Treatment of fabrics so that size will not be appreciably altered by washing or dry-cleaning.

Prick Stitch *See* Hand-Pricking.

Q

Quilting Stitching several layers of fabric together in an all-over design.

R

Ravel To draw yarns out from along the edge of the fabric to form fringe.

Regulation Stitch The permanent stitching placed in a garment, usually 12 stitches per inch. May be varied in length to suit the fabric.

Reinforce To add strength to corners and areas of great stress by adding rows of stitching or a patch of fabric.

Revers Wide shaped lapels on a garment.

Reversible Fabric that has been finished so that either side may be used or a garment finished so that it may be turned and worn on either side.

Rick Rack A saw-tooth-edge braid made in cotton or metallic thread. Can be applied as a flat braid or set into a seam.

Rip To open a seam by pulling out or cutting the stitching.

Rolled Hem *See* Hand-Rolled Hem.

Ruffle A band of fabric that is gathered or pleated and applied to an edge as trimming.

Running Stitch The simplest form of hand-stitching; small stitches that appear the same on both sides of the fabric, used for gathering.

S

Saddle Stitch   A decorative top-stitch made by taking longer stitches on top and shorter ones underneath.

Sag   The stretch that occurs in the bias grain of garments after hanging, or the effect of strain on any part of a garment.

Satin Stitch   An embroidery stitch made by rows of flat stitches placed close together.

Scallop   An edge finish made up of a series of semi-circles.

Seam   The line or fold formed by stitching two pieces of fabric together.

Seam Allowance   The fabric edge that extends beyond the stitching line. The normal seam allowance in all patterns is ⅝ inch unless it is marked and printed otherwise on the pattern.

Seam Finish   The finish applied to a raw edge to control fraying and raveling.

Seam Roll   A long, firmly padded cylinder that is used for pressing seams.

Selvage   The narrow woven border on the lengthwise edges of the fabric.

Shank   The stem between the button and the fabric to which it is sewn; may be part of the button or can be made with thread when the button is sewn on.

Shaping Materials   Appropriate fabric used as interfacing, underlining, interlining or lining in a garment.

Shell Edge   A narrow hem that is stitched by hand and stitched over the edge at measured intervals to form scallops. Used on lingerie.

Shell Tuck   A tuck that is sewn by hand with a stitch taken over the edge at measured intervals to form scallops.

Shirring   Two or more rows of gathers.

Shrinking   Contracting of fabric usually resulting from washing or dry-cleaning. Most fabrics are now treated by manufacturers to control shrinkage.

Side Pleats   Also called Knife Pleats.

Size   The measurement classification within a figure type which allows for variations in body measurements such as bust, waist, and hip. Each figure type has a range of sizes.

Sizing   A chemical finish applied to a fabric to give it added body or stiffness.

Slash   An even cut in the fabric along a straight line. This is a longer cut than a clip. Slashes are usually finished with a seam or facing.

Sleeveboard   A small, narrow, well-padded board for pressing sleeves.

Slip-Basting   Invisible hand-basting, put in from the right side.

Slip-Stitch   Tiny hand-stitches taken through and under a fold of fabric where the stitching must be invisible.

Slot Seam   A seam which has an underlay of fabric and resembles an inverted pleat.

Smocking   A decorative way of gathering a piece of fabric into regular folds; done before the garment is made up.

Soutache   A narrow rayon braid with rounded edges used for decorative effect. Can be curved or shaped easily.

Spanking   Pounding or flattening fabric with heat and steam to shape it. Used primarily on woolen fabrics.

Stab-Stitch   A stitch in which the needle is brought in and out of the fabric at right angles. Used for sewing on buttons or as an edge stitch.

Stay   Tape or fabric sewn into a section of the garment to reinforce the section and hold it securely in position. Used at waistlines, under gathers or shirring.

Stay-Stitching   A row of machine stitching placed on the seamline. Used as a reinforcement or as a guide for turning an edge accurately.

Steam Press   To press a garment using steam produced by moisture and a hot iron to remove creases, raise nap in pile fabrics and shrink out fullness in woolens.

Stiffening   Fabric such as crinoline, horsehair or non-woven interfacing used to stiffen parts of a garment.

Straightening   Manipulating fabric to correct grain-line; pulling out a crosswise thread of the fabric and then cutting along that line.

Straight of Goods   This refers to the lengthwise grain or crosswise grain of the fabric.

Sunburst Pleats   Pleats that are wider at the bottom than at the top.

Surplice   Front closing that is cut on the diagonal.

T

Tack   To hold two pieces of fabric together at a point with tiny hand-stitches.

Tailor's Tack   Method of marking pattern symbols with temporary loose basting stitches sewn through double layer of fabric and cut apart when pattern is removed.

Tailoring   The technique of shaping and molding the garment throughout the construction processes in making a suit or coat.

Taping Sewing tape on the back of fabric for reinforcement at points of stress.

Tension The degree of looseness or tightness of bobbin thread and needle thread in machine-stitching. The bobbin thread and needle thread should lock evenly together in the fabric.

Termination Point Marking placed at the end of a tuck or dart to guide in matching the layers of fabric exactly.

Top-Stitching A line of stitching on the outside of the garment, usually placed close to a finished seam or a finished edge.

Trapunto Quilting in which only the design part is padded.

Trim To cut away excess fabric in the seam allowances after the seam has been stitched.

True Bias Exact 45-degree diagonal of the fabric. When cut on this line, material will have the most "give."

Tubing A hollow cylinder of fabric used for button loops and decorative trim.

Tucks Straight folds of fullness evenly stitched.

Twill Tape A woven cotton tape used as a stay, drawstring or ties.

U

Underlap A part of a garment that extends or laps under another part.

Underlay An additional piece of fabric placed under a section for the purpose of joining as in a pleat or slot seam.

Underlining A suitable fabric used to back a section or an entire garment. It is used to give body and shaping and to prevent sagging and stretching of the outer fabric.

Understitching A row of machine-stitching through the facing and seam allowance close to a seamline. This holds the facing to the seam allowances and prevents the facing from rolling to the outside.

Unit Construction Organization of sewing procedure so that an entire garment section is completed before it is joined to another.

V

Velvet Board Another name for a needle board.

Vent A lapped, finished opening on the hem edge of a sleeve, jacket or skirt.

W

Warp The yarns that run lengthwise in a woven fabric. The filling yarns are interlaced with them at right angles.

Weights Metal discs which are covered with fabric and sewn in cowl necklines or in the hemlines of coats and jackets.

Welt An applied strip of fabric used to finish the lower edge of slashed pocket. It is stitched on three sides and left open at the top.

Whip Stitching two finished edges together securely with tiny slanting stitches.

With Nap Designation for fabric that must be cut with all the pattern pieces laid in one direction. This includes napped fabrics, pile fabrics and those with a one-way design produced by light reflection (sateen, satin), printed or woven with an up-and-down direction.

Woven Seam Binding A straight-edged rayon, silk or nylon binding used to finish raw edges of hems or as a stay. It cannot be shaped or used on curved edges.

Y

Yardage The amount of fabric needed to make a particular garment. The back of the pattern envelope has a yardage chart. This gives the exact amount of fabric necessary for each view and size for the various widths of fabric.

Z

Zigzag Stitch A machine-stitch made by the movement of the needle from side to side rather than in a straight line. The stitch is made with a zigzag attachment or an automatic machine. Used to stitch two edges of fabric together, finish the raw edges of seams, stitch plain seams for greater elasticity, apply appliqués, mend tears or make decorative stitching.

Zipper A closure made of metal or nylon chains attached to tape so that it can be stitched into a placket.

Zipper Foot Machine foot with one prong for stitching in zippers or cording. Right, left or adjustable attachments are available.

CHAPTER 3

THE RAW MATERIALS— FABRIC, SHAPING MATERIALS, NOTIONS

The basis of any fashion is, of course, the materials of which it is made. Fabric, thread, buttons, trimmings and the like are the seamstress' raw materials—her paint and canvas. Top designers use fabrics as fine artists do paint—subtly, skillfully, dramatically creating fashions that are exciting and beautiful. Many home-sewers haven't achieved this perfection, but everyone should understand how different materials handle and the effects they create. Then putting a costume together will not be thought of as a flat jigsaw puzzle, but instead, as the molding and draping of fabric to create the desired result.

THE ART OF FABRIC SELECTION

Fabrics are a lot like people. They have very distinct personalities and behavior patterns. They can be stiff and unyielding; crisp and businesslike; soft, fluttery and feminine; even whimsical and fun. Studying the personality of fabrics is almost as interesting and profitable as studying people. The more you know about them, the more you enjoy them, and the more success you have in dealing with them.

If a garment is to be completely successful, the personality of the fabric must be used to full advantage. It should be flattering to you, expressive of your personality, and completely suitable to the design and the occasion. In short, the fabric in a garment as well as the design must be in good taste. Developing perfect taste in fabric selection is not an easy task, but neither is it an impossible one. It takes study, experimentation and probably a few mistakes before one unerringly selects the right fabric for every design.

Suggested Fabrics

When choosing fabric for a particular design, check the pattern envelope for "Suggested Fabrics." Here are listed the designer's choices of fabrics having the proper weight and drapability for the design. Your choice needn't be confined to these selections, but you should look for fabrics similar in weight and drapability. In Chapter 4, you will find a complete "Glossary of Familiar Fabrics" with their descriptions and suggestions for their use.

Before you decide on a fabric, study the sketch of the design and determine the general silhouette of the garment. Hold the fabric in these same general lines. Does it poke out when it should fall in graceful folds? Will it gather softly into shirring at the waist? Will it hold crisp pleats? Will it pouf if a bouffant effect is needed? If the design is a molded one, will the material be firm enough to retain the shape?

Learning to understand fabric and how it will shape in a garment takes two things—practice and observation. Practice feeling fabrics, all sorts of fabrics. Observe their behavior carefully. Look at the fabrics used in ready-to-wear garments. Check pattern publications to see which fabrics the experts select for various styles. Soon you will be able to look at a fabric and visualize it in a specific design, or look at a pattern and see it in a particular fabric.

There are two artistic factors that play a part in fabric selection—texture and color. Four basic elements are involved in texture: the light reflection which determines a fabric's sheen or dullness; the touch, its roughness or smoothness; the look, its richness or plainness; and the hand, which means the weight, body and drape. As to color, in addition to the optical illusions you can create with the right choice of color, as outlined in Chapter 1, there are other considerations in selecting color for your wardrobe. Which colors go well with each other and how much of each to use is an important decision you will have to make.

TEXTURE

Each of the elements of texture will have an influence on the total appearance of the garment and the figure wearing it. Whether a fabric is shiny or dull, whether it has a look of elegance or an everyday air, will make it more or less suitable for you and for the occasion. Surface roughness or a smooth silky look will determine to a large degree the type of garment for which a fabric can be used, as will its body and its ability to be draped softly, pleated crisply or molded sleekly.

Texture and Individuality

Just as certain styles seem more suitable for certain personalities, so do textures. For instance, three career women with comparable figures may select the same suit pattern. The first wants to look cool, crisp and efficient. She selects a smooth worsted wool in a conservative color. The second likes casual clothes with a bit of country about them. Her choice is sturdy, casual wide-wale corduroy. The third prefers the feminine look, and chooses a soft, airy bouclé woolen. Each suit is in good taste. The fabric is appropriate for the style and expresses the personality the individ-

ual wishes to convey. Always select the texture that makes you feel your best at all times.

Texture and the Design

Texture and a pattern design should be thought of together, so that they will not be in conflict. If a design calls for a bouffant effect, select a fabric that creates poufs naturally. However, if the design shows soft folds, be sure not to use a crisp or stiff fabric. Just like people, fabrics are more successful if they are doing what they like to do.

In defining texture, the word "hand" is frequently used. The hand, or weight and draping quality of the fabric, will determine to a great extent the designs for which it may be used. The way to determine and understand the hand of a fabric is to become a "fabric feeler." Touch it, drape it in folds, hold it up to see how it falls.

Textures for the Occasion

Usually one thinks of selecting the right clothes for an occasion, without consciously considering the appropriateness of the fabric. Obviously, there are certain elaborate fabrics which are never worn in the daytime. Satins, brocades, sequined fabrics are strictly for evening wear. On the other hand, there are fabrics and textures which seem more suited to city, country or resort wear.

Generally, clothes for the city and for business are best fashioned in fine-textured fabrics that are conservative in feeling. Recently, the range of "city" fabrics has been considerably extended. Tweedy materials, homespun fabrics, nubby* woolens are being used to create more casual-looking city clothes. Textures which wear well, resist soil and keep their shape are not only more practical for city wear, but more appropriate.

For the country, the rougher, sturdy fabrics look marvelous, and are in the right setting. The style of clothes for the country is more casual because living is more leisurely there. The textures should carry out the same theme of casual comfort.

Resort wear is the most fun of all. Here all the whimsical, funny, even bizarre fabrics and textures look right at home. The wild prints that are wrong for the suburbs are very right in the carefree atmosphere of the resort. For those who don't visit resorts, the same sort of textures can be used for at-home enter-

taining. Again, when the whole atmosphere is one of fun and relaxation, let the fabrics help set the mood.

Although certain fabrics are strictly evening fabrics, many popular daytime fabrics are now appearing in very effective evening fashions. The plaid woolens, formerly worn by school girls in skirts and dresses, appear in sleek, informal evening sheaths. Soft, drapable wool jersey is cut into a "little nothing" dress that is perfectly right for today's casual entertaining. However, many of these fabrics can be called "novelty" fabrics as far as evening wear is concerned, and usually look right only on younger girls or women with youthful figures and appearances. Soft flannel sheaths can be very striking for informal evening wear with the right sparkly jewelry; in summer many of the new "dressy" cottons and silky synthetics are perfect choices for evening ensembles. But when you want to feel really dressed up and ready for a big night, try the real evening fabrics. You'll feel more gala. There is something special about the luxurious feel of a silk crepe or satin, the rustle of taffeta or brocade, that makes you feel your elegant best.

Combining Textures

Being well dressed would be a simpler task if someone could just devise a hard-and-fast rule about combining textures, colors and lines. There just isn't any. Some women seem to have a sixth sense when it comes to coordinating a costume; most of us have to work at it.

The basic concept in combining the elements of any artful creation, be it a painting or a Paris costume, is unity of idea, with some variety. When working with textures, it generally means using sheers with sheers, heavyweights with heavyweights. Quite obviously, you do not add a wool tweed cummerbund to a nylon chiffon gown, nor a draped chiffon blouse to a cotton corduroy suit. However, some of the subtleties of selecting just the right textures in a costume are less obvious.

The only way to become adept at combining textures is to study the effect of one texture on another, and to observe various textural combinations used in fashion. Experiment with different combinations when planning a costume. When you sew your own, this is easier to do than when purchasing garments. You can take swatches of your garment along with you as you shop for blouses, accessories or other fabrics which will be combined with the garment you make.

COLOR

The second factor you have to consider in choosing a fabric is color. While the color is often more obvious than the texture, it creates just as many problems because of the profusion of colors that exist. It is so easy to employ too much color or the wrong kind, unless you learn to follow a few basic guides based on the principles of design.

Chart a Color Scheme

In planning your wardrobe, it is most important that you have a definite color scheme in mind. Unless you do, the various garments and accessories you make or buy will not seem to belong together. This lack of co-ordination will cause colors to clash or, what may be even worse, leave you with gaps in your wardrobe. A lovely suit without the right blouse can hang in the closet for months.

In order to avoid this unhappy situation, there are certain things you can do. First, decide on the colors which are most becoming to you. If you like one especially well and it can be used as a basic color, then make this your background color. Naturally, a basic color should be one which will combine nicely with a variety of other colors.

Usually, you will use the basic color for garments you plan to wear for several years, such as a coat or a suit. This is the most satisfactory plan for "carry-over" clothing, for it allows you to introduce unusual or livelier colors as accents in your wardrobe and change them from time to time without discarding the major garment.

Dark colors and those that create a neutral effect are the ones most frequently used for basic colors. Black, navy blue, brown and gray fall into this category. Although brighter colors can be used as basics, it is usually best to avoid them unless you can afford to change your entire wardrobe frequently. A person seems to tire of colors of high intensity more quickly than of those in more subdued hues. There is no reason for a basic color to give your wardrobe a monotonous look if you learn to employ color wisely and with imagination.

As soon as your basic color is chosen, you should look at all other colors with it in mind. Each new piece of apparel you select should be chosen to blend with your basic color. Gradually, you will evolve a color scheme which will make your entire new wardrobe more attractive and satisfying to wear.

Color in the Balance

Proper balance of color is important, especially when forceful and weak hues are used together. A good rule to follow at such time is that the larger the area to be covered, the less intense the color should be; the smaller the area, the brighter the color can be.

The amount of a color to use is also a matter of proportion. Subtle variations in the tone and the amounts of color used will create an interesting effect, while too much repetition of one color can become monotonous. For instance, the identical hue used for a hat, bag, gloves and shoes will create a less pleasing effect than if you were to choose one dark, one light and one bright tone of the same color.

Remember, too, that a light color has power to attract the eye and hold attention. This makes it possible for you to camouflage figure irregularities by drawing the eye to your most attractive feature. If several light areas are used, the eye will dart from one to the other. Unless they are placed advantageously, they can cause the figure to appear shorter and stouter. But a rhythmic feeling can be developed in a design if the colors are placed properly and used in correct amounts. The eye will seem to glide from one hue to the repeated one.

Color Harmony

Naturally, it is important for any color combination to give a feeling of harmony. To produce such an arrangement, colors should seem to belong together. This may be done by combining related colors in a monochromatic or an analogous harmony. It may also be achieved by using contrasting colors in a complementary harmony. Whichever you choose, one color should be emphasized with the others playing subordinate roles.

PATTERNED FABRICS

Prints, plaids, checks and stripes can add a delightful excitement to an otherwise drab wardrobe. However, it is important to select a patterned fabric that is flattering to the wearer.

Analyze the Design

The size of the fabric design should be in proportion to the size of the wearer. Small prints, miniature checks, narrow stripes seem best for the petite figure, larger designs for the taller. Large, bold prints, dramatic plaids and stripes should be worn only by someone with a Miss America figure. Usually the medium-sized print with an indefinite outline will be most flattering to the average figure.

Because of their versatility, prints have become a part of everyone's wardrobe. However, to select one which embodies the elements of good design is not always easy. The oft used principle of "unity with variety" is a good rule to follow. Motifs should be related. They should be placed so that the eye glides rhythmically from one motif to the next. Try an artist's trick. Hold the fabric at arm's length and study it through half-closed eyes. Do the designs and colors seem to blend in a pleasing harmony? If they do, you have probably chosen a good design.

Then the mood of the print should be considered. Some create a formal or conservative feeling; others a frivolous, gay spirit. Some seem demure; others exotic. Never allow the design to seem more important than you. Remember, you are simply selecting a background for your personality.

THE PRACTICALITIES OF FABRIC SELECTION

Once you have chosen a fabric that you like, one that is suitable for your pattern and appropriate for you, there is another point you will have to check at the store, and this is whether or not the fabric has a straight grain.

THE IMPORTANCE OF GRAIN LINES

Since the entire appearance of the garment may depend on whether the various sections are cut properly on the straight grain of the fabric, you should check fabric before purchasing it to see if the grain is straight. If it is not, then you will have to decide whether you can successfully straighten it yourself. Although fabrics are always originally woven on grain, finishing or printing processes will often pull them off-grain. In some cases a permanent finish may lock the threads in the off-grain position and the fabric can never be straightened. Wash-and-wear fabrics, in particular, should be carefully checked.

Testing for Position of Grain Lines

To test the grain of a fabric before you buy it, fold the fabric back on itself, matching the selvages. If the end of the fabric has been torn, see if the torn end is exactly at right angles to the selvage. If the fabric has been cut straight across the end, then try to follow a single crosswise thread to see if it is exactly parallel to the end of the fabric. Be sure to check carefully any prints with a regular design. It may be that the fabric was printed in an off-grain position and when straightened, the print pattern will be distorted.

On plaids or prints having a regular design at right angles to the selvage, make the following test. Unroll about a yard of the fabric from the bolt. Fold back about one-half yard. Match the selvages carefully, mak-

ing the fold at right angles to the selvage. Now, see if the design is parallel to the folded line. If it is a wash-and-wear or permanently finished fabric and is more than one-half inch off grain, don't buy it. You will never be able to straighten it and have a satisfactory garment.

It is rather difficult to determine grain straightness in knits, since most of them are produced in circular or tubular form with no lengthwise finished edges. The only way to check grain, before you buy the fabric, is to fold back about one-half yard and match the lengthwise folded edges carefully. This makes a fold at right angles to the edges. See if a single rib is at right angles to the folded line.

SHAPING MATERIALS

Shaping materials have been in existence for centuries. Look at the costumes in a museum. Elaborate metal and bone hoops, bustles and other contraptions gave fantastic shapes to garments of the past. Shaping materials are no less important today than they were in the days of Marie Antoinette, but fortunately for us, light-weight, shape-retaining fabrics do the job. They are much more comfortable to wear and work with.

Not only do shaping materials help shape the garment, but they also add to its durability. Below is a list of the jobs that shaping materials can be expected to do.

☐ Prevent sagging and stretching of knitted or loosely woven fabrics at points of strain, such as skirt backs.
☐ Give greater crease-resistance to all fashions.
☐ Add firmness and body to fashion details such as necklines, pockets or to the entire silhouette.

☐ Create fashion effects such as yokes, stand-up collars, peplums and stand-away flares.
☐ Strengthen edges where buttons, buttonholes, hooks and eyes are used.
☐ Tailor a fashion and help assure perfect fit.
☐ Increase the life of the garment.
☐ Add warmth to a garment.

Selecting Correct Shaping Fabric

Choosing the proper shaping materials for a garment is almost as important as selecting the right fashion fabric. Picking just the right one will take almost as much thought and consideration. You will have to choose a shaping material with two major points in mind. First, is it right for the fashion fabric—the proper weight and color—and second, what effect will it create in the garment? Will it stiffen it, make it soft and drapable, or just firm enough? The basic criteria for selecting shaping materials are:

☐ Correct weight—no heavier than the fashion fabric, unless you want a very crisp, standing effect.
☐ Proper finish and texture—should be somewhat similar to the fashion fabric.
☐ Right degree of stiffness and flexibility—it should suit the silhouette of the garment, or be able to take the shape of a specific detail.
☐ Shrinkage control—be sure to read the hang tags to see that the cleaning is the same for fabric and shaping material.
☐ Color—try to match the fabric color as nearly as possible; shaping materials may show through some fabrics.

The best way to determine which shaping material to use is to test the effect by draping the fabric and shaping material over your hand. Decide how they combine. Feel the two together to get an idea of the weight and texture; hold them up to see how they drape. Carefully consider how the two will shape into the silhouette of the garment.

How to Use

Shaping materials are used in a garment in four different ways, each having a slightly different purpose. They can be used as underlining, lining, interfacing or interlining.

UNDERLINING. A piece of shaping material usually cut in the shape of the design section of the garment, and used to back that section. The main purpose of underlining is to give shape to the garment and add to its crease-resistance and wear. The two pieces, garment section and underlining, are treated as one during construction.

LINING. Similar to underlining, except that it is constructed separately from the garment pattern pieces and joined to a major seam. Lining will not only shape the garment and add to its wear, it will provide a nice finished look to the inside of the garment.

INTERFACING. A piece of shaping material cut in the shape of a facing section and placed between the facing and the garment. Its purpose is to add firmness to the section, usually an edge, and help it retain its shape.

INTERLINING. Cut in the shape of a lining section and used between a lining and the design section. It is often used in coats or jackets when shape and added warmth are needed. Interlining is constructed separately and catch-stitched to the garment facing before the lining is sewn in.

Usually patterns indicate when shaping materials should be used. Study the chart shown here before choosing your shaping material.

WHAT MAKES THE SHAPE

SHAPING MATERIALS

USES	WOVEN	NON WOVEN	IRON ON
1. To tailor heavy coats and heavy suiting fabrics	1. Hymo "Special" Hair Canvas P-20 Bravo	Pellon—heavy weight Interlon—heavy weight	Shape-Flex Hair Canvas P-93
2. To tailor medium-weight woolens and synthetics; to give crisp effect to firm cottons and linens	2. Hymo "Regular" Veriform—crisp Undercurrent—crisp Si Bonne—crisp Sta-Shape—medium weight Veri-Super—crisp Super Siri—firm Hair Canvas—P-17, P-26 Acro Fino Formite	Interlon—regular weight Pellon—medium weight	Hair Canvas P-92 Detail Pelomite Shape-Flex
3. To give soft shaping to medium-weight fabrics; to give crisp shaping to lightweight fabrics	3. Si Bonne—soft Super Siri—soft Finolite Hair Canvas P-27 Undercurrent—medium soft Veriform—medium soft Veri-Super—medium soft Sta-Shape—lightweight durable press Also: organdy, permanently finished cotton, crepe, batiste, muslin, China silk	Pellon—lightweight all bias Interlon—lightweight all bias	Hair Canvas— P-91 P-94 Detail Pelomite Shape-Flex
4. To give soft shaping to lightweight fabrics; to give crisp shaping to sheers and laces	4. Si Bonne—soft Super Siri—super soft Also: net, organdy, organza, marquisette, lawn		

NOTIONS AND TRIMS

Patterns and fabrics do not cover the entire list of items you'll need for your sewing. There is a whole group of interesting items called notions and trims which are essential to the completion of a garment.

The essential notions which you must have for a garment are listed on the back of the pattern envelope. Thread, zippers and seam binding will almost invariably be mentioned. Buy these, plus any others listed, at the same time you purchase your fabric.

Zippers

Zippers are typed according to their purpose: neck zippers, dress placket zippers, skirt placket zippers, trouser fly zippers, and light-weight and heavy-weight separating zippers for jackets.

You'll have no problem selecting the type and length zipper you need. Your McCall's pattern tells exactly which to choose in the section marked "Notions" on the back of the envelope. Select one in the color closest to your fabric color. If you can't find an exact match, then select a shade darker.

Recently there have been developments in the zipper industry resulting in two new zippers which are going to add a great deal to the fashion look of garments. The "invisible" zipper is as thin as a seam line and the zipper teeth are completely invisible behind tapes. The conventional lap covering usually required to conceal a zipper is not even necessary. Currently it is only available in 7-inch and 9-inch lengths and is used for skirts, slacks and shorts. The application of this zipper is somewhat different from standard, so be sure to check the instructions accompanying the zipper.

Even more recent is the nylon zipper with nylon coils that mesh. It is a lighter, more flexible zipper than the metal chain and is easily repaired in a few seconds. It takes color beautifully and keeps the coils permanently colored.

Nylon Tape Closure

This type of closure is especially useful for fastening openings on belts, waistbands, jackets, slipcovers and for attaching removable collars and cuffs. It is a bit too bulky to use in most dresses or skirts. The tape is an inch wide and comes in yard or more lengths which can be cut to the size you need. There is a wide color range; select the one closest to your fabric color.

Snaps

Snaps are available in silver and black and should be rustproof. They should be used where there is little strain, never to replace a button. Sizes vary from size 4/0, the finest, to 4, the largest. Sizes 4/0 and 0 are used for sheer and medium-weight fabrics, and 1 to 4 for heavier weights.

Hooks and Eyes

These also come in silver and black. Again, select ones that are rustproof. They are useful where there is tension on a garment or an inconspicuous closing is needed. The eye can be either a straight bar type for use on overlapping edges, or the round type for edges that just meet. Hook and eye sizes vary from 00, the finest, for use on light-weight materials, to 12 for very coarse heavy-weight fabrics.

Gripper Snaps

These may be bought in separate units, or they can be purchased already applied to tape. A kit is available for applying the fasteners. A wide color range is available and some have decorative designs on them. Although grippers can replace buttons, they are mainly used in women's sport jackets, children's playclothes, baby clothes or men's shorts.

Buttons

The size and number of buttons needed for a garment are listed on the pattern envelope. There are two basic types of buttons: the shank, which is sewn to the garment under the button face, and the sew-through type. Buttons are available in wood, bone, plastic, metal, glass, leather, jet, pearl, fabric or crocheted, and there are kits for covering your own buttons easily and quickly.

Choose buttons that are best suited to your fabric and your size, considering the color, texture, design and style of the garment. Be sure to select washable buttons if they are to be placed on a washable garment.

Bias Seam Tape or Binding

This is used as a trim edge finish or as a finish for raw

edges on the inside of garments. It comes in assorted colors and is available in cotton percale, pima and nainsook, rayon or silk. The fabric closest to your garment fabric should be selected, so it will react to washing or cleaning the same as the rest of the garment. It is purchased as single-fold, double-fold or wide bias tape. Rayon and silk bindings are single fold and are used to finish curved seam edges and hems. Double-fold cotton bias tape is most useful as a trim since it is already folded and easily applied. For use as a facing, it is best to use the single fold. The cotton percale tape used for trimming is also available in stripes, checks, plaids and small prints and can add a gay finish to summer sportswear or children's clothing. The wide bias tape is used for quilt binding or edge trimming. See page 230 for complete directions on how to apply bias seam bindings.

Woven Seam Binding

A straight woven tape with finished edges. Used to finish hem edges, and as a stay to eliminate stretching of a seam. It is available in rayon, silk or nylon, and in assorted colors. Commercially, the ½-inch width is usually the only size available.

Bias Skirt or Hem Facing

This is a bias strip 2½ inches wide with folded edges. It is used for facing hems when the skirt is not long enough for a self hem or when a very bulky fabric is used and a hem would produce an unsightly bulge. It comes in assorted colors and is of percale, nainsook or rayon taffeta.

Twill Tape

A cotton tape used in tailoring to tape edges and roll lines as well as seams to prevent stretching, especially in heavy-weight fabrics or very stretchable materials. It has a sturdy twill construction that has no stretch or give. It is available only in black or white and in widths of ¼ to 1 inch. The ¼ inch is used for tailoring, the ⅜ to ⅝ inch for making ties on garments or for taping seams. The 1-inch is not readily available, since it is used mainly in upholstery work.

Cording

Cording is used to pipe edges and seams, tucks, buttonholes, in loops and frogs, and in shirring. It is available in sizes 40 to 300. The fine cable cord (No. 40) is excellent to use for cording buttonholes and for fine piped edges. The heavyweights can be used for drawstrings or heavy cord belts. When using cord for seams at the waistline or for edge trims, select the size cord needed for your fabric and for the effect you desire. Cording comes in white only because it is covered by the fabric.

Corded Piping

This is a fine cording covered in bias cotton for use as a decorative edge trimming. It is available in assorted colors and provides a neat decorative finish for faced edges and seams.

Braid Trims

There is a wide assortment of novelty braid trimming available, including fold-over braid, middy braid, soutache (very fine braid), shell and novelty trims. The pattern may indicate the type of trim needed, or you can use your own judgment.

Elastic

Available as thread or in various widths up to several inches. Ordinarily it is made of nylon or rayon and is limited to white, pink and black. The elastic thread is sometimes found in light blue, brown, navy and gray in addition to the regular white, pink and black.

Belting

The width and yardage needed for making belts is listed on the back of the pattern envelope. You may cut your own belt interfacing or backing from heavy interfacing fabrics, buckram, heavy canvas or grosgrain ribbon. However, the commercial beltings are quite fine and easier to use. They come plain, rubberbacked or leather-backed and are made of heavy cotton or rayon. Belting can be purchased by the yard or in standard belt length packages. Also very popular are belt and buckle kits that come by waist size and in widths from ½ to 3 inches.

Buckles

The size buckle needed will depend upon the width of the belt. The inside measurement of the buckle should be slightly wider than the width of the belting used. Buckles are available in bone, wood, plastic, metal, leather, pearl or fabric-covered, and with or without a prong. The kits for covering buckles are very easy to use, and provide a nice self-belt finish to a garment. Select the type and shape buckle which is best suited to the garment style and any buttons or trims used.

Shoulder Pads

The style in shoulder padding changes with the look of fashion. The size, shape and thickness will vary according to the fashion of the shoulder line and to the shape of your shoulders. Today, pads are used mainly to correct figure faults, for example, to build up narrow or rounded shoulders in garments which normally do not require their use. Commercially, several shapes of shoulder pads are available in styles for blouses, dresses, suits or coats. Dress and blouse pads are usually covered in fabric, or you can cover them in the dress fabric. Suit and coat pads are usually purchased uncovered; they are placed between the garment and the lining.

Featherboning

Featherboning is used wherever stays and stiffening are needed—in strapless bodices, hoop skirts, high collars, wide belts and cummerbunds. The boning is covered in cotton or synthetic fabric (white or black) and it can be stitched to the garment or encased in a lining. The width and yardage needed is listed on the pattern envelope of the garment requiring it.

Stays

These are metal, plastic or bone strips in various pre-cut widths and lengths and are used for strapless bodices, points in collars, cummerbunds. The length, width and number needed are listed on the pattern envelope.

Zigzag Wire Stays

These are spring wires which are flexible and adjustable in length. Because of their flexibility, they are almost invisible when used in necklines or collars or for formal gowns. They are inserted inside the seam and attached to the seam allowance. They come in either black or white and in several lengths.

Horsehair Braid

Horsehair braid is a stiff woven braid used for hemming the edge of light-weight full skirts and lace garments to give the hem support. It is available in widths from ½ inch to 3½ inches in black or white.

Weights

Round lead weights available in various sizes are used to weight the hem edges of jackets and coats, or for weighting necklines and collars for a particular fashion effect.

CHAPTER 4

FABRIC FACTS

"Little lamb, who made thee?" might be a logical question to ask today when viewing a mound of fuzzy lamb's wool in a fabric department. Years ago the question would have been silly because everyone knew a sheep on a hillside provided the origin. Today it may come from a laboratory and be composed entirely of man-made fibers.

Although the vast, wonderful array of new fabrics which appear each year are a delight to see, they can at the same time be bewildering. Years ago, women took pride in being able to identify a fabric by looking at it and feeling it. Now, this is almost a lost art. Because of new methods of manufacture, identities have become confused so that synthetics may resemble wool; cotton, silk; silk, linen. In fact, fabrics can look, behave and feel just about any way man wants them to. It all depends on what is done to the fiber when converting it to cloth.

Because sewing and pressing techniques vary according to the material, it is important that you understand the three factors—fiber, construction and finish—which influence the manner in which a fabric is handled. Try to be as knowledgeable as possible about these matters. It will make your sewing easier, and make you a better-dressed woman.

THE FIBERS

Less than fifty years ago, all fabrics were made of natural fibers. There was wool from the sheep; cotton from the cotton plant; silk from the silkworm cocoon and linen from the flax plant. Today we have the same natural fibers and a tremendous variety of new synthetics which originate in a test tube. Terms such as "polyamides," "cellulose triacetates," "polyesters" and "acrylics" appear everywhere. You may never see a polyamide or care to see one, just as you may never see a cotton plant or care to see one, but you really should know what these fibers will do for you.

The first place to start checking is the bolt of fabric. It is a Federal Trade Commission ruling that fabrics must have the fiber content identified before they are sold to retail outlets. Carefully check labels and hang tags before you buy. This knowledge may affect your purchase.

To help you obtain this information a list of the popular fibers and fabrics is given here. Important characteristics and general tips on sewing and care are also noted. New fibers and fabrics will be appearing regularly. Try to keep up-to-date by reading magazines, such as *McCall's Pattern Fashions.*

FIBER AND SOURCE	EXAMPLE	CHARACTERISTICS	SEWING TIPS AND GENERAL CARE
■ NATURAL FIBERS *ANIMAL* (protein): WOOL (hair fibers of various animals, most commonly, sheep). Others include mohair, cashmere, vicuna, camel's hair and alpaca		Warm, absorbent, wrinkle-resistant. Dyes well. Shrinkage tendencies reduced when treated or blended with nylon and other synthetics. Synthetic blends have tendency to pill.	Dry-clean unless labeled washable, then follow manufacturer's instructions. Use press cloth and moderate iron when pressing. Dry away from heat. Sponge before sewing, unless fabric has been pre-shrunk.
SILK (cocoon of silk worm)		Lustrous, smooth, drapes well. Is naturally resilient and strong. Takes brilliant dyes. Blends with wool, cotton and man-made fibers.	Dry-clean unless labeled washable. Press on wrong side with moderate iron, when damp. Sew sheers over tissue; use silk or mercerized thread. Place sharp pins in seam allowance to avoid holes.
VEGETABLE COTTON (seed pod of cotton plant)		Versatile, strong, long-wearing; blends well with most fibers. Can be finished so that it is crease-resistant and needs little or no ironing.	Shrinks, unless Sanforized or otherwise treated. Washable, can be pressed with hot iron while damp. Resin-finished cottons have wash-and-wear properties; need little ironing. With these finishes, follow sewing hints for man-made fibers.
LINEN (flax fibers)		Cool, comfortable, absorbent. Has a crisp, fresh appearance. Can be blended with natural and man-made fibers. Shrinks unless treated. Frequently has crease-resistant finish applied.	Washable. Press with hot iron while very damp, on wrong side. Shrink (if not treated) before cutting. Cut, don't tear, to straighten ends. Raveling edges need special finishing; zigzag stitches are satisfactory.

FIBER AND SOURCE	EXAMPLE	CHARACTERISTICS	SEWING TIPS AND GENERAL CARE
■ MAN-MADE FIBERS RAYON (regenerated cellulose)	Rayon (variety of manufacturers) Coloray (Courtaulds) Solution-dyed yarn giving superior color-fast properties. Cupioni (American Bemberg) A thick-and-thin rayon filament giving a slubbed appearance. Bemberg (American Bemberg) A rayon filament made by the cuprammonium process. Jetspun (American Enka) Rayon yarn solution-dyed.	Drapes and dyes well. Blends with all natural and synthetic fibers. Characteristics similar to cotton. Can be textured, creped, moiréed; variety of finishes applied.	Dry-clean or wash, depending on manufacturer's instructions. Use warm iron. Handle carefully when wet since rayon loses strength in wet state; do not wring; dry-roll in a towel.
ACETATE (acetylated cellulose)	Chromspun (Tennessee Eastman) Solution-dyed acetate yarn. Celaperm (Celanese Corp.) Filament and staple acetate yarn. Estron (Tennessee Eastman) White acetate yarn colored by conventional dyeing methods.	Soft, luxurious and smooth. Drapes beautifully. Takes sharp and brilliant colors. Blends well with synthetic and natural fibers. Heat-set pleats are permanent. Moth- and mildew-resistant. Fades on exposure to atmosphere unless solution-dyed.	Hand-wash or dry-clean. Use cool iron and press while quite damp. Use tissue under seams to avoid marking right side. Keep away from heat and acetone (nail polish removers) to prevent melting and dissolving of acetate fabric.
TRIACETATE (cellulose base)	Arnel (Celanese Corp.)	Excellent wet strength. Won't shrink or stretch. Takes permanent pleats well, resists wrinkles. Blends well with natural and most synthetic fibers, giving fabric a soft, comfortable feeling and beautiful drape.	Washable, quick-drying; easily pressed with iron set at "wool." In blends, treat as for the other fiber; sew as for synthetics. Use tissue under seams to prevent marking right side.

FIBER AND SOURCE	EXAMPLE	CHARACTERISTICS	SEWING TIPS AND GENERAL CARE
■ DERIVATIVES OF CELLULOSE	Zantrel (American Enka)	Luxurious soft hand; drapes well. Strong; low water absorption. Dimensionally stable.	Dry-clean unless marked washable.
ACRYLIC (more than 85% acrylonitrile)	Acrilan (Chemstrand Corp.) Orlon (DuPont) Creslan (American Cyanamid) Zefran (Dow Chemical)	Used alone or in blends with natural or other synthetics. As a group have natural, luxurious feel; warmth and bulk but light in weight. Good crease recovery; retain pleats and press. Resist damage by moths, sunlight and mildew.	Most blends are washable, using warm water and a detergent; rinse thoroughly to prevent graying. If ironing seems necessary, use low setting. Mercerized thread may be used; fine needles, sharp pins and scissors are necessary. Choose washable notions. Perfect machine tension is essential to prevent seam puckers. Avoid ripping out or pressing until fit is assured.
MODACRYLIC (35-85% acrylonitrile)	Verel (Tennessee Eastman)	Warm, strong; resistant to sunlight, moths and wrinkling. Bulk without weight.	Wash easily, dry quickly. In fur-like form should be treated as fur. Follow Acrylic washing instructions; use very low iron or shriveling will result.

FIBER AND SOURCE	EXAMPLE	CHARACTERISTICS	SEWING TIPS AND GENERAL CARE
	Dynel (Union Carbide Corp.)	Coatings (fur-like fabrics of 100% Dynel or Dynel blended with Orlon). Has soft, luxurious feel; drapes well. Reduces static electricity, has good wrinkle recovery. Dyes beautifully; fire-resistant.	
NYLON (polyamide)	Nylon (DuPont, Chemstrand) Caprolan (Allied Chemical) Antron·(DuPont) trilobal nylon multifilament.	Noted for toughness, elasticity and strength. Takes a durable pleat, resists moths and mildew. Blends well with both natural and synthetic fibers, giving added strength. Dry, silk hand, drapes and takes color beautifully.	Easily washed, using moderate temperature and mild soap. Rinse thoroughly. Wash white with white since nylon pulls color from other fabrics. Quick-drying, little or no ironing. Use low heat in pressing. Sensitive to strong sun. (See Acrylics for sewing.)
POLYESTER	Dacron (DuPont) Kodel (Tennessee Eastman) Fortrel (Celanese Corp.) Vycron (Beaunit Mills) T62 (DuPont) (trilobal extended Dacron filament)	Usually found in blends. High tensile strength. Has excellent wrinkle resistance and retains heat-set pleats. Good draping qualities and resistance to shrinking or stretching. Light-weight. Absorbs little moisture. Sensitive to heat. Resists moths, mildew and sunlight.	Spot cleans and washes easily in warm water; rinse thoroughly to prevent graying. Quick-drying, needs little or no ironing. Use iron on "warm" setting if you must press. Cannot be eased in or shrunk during construction, so correct pattern selection is important.

FIBER AND SOURCE	EXAMPLE	CHARACTERISTICS	SEWING TIPS AND GENERAL CARE
STRETCH YARNS	Helanca Yarn (Heberlein Patent Corp.) Nylon 288 (DuPont) Agilon (Deering Milliken)	Warp stretch pulls parallel to selvage edge. Filling stretch pulls across the fabric width. Two-way stretch pulls in both directions.	Use the type of stretch the pattern calls for. Check manufacturer's directions for care. See Chapter 7 for full instructions on handling stretch fabrics.
RUBBER	Lastex (Uniroyal) (elastic yarn)	Lastex yarn is the rubber core and is wound with cotton, wool, silk or yarns to produce a permanently elastic yarn. Used in warp or filling, the fabric will stretch in the direction of the lastex.	Washable, dry-cleanable; use moderate temperature iron. Use nylon thread, a fine needle and stitch at slow even speed with a small stitch (14 to the inch.) Adjust tension. A zigzag machine is very satisfactory to stitch seams and as a seam and hem finish.
METALLIC	Lurex (Dow Chemical)	Yarn in which bright aluminum foil is put between plastic film. Woven or knitted into fabrics.	Usually washable if fabrics in which they appear can be washed. Test first, then press with moderate iron.
	Mylar (DuPont)	Metal foil covered with polyester film to produce a metallic yarn.	
	Metlon (Metlon Corp.)	Aluminum foil between two layers of plastic film.	

FIBER AND SOURCE	EXAMPLE	CHARACTERISTICS	SEWING TIPS AND GENERAL CARE
GLASS	Fiberglas (Owens-Corning Fiberglas Corp.)	Glass yarn for home furnishings, curtaining and industrial uses. Resists moth, mildew, sunlight; fireproof and non-absorbent. Does not deteriorate with age.	Avoid rubbing, machine-washing, dry-cleaning, ironing. Test fabric for correct stitch, tension. Use mercerized thread, long stitch, loose tension, light pressure, sharp needle. Line with Fiberglas only.
URETHANE FOAM	Scott Apparel Foam (Scott Paper Co.) Curon (Reeves Bros.)	Rubber-like material used for interlining and interfacing. Light-weight, non-allergenic, non-toxic, odorless, gives warmth without weight. When bonded to another fabric, gives resilience and shape retention to the fabric.	Follow manufacturer's instructions for care. See complete instructions for handling in Chapter 7.

THE BLENDS

Technicians in the textile industry are constantly experimenting with blends to improve the appearance and serviceability of fabrics. Wool is blended with Dacron to make it washable, more crease-resistant, lighter in weight. Cotton is blended with nylon to make it stronger, quick-drying and silkier in appearance. Some of the blendings are quite successful, but others may fail to give the performance expected.

The secret of perfect blending is in the balance of fibers. A 100 per cent synthetic of Dacron, Orlon, Acrilan, Arnel, nylon and others less well known will do exactly what is claimed. These synthetics are usually washable and highly crease-resistant. They won't shrink, stretch or lose shape. When they are combined with other fibers, usually the natural fibers, these same characteristics are partially added to the fabric, but only in proportion to the percentage of synthetic fiber in the fabric. If the fabric is to give the performance of the synthetic, the synthetic fiber must compose at least 50 per cent of the blend. In many cotton and rayon blends, the synthetic fiber must constitute 65 per cent of the fabric for the blend to react as the synthetic.

When confronted with a fabric that is composed of two or more fibers, it is often a problem to know just how to handle the combination of fibers to get the best results in your garment. Again, check those hang tags and labels. The various percentages of fibers in the fabric will be listed, and reliable manufacturers will state how the fabric should be cleaned. Don't think that just because a woolen has some Dacron in it, the fabric is washable. Be sure that the Dacron is at least 50 per cent of the fabric and the tag clearly states that the fabric may be washed. Don't assume that just because a cotton contains a little nylon, it won't shrink. The nylon may be there just to add sheen or to make the fabric stronger. Be sure that the tag or label states that the fabric will not shrink more than one per cent. Even then, it's often best to test the fabric for shrinkage. (See the shrinkage test on page 97.)

FIBERS INTO FABRIC

Man has been making cloth to cover himself since his very earliest history. He probably started with the skins of animals and then learned how to pound fibers from bark, bonding them into cloth. Weaving and knitting followed. Despite all our wonderful scientific advances, we still haven't found any new methods of making cloth. Man still must weave, knit or bond fibers into fabric.

From these three basic methods of making a cloth, a huge technology has evolved. Man can weave fabrics in an endless variety of textures; he knits them in all sorts of interesting stitches, and bonds them with heat, moisture and chemicals.

Woven Fabrics

Most of our fabrics are woven. In weaving, two systems of yarns are interlaced at right angles to each other. The type of yarn used, the way the yarns are interlaced, even the colors of the yarn produce an infinite variety of interesting fabrics in look, feel and reaction.

It isn't so important for you to know how these weaves are made, but it is important to know what they will do, how they will look when you make them up in a garment. When you purchase fabric you should know if the weave is a sturdy one or if the very nature of the weave allows the fabric to stretch, and what will happen when the garment is worn. Although less important, it's nice to know what the different weaves are and what they are called, so when you read and hear about various fabrics you can at least have a mental picture of what the fabric looks like.

Surprising as it may seem, there are basically only three methods of weaving: the plain weave, the twill weave and the satin weave. They vary in the way the lengthwise threads or warp yarns are crossed by the crosswise threads or filling (weft) yarns. But there are many, many ways to vary each of these basic weaves.

PLAIN WEAVE. This is the most common of all weaves. Each filling yarn goes over one warp yarn and under the next alternately. Every second warp yarn is raised in the loom, the filling shot across, then the alternate warp yarns are raised, and the filling shot across again.

When warp and filling yarns of the same size are closely woven and equally spaced, the plain weave is the strongest of all weaves.

Familiar fabrics made with a plain weave are: batiste, broadcloth, challis, gingham, muslin, madras. And there are many, many more.

One major variation of the plain weave is the *Basket*

Weave. Double yarns are used in a plain-weave pattern, instead of the usual single yarn. This produces a very loosely woven fabric, which stretches easily and drapes well. The looseness of the fabric makes it less durable and not very satisfactory for clothing; it is very likely to stretch out of shape quickly in a garment.

The *Rib Weave* which has ribbed or corded effects in either the warp or filling direction is another variation of the plain weave. The rib may be produced by alternating fine yarns with coarse yarns, or single yarns with double yarns. In general, ribbed fabrics are not as long-wearing as plain-woven ones, especially when

WEAVES

Plain weave

Plain weave variation:

    Rib

    Basket

Twill weave

Satin weave

Pile weave

Double-cloth weave

Leno/gauze weave

Swivel weave

Dobby weave

Jacquard weave

Knitted fabric

Bonded fabric

the ribs are rather thick, because the coarser yarns tend to pull away from the finer ones, resulting in splits and tears in the fabric. The entire yarn is also exposed to abrasive wear and is less durable.

TWILL WEAVE. This weave is formed by the filling crossing at least two warp yarns before going under one or more yarns, with a shift to the right or left in succeeding rows forming diagonal ridges on the face of the fabric. Basically, twills are not as tight a weave as the plain weave, since the yarns are not as tightly interlocked. However, most twills are woven of sturdy yarns and give good service. They are often preferred for suits, coats and work clothes because of their rough and interesting texture. A few fabrics representative of the twill weave are: gabardine, drill, serge, whipcord, foulard, surah.

Changes in the direction of the twill weave's diagonal lines produce variations such as the herringbone, corkscrew, entwining and fancy twills.

SATIN WEAVE. This is the weakest type of weave. Similar to the twill in construction, the yarns are more widely spaced, producing long floats which lie on the surface and receive most of the wear. Satin weaves produce smooth, lustrous fabrics. Satin and sateen are made with a satin weave.

There are many variations of each of these weaves. To help you recognize the most popular of these special weaves a brief description of each is given here:

PILE WEAVE. This fancy weave uses both the plain and the twill weaves in construction. An extra warp or filling yarn is woven into the basic construction. This additional yarn is drawn up from the surface of the fabric forming loops. The loops may be cut or closely sheared as in velvet, or left uncut as in terry cloth.

DOUBLE-CLOTH WEAVE. In double-cloth, two fabrics are woven on the loom at the same time, one on top of the other and interlaced in construction. Two different weaves can be used; for example, a twill on one side, a plain on the other. These fabrics are frequently bulky. If made of warm, woolly fibers, they can give great warmth. Fabrics representative of double-cloth weaves are blanket cloth and upholstery fabrics of all types.

LENO WEAVE; GAUZE WEAVE. Very light-weight meshy fabrics are woven with the leno loom. Basically the plain weave is used with the second warp yarn twisting around the first warp as it passes alternately over and under the filling yarn, locking the filling in position. Some major fabrics woven on leno looms are marquisette, netting, mesh shirtings.

LAPPET and SWIVEL WEAVES. In both these weaves, decorative dots, circles or other small figures are woven on the surface of the fabric while it is being constructed in the loom. In the swivel weave, yarns are cut when the fabric is completed. Since the yarns cannot be securely fastened, the designs may pull out when the fabric is handled in washing. The lappet weave has the designs stitched in the fabric while it is being woven. The ends of the threads are fastened so they will not pull out easily. Dotted swiss is produced by both these methods. The lappet weave dotted swiss is preferable to the swivel weave.

DOBBY WEAVE. Special looms are needed for dobby weaves, which produce small geometric designs in the fabric. Although this weave does make use of floats, they are usually small enough not to affect the wear of the fabric. The most familiar of the dobby weaves is the popular bird's-eye, which is a small diamond pattern with an eye in the center.

JACQUARD WEAVE. The marvelous damasks, brocades and tapestries are made on the Jacquard loom. The easiest explanation of the loom is that it is controlled by perforated paper patterns similar to player piano rolls, and is capable of producing intricate patterned designs. Floats are inevitable in the Jacquard weave because of the elaborate designs and may affect durability unless the fabric is compactly constructed and of good quality. Damask, brocade, tapestry and matelassé are all Jacquard weaves.

The Knits

Knitted fabrics are in fashion. They seem to answer a demand for clothes that are practical, comfortable and still good-looking. More and more fibers are being turned into attractive knit patterns and made into all types of garments from underwear to evening clothes.

When buying a knit, remember that it is a resilient fabric. The fact that it is formed of loops makes it springy, stretchy and more elastic than woven cloth. These qualities can be both an advantage and a disadvantage. Knits stretch and contract with the body, making them wonderful for active wear. They usually spring back into shape. After long wear, however, they may become stretched and start to "bag."

Knits come in marvelous patterns, in all sorts of weights and in a myriad of textures. They drape well and do not wrinkle easily. However, because of their elasticity they may cling to the body and they do require special handling. Before sewing a knitted fabric be sure to read the special directions on page 99.

Bonded Fabrics

The oldest method of making cloth is by bonding fibers. Early man pounded the bark of trees and through pressure created a cloth. A French monk placed wool in his sandals to relieve foot pain. He discovered that the moisture, pressure and heat matted the wool fibers, interlocking them to form a sort of wool cloth. Thus, felt was born.

For dressmaking there are only two types of bonded fabrics you are likely to work with: felt and the non-woven shaping materials. There is no elasticity or resilience to these fabrics, and they will tear under stress. The edges will not ravel or fray. They will not drape, but many are thermoplastic, which means they shrink and shape with the application of heat and moisture. This quality is fine if you are making a shaped garment, but it can present problems in pressing.

FABRIC FINISHES

If you've mastered the fibers, and know about weaves, you have one more step to go. There is another process involved in the manufacturing of fabrics which will have a decided effect on a fabric's action and behavior—the finishing. This includes all those wonderful treatments which make fabrics shrink-resistant, crease-resistant, color-fast, drip-dry, mothproof.

Once more, check the labels. You will discover a host of trade names, like Mitin, Zeset, Lanaset, Everglaze. Most of these finishes are patented processes and the only way to discover what the name means and the purpose of the finish is to consult a list, such as the one here. Many of these finishes accomplish several purposes. New finishes appear almost daily, so keep up to date by reading about them in current magazines.

Drip-dry Finishes

Belfast *(Deering Milliken)* A chemical modification of cotton fibers for permanent wash-and-wear qualities. Fabrics can be machine-washed, tumble- or drip-dried.

Dip 'n Dry *(Fuller Fabrics)* A finish applied to make fabric fast-drying, easier to iron and crease-resistant.

Dri-Don *(Dan River Mills)* A resin finish applied to cottons to increase wash-and-wear properties and add to crease-resistance.

Crease-Resistant Finishes

Disciplined *(Bates Fabrics)* A finish applied to give resistance to creasing, soil, mildew and perspiration.

Dri-Smooth *(Cranston Print Works Co.)* A finish applied to cotton fabric for crease-resistance and soil and perspiration control.

Everglaze *(Jos. Bancroft and Sons)* A trademark that identifies fabrics treated for crease-, stretch- and shrink-resistance.

Good Conduct *(Wamsutta Fabrics)* A finish applied to fabrics to give crease-resistance.

Perma Pressed *(Avondale Mills)* A finish applied to make fabric crease-resistant and fast-drying.

Tebilized *(Tootal Broadhurst Lee Co. Ltd.)* Trademark applied to cottons, linens, rayons and mixtures indicating permanent crease-resistance and improved hand and drape.

Wrinkl-Shed *(Dan River Mills)* A finish which gives crease-, soil- and mildew-resistance, and shrinkage control.

Shrinkage-control Finishes

Sanforized *(Cluett, Peabody and Co.)* Trademark appearing on woven cottons and cotton blends indicating that the fabric has been treated so it will not shrink more than one per cent when washed.

Lanaset *(American Cyanamid Co.)* Process used to control woolen shrinkage.

Zeset *(DuPont)* Process used on rayons and cottons giving wrinkle-resistance, and stability against shrinking, sagging and stretching.

Water-Repellent Finishes

Zelan *(DuPont)* A finish for water- and spot-repellency.

Cravenette *(Cravenette Corp.)* A water-repellent finish.

Mothproofing Finish

Mitin *(Geigy Chemical Corp.)* A lasting, non-toxic mothproofing compound applied by the manufacturer when fabric is being dyed.

Insulating Processes

Milium *(Deering Milliken)* A lining fabric with a metal insulating treatment that gives warmth in winter, coolness in summer.

Texturing Processes

Lanolized A process that impregnates fabric with lanolin giving a softer, smoother finish.

Mercerized A chemical treatment of cotton giving added luster, strength and dye retention.

Taslan *(DuPont)* A process applied to synthetic fibers to produce a bulkier, more textured appearance.

Ban-lon *(Joseph Bancroft & Sons)* Fiber bulking process to give textured yarns for knitted and woven fabrics.

Color-Fast Processes

Vat Dyed *(Vat Dye Institute)* A dyeing process used on cotton, washable rayon, and linen fabrics to keep them color-fast to laundering, sun fading, and rubbing.

Avisco Integrity Tag *(American Viscose Corp.)* Rayon or acetate fabrics bearing this label meet standards for color-fastness, strength, shrinkage and chlorine-damage control.

GLOSSARY OF FAMILIAR FABRICS

We've talked about fibers, we've talked about finishes, we've talked about weaves, now let's talk about specific fabrics. When you read the list of suggested fabrics on a pattern envelope you should know what is meant by dimity, voile, madras, corduroy. This glossary has been compiled to help you identify the fabrics which you are most likely to use.

Barathea Made of silk or rayon warp with a woolen or worsted filling. Various weaves are used to produce this fine-textured cloth, which is usually of high quality. It comes most often in black.

GLOSSARY OF FAMILIAR FABRICS

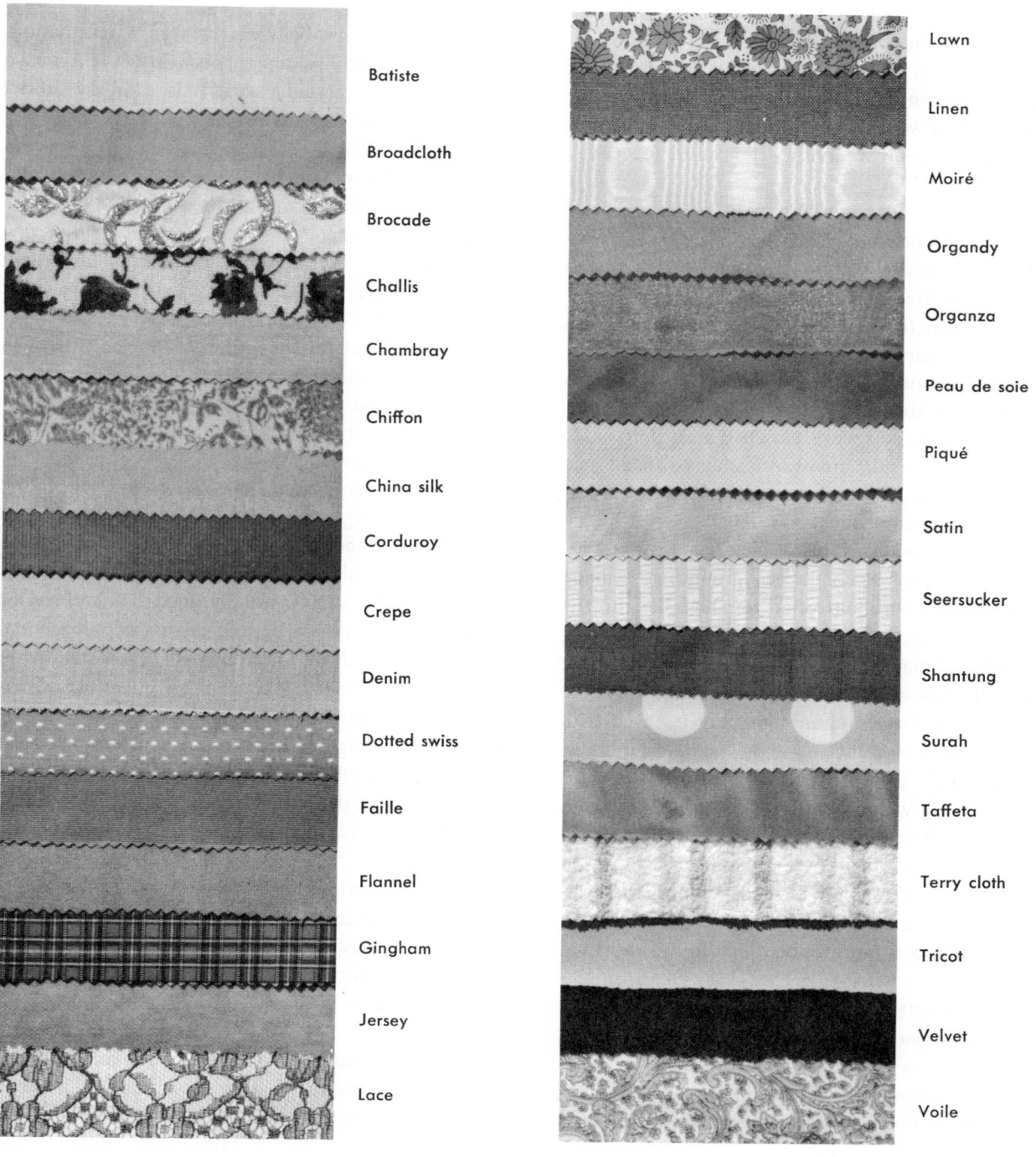

Batiste	Lawn
Broadcloth	Linen
Brocade	Moiré
Challis	Organdy
Chambray	Organza
Chiffon	Peau de soie
China silk	Piqué
Corduroy	Satin
Crepe	Seersucker
Denim	Shantung
Dotted swiss	Surah
Faille	Taffeta
Flannel	Terry cloth
Gingham	Tricot
Jersey	Velvet
Lace	Voile

Bark Crepe   A woolen or rayon fabric that has rough, barklike surface interest. Used for coats and in upholstery.

Batik   This is a method of printing cloth, rather than a special weave, fiber or finish. Design areas are covered in wax and color applied. When the wax is removed, the design appears in white on a colored background.

Batiste   Soft, sheer cotton fabric woven in a plain weave. It comes in white, solid colors and prints, and is very suitable for soft dresses.

Bedford Cord   A cloth made by using a variation of the plain weave in which cords run the length of the fabric. It can be woven of any of the major fibers, but is generally of wool or cotton. It is used for coats, suits, uniforms.

Bengaline   Cross-rib material with filling yarn coarser than the warp to produce the corded effect. It is usually made of silk, rayon, wool or cotton in various widths and is used for dresses, coatings and ribbons.

Bouclé   Usually found in woolens, this cloth is woven with a novelty yarn which has tightly curled loops. It does appear in some cottons and other fibers, and is very popular in knitted fabrics.

Broadcloth   Usually a plain, closely woven cloth made of wool, cotton or silk, broadcloth may be made in a number of weaves. Cotton broadcloth has a fine crosswise rib and a lustrous finish.

Brocade   A decorative fabric which has a raised pattern woven in relief against a background. It is made of a variety of fibers and often has metallic threads forming the raised or embossed pattern. Depending on its weight, it may be used for clothing or upholstery.

Burlap   A plain-weave coarse fabric made from jute or allied yarns. Comes natural or may be dyed in a variety of colors or prints.

Butcher Rayon   Rayon fabric with a linen weave.

Calico   A plain-woven cotton which is printed with small designs. It comes in various qualities depending on the texture and fineness of the yarn used.

Camel Hair   A coating fabric made from the natural-colored hair of the camel, frequently mixed with wool. It is a soft napped fabric, noted for its warmth and light weight.

Cashmere   A soft finish fabric made entirely from the hair of goats from Kashmir or from fine wool mixed with the hair widely used in coats, suits, sweaters.

Challis   A light-weight soft wool, cotton, rayon or combination of fibers made with a plain weave and usually printed with a small design. Usually used for dresses and blouses.

Chambray   Smooth, lustrous fabric made of colored or dyed warp threads, and white or contrasting color threads in the filling, producing an irridescent effect. Usually, it is a cotton fabric, but may be made in a combination of fibers. It is sturdy, launders well, and is easy to work with.

Cheviot   A heavy-weight twill-weave woolen or worsted with a rough, hairy surface, similar to tweed. Ideal for sportswear.

Chiffon   Very sheer, light-weight, transparent cotton, silk, rayon or blend of fibers made in a plain weave with fine, highly twisted yarns. It is a dressy fabric, and is often used for soft draping over other heavier firmer fabrics.

China Silk   A very soft light-weight plain-woven silk, used primarily for linings. It is simulated in some rayon lining fabrics.

Chino   A sturdy cotton fabric, made in plain or twill weave and fairly lustrous. It is used extensively for summer uniforms and sportswear.

Chintz   A glazed, crisp cotton of a closely woven plain weave, usually printed with bright and gay colors. It is used a great deal for drapery and slipcovers. In lighter weights, it is very adaptable to gay summer dresses and sportswear.

Corduroy   A very strong, durable cotton pile fabric with rounded ridges or wales of pile running lengthwise. The wales come in various widths. Suitable for casual clothes and sportswear.

Covert   A twill weave usually made of woolen or worsted yarn but can be cotton, rayon or spun acetate. Fabric woven with yarns of two shades of the same color so that fabric has a speckled effect. Used for coats, suits, sportswear.

Crepe   Light-weight fabric of silk, rayon, cotton, wool, synthetic or a combination of fibers. It is characterized by a crinkling of the surface, obtained by using either hard-twisted yarns, chemical treatment, special weaves or embossing.

Damask   Woven designs similar to those of brocade are found in damask, but the cloth is a finer, thinner construction. It is made of silk, cotton, linen, rayon and some blends of synthetics. Widely used for table linens, damask is available in various qualities at all price ranges.

Denim   Twill-weave cotton woven with colored warp and white filling yarns. Gives a strong fabric that launders well. Popular for work and play clothes.

Dimity   Thin sheer cotton fabric with corded stripe

or check effects made by weaving heavier threads in a pattern using a plain weave. Popular for dainty dresses, lounge wear.

Dobby   Any fabric woven on special dobby looms. Can be of cotton, rayon and silk. Fabrics have small woven designs such as dots, geometric figures, floral motifs. Widely used for shirts, blouses, dresses.

Doeskin   A fine quality, smooth finish, satin weave wool fabric with a slight nap. Used for coating, suiting or sportswear. Also made in twill-weave rayon napped on one side.

Dotted Swiss   Sheer cotton fabric made of a lappet or swivel weave, with woven dots in it. Used for blouses, dresses, children's clothes, curtains.

Doupioni   A silk yarn which is uneven, irregular and of a large diameter. It is used in cloth of the same name, as well as pongee, shantung and other slubbed silks.

Drill   A durable closely woven cotton fabric of medium weight; when dyed, drill is the basic cloth of khaki and ticking.

Duck   A closely woven, durable, heavy cotton fabric. Use depends on its weight.

Duvetyn   A very softly napped wool fabric, or a silk which has a suede-like downy nap. It looks like a compact velvet, drapes well and wears well.

Faille   Silk or rayon fabric with a flat crosswise rib effect, similar to grosgrain. Used for dresses, suits and coats.

Fake Fur   Woven or knitted fabrics made of cotton or synthetic fibers to simulate the fur of animals. Used wherever real fur might be used.

Felt   Bonded fabric created by interlocking threads through moisture, heat and pressure. Widely used in millinery, most felt has wool fiber as the base, but it can be made of almost any fiber.

Flannel   A soft, loosely woven cloth of either plain or twill weave which the dull finish may conceal. Flannel comes in many weights and textures, is usually slightly napped, and can be made of cotton, wool or rayon. Used for suits, dresses, coats and, in cotton, for sleepwear and sport shirts.

Fleece   A heavy-weight woolen with very long nap used for coats. It is inclined to be bulky, and may be difficult to sew.

Foulard   A soft, twilled silk or rayon, usually printed in small figures. It is very popular for neckwear, and is also used for soft dresses, blouses, robes.

Gabardine   A sturdy cotton, rayon or wool fabric with a simple twill construction, giving steep diagonal lines on the face of the cloth. It is widely used in suits, coats, sportswear of all kinds.

Georgette   A light-weight silk crepe with a pebbled effect. Has exceptional stiffness and body for its weight due to the yarn twist in weaving. Can be white, dyed or printed.

Gingham   Plain-weave cotton of medium weight, which comes in checked, plaid or striped designs. It comes in various grades; better ginghams are soft, finely woven.

Homespun   Usually a plain-weave wool or cotton fabric which looks as if it were hand-loomed. The yarns used are rather thick, producing a fairly heavy-weight fabric.

Hopsacking   A coarse plain-weave cloth of wool or cotton which is not very closely woven. Some hopsacking may be of a basket weave. It is used primarily for coats and suits.

Jacquard   Any fabric woven on the looms named for the inventor, Jacquard, which make it possible to weave intricate and fancy designs into cloth. Brocades, damasks and tapestries are all the result of Jacquard weaving.

Jersey   A smooth, plain-knit fabric of wool, cotton, rayon, or synthetic blends. Usually jersey has a dull surface and excellent draping qualities. Widely used in dresses, shirts, sportswear, underwear.

Lace   Open-work fabric made with bobbins, needles or hooks. The threads form a design. Can be hand- or machine-made. Used for trimming or for entire garments.

Lamé   Any fabric in which metallic threads are used in the weaving for decorative purposes. Used mainly for evening wear.

Laminate   A layer of fabric which has been fused with a layer of foam; currently the term is widely used for fabrics fused with foam rubber. Used to give warmth without weight.

Lawn   Fine, sheer, crisp-finished cotton or linen of plain weave. It is crisper than voile, less crisp than organdy. Comes in white, solid colors and prints. Popular for children's clothes, summer dresses, sleepwear.

Linen   Strong, lustrous fabric of plain-weave flax fiber. It comes in three major weights: handkerchief linen, which is very sheer; medium-weight, dress-weight linen; and heavier-suiting-weight for tailored garments.

Madras   A plain cotton weave, usually in strongly colored plaids, stripes and checks which will "bleed" slightly when washed. Name comes from the section in India, where it was originated. Used for shirts, dresses, blouses.

Marquisette   A gauze-weave mesh fabric, very light in weight. It is made of cotton, rayon, silk or nylon and is used for curtains or dressy evening fashions.

Matelassé   Fancy fabric made on dobby or Jacquard looms. The patterns are raised, giving a quilted effect. It is made of silk, rayon, cotton or wool.

Melton   A dull, non-lustrous wool fabric used for coatings and outer garments. Fabric gives excellent wear since the finishing process covers up all interlacings of the yarns giving a "solid" fabric.

Mohair   Generally a soft, woolen fabric, made in plain and twill weaves, which is napped with goat hair. Fabric is glossy and lustrous, sometimes formed in loops on the surface.

Moiré   Any fabric which has a wavy, water-marked finish. Most moiré is taffeta, treated to have a wavy, watery effect.

Monk's Cloth   A rough basket weave, made of coarse cotton or linen fibers. Used mostly for slipcovers, draperies.

Mousseline de Soie   Muslin made of silk or rayon with a crisp, firm finish; resembles chiffon. Used primarily for evening wear.

Muslin   A substantial plain-weave cotton, fairly strong and heavy. It comes in various grades and qualities. Cheap muslin is sized or filled with a starchy substance which washes out; better grades are made of stronger, finer fibers.

Nainsook   Soft, fine cotton fabric similar to batiste, but of coarser yarn. Light in weight, of plain weave, it resembles a soft-finished dimity. It is durable and launders well.

Net or Netting   Open-weave fabric with knots coming at each corner of the square. Can be cotton, rayon, silk, or nylon and ranges from very light-weight to heavy fabric.

Nonwoven Fabric   Fabric made by bonding fibers together with an adhesive agent or by fusing rather than weaving, spinning or knitting.

Organdy   Sheer, stiff, transparent plain-weave cotton cloth, which usually is treated for permanent stiffness.

Organza   Thin, transparent, stiff fabric of rayon or silk used for evening wear.

Ottoman   A crosswise-ribbed fabric similar to faille or bengaline, but with much heavier ribs, often spaced with finer ribs between. It can be made of wool, cotton, silk or rayon covering cotton cords.

Oxford Cloth   Plain-, basket- or twill-weave cotton, often used for shirting. It is fairly heavy cloth in which two yarns travel as one in the warp, and one filling yarn is equal in size to the two warp yarns.

Paisley   Any cotton, wool, or rayon which is printed with the traditional scroll design which originated in Paisley, Scotland.

Peau de Soie   The name means "skin of silk" and denotes a soft, good-quality silk satin cloth which has a rather dull, grainy appearance.

Percale   Closely woven plain-weave cotton fabric of smooth yarn. Widely used in white and pastels for fine sheets, it may also be printed for dress fabric.

Pile Fabrics   Any material that to some degree resembles fur in that it has a fairly heavy nap or loops, cut or left uncut, on the face of the fabric, hiding the basic weave underneath. Fur fabrics, terry, velvet, corduroy are all classed as pile fabrics.

Pima   A very fine quality cotton fiber, strong and lustrous, named after Pima County, Arizona, where it was originally grown.

Piqué   A medium- or heavy-weight cotton fabric with raised cords running lengthwise. The cords can be of various widths, and several novelty weaves are available, such as waffle and bird's-eye piqués.

Plissé   Cottons with a puckered effect put in by a special finish. They may be plain or printed in cottons ranging from lawn to organdy weights. Most plissés have permanent puckered effects; in cheaper plissés, puckers may wash out.

Polished Cottons   Generally, a plain-weave cotton which has a glazed finish, mechanically applied. Many weights and grades of cotton fabric are polished through these methods.

Pongee   Usually raw silk in a natural tan color which has a rather uneven, crude texture. It also refers to cotton or rayon cloth of similar weight and texture, which comes in solid colors or prints.

Poplin   A standard dress goods material in which the filling is heavier than the warp, producing a somewhat uneven ribbed effect. It can be of wool, silk or rayon, but is most commonly a medium- or heavy-weight cotton fabric.

Puckered Nylon   A fabric originally made by weaving pre-shrunk and non-shrunk nylon yarns together. Other methods are also used to create permanent puckering, usually in stripes.

Pure Dye Silk   Silk goods which are not weighted more than 10 to 15 per cent with metallic finishes to give them a heavier hand and stiffness. Too much weighting reduces the strength of the fabric, making the fibers break.

Raw Silk   Silk from the cultivated silk worm, before any processing has been done to remove gum.

Rep   A fabric with a ribbed effect.

Sailcloth   A very strong, durable canvas. Can be made of linen, cotton, or nylon. Used largely for play clothes and in upholstery.

Sateen   A cotton cloth woven with the standard satin weave used for silk and rayon satin. It is highly lustrous, used widely for linings in washable garments.

Satin   Silk or rayon in satin weaves, producing a highly lustrous, slippery fabric used for evening wear and linings.

Seersucker   A dull-surfaced medium-weight cotton with crinkly stripes on a plain surface, produced by a plain-weave crepe variation. Widely used for summer clothes.

Serge   Diagonal worsted, wool, rayon or silk in a fine twill weave. It is used as a standard fabric for tailored suits; it is rugged, of high texture and smooth appearance.

Shantung   A rough silk in a plain weave which has large irregular filling yarns which give it a slubbed effect. Cotton and rayon are often used to simulate this fabric.

Sharkskin   A medium- to heavy-weight sleek fabric with a slightly lustered and textured weave. It is made in wool, rayon, silk and synthetics. It is very popular for tailored suits, slacks and sportswear.

Suede Cloth   Plain-weave cotton napped on one side to look like leather suede. Used in jackets and sportswear.

Suiting   General term used for any fabrics which are suitable for coats, suits. Includes many weaves, textures and various fibers.

Surah   Twill-weave silk, rayon or synthetic which is suitable for soft, tailored garments. It is available in solid colors, prints, and plaids, and is often used for neckwear.

Taffeta   A closely woven, smooth fabric of plain weave with a crisp finish, and usually with a sheen to its surface. Formerly all taffeta was silk; now, rayon or synthetic fibers compose much of the cloth.

Terry Cloth   A cotton fabric with uncut loops on one or both sides used extensively for towels since it is absorbent and requires no ironing. It is popular for beach and sportswear as well.

Ticking   A drill cloth of twill construction which has alternate stripes of white and colored yarn. Used

mainly for pillow and mattress covers, in recent years it has become a novelty sportswear fabric for shorts, slacks and dresses.

Tricot   A fine-waled knit fabric, used a great deal for underwear and sleepwear, also for gloves. It is commonly made of rayon, nylon or cotton.

Tulle   Silk, nylon or rayon sheer cloth with a hexagonal mesh construction. It is a stiff fabric, used for bouffant gowns, bridal veils and for dance costumes.

Tussah   A sturdy, rough silk fiber sometimes called wild silk. The cloth is very coarse, rough and usually quite loosely woven.

Tweed   A rough-surfaced fabric, usually woven in two or more colors to obtain some sort of pattern, check or plaid. Originally tweed was a rough homespun of heavy woolen, but today the term covers almost any fabric which is nubby, of variegated colors and has a roughened look. Tweeds are usually woolens; however, cotton tweeds, silk tweeds and synthetic tweeds have become popular in the past decade.

Velour   Thick-bodied, soft, close-napped fabric, mainly used as a suit or coat fabric. Wool velour is constructed like a broadcloth with an erect nap that is thick and full. Nylon velour is also very popular for dressy at-home fashions.

Velvet   Pile fabrics with plain or twill back and warp yarns forming the pile. They may be of all silk, rayon, nylon or cotton, but are usually made of a silk or synthetic fiber with a cotton back.

Velveteen   Cotton velvet with short, thick pile and a dull surface. Widely used for evening fashions.

Voile   Light, sheer, thin, transparent cloth, which is similar to organdy and lawn. It is less stiff than these, drapes well and tends to cling to the body.

Waffle cloth   A textured cotton similar to piqué that is woven on a dobby loom in a fine honeycomb weave.

Wash-and-Wear   Any fabric which can be washed, dried and then worn again with little or no ironing.

Whipcord   A worsted similar to gabardine but with a steeper or more pronounced twill. Dry and harsh to touch, it is a strong, springy fabric preferred for riding clothes and sharply tailored garments.

Woolens   Woven wool fabrics of short, fuzzy fibers which have not been highly twisted.

Worsteds   Popular class of wool cloth made of choice wool fibers which are smooth, strong and more highly twisted than the woolen fibers.

Zibeline   A wool coating fabric with a long, rather wiry, lustrous nap of straight fibers laid over in one direction.

CHAPTER 5

THE TOOLS OF THE TRADE

A pleasant place to work and the correct tools are a "must" for sewing enjoyment. Try to establish a sewing center in your home. It will make it possible for you to sew efficiently and to utilize moments snatched from a busy schedule.

A PLACE TO SEW

Years ago a special room was set aside for sewing. Equipment was always ready to be used and sewing could be left in place for future work. Today few women are lucky enough to have this ideal arrangement. Usually, sewing and equipment must be packed away between sewing sessions. However, if you give this matter careful thought, perhaps you can find a tiny space in a closet, a hall, a corner of the kitchen or a guest room which can be fitted for sewing. Use your ingenuity and design a sewing nook for yourself.

Organization and planning are the keys to good results in a limited space. Utilize as many portable aids as possible. A sewing screen placed in a corner of a room can be decorative on one side but very functional on the other. Put pegboard on the back with hooks to hold yardsticks, tapes and small shelves for boxes and tools. Hide your sewing table, machine and pressing equipment behind the screen. Although the equipment is out of sight, it will always be handy for using.

Be sure the area where you sew is well lighted. Don't depend on machine lighting alone. Select a straight-back chair without arms. It should fit your back adequately, so that you will be comfortable for long sewing sessions. A full-length mirror convenient to your sewing area is a must.

If you can arrange a three-way mirror it will be even better. The mirror panel needs to be only wide enough to take in your figure, but it must be long enough so you can stand quite close and see yourself from the top of your head to your toes. Then you will be able to judge the entire effect of your garment and make the necessary adjustments in length or placement of details easily and accurately.

ESSENTIAL TOOLS

The equipment you need depends on the amount and type of sewing you do. Each year new devices appear on the market. Watch for these on notions counters of your local stores. Often you will find an inexpensive item that can save hours of sewing time and help create a more professional look.

Not every seamstress needs every piece of equipment. However, these items are essential to successful and easy sewing:
- Sewing machine.
- Attachments—adjustable zipper foot and seam guide.
- Dressmaker's shears—bent handles, 6½ to 8 inches long.
- Scissors—sharp points, 3 to 6 inches long.
- Tape measure—folded, 60 inches long, reversible.
- Yardstick.
- Ruler—transparent with ⅛ inch markings, 6 inches long. Also one 12 inches long.
- Tracing wheel.
- Dressmaker's carbon paper (tracing paper).
- Tailor's chalk or chalk pencil.
- Dressmaker or silk pins.
- Thimble.
- Pin cushion.

- Needles—assorted sizes.
- Thread—various types and colors.
- Pressing equipment—iron, ironing board, pad, cover, sleeve board, press cloth, tailor's ham, sponge.
- Full-length mirror.

In addition to the necessary equipment, there are many other sewing aids which are useful. The items below do not comprise a complete list of available equipment but are among those you may find most helpful.

- Sewing machine attachments other than those listed above.
- Pinking or skalloping shears.
- Buttonhole scissors.
- Seam ripper.
- Thread clips.
- Cutting board.
- Hem marker.
- Hem gauge.
- Emery bag.
- Needle threader.
- Loop turner.
- Bodkin.
- Stiletto.
- Tweezers.
- Seam roll.
- Clapper.
- Point presser.
- Needle board.

Keep your small equipment neatly arranged in a handy sewing box or basket. If you do not have a specially designed one, divide the area with smaller boxes to insure tidiness. Be sure thread ends are caught in the notch on each spool.

Whenever you purchase equipment, check the quality. Buy good tools and give them excellent care. They are a form of investment which should pay dividends in length of service and performance. To help you shop wisely, here are some helpful suggestions for selecting various types of equipment.

Cutting Tools

Look for shears and scissors made of steel by the hot-drop forge method, which insures a sharp cutting edge that can be reconditioned. The manufacturer's literature accompanying the cutting tool will give this information. Take along a few scraps of fabric when purchasing shears or scissors. Cut with the entire length of the blades and release the fabric. If a thread of the fabric is caught, the cutting edges of the blades are imperfect. Check the points. Select cutting tools joined with a bolt or screw rather than rivets, which may loosen and cannot be tightened.

CUTTING TOOLS

Thread clips
Scissors
Scissor cutting gauge
Ripping scissors
Tweezers
Buttonhole scissors
Seam rippers
Pinking shears
Dressmaker's shears
Electric scissors

Shears and scissors do require some care. Handle them as you would surgical instruments. Lay them down; don't drop them. Keep them dry and occasionally oil them at the screw. Reserve them only for your sewing; don't use them for cutting paper or other general household tasks. When they become dull, have your cutlery repair shop sharpen them.

DRESSMAKER'S SHEARS. Select bent-handled shears that have a small ring handle for the thumb, a large ring handle for the second and third fingers. Do not buy straight-handled shears; the blades won't rest flat on the table when cutting, and you will not get as accurate a cutting line. Choose a length of 6½ to 7 or 8 inches; these will be better than the shorter 6-inch length. Left-handed sewers should take advantage of the left-handed shears which are available in the 7½-inch length.

SCISSORS. In contrast to shears, scissors are straight and have identical rings for handles. Select scissors 3 to 6 inches long with double sharp points. Keep your scissors handy at the machine for trimming, clipping threads and light cutting.

PINKING OR SKALLOPING SHEARS. Pinking shears have zigzag edges, and skalloping shears scalloped cutting edges. They are excellent in finishing seams to prevent raveling of fabric edges. Pinking shears are available in lengths from 5½ to 10 inches. The 9- and 10-inch lengths will give a deeper zigzag than the standard 7½-inch size. Skalloping shears come only in 7½- or 9-inch lengths.

BUTTONHOLE SCISSORS. A handy item if you make a lot of garments with machine-made buttonholes, these are designed to cut open buttonholes accurately, and can be adjusted for different buttonhole lengths.

RIPPING SCISSORS. With care you won't be subjected to much ripping, but if you must, these will be helpful. The blunt point cuts open stitched seams without cutting the fabric. They hold and pull the threads as you cut the seam stitches.

SEAM RIPPER. This inexpensive item is used for ripping seams and can sometimes be used as buttonhole cutters. Although it is efficient, it should be used with great care. Otherwise you may find yourself cutting the fabric.

THREAD CLIPS. A real time-saving little clipper that can be used effectively for snipping threads and making the small clips needed for marking or for curved seams. It has one ring which fits over the little finger, and is operated by squeezing with the palm of the hand.

ELECTRIC SCISSORS. This is a relatively new and expensive item. It is valuable to sewers who may have arthritis or find some difficulty in manipulating shears for long periods of time. For general sewing, electric scissors really are not a necessity, but may be a useful luxury. They operate on AC current; cut thin or heavy fabric.

SCISSOR CUTTING GAUGE. When long strips of fabric need to be cut, this gauge is a tremendous help. It fits on the point of the scissors and may be adjusted to various widths. It insures even widths of cloth and facilitates cutting a large quantity of material in a short time.

CUTTING BOARD. A real boon to the person with no cutting space. The board folds easily for storage, and is marked with inches in each direction to allow for accurate placement of fabric. Material can be pinned right to the board. It measures 40 by 72 inches and folds to a mere 12½ by 40 inches for storage.

Measuring Tools

Custom fit in garments requires custom measurements of body, pattern and fabric. Accurate measuring tools are essential for accurate sewing so be sure you have the ones you need.

MEASURING TOOLS

TAPE MEASURE. Select an oilcloth or plastic tape measure; paper ones may tear and linen ones may stretch. The fold-up type is the easiest to use and store. You'll need one which measures 60 inches and has the numbers clearly printed on both sides of the tape. Metal tips on either end will help the tape to lie flat and keep ends from fraying.

YARDSTICK. The best yardsticks are made of maple or hickory and finished to a satiny smoothness which will not catch on even the most delicate fabrics. Since they are inexpensive, take time to find a good one. You'll need your yardstick for checking grain lines and for other general marking purposes.

RULERS. Transparent, flexible rulers are best. You can see to mark details such as buttonholes, and the flexibility makes it possible to measure slight curves. Buy those with ⅛-inch markings, since sewing directions are given in ⅛-inch measurements; you need a 12- or 18-inch ruler and a short 6-inch one. A little metal gauge with a sliding marker is also handy. It may be adjusted to fractions of an inch and is useful for measuring tucks, spacing buttonholes and other small construction details.

SKIRT MARKER. If you do a lot of sewing for others, or have to do your own hem marking, you'll find this instrument more than worth its weight in gold. It provides a much quicker and more accurate method of marking hems than when a yardstick is used. Skirt markers come in various types—pin markers, chalk markers, and combination pin-chalk markers. The pin marker gives a more accurate marking. Chalk marks tend to be too thick, and the chalk does not come out of some fabrics.

Marking Tools

Because of the many types of fabric you use, you may need several different devices for marking pattern

DRESSMAKER'S CARBON. The dressmaker's carbon comes in packages of one color or assorted colors. It is wisest to buy the assorted packs and use

MARKING TOOLS

Dressmaker's carbon paper
Tailor tacker
Tailor's chalk holder
Tailor's wax
Chalk tailor tacker
Tailor's wax container
Smooth-edge tracing wheel
Saw-tooth edge tracing wheel
Saw-tooth edge tracing wheel with guide
Chalk pencil
Marking pencil
Tailor's chalk

symbols. Not all fabrics can be marked in the same way, just as they can't be cut and stitched in the same way.

TRACING WHEEL. The tracing wheel is available in needle-point and saw-tooth edges as well as with a smooth edge. The needle-point style is used for marking heavy fabrics; the saw-tooth style for most light- and medium-weight fabrics.

The newest tracing wheel has a smooth edge, allowing the pattern tissue to remain intact. The wheels rolls along pattern markings and transfers them through the dressmaker's carbon to the wrong side of the garment fabric. (Complete instructions for marking appear in Chapter 7.)

the color closest to your fabric color when tracing. Carbon markings may show through very sheer fabrics, so always test a scrap of fabric before tracing on the garment pieces.

TAILOR'S CHALK OR CHALK PENCIL. Chalk is used on fabrics which cannot take the carbon, or for marking which will later be removed (trims, grainlines, etc.). It rubs off very easily when the marking is no longer needed. Tailor's chalk is made in flat 2-inch squares in white, black, red and blue. White and blue are least likely to stain fabric. You should have both of these colors. The chalk pencil gives a thinner, more accurate mark. It is easier and less messy to handle.

TAILOR'S WAX. Use this with caution; it does not wash out and may not disappear with dry-cleaning. The wax is clear or white in color and should be used only on woolens which will not take the softer chalk. Be sure you mark only on the wrong side of the fabric.

TAILOR TACKER. This metal tool marks both sides of the fabric through dressmaker's carbon. Dots are marked by placing the point sharply down on the fabric; straight lines by drawing the tool along. The tracing wheel is actually easier to use.

packages of 100, but if you're going to do a large amount of sewing, buy them in the large economy one-pound box. For very heavy fabrics, there are coarser pins, size 14 and lower numbers for upholstery work.

NEEDLES. Buy the big assorted packages of needles that have all of the 10 sizes you'll need. Generally "sharps" of medium length are used for sewing; 9 or 10 for sheers; 6 or 8 for medium-weight fabrics; 1 to 5 for heavy materials. For very fine hand sewing use "betweens," which are short needles. For basting and millinery, select "milliners," which are no longer than sharps. "Calyx-eyed sharps" have large eyes,

SEWING EQUIPMENT

Sewing Equipment

Sewing is a meticulous craft, so select your tools with care. Many a fine dress has been marred by such a small item as a wrong pin or needle.

PINS. Select only the sharpest and the finest rust-proof dressmaker or silk pins. Numbers 15, 16 and 17 are suitable for most fabrics. You may buy small

making them easier to thread. When sewing on delicate silks, you may wish to purchase enough very fine needles to use in place of pins.

SPECIAL NEEDLES. Special tasks require special needles:
☐ Embroidery — long, sharp, large-eyed crewel needles. Similar to "sharps," these have a large eye

for easy threading of embroidery yarn or thread.

☐ Upholstery—large, curved needles which are designed to slip in and out of heavy fabric easily.

☐ Darning—long, coarse needles with large eyes.

☐ Leather and Fur—three-cornered pointed needles called "Glover's needles."

☐ Beading—needles which are very fine and long, especially designed for beading.

☐ Quilting—short, between-type needles.

☐ Millinery—long, thin needles used for millinery tacking.

NEEDLE THREADER. If you have an eyesight problem, or just find threading needles a chore, use a needle threader.

THIMBLE. You should always use a thimble for hand sewing. Your sewing will be more comfortable, and the results more perfect. The metal ones are more durable than the plastic type. Find one which fits the middle finger of the hand holding the needle. Look for a firm, snug fit. If the thimble seems to slip off easily, wet the end of your finger. The moisture creates suction and holds the thimble in place.

PIN CUSHION. If you want a purely decorative pin cushion, then select at random the one which you find the most attractive. If you want real service, then use the wrist type. A plastic or elastic wrist band keeps it in place. It never slips away or gets hidden among patterns and fabric just at the time you need it. The cushion is usually sponge rubber or sawdust.

EMERY BAG. You may find one on your pin cushion. This is a small bag with an abrasive inside which removes rust from pins and needles. You can also purchase them separately. Use it to keep pins and needles clean and free from rust.

THREAD. Thread, like fabric, is made of various fibers and in various weights suitable for certain types of sewing. Always select the one best for your fabric.

Thread is made in almost as many colors as fabrics are. Select a color slightly darker than the cloth with which it is to be used. The thread sews in lighter than it appears on the spool. Use a contrasting color for basting—one which is easily seen when it is time to remove the stitches.

Mercerized Cotton Thread. Most often used for general sewing.

Silk Thread. May be used on fine woolens and silk fabrics, since it produces a finer stitching line. When working on fine fabrics, silk thread is an excellent choice for basting because it slips in and out of fabric easily and can be pulled out without marring the fabric. It's also good for basting pleats because it does not mark fabric when pressed.

Synthetic Thread. Should be used on synthetics and their blends. Never use a synthetic thread on cotton or linen which will have to withstand high temperatures in pressing. Synthetic threads usually require a looser upper and lower tension on the machine, and a fine needle.

Elastic Thread. Used for gathering or for shirred effects which are either machine- or hand-stitched. It is used only as bobbin thread.

Buttonhole Twist. Silk thread (Size D) comes on 10-yard spools. Use it for decorative stitches, handworked buttonholes, sewing on buttons and as the bobbin thread when gathering large sections of fabric. It is stronger than cotton thread and slips easily through the fabric, making gathering a much easier task.

Embroidery Floss. Used for decorative stitches and most embroidery. It comes in 6-strand twists; your pattern will indicate the number of strands to use in embroidered designs.

Needles and Thread

Thread and needle should be considered together. The weight of the fabric determines the size of needle and thread. To help you find just the right size, a special chart is shown here. In using the chart, remember that fabrics of the same general description may vary. You should always test the thread on a scrap of the fabric you are using. You will notice that on the chart there is a column showing the approximate number of machine stitches to the inch. Use this guide for fine sewing.

WEIGHT OF FABRIC	TYPES OF FABRICS	THREAD	NEEDLES		
			HAND	MACHINE	MACHINE
Very Sheer	Batiste, chiffon, fine lace, marquisette, organdy, net	mercerized cotton silk white and black six cord—100,120,150	10	Fine 9	16 stitches to inch
Sheer	Dimity, dotted swiss, handkerchief linen, lawn, sheer crepe, voile	mercerized cotton silk white and black six cord—100,120,150	9	Fine 9-11	14-16 stitches to inch
Light Weight	Chambray, gingham, percale, taffeta, satin, sheer wools, challis	mercerized cotton silk white and black six cord—60,70	8,9	Fine 9-11	12-14 stitches to inch
Medium	Muslin, chintz, dress linen, piqué, flannel, jersey, broadcloth, corduroy, crepe	mercerized cotton silk heavy-duty cotton white and black six cord—50,60	7,8	Medium 11-14	10-14 stitches to inch
Medium Heavy	Denim, velveteen, terry cloth, tweeds, drapery fabrics, twill, gabardine, coatings, fleece	mercerized cotton silk heavy-duty cotton white and black six cord—36,40	6,7	Medium Coarse 14-16	10-12 stitches to inch
Heavy	Upholstery fabric, sailcloth, ticking, heavy denim	heavy-duty cotton white and black six cord—24,30,36	4,5	Coarse 14-18	8-10 stitches to inch
Very Heavy	Canvas, duck, awning fabric	white and black six cord—8,10,20	1,2,3	Coarse 16-18	6-8 stitches to inch

Miscellaneous Equipment

The more you sew, the more uses you will discover for various other pieces of equipment. A few which are most helpful are:

☐ Loop turner to help in turning tubing to the right side.

☐ Stiletto for punching eyelets and holes in fabric and leather.

□ Bodkin for threading elastic, fabric and tape through casing.

□ Tweezers for removing threads from ripped seams.

Sewing Machine

With the many brands and models available, it may be difficult for you to select a new machine and be confident you have purchased the best machine for your money and one which will meet your needs for years to come. Visit the dealers in your area and request demonstrations of their machines. Consult consumer reports. After you have narrowed your selection down to one or two machines, you may find it advisable to rent a model so you can test its performance.

In making your decision, you will have to decide between a straight-stitch and a swing-needle (zigzag) machine and between the cabinet and portable models. The type and amount of sewing you do, the space you have for a machine and your budget will influence your choice.

If you use the machine only for plain sewing, patching and mending, you may find the straight-stitch sewing machine satisfactory. This type sews forward and backward and usually can be released for some free-motion darning. The needle moves up and down in a straight line. Usually some attachments are available for the various machines.

The more versatile swing-needle or zigzag machines have a needle that moves from side to side as well as up and down, making it possible to do many of the finishing details and decorative stitches without the use of attachments. The swing-needle or zigzag machines vary greatly in the amount of decorative stitching they will do. Some machines are built to use templates, which produce distinctive patterns; others require just a twist of a knob. If you plan to purchase a zigzag machine consider the difficulty of operating the decorative controls in case you expect to do specialty stitching. If you are not mechanically inclined, choose a machine that is easy to set.

Some machines are constructed with slanting needles, allowing for better visibility. Both straight-needle and swing-needle machines can be obtained with this type of needle.

Your next decision will be whether to select a cabinet or portable model. The cabinet model costs more, but it does provide extra work space, a convenient storage space for your equipment, and is easier for quick use. Cabinets are available in all periods of furniture style, and can be a decorative piece of furniture. Usually the cabinet model machine is a heavier machine, capable of handling heavy and bulky fabrics.

When space is limited, budgets limited, or the machine must be moved frequently, the portable is a more practical purchase. Take care to select a portable that is capable of handling fairly heavy and bulky fabrics. Inexpensive, light-weight portables may be too light to handle any but light- or medium-weight fabrics and will "slip" around the table when in operation. Beware of second-hand portables that are merely the regular heavy sewing head set into a cheap, unwieldy carrying case. These may be inadequately wired, and have a cheap motor attached that cannot be efficiently controlled.

Before you purchase your machine, test and check the construction and performance. A diagram of a standard model machine with the major parts identified is shown here. Become familiar with all the parts, then use the following questions as a checklist for judging the quality of a machine.

Long-Life Design

□ Is the wiring located where it will not be pinched, and is it protected against wear and oil drip?

□ Are service parts carried in stock and is repair service readily available?

□ Is the cabinet well constructed; hinges sturdy; legs well braced; leaf well supported and level when opened?

□ Is a guarantee offered on the machine?

Easy-to-Use Features

□ Are the upper tension setting and stitch-length controls easy to see and read?

□ Is the lamp well placed to throw light where needed?

□ Are there adjustable lock positions for the forward and reverse stitching controls?

□ Does the machine stitch forward and backward, plus have a quick release mechanism for darning and embroidery?

□ Is the foot or knee speed control comfortably placed?

Good Operation

□ Is the machine quiet and free from objectionable noise and vibration?

□ Is the machine easy to start and stop, and does it run smoothly at all speeds?

☐ Are the needle and bobbin easy to thread?
☐ Do two pieces of fabric stitched together travel between the foot and feed dog evenly at the same rate?
☐ Is the bobbin winder easy to use and does it fill the bobbin evenly?

Easy-to-Care-for

☐ Are the coverplates easily removable and all parts readily accessible for cleaning, oiling and greasing?
☐ Is the light bulb easy to replace?
☐ Is the machine easy to dust and wipe clean?

After you purchase your machine, it is important that you learn to operate and care for it efficiently. All new machines have accompanying instruction manuals which illustrate the parts of the machine and give full instructions for all phases of operation and care. If you buy a second-hand machine and receive no manual, contact a dealer in your area who handles the brand machine you purchased. He will either be able to provide a manual or demonstrate the operation of the machine. Remember that each machine may vary in the placement and type of parts, so no matter how many machines you have operated in the past, study the manual before attempting to operate one that is unfamiliar.

Winding the Bobbin

Wind the bobbin using thread which is identical to upper thread. It must be wound evenly and should never be so fully wound that it is tight in the bobbin case. If the bobbin has thread on it, remove it before winding new thread, or the new thread will not wind evenly or feed easily when stitching. Bobbins wind differently on the various machines, but generally there is a spool pin for the thread located below the balance wheel. The thread is placed on the spool pin, run through a bobbin tension disc, and then to the bobbin which is placed on a spindle. Always release the stop-motion screw on the balance wheel by turning it toward you. Raise bobbin winder and press it against the handwheel. Hold thread end to start winding, and wind until the bobbin is full.

Threading the Machine

Always check your instruction manual for proper threading. Your machine simply won't work if it isn't threaded exactly according to plan. Although upper threading of machines may vary according to the placement of the parts, it does follow a general pattern. The thread is placed on the spool pin on top of the machine head, then through a thread guide to the tension mechanism, through another thread guide to the take-up lever, through another thread guide, and inserted into the needle. Be sure that the thread is placed through the needle in the correct direction. After the machine is threaded, draw about 5 inches of thread through the needle.

The bobbin should be placed in the bobbin case carefully, so that the bobbin will move in the correct direction. Follow the directions in the manual for the machine you are using. It is important that the bobbin thread be placed in back of the presser foot before stitching begins. To draw bobbin thread up through the needle hole, insert the bobbin in the bobbin case, leaving about 3 inches of bobbin thread outside the bobbin, as shown in your manual. Close the bed plate. Raise take-up lever to its highest point. Turn the wheel by hand until the needle goes down and up so take-up lever is again at its highest point. Pull the end of the needle thread and a bobbin thread loop will appear through the needle hole. Pull end of bobbin thread through needle hole with scissors, and place both bobbin and needle threads diagonally back and under the presser foot.

Inserting the Needle

You will have to change needles in your machine when one breaks or when you need a different size for various weights of fabric.

Generally size 14 needles are used for normal sewing, but various fabrics may require a heavier (size 16) or a finer (size 11) needle. If you are in doubt about what needle size to use for your fabric, check the chart on page 67. In case a different numbering system is used for the needles on your machine, the manual will give you the necessary information.

Every sewing machine needle has a short groove at the eye on one side, and a long groove on the other. When inserting a needle in a machine, the long groove must always face the side from which the machine is to be threaded. On most machines, the last thread guide will indicate the direction in which the thread must enter the needle. Be sure the flat side of the needle is facing in the direction opposite to the thread. Raise the take-up lever to its highest point, and insert the needle upward into the needle clamp as far as it will go and tighten needle clamp screw.

Stitching

Test the stitching on a scrap of fabric. Never operate

a threaded machine without fabric. The threads will become tangled and the feed will be damaged.

To stitch, raise the take-up lever to its highest point, place the needle and bobbin threads diagonally back and under the presser foot. Place the larger amount of fabric to the left of the head and the part to be stitched to the right. Lower the needle into the fabric by turning the balance wheel toward you. Lower the presser foot and start stitching with a slow, even speed. Place your hand so your fingers are guiding the fabric lightly. Be sure the weight of the left arm is not resting on the fabric causing uneven feeding. Guide the fabric, but do not force or pull it through the machine.

When you have completed the stitching, raise the take-up lever to its highest point by turning the balance wheel toward you so the tension is released. Raise the presser foot; remove the fabric by drawing it to the back and left of the needle; cut threads.

There are various types of seam guides to help you stitch in a straight line. Lines on bed plate, a special attachment, or tape placed on bed plate can be used.

Correct Tension

After you have stitched your scrap of fabric, check it for correct tension. If the tension is correct, the stitch will be perfectly locked in the fabric and the needle and bobbin threads perfectly balanced so that the stitch appears the same on both sides of the fabric. When tension is incorrect, with either the needle or bobbin thread too tight or too loose, stitching will not appear the same.

Inspecting the line of stitching is the only way to check tension. It is important that the tension be checked on each type of fabric used, since tension requirements vary for some fabrics. If your stitching on the test scrap does not appear exactly alike on both sides of the fabric, then determine if the needle or bobbin thread needs adjusting. To do this, stitch diagonally across a square of your fabric, folded on true bias. Hold the stitching tightly at each end between thumb and forefinger and pull with an even gradual force until the thread breaks. The broken thread is always the one with tight tension. When the tensions are balanced, both threads break together and require more force to break.

If tension does need adjustment, it is better to try to adjust the upper tension. Most machines have a numbered tension dial with numbers ranging from 0 to 9. To increase turn upper tension toward the higher numbers; to decrease toward the lower. Never move more than two numbers at a time, then recheck the tension by stitching a scrap of the fabric.

Adjusting bobbin tension is more difficult, and should only be attempted if tension cannot be corrected with an upper tension adjustment. The bobbin case has a small tension screw which, when turned in the correct direction, will increase or decrease tension. Be sure to check your manual or ask your dealer to find the proper bobbin tension screw and direction for increase or decrease.

Correct Pressure

The amount of pressure influences the ease with which fabric will flow through the machine when stitching. Pressure should be heavy enough to keep two thicknesses of fabric traveling at the same rate; light enough to keep fabric from being marred by the feed dog. The surface finish, weight and texture of the fabric will determine the amount of pressure needed. To test for correct pressure, feed a double thickness of fabric through the machine and adjust the thumb screw until the fabric moves under the presser foot easily and shows no feed marks.

The pressure thumb screw is located on the top of the machine head and controls a spring which connects with the presser foot mechanism. It can be raised and lowered either by turning or a press-release mechanism. Check your manual or with your dealer on the correct operation of pressure control.

Stitch Length

There is no test for checking the correct stitch length for various fabrics. However, the chart on page 67 prescribes the proper stitch length for most fabrics. Generally, a shorter stitch (16 to an inch) is needed for sheer, fine fabrics; a medium stitch (12 stitches per inch) for medium weights; a long stitch (8 to 10 to the inch) for heavy, coarse fabrics. There are also certain specialty stitches used for basting, gathering, reinforcing which require different lengths of stitches.

The stitch regulator is usually placed on the right side of the machine. It lists numbers from about 7 to 20. A bar is placed in the center of the numbered plate and stitch length is regulated by moving the bar to the number indicating the number of stitches desired. The stitch regulator also controls the forward or backward motion of the feed dog. Usually by raising the stitch regulator to the highest point, you are able to stitch backwards.

Care of the Machine

A sewing machine, like any piece of equipment, needs some care and cleaning. When not in use, keep your machine covered to prevent dust from settling on it. Also, fabric will leave deposits of lint around the feed dog and bobbin case, which must be removed fairly often.

You should have a lint brush especially designed for cleaning sewing machines, and a piece of cheesecloth or lintless cotton. If a brush was not provided with your machine, you can purchase it at most sewing notions counters. To remove lint deposits, remove the throat plate of the machine and brush the lint and dust from the bobbin case and feed mechanism. Following the instructions given in your manual, remove the entire bobbin case if possible, and remove all lint, fluff and loose threads or foreign matter which has collected. Dust the entire machine, using the cloth, and brush out hard-to-get-at crevices.

Periodically, it is necessary to oil and lubricate the machine. If you use it every day, do this about every six weeks. If you use it infrequently, then every three to four months should be sufficient. Use only regulation sewing machine oil. Apply it sparingly, using only one drop of oil for every oiling point. Although machines vary greatly, the places which require oil on most standard models are noted in the illustration here.

When the machine has been thoroughly oiled, run it slowly for several minutes to allow the oil to work into the moving parts. If you do not plan to use the machine immediately, place a scrap of fabric under the presser foot and lower the needle. The fabric absorbs the excess oil that might drain down through the machine. The machine will be ready to use when you take it out again and there will be no danger of getting oil spots on your garment.

Repairing Tips

There is nothing more frustrating than to be in the middle of constructing a garment and have the machine start to "act up." Although major repairs should only be made by qualified repair men, there are certain minor adjustments you can make yourself when a machine operates improperly. If your machine develops one of these common ailments, check the possible causes suggested. If these remedies do not correct the trouble, then call your service-repair man.

Breaking of Needle - Causes:

• Improper size of needle for thread and material (see chart, page 67).
• Needle bent.
• Pulling of material when stitching.
• Needle striking improperly fastened presser foot or attachments.
• Crossing too thick a seam using too small a needle.

Breaking of Needle Thread - Causes:

• Knot in needle thread.
• Improper threading.
• Upper tension too tight.
• Needle not inserted in needle clamp as far as it will go.

- Needle blunt or bent.
- Needle in backwards.
- Thread too coarse for needle.
- Roughened hole in throat plate.
- Improper arrangement of thread when starting to sew.

Breaking of Bobbin Thread - Causes:

- Improper threading of bobbin case.
- Bobbin thread tension too tight.
- Knot in bobbin thread.

Skipping of Stitches - Causes:

- Needle not inserted in needle clamp as far as it will go.
- Needle in backwards.
- Needle threaded incorrectly.

- Needle blunt or bent.
- Needle too small for thread.
- Needle too short.

Puckered Seams - Causes:

- Tension too tight.
- Stitch too long for material being sewn.
- Wrong presser foot. Use only the presser foot provided for each particular machine; they are not interchangeable.

Sewing Machine Attachments

When you purchase your new machine, check the attachments included in the price of purchase, and those which are available at additional cost. Attachments make sewing easier and provide opportunities for decorative sewing. Don't neglect them; learn to use them effectively. They not only save time, but make sewing a more creative and interesting experience.

MACHINE ATTACHMENTS

Quilting guide
Zigzagger or decorator
Gathering foot
Button sewing foot
Narrow or foot hemmer
Tucker
Seam guide
Multiple-slotted binder
Edge-stitcher
Ruffler
Buttonholer
Cording-zipper foot

Before purchasing any additional attachments, talk to your dealer about the work each will do and have him demonstrate the operation of each. Decide which of the attachments will be practical for your needs. If you make only simple garments with few decorative details, then you will probably use only a few of the attachments. However, if you enjoy making garments with your own original ideas for trimming, you will use many of them. In selecting attachments, be sure that they will fit your make and model machine.

The zigzag machines require fewer attachments than the straight-stitch type, while the automatics vary widely in the amount of work they do without attachments, so that no accurate list can be made to apply to all automatics. However, listed below are the ones most frequently used on the straight-needle machines, what they do, how to use them and whether they are necessary or optional equipment.

CORDING-ZIPPER FOOT. The cording-zipper foot is designed for stitching close to a raised edge and can be adjusted to either the right or left side of the needle. The hinged feature of the foot insures even feeding over pins or heavy layers of fabric formed by crossed seams. It is used for covering cord, applying cording into seams, and most frequently for zipper application. It is essential to have one, since no zipper can be successfully applied by machine without it.

SEAM GUIDE. Seam guides help insure more accurate seam widths on both straight and curved seams, as well as provide a guide to accurate top-stitching. Most new machines have the seam markings on the plate of the machine, but if yours does not, you can purchase an inexpensive type which attaches to the machine bed, or you can make your own simply by placing cloth adhesive tape across the bed of the machine, with accurate markings on it, $5/8$ inch and $1/2$ inch from the needle. In stitching, keep your eyes at the edge of the seam guide or marking on the tape to direct the fabric correctly.

BUTTONHOLER. Standard models have templates which are inserted in the buttonholer and guide the machine in making various sizes of buttonholes from $5/16$ to $1\,1/16$ inches. There is also a special template for eyelets. Each buttonhole attachment has a dial which makes it possible to adjust the bight (width) of the stitch used. Both straight and keyhole buttonholes can be made. The buttonholer is easy to operate and works well on most fabrics. If you wish to make even, attractive buttonholes, you'll definitely need this attachment. The buttonholes are not only quicker to make than the hand-worked type, but they're stronger. For best results, use two rows of stitches.

ZIGZAGGER OR DECORATOR. A variety of decorative as well as straight stitches can be made without removing the attachment from the machine. The attachment is equipped with stitch patterns, or cams, which can be changed according to the design of the stitch desired. There is a dial which adjusts the bight (width) of the stitch, and a stitch length regulator which may be used to produce variations on the basic stitch design. The attachment offers many ways to do decorative work such as border trims, appliqués, decorative tuck edgings. It also is most useful for zigzag seam finishes, and for sewing seams on stretchy fabrics.

NARROW OR FOOT HEMMER. The attachment forms and stitches a perfectly turned hem, without previous basting or pressing. The hem formed is about $1/8$ inch in width, and is very useful when finishing the edges of ruffles, and for applying lace, rickrack or any finished trim to an edge in one operation. Hemmers which make wider hems are available for some machines.

RUFFLER. This attachment is capable of making uniform gathered or pleated ruffles, and will make and apply ruffles to another section at the same time. Some models are also equipped to apply piping to a ruffle, or to make a ruffle and attach it with a facing in one operation. It is a relatively simple attachment to operate, and is most valuable in making household items such as curtains, slipcovers and bedspreads which require long lengths of ruffling. It is also useful in making children's clothes which have gathered skirts with ruffled trims and petticoats.

MULTIPLE-SLOTTED BINDER. Excellent for applying various widths of commercial or self-fabric bias binding to a straight or curved edge, the binder ensures uniform application and eliminates tedious pinning and basting of binding. It is most often used to add decorative bound edge-trims and to bind seams on fabrics which ravel a great deal. It is particularly useful for making household items such as café curtains with bound edge-trim, aprons, toaster covers, and for adding neat, bound finishes to all types of garments.

GATHERING FOOT. Do not confuse this attachment with the ruffler. The gathering foot does what its name implies—gathers fabric as it is stitched. It will produce uniform rows of shirring with the fullness locked in every stitch.

EDGE-STITCHER. This has five slots that serve as guides when stitching must be uniform and accurate on the edge of the material. It is most helpful when sewing together bands of lace, making lace insertions, making French seams, piping edges, or for making pin tucks up to ¼ inch deep.

TUCKER. Used for making uniform tucks from ⅛ to 1 inch in width; the tucker is equipped with two scales: one regulates the width of the tucks, the other ensures equal spacing between tucks. It can be used effectively for creating cross tuck effects, pin tucks or regular tucks.

QUILTER. The quilter has a short open foot and an adjustable or removable space guide that may be used to the right or left of the needle to guide the quilting stitches in even rows. It is especially useful for quilting padded fabrics, and some models are adaptable as an embroidery foot which permits following curved lines with ease and accuracy.

PRESSING EQUIPMENT

Expert pressing is as essential to the good looks of a garment as expert sewing. Keep pressing equipment as handy as the sewing machine; it should be used almost as often as the machine. For tips on how and when to press, check Chapter 8.

PRESSING EQUIPMENT

Adjustable ironing board
Press cloths
Needle board
Steam and dry iron
Press mitt
Tailor's ham
Seam roll
Point presser
Sponge
Hand point presser
Wooden clapper

Iron

A combination steam-dry iron is best; one with a temperature control essential.

Ironing Board

Obtain an adjustable one. They are most comfortable because you can adjust them to your height. Metal boards are more durable than wooden ones and do not warp.

Ironing Board Pad and Cover

Select a pad that will last. The foam rubber or plastic foams are quite durable. Heavy cotton padding is inclined to wear more quickly and scorch easily. The best covers are the silicone-coated ones or the asbestos type, since they do not become scorched as easily as the cotton drill or duck ones. Be sure that the cover and pad you select fasten securely to the board and fit it well.

Press Cloths

The commercially treated cloths are very inexpensive. Closely woven cheesecloth also makes an excellent press cloth. The open texture allows the steam to go through but the weave keeps fabric surface from shining. A dry wool press cloth under a damp cheesecloth is helpful for problem materials that shine.

Sponge

Used to dampen fabric as you press. It gives an even amount of moisture to an area.

Press Mitt

If all garments were composed of straight or angled pieces, these wouldn't be essential. Since garments curve as often as they lie straight, you need a curved cushion to press and shape the curved detail. The mitt is a small padded mitt that slips over the hand.

Tailor's Ham

This is a ham-shaped cushion also used for pressing curved and shaped details. It is essential if you plan to do any sort of tailoring. Inexpensive hams are available commercially, or you can make your own. Cut two oval pieces of firmly woven cotton or lightweight wool about 8 by 12 inches. Sew the ovals together and leave an opening. Turn right side out and stuff firmly with wool scraps, kapok or sawdust. The secret of a successful ham is packing it firmly. For best results soak the scraps and stuff them into the ham while still wet. Shape it as you pack and pack until it is solid. Then sew the opening closed with an overhand stitch.

Seam Roll

This is a padded rolled cushion to place beneath the seam when pressing. It will keep ridges from forming along the seam line. Commercial ones are available.

Wooden Clapper

When tailoring garments, purchase the clapper. It is a shaped wooden block which is pounded against steam-dampened fabric for the purpose of flattening edges and pressing seams flat.

Point Presser

Again, this item is mainly used for tailoring, but is useful for almost any garment making. It is a thin, shaped wooden board used to press open the seams in corners, points and other difficult areas.

Needle Board

To prevent the pile of velveteen, velvet and other pile fabrics from matting, use the needle board. The fabric is placed face down on the needles so that the pile fits between the needles and can be pressed without marking.

CHAPTER 6

THE EASY RULES OF PATTERN ALTERATION

If you have purchased your pattern in the correct figure type and size for your type of figure, most of your pattern worries should be over. However, the pattern is made for the average person, and since everyone differs in contour, you may find that your figure deviates slightly from the average. This makes it necessary to make a few adjustments to the pattern to achieve a custom-made look. Having a garment that is custom-cut and custom-fitted to your individual figure is half the joy of sewing.

Knowing exactly what alterations to make in your pattern to achieve this perfect fit comes with experience . . . sometimes sad experience. Often a beginner will blithely cut a pattern in expensive fabric, only to find, when it is completed, that the garment just doesn't fit properly. It may be too late, then, to do anything about it. This will never happen if you become familiar with your own individual contour and learn the simple adjustments to make in your tissue pattern so that you can cut correctly for a perfect fit.

A BASIC PATTERN

If you truly want to make clothes with a custom fit, you should first make a basic pattern. Although this takes time in the beginning, it will save a great deal of time and even money as you continue to sew. No longer will your sewing be experimental. It will have a professional look.

The basic pattern can be made in two ways: by using inexpensive fabric for a slim skirt and a standard bodice with set-in sleeves; or by using the McCall's Try-on pattern made of non-woven material. Naturally the Try-on will be easier to use because it is designed especially for this purpose. All the pattern markings are printed on the pattern. The pattern can be cut, adjusted to the figure, stitched and used again and again as a guide for altering other patterns of a similar silhouette. Try-on patterns are available in Misses' and Junior sizes, Number 300; Half sizes, Number 400. They can be ordered through any McCall's pattern dealer.

One big advantage in purchasing the Try-on is the instruction booklet which accompanies it, giving directions for altering the pattern for various figure irregularities.

However, if you decide you would rather make your basic from cotton fabric, buy a tissue pattern of a simple, basic dress in your figure type and size. Use firmly woven fabric such as percale or muslin. Lay out the pattern and cut. Transfer all pattern markings to the fabric.

Using the Basic Pattern

EASE. In order to use a basic pattern successfully you must understand the meaning of "ease." Ease is the amount of fullness built into every pattern to allow room for a person to move. It is the amount added to body measurements so that a garment isn't skintight. Even a very fitted sheath has ease.

Although body measurements are standardized, the amount of ease isn't. Each pattern company decides how much ease is needed in its patterns. This is the reason why the fit of a garment in one brand of pattern is not identical with another although the size is the same.

The standard amount of ease in a McCall's pattern is:

Bust—3 inches in a basic bodice. Evening bodices which are designed to fit snugly may have less.
Waist—½ inch.
Hip—Approximately 2 inches in slim skirts.
Back Waist Length—¼ to ⅜ inch.

You may want a little more or less, depending on how tight you wear your clothes; however, these are average amounts of ease for today's fashions.

The style and the design of the pattern also influ-ence the ease allowance. A garment with the sleeve and bodice cut in one piece will have more ease through the bodice than a fitted garment with a set-in sleeve. A blouson style will have more length than a fitted bodice. This is known as design ease and changes with fashion.

ADJUSTMENTS. Trying to measure pattern pieces and decide whether the ease allowance is correct for you is a difficult and uncertain task. The use of a basic pattern avoids this confusion because it can be adjusted until it fits perfectly. After the basic has been fitted, identical alterations can be made on each pattern you use. If you add ½ inch to the waist length of the basic, then you will add ½ inch to the length of other bodice designs, such as blouson, a dropped waistline, an Empire line, in order to retain the same proportions the designer intended. The same thing applies to horizontal or around-the-figure measurements.

FITTING. Assemble the basic garment by machine-basting the seams together. Then the stitches may be pulled out easily to make adjustments. It is impossible to fit a garment accurately if it has been pinned or hand-basted together. Try the garment on and check

POSITIONS OF GRAINLINES

these points to determine if the basic pattern fits:

☐ Grainlines at chest, bust, waist, hip and upper arm are straight and parallel to the floor.

☐ Grainlines at center front and back are perpendicular to the floor.

☐ Garment hangs gracefully and smoothly when you are standing straight.

☐ Garment has sufficient fullness throughout for movement in sitting, bending and walking.

☐ Bodice length is correct both above and below the grain line at front and back bustline.

☐ Skirt is correct length.

☐ Sleeves are correct length above and below the elbow.

☐ Neckline fits smoothly, without gaping or pulling.

☐ Center front and back seams are in the center of the figure.

☐ Side seams lie halfway between front and back, perpendicular to the floor.

☐ Shoulder seams lie straight across the shoulder.

☐ Sleeve seams lie across the tip of the shoulder for normal unpadded shoulder. As amount of padding increases the sleeve seam moves out on the shoulder.

☐ Bodice darts point directly to the fullest part of the bust.

☐ Hip darts end just above fullest part of the hip.

☐ Elbow darts are even, with center dart pointing directly to point of elbow when arm is bent.

ADJUSTING YOUR PATTERN

Whether you are using a tissue paper pattern or altering your basic pattern, the adjustments will be made in the same way. To help you solve your adjustment problems, below are described the most common fitting ailments that women have, and the pattern adjustments which will remedy each situation.

Since many of these adjustments suggest the use of the McCall's Easy-Rule Guide, you should understand how it is used to shorten and lengthen pattern pieces.

This simple device ensures accuracy.

Length

Problem

Too Long   If the bodice is too long, it will fold over at the waistline. If the skirt is too long, the whole garment looks large.

Adjustment

Shorten   If you need to shorten a pattern, crease tissue on the line marked on Easy-Rule guide. Using the printed ruler, fold a pleat taking up the necessary amount. Tape in place. Redraw seams and construction markings to retain the original shaping of pattern.

Problem

Too Short   If the bodice is too short, it will ride high and look skimpy. If the skirt is too short, the whole garment looks too small.

Adjustment

Lengthen   To lengthen a bodice or skirt pattern, cut apart on dotted lines of Easy-Rule guide. Using the printed ruler as a guide, spread the pattern the amount to be lengthened. Tape over paper. Redraw seams and construction markings to retain original shaping of pattern.

Bustline

The bust area of the bodice should fit smoothly with enough ease to move comfortably. Darts should point toward the fullest part of bust.

Problem

High Bust Bodice fullness for bust falls below bust so that bodice is too tight at actual bustline and too full below bustline; bust darts too low.

Adjustment

Raise Bust Dart Draw lines through center of each dart. The lines will cross at bust point of tissue pattern. Mark the position of point of your bust on pattern. Measure the distance between original bust point and new bust point. This is the amount for dart to be raised. Raise side dart, keeping it parallel to original dart. Raise point of waistline dart same amount. Redraw darts and side seams.

Raise French Dart Mark new bust point on pattern. Draw a line from mark to center fold line at base of original dart. Measure back ½ inch on this line and mark point of new dart. Redraw new dart from this point to stitching line at base of original dart. Fold and pin new dart. Redraw side seam on right and wrong side. Unpin dart and you have the correct angle at base of dart.

Problem

Low Bust Bodice fullness for bust is above bust; bust darts too high.

Adjustment

Lower Bust Dart Mark bust point of pattern and position of point of your bust on pattern same as for raising dart. Measure distance between two points to determine amount to lower dart. Lower side dart, keeping it parallel to original dart. Lower point of waistline dart same amount. Redraw dart and side seams.

Lower French Dart Mark new bust point on pattern. Draw line from mark to center fold line at base of original dart. Measure back ½ inch on this line; mark point of new dart. Redraw new dart from this point to stitching lines at base of original dart. Tape over paper. Fold and pin new dart. Redraw side seam same as for raising French dart. Unpin dart.

Problem

Large Bust Wrinkles pulling across bust; dart fitting not sufficient for curve of bust; grainline of fabric pulls up at bust.

Problem

Smaller Than Average Bust Folds falling across bust; dart fitting too full for curve of bust; grainlines of fabric droop at bustline.

Adjustment

Larger Than Average Bust Slash pattern as directed for the small bust. Spread the pattern on vertical slash at bust point, one half the needed amount, tapering from shoulder line to waistline. This will automatically spread the underarm slash. Tape over paper. The underarm and waistline darts have been increased which is desirable as a large bust needs additional dart shaping. Mark new point of dart ends in center of slashes. Redraw the darts from new point to the waistline and underarm.

Adjustment

Smaller Than Average Bust Draw line through center of underarm dart and waistline dart until the two lines meet. This marks the point of bust. Draw a line from point of bust to shoulder, halfway between shoulder and neck edge. Slash from waistline edge along the vertical line to within ⅛ inch of shoulder seam. Slash on horizontal line to within ⅛ inch of bust point. Lap cut edges of vertical slash at bust point the needed amount, tapering slash from shoulder line to waistline. This will lap the underarm slash edges automatically.

Larger Than Average Bust With French Dart Draw line through dart and slash same as for smaller than average bust. Spread dart half the necessary amount, keeping neck edge on original center front. Tape over paper. Mark new bust point in center of slash. Redraw dart from new point to original stitching lines at base. Redraw center front line.

Smaller Than Average Bust With French Dart Draw a straight line on center fold line of dart, extending to center front. Slash on this line. Lap edges of dart half the necessary amount, keeping neck edge on original center front. Tape in position. Redraw center front line. Redraw dart from point of original stitching lines at base.

Shoulder

As soon as the correct bust dart position and amount of ease are established, proceed to the shoulder area. The area between bust and shoulder should be free of wrinkles. The shoulder should conform to slant and width of your shoulder.

Problem

Sloping Shoulders Wrinkles slope from neckline to armscye and fall in folds; fabric grainline drops at armscye in both bodice front and back.

Problem

Square Shoulders Bodice has wrinkles pulling from the shoulder to bust and shoulder blades; fabric grainline pulls up at armscye in front and back.

Adjustment

Sloping Shoulder Determine amount you will need to lift shoulder. Armhole must be lowered same amount. Measure down this amount from armhole edge of shoulder and mark. Measure down from armhole at side seam; mark same amount. Redraw shoulder seam, tapering from mark to neckline. Redraw armhole, tapering from mark to notches. Size and shape of armhole have been retained so sleeve will fit.

Adjustment

Square Shoulder Determine amount shoulder must be released. Armhole must be raised same amount. Tape pattern over paper. Measure up this amount from armhole edge of shoulder and mark. Measure up from armhole at side seam; mark same amount shoulder was released. Redraw seams from mark to neckline and armhole, from mark to notches.

Sloping Shoulder on a Raglan Sleeve Determine the amount you will need to lift shoulder. Starting at original dart stitching line at neck edge, redraw a new line making dart longer and deeper over tip of shoulder. The amount dart is lengthened depends on the amount it was increased in depth. Dart must be tapered to a gradual point. If you take the dart deeper and then curve it back to the end of original dart, you will get an unsightly bulge on the sleeve at end of dart.

Square Shoulder on a Raglan Sleeve Determine the amount you will need to drop shoulder. Starting at original dart stitching line at neck edge, draw a new line making dart more curved over tip of shoulder and more shallow. Taper to end of original dart. Curving of the dart stitching line gives the greatest possible amount of fabric at tip of shoulder in this type of sleeve.

Sloping Shoulder on a Kimono Sleeve The point at which alteration is made is determined by width of shoulder. Hold pattern up to you, matching center front to center front of your body. Mark tip of your shoulder on shoulder seamline of bodice front.

Draw a diagonal line from mark indicating tip of your shoulder to high point of underarm seam. Slash pattern on this line. Lower sleeve section the amount that must be removed from shoulder, keeping slash edges even. Tape over paper. Redraw shoulder line from top of sleeve section to neckline. Redraw underarm seam from bottom of sleeve tapering to waistline.

Square Shoulder on a Kimono Sleeve Locate tip of shoulder same as for sloping shoulder. Draw a diagonal line from mark, indicating tip of your shoulder, to high point of underarm seam. Slash on this line. Raise sleeve section the amount that must be added to shoulder, keeping slash edges even. Tape over paper. Redraw shoulder line from top of sleeve section to neckline and underarm seam from bottom of sleeve tapering to waistline.

Problem

Narrow Shoulders Seamline extends beyond tip of shoulder; sleeve seam falls over edge of shoulder.

Adjustment

Narrow Shoulder Measure amount that seamline drops off tip of shoulder. This is the amount shoulder seam must be shortened on bodice front and back. Draw a line through Easy-Rule to a point even with armhole notch and another line from this point straight across to armhole seamline. Slash on line. Lap shoulder seam edges to shorten needed amount. Tape in place. Redraw shoulder seam from neck to armhole. Size of armhole has not been changed; sleeve will fit.

Problem

Broad Shoulders Bodice pulls from armhole to shoulder seam; shoulder seamline does not reach tip of shoulder and sleeve cap rides up.

Adjustment

Broad Shoulders Measure from armhole seamline to tip of shoulder. This is the amount shoulder seam must be lengthened on bodice front and back. Cut pattern as directed for narrow shoulder. Spread slash to lengthen needed amount. Tape over paper. Redraw a straight shoulder seam from neck to armhole. Shoulder is now long enough to allow seamline to reach tip of shoulder.

Narrow Shoulder on a Raglan Sleeve Draw a line across center of shoulder dart, perpendicular to grainline of sleeve. Pin bodice front and bodice back to corresponding sleeve seams, neck edges and matching notches. Mark bodice pieces at point at which line on sleeve touches bodice seam. Unpin sleeve. Draw a line on bodice front from mark to point of bust, then across fold line of bust dart to underarm seamline. Draw a line on bodice back from mark, down and across to underarm seamline, in same position as on front. Slash along line on sleeve and on bodice pieces from diagonal seam to underarm seamline.

Lap slash edges on sleeve to shorten the needed amount. Tape in place. Redraw seams. Lap diagonal seam edge of bodice front and back same amount as sleeve. Tape in place. Redraw diagonal seams from neck edges to notches.

Narrow Shoulder on a Kimono Sleeve Locate tip of your shoulder on pattern same as for sloping shoulder. Draw a diagonal line from mark, indicating tip of your shoulder, to high point of underarm seamline. Slash pattern on this line. Lap shoulder seam edges to shorten needed amount. Tape in place. Redraw shoulder seam.

Broad Shoulder on a Raglan Sleeve Draw lines and slash pattern pieces same as for narrow shoulder on a raglan sleeve. Spread slash edges of sleeve to lengthen needed amount. Tape over paper. Redraw seams. Spread diagonal seam edges of bodice front and back same amount as sleeve. Tape over paper. Redraw diagonal seams from neck edges to notches.

Broad Shoulder on a Kimono Sleeve Locate tip of your shoulder on pattern same as for sloping shoulder. Draw a diagonal line from mark indicating tip of your shoulder to high point of underarm seamline. Slash on this line. Spread slash to lengthen needed amount. Tape over paper. Redraw shoulder seam.

Neckline

Necklines should fit smoothly and hug the body closely. If alterations are made on the neckline, the same alterations are made on the facings.

Problem

Thin Neck   Neckline falls away from neck and falls in folds.

Problem

Full Neck   Neckline pulls and wrinkles around neck and is too tight.

Adjustment

Thin Neck   Tape paper under the neckline edge. Build up the neckline the desired amount. Add the same amount to bodice front and back. Alter the facing in the same manner and restore the original width of the facing.

Adjustment

Full Neck   Cut out neckline of bodice front and back the necessary amount to fit neck smoothly. Alter facing in the same manner and restore the original width of the facing.

Problem

Open Neckline That Gaps   Neckline is too big and hangs away from the neck.

Adjustment

Gapping Neckline   Slash from neckline down to point of bust. Then slash from waistline up to point of dart along center fold line. Lap pattern half the necessary amount at neckline edge. The waistline dart will be deeper because you are transferring the extra fullness from neckline to the dart. Redraw neckline curve. Stitch dart on the original stitching line. Slash facing pattern and lap same as for neck edge of bodice. Redraw neckline curve of facing.

Back

Many times the pulling and wrinkles in a bodice are caused by too little ease in the bodice back.

Problem

Broad Back Bodice pulls across back, restricting movement.

Adjustment

Broad Back Slash the pattern from shoulder seam straight down for about 10-12 inches. Spread the pattern half the desired amount to be added. Bring shoulder edges together, forming a small dart on side of slash nearest armhole. Clip seam allowance of armhole to allow the pattern to lie flat. Tape over paper. Redraw shoulder seam.

Broad Back on a Kimono Sleeve Measure 2 to 2½ inches from neck edge on shoulder seam and mark. Draw a line straight down from mark, parallel to grain-

line. Draw a horizontal line from first line across to high point of underarm seam. Slash pattern on this line. Spread pattern half the needed amount on vertical slash. Tape over paper. Make a dart at shoulder seam about 2½ inches long and the width of amount added at shoulder seam. Redraw underarm curve.

Broad Back on a Raglan Sleeve It is possible to add as much as ½ inch to back of a raglan sleeve bodice but more than that will not be satisfactory. Tape bodice back over paper. Add as much as ¼ inch to center back from neck to waistline. This makes neckline and waistline larger. Decrease neckline by ¼ inch at edge joining sleeve. Taper to nothing on diagonal seam from neck to underarm. Increase dart ¼ inch to bring waistline back to original size.

Sleeve

If sleeve pulls and wrinkles across the upper arm, the sleeve should be made larger.

Problem

Large Upper Arm Sleeve pulls and wrinkles across fullest part of sleeve; fabric grain pulls up at the center of sleeve.

Adjustment

Large Upper Arm Slash sleeve pattern through center from circle at cap to lower edge. Slash straight across sleeve cap from seamline to seamline. Spread pattern on vertical slash, increasing sleeve necessary amount at widest part. Tape over paper. This has automatically lapped edges of the horizontal slash on sleeve cap. Measure amount sleeve cap was shortened by the lapping of edges of the horizontal slash. Add this amount to sleeve cap to restore it to its original length. Redraw curve of cap.

Bodice front and back side seams must be altered so sleeve will fit with normal ease allowance. Add half the amount of the increased width of sleeve to underarm side seams, tapering to nothing at waistline.

Large Upper Arm on a Kimono Sleeve You may enlarge a kimono sleeve up to 1½ inches; any more than this is not satisfactory. Divide the amount to be added by four. Add this amount at shoulder and underarm of sleeve. Taper from shoulder to lower sleeve edge and to original seam allowance at neckline. Taper from underarm to lower edge of sleeve and to original seam allowance at waistline. Make same alteration on bodice back.

Large Upper Arm on a Raglan Sleeve Draw a line parallel to grainline from lower edge of sleeve to point of shoulder dart. Draw another line across sleeve from underarm to underarm. Slash on line from lower edge of sleeve to the point of dart. Then slash on line across widest part of sleeve between underarm seamlines. Spread pattern on vertical slash, increasing sleeve necessary amount at widest part. This automatically laps edges of horizontal slash. Redraw dart.

Problem

Sleeve Width Too Narrow   Sleeve is too narrow; pulls and wrinkles at lower edge.

Adjustment

Alteration for Narrow Sleeve   Slash the pattern through the center of sleeve to the circle at seamline of cap. Spread the slash, increasing the sleeve the necessary amount at hem and tapering to sleeve cap. Insert tissue under the slash and pin or tape in position. Redraw grainline parallel to center of sleeve and straighten the lower edge of the sleeve.

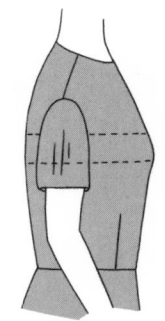

Problem

Sleeve Width Too Full   Sleeve is too full and too wide at lower edge.

Adjustment

Alteration for Full Sleeve   Slash the pattern through the center of the sleeve to the circle at sleeve cap seamline. Overlap the slash edges decreasing the necessary amount at hem and tapering to seamline at cap. Pin or tape in position. Redraw grainline straight and parallel to center of sleeve and straighten the lower edge of the sleeve.

Problem

Binding Sleeve Cap   Sleeve pulls and wrinkles across top of sleeve.

Adjustment

Binding Sleeve Cap   Raise the underarm edges of sleeve about ⅜ inch and add ⅜ inch to side seams of sleeve. Redraw the line, tapering to nothing. Adjust bodice front and back to match sleeve. Add ⅜ inch to lower edge of armhole seam and ⅜ inch at underarm side seam. Taper to nothing at armhole and waistline.

Posture

Problem

Straight Back Fold falling from neckline to shoulder blades in bodice back; fabric grainline drops at shoulder blades in center back.

Adjustment

Straight Back Slash pattern back, straight across from center back to armhole seamline, about 4 inches below neckline. Lap slash at center back to remove necessary amount. Tape in position over paper. Redraw grainline and straighten center back. This will make the neckline edge smaller. Trace the outline of pattern at center back, neckline, shoulder and armhole edges above the slash. Match center back neckline seam of tracing to new center back line. Using tracing as a guide, restore neckline to its original size and redraw shoulder and armhole edges.

The extra length in the back of a one-piece dress, whether it is caused by a straight back or a swayback is removed by slashing and lifting the necessary amount at the shoulder blades same as for a straight back.

Problem

Round Shoulders Bodice wrinkles pull from neckline in back toward shoulders; grainline pulls up at the shoulder blades in center back.

Adjustment

Round Shoulders Slash the pattern back, about 4 inches below neckline, straight across center back to armhole seamline. Spread the slash the necessary amount at center back. Tape pattern over paper. Redraw grainline and straighten center back. This makes the neckline edge larger. Trace the outline of pattern at center back, neckline, shoulder and armhole edges above slash. Match center back neckline seam of tracing to new center back line. Using tracing as a guide, restore neckline to its original size and redraw shoulder and armhole edges.

When a one-piece dress pulls up at center back, adding to the lower edge will not make the dress hang correctly. Slash the pattern at the shoulder blades and spread the necessary amount same as for round shoulders.

Waistline

After bustline and shoulder area have been fitted, proceed to waistline. Waistline seam should fit comfortably at natural waistline with no wrinkles above or below the waist.

Problem

Large Waistline Waistline of skirt rides up above natural waistline and wrinkles pull around waist.

Adjustment

Large Waistline Add 2 inches or less to your waistline by dividing the total amount by four and increasing each side seam this amount. Taper from waistline to underarm seam of bodice and from the waistline to hipline of skirt. If you need to increase the waist more than 2 inches, let out each dart slightly (not more than ¼ inch) at the waistline; taper to point of dart.

Waistline with French Dart—Too Small Divide total amount to be increased by four. This amount will be added to each side seam. Tape pattern over paper. Fold and pin dart in pattern front, matching stitching lines. Measure out from natural waistline marking on front and back. Mark amount to be added. Redraw side seams, tapering to armhole and to hipline. Unpin dart on front and you have new cutting line.

Problem

Small Waistline Skirt falls below natural waistline; bodice too full at waistline.

Adjustment

Small Waistline If your waistline measures less than the pattern size you are using, take in the waistline 2 inches or less by dividing the total amount to be decreased by four and removing this amount from each side seam allowance. This will evenly decrease the waistline. Taper from waistline to underarm seam in bodice and from waistline to hipline in skirt. If you need more than 2 inches removed, take in each dart slightly (not more than ¼ inch) at waistline, tapering to point of dart.

Waistline with French Dart—Too Large Divide the total amount to be decreased by four. This is the amount that will be removed from each side seam. Fold and pin dart in pattern front, matching stitching lines. Measure in from natural waistline indication on front and back and mark amount to be removed. Redraw side seams, tapering to armhole and to hipline. Unpin dart on front and you have the new cutting line.

Skirt

When making skirt alterations, remember that you need an ease allowance at hipline for movement and comfort.

Problem

Large Hips Skirt pulls across hipline and tends to ride up; fabric grainline goes up at side seams.

Adjustment

Large Hips To increase hipline 2 inches or less, divide the total amount to be added by four and add an equal amount to each side seam allowance, front and back. Taper from waistline to hem.

Problem

Large Derrière Skirt wrinkles across the derrière, tends to ride up in the back; fabric grain goes up in the back; side seams swing toward the back.

Adjustment

Large Derrière If you have this problem, increase both width and length in the skirt back at fullest part of derrière. Slash pattern through center of dart nearest

center back and spread pattern half the necessary amount. Cut straight across pattern 7 inches below waistline from center back to side seamline. Spread pattern enough to return center back to its normal straight grain. Tape over paper. This has increased size of the waistline. To return waistline to its original size, divide the total amount added by number of darts and increase each dart an equal amount. Redraw darts lengthening them so that fullness falls at fullest part of figure.

Problem

Small Hips Skirt too full over the hipline, falls in folds over hip; fabric grain drops at side seams.

Adjustment

Small Hips To decrease hipline 2 inches or less, divide the total amount to be decreased by four and take an equal amount off each side seam allowance, front and back. Taper from waistline to hem.

Problem

Small Derrière   Skirt falls in folds across the derrière and tends to sag in back; grainline drops in center back of skirt.

Adjustment

Small Derrière   To adjust for this, decrease length and width at center back of skirt. Slash the pattern back through center of waistline dart. Lap slash edges to remove necessary amount of fullness. Slash straight across pattern about 7 inches below waistline from center back to side seam. Lap edges of slash enough to bring the center back grain to its normal straight grain position. Tape in place. This will decrease the size of the waistline dart. Redraw the dart from waistline marking to point.

Problem

Sway-Back   Folds or wrinkles form across the center back between waist and hip.

Adjustment

Sway-Back   The sway-back is a very common problem which requires shortening center back of skirt. Slash pattern about 3½ inches below waistline, straight across from center back to side seamline. Lap slashed edges to remove the necessary amount.

Tape in position. Redraw the center back line to restore original grainline. This will decrease the back waistline measurement which is usually desirable for this figure. Take in the bodice darts at the waistline the amount you have removed from center back to make bodice back waistline fit skirt.

If you need the original waistline measurement, increase the side seam of the skirt the same amount as removed from center back. Taper from waist to hip. Redraw the skirt dart to straighten it.

See straight back alteration to correct swayback on a one-piece dress.

Problem

Large Abdomen   Waist pulls across the front in bodice and skirt, and waistline rides up at center front; side seams of skirt swing toward front; fabric grainline goes up at center front.

Adjustment

Large Abdomen   Draw a line through waistline darts and another one from center front to side seam about 3 inches above and below waistline on both bodice and skirt. Slash on markings. Spread this slash at dart half the necessary amount to be added. Then spread slash to side seam enough to bring center front back to normal straight grain. Tape pieces in position over paper. Redraw waistline darts in center of slash, bringing them back to their normal position and size.

Pants

The pants fashions of today create special fitting problems. A snug fit is demanded, but the garment must not be too tight at any point. It is important that major alterations be made on the tissue, since little can be done once the garment has been cut. If you have a number of fitting problems, it would be wise to test the pattern in an inexpensive fabric. Once you achieve the perfect fit for your figure, use this as a basic pattern for all kinds of pants in your wardrobe.

Pants patterns should be bought by hip measurement. However, there are other measurements which are needed to alter your pattern properly, so have somone take the following measurements for you.

□ Waist—The waistline can be taken in or let out very easily, so do not use this measurement as a guide for buying your pattern.

□ Hip—This is the important measurement to keep in mind when buying your pattern. Take the measurement 7 inches down from the waist.

□ Instep—This measurement is taken over the instep and around the heel. It determines how narrow the pants can be at the ankle and still be able to get over the foot without an opening.

□ Length of Crotch—Take this measurement in sitting position. Take the measurement from the side waistline down to the seat of the chair.

□ Waist to Ankle—Take this measurement from the side waistline to the ankle to get the total length.

Before cutting your fabric, check your pattern according to the procedure listed below. Make the alterations necessary for your figure. Some further adjustments may be necessary in the first fitting, but at least you can cut with the assurance that the pattern has been proportioned to your individual measurements.

Start by making all lengthwise adjustments on your pattern. Once the length of the crotch and the length of the pants have been established, you will be able to mark the location of the hipline on your tissue.

CROTCH LENGTH. Draw a line across the patterns at right angles to the grainline from the widest part of the crotch to the side seam. The length of the tissue from the waistline to this pencil line should be the same as your crotch length taken in the sitting position plus ¾-inch ease.

If the pattern is too long, crease along the Easy-Rule Guide line and fold a tuck to take up the desired amount.

If the pattern is too short, cut apart along the dotted lines indicated by the Easy-Rule Guide. Spread the pattern apart the desired amount and insert a piece of tissue.

LEG LENGTH. Measure the length of the pattern from waistline to lower edge. This should be the same as your measurement from waist to ankle.

If the pattern is too long, take a tuck along the Easy-Rule Guide line in the leg.

If the pattern is too short, cut and spread the tissue using the Easy-Rule Guide.

HIPLINE. Measure down 7 inches from the waistline and draw a horizontal line on the pattern. A colored pencil will make this line more visible. The hip measurement of your pattern will be taken at this point.

Now you are ready to make the crosswise adjustments on your pattern. Your pattern was purchased by hip measurement so we will start from the hipline and make all other adjustments accordingly.

Take the hip measurement of your pattern at the hipline marking you made on the tissue 7 inches down from the waist. There should be a 2-inch ease. If the tissue does not measure 2 inches more than your body measurement then the pattern will have to be adjusted.

If the pattern is too big, take a vertical tuck parallel to the grainline and avoiding any dart markings. Carry the same width tuck down the entire length of the pattern.

If the pattern is too small, slash the tissue in a vertical line parallel to the grainline and avoiding any dart

markings. Spread the tissue the necessary amount and insert a piece of tissue down the entire length of the pattern.

WAISTLINE. You will have a better fit if the waistline is eased to the waistband. Make the waistline of the pants ½ to ¾ inch larger than the waistband measurement. The waistline can be increased or decreased by adjusting the darts. Each dart can be taken in or let out as much as ¼ inch but no more. If this adjustment is not sufficient, the side seams can be altered also. Divide the additional amount needed by four and increase or decrease each side seam edge this amount. Taper to hipline, being careful not to change the hip measurement.

WIDTH OF THE LEG. There is no standard amount of ease required for the width of the leg. This is a matter of personal preference and depends so much on the size and shape of the leg muscles. A person with heavy legs will not be able to fit her pants as tight as the person with very slim legs.

If you have heavy thighs, add to the inside leg seems, front and back, at the crotch, tapering to the lower edge. Do not add to the side seams. This will do nothing for tightness through the thigh area. Tightness in the thigh means that you need more width in the crotch as well as the leg, and adding at this point will give you both. Width of crotch refers to the thickness of the body from front to back. This cannot be measured but it is important to the fit of pants. It cannot be adjusted by adding to the side seams of a pattern.

Thigh muscles that bulge in the front even on a slim leg can cause a fitting problem. Add to the inside leg seam of the front only and taper to the hemline. Do not add to the inside leg seam of the back. This will only succeed in giving a baggy seat.

If you have very slim thighs, you will need to decrease the inside leg seams front and back at the crotch and taper to the lower edge. You need less width in the crotch and the leg, and this can never be accomplished by fitting it out at the side seams.

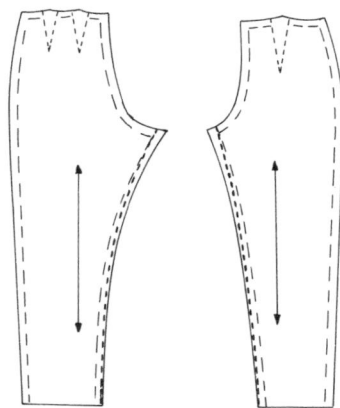

In addition to these general basic rules for adjusting pants patterns to your figure, there are a few special alterations that some women may need in order to take care of specific figure problems. If you have one of the problems listed below, adjust your pattern accordingly.

SWAY-BACK. This problem is handled in the same way as for a skirt. The wrinkles across the back are removed by taking out the extra length at center back. Slash straight across the back to the side seam about 3½ inches below the waistline. Overlap slash lines to remove the necessary amount. Redraw the center back seam and the darts if they have been affected. This has decreased the back waistline which is normally desirable with a sway-back. However, if you need the normal waistline width, add the amount trimmed from the center back to the side seam tapering to the hipline.

LARGE ABDOMEN. This adjustment may also apply in a lesser degree to the average figure wishing to wear fitted pants without a girdle as well as to the person who wants to wear a lighter-weight one than she is in the habit of wearing. You may never need to consider such an alteration for a skirt but fitted pants emphasize the slightest figure fault. Slash through the center of the waistline dart and spread the tissue the necessary amount. Slash straight across the front about 3 inches below the waistline seam. Spread the amount necessary to bring center grainlines back from normal straight grain. Insert tissue under slashes. Adjust waistline darts in the middle of the slash bringing them back to their original position and size.

PROTRUDING HIP BONES. Extra dart fullness released at the point of the hip bones will take care of this problem. Reposition the dart so that it comes in line with the hip bone. Increase the width of the dart and for some figures the dart may need to be shortened. The larger dart releases more fullness over the hip bone. This makes the waistline smaller, so now you will have to add the difference at the side seam and taper to the hipline.

LARGE DERRIERE. There are several adjustments for this, depending on the degree of your problem. First try making the back darts deeper and longer. The deeper darts will give more fullness and the longer darts will drop that fullness lower where it is needed. Add to the side seam to compensate for the amount lost in the waistline measurement by taking the darts deeper. Taper from waistline to hipline. If more fullness is needed, then add at the inside leg seam on the back. This will add length and width to the back crotch measurement without getting a baggy seat.

FLAT DERRIERE. For this type of figure, the pattern is going to have too much length and width across the back. Lift the pattern across the back to take out the extra length. Do this by slashing straight across the back to the side seam about 3½ inches below the waistline. Overlap slash lines to remove the necessary amount and redraw the center back seam. Shallower darts will give less fullness across the back. Decrease the darts and take out the extra waistline width at the side seam. Taper from waistline to hipline. For this figure problem, make the dart nearest the center about 1½ inches longer than the other dart. This distributes the dart fullness and gives a smoother fit. Remove the extra fullness below the hipline by increasing the inside leg seam of the back at the crotch and tapering to the lower edge.

FITTING BASIC PATTERN FOR PANTS. Machine-baste the pants together for the first fitting. Hand-basting will not give an accurate fit for such a snug garment. The way you assemble the pants is very important to the fit. Stitch the side seams first and then stitch the inside leg seams. Stitch the front and back crotch in a continuous seam. All men's pants are made this way and it makes pants hang better. Baste the waistband in place for the first fitting.

During the first fitting make any necessary adjustments. The legs can be tapered to the most becoming width for you. When tapering the legs, pin-fit the same amount on the inside and outside leg seams. Do not do all the tapering from the side seam.

Make all necessary adjustments and try the garment on again to check the fit. When you achieve perfect fit, take the time to transfer all the adjustments made on the fabric to your tissue pattern. Now you have a pants pattern perfect for you. You can use this basic pattern for all pants that you make and save a lot of time in experimenting with alterations on new patterns.

CHAPTER 7

GROUNDWORK FOR ACTION

You have your pattern altered to fit you; you've bought your fabric, and now you're more than ready to start cutting and sewing . . . and that is exactly what you wil! be able to do after one more preliminary step. Before you can put your shears to work, you will have to be sure the fabric is ready to cut. Each of the three types of fabric—woven, knitted and bonded—requires slightly different handling when you prepare it for cutting, as well as when you cut, mark, and finally sew.

PREPARING WOVEN FABRICS

Most of the fabrics you use will be woven, composed of lengthwise and crosswise threads interlaced at right angles to each other. These lengthwise and crosswise threads are referred to as the grain of the fabric. The lengthwise grain runs parallel to the selvages, the crosswise grain from selvage to selvage.

Fabrics are always woven with the crosswise grain at exact right angles to the lengthwise grain; the lengthwise threads are held taut in the loom and generally there are more of them than crosswise threads. These additional threads make the lengthwise grain stronger than the crosswise grain and less likely to stretch. Because of this, it is best to have the lengthwise grain follow the length of the body, since greater strength is needed lengthwise when stretching, bending and sitting. You will want the additional stretch of the crosswise grain across the body for movement.

Checking Position of Grain Line

After you have purchased the fabric, be sure to check the grain again by either tearing or cutting it along one crosswise thread. To tear it, clip the selvage; then place the left thumb on top of the material and the right thumb underneath and tear quickly, straight across the fabric. Sheer, pile, ribbed and loosely woven fabrics should not be torn, but should be checked by pulling one crosswise thread. Clip the selvage and gently pull one crosswise thread. Ease the fabric along the thread as you pull it out to help prevent breaking the thread. Cut across the fabric on the pulled thread from selvage to selvage.

After each end has been torn or cut along one crosswise thread, lay the fabric flat on a large surface. Fold it in half lengthwise matching the selvages accurately. If the crosswise ends match evenly and are at right angles to the selvage edge and the fold, the grain of the

ON GRAIN

fabric is straight. If the crosswise ends do not match evenly or are not at right angles to the selvage edge and the fold, the fabric is off-grain.

TORN EDGE — OFF GRAIN   PRINTED OFF GRAIN

Straightening Fabrics

There are several ways to straighten off-grain fabrics, depending on the type of the material. For cottons, silks, linens, wools and some synthetics which have no permanent finishes, first try straightening the grain by stretching the fabric. Place the fabric on a flat surface and pull the fabric on the true bias in the direction opposite to the higher off-grain edges. Continue stretching until the crosswise threads are at right angles to the lengthwise threads. If this method does not work, you will have to use one of the other methods suggested here.

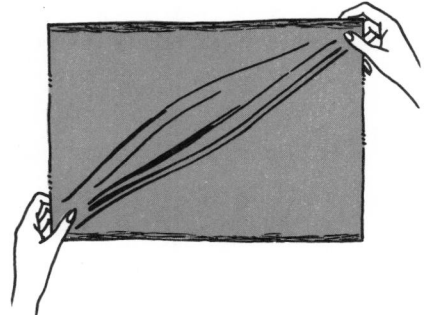

If the fabric is washable, fold the piece in half lengthwise matching the selvage and ends of the fabric evenly. Baste the selvage edges together, and the ends together evenly. Fold the fabric loosely and immerse in water until it is completely wet throughout. Place it on a flat surface and pull gently on the bias in the direction opposite to the higher off-grain edges until the crosswise threads are at right angles to the lengthwise threads. Drape straightened fabric over clothes line, clothes rack or shower rod until it is dry. Do not try to dry it in an electric dryer; the motion may distort the material again. When dry, press smooth and flat with a steam iron or a dry iron and damp press cloth. After the fabric has been completely pressed, remove the bastings along the edges.

For woolens and other fabrics that are not washable, you should follow a slightly different procedure. Fold the fabric in half lengthwise, matching selvages and ends evenly, and baste together along the selvage edge and ends. Place a sheet in warm water and wring it as dry as possible. If the sheet is too wet, it will give the wool fabric a puckered, washed look. Lay sheet on a flat surface and place folded fabric flat on sheet. Fold sheet in half over fabric. Fold loosely and allow it to remain folded for eight to ten hours. Remove the fabric carefully and place it on a flat surface to dry, first pulling gently on the bias to straighten the grain. When completely dry, press flat and smooth with steam iron or dry iron and damp press cloth.

Shrinking Fabrics

Another important point to check before you purchase any type of fabric, woven or knitted, is whether the fabric has been pre-shrunk. Most fabrics today have been processed for shrinkage, but you will still find some inexpensive cottons, linens, washable rayons and blends of less than 65 per cent synthetic fiber which may not have this noted on the bolt. They may very well have been processed, but unless it is specifically stated that shrinkage is less than one per cent, be careful. You may still buy the fabric, but be sure you test it for shrinkage before you cut it for a garment.

To test for shrinkage, cut a 6-by-6-inch square of

the fabric and trace its exact outline on a piece of paper. Wash the square of fabric in warm water, let it dry and press it. Compare it with the tracing to see how much, if any, shrinkage has occurred. If you do find the fabric shrinks, then shrink the entire piece by one of the methods described above for straightening the grain. Use the immersion method for washables; the damp-sheet method for non-washables.

Woolens will often require some shrinkage, unless they are tagged "ready for the needle" or have some sort of label or tag stating that they have been shrunk. Even when you plan to have the garment dry-cleaned, you will need to shrink woolen if it has not been pre-shrunk. The steam-pressing used in shaping the garment during construction will cause the fabric to shrink if it hasn't been treated. It is safest and easiest to have a dry-cleaner shrink wool fabrics. However, you can shrink it yourself using the damp-sheet method outlined above.

Silks which are to be dry-cleaned, synthetics or blends containing 65 per cent synthetic fibers require no shrinking. Felt is created by a bonding and shrinking process, so any further shrinkage should be avoided.

Be sure to shrink and straighten any inner shaping materials you use, if they are not pre-shrunk. Do the same for any notions such as zippers, grosgrain ribbon or tape which will be placed in a washable garment. Most of these items, except the ribbon, have the notice "washable" on the package, and will not need shrinking, but be sure to check.

PREPARING KNITS

Knits, too, should be checked for straightness of grain and shrinkage. Remember in the knitting process, the fabric is produced by a series of interlocking loops formed by one or more yarns. As the loops are interlocked they form chains in both directions of the fabric. The chains running the length of the fabric are called "wales," and correspond to the lengthwise grain of woven fabric. The chains running across the fabric are called "courses" and correspond to the crosswise grain of woven fabrics. The bias of the knitted fabric is the diagonal grain formed by placing the wales on top of and parallel to the courses, the same as in woven fabric.

If the knit is a synthetic such as Arnel or nylon jersey, the fabric occasionally becomes distorted and locked in an off-grain position. It is impossible to straighten, so you should avoid buying such fabrics if they are much off-grain. If you do buy one, you will have to cut each pattern piece individually following a lengthwise rib to preserve the grain lines. The same is true for wool or cotton knits termed "washable." They have been permanently finished and cannot be straightened.

Wool and cotton knits which have no permanent finish can be straightened by folding the fabric along a single lengthwise wale, basting it in position and steam-pressing the folded edge. Using this as a selvage, straighten the knit as you would a woven fabric by stretching it into position.

PREPARING BONDED FABRICS

Felt and non-woven fabrics, such as Pellon, Keybak, Interlon and other bonded shaping fabrics, are formed by several methods, but none of them have a grain since the fibers are meshed and locked together. Pattern pieces may be laid and cut in any direction. The commercial products usually have been treated to prevent shrinkage, but check the hang tags or bolt to make sure. With wool felt, avoid steam pressing as much as possible, since this tends to shrink the fabric a great deal.

SPECIAL HANDLING FOR PROBLEM FABRICS

Although most fabrics you will be using are easy to handle, there are a few types that require special attention. Beginners would do well to avoid these fabrics until they have had a little practice on easy-to-work-with, firmly woven cottons and woolens. Then these problem fabrics will offer little or no difficulty if you follow a few simple suggestions in preparing, cutting and sewing them.

Chiffon

Chiffon tends to be slippery and will slide when being cut, unless a non-slippery surface is used. An old sheet or tablecloth on the cutting surface should suffice. Be sure to use fine dressmaker pins and cut with very sharp shears. Use a fine machine-stitch (15 to 18 to the inch) and a fine machine needle. The feed dog may catch the fabric surface, so it's best to stitch over tissue paper, which may be torn away after stitching. Preferred seam finishes for sheers are the French seam and hand-rolled edges, since these are the least conspicuous. Wider seams show through the sheer. When facings are needed, it is best to make the entire garment section double, rather than have the edges show through to the right side of the garment.

Crepe

The spongy quality of crepe, which makes it drape so beautifully, also tends to make it stretch when being machine-stitched. To prevent stretching, stitch over tissue paper. Fit crepe garments fairly snugly; they usually stretch after wearing. However, don't fit too tightly, or your garment will pull and stretch in all the wrong places. Allow crepe garments to hang at least overnight before marking the hem, since the fabric tends to stretch when hanging. Press it lightly, always using a press cloth to prevent shine.

Felt

Felt does not present many difficulties in construction. It may be cut in any direction since it has no grain. It does not ravel, needs no edge finish, and usually felt garments have no hems. Choose very simple patterns for felt, without a great many construction details. It is hard to ease seams in felt. Use lining fabric or iron-on tape for facings when required to avoid bulky seams. Use a fairly long machine-stitch and medium tension. Press felt with a warm, dry iron; steampressing tends to shrink it.

Fur Fabric

When working with the fabulous fakes, follow the layouts and directions for cutting napped fabrics. Baste seams together by hand before stitching, since the pieces tend to slip when machine-stitched. Use a light tension on the machine, and a long stitch (8 to 10 to the inch). Use a needle to smooth pile out of the seams on the right side of the fabric. Slash darts and press open with tip of iron and a dry press cloth. Never use a steam iron; it will mat the fabric. Use lining fabric for facings, and hooks and eyes, snaps or loops for closings. Buttonholes should be avoided, since they are very difficult to manipulate in heavily napped fabric.

Jersey

For jersey or any knit fabric that comes in a tubular form, you may have to cut the tube open following a lengthwise rib if the pattern layout shows the pieces cut singly. Open flat, square off ends, and steam-press to remove fold creases. Pin pattern securely to wrong side of the fabric to keep edges from rolling. Staystitch each piece immediately after cutting to prevent its stretching out of shape. For permanent stitching, use a long machine-stitch (10 to 12 to the inch) with loose tension. Stretch the material slightly without pulling while machine-stitching to keep seams from breaking later. For reinforcement, double-stitch or tape seams at points of stress such as waistline, underarm, elbows of long sleeves. Hang garment for at least twenty-four hours before marking hemline. Underline jersey garments to prevent their stretching out of shape.

Double-Knits

Double-knits are wonderful fabrics for the homesewer, and present few problems in handling. Choose patterns suitable for jersey or light-weight wools, avoiding bias-cut skirts because of the excess stretching. If your double-knit is very light-weight, you may want to underline it with China silk, but in general, these knits are not underlined because you want to retain the suppleness of the fabric. You may line suit jackets with soft silk crepe or China silk. Pre-shrunk muslin makes a good interfacing, but you may choose any woven interfacing that is not too firm or bulky. A firm, straight taffeta petticoat or fitted slip is recommended for wear under the knits.

Follow a lengthwise rib for correct layout; straighten knit by pulling on the true bias. Stay-stitch all curved or bias edges. Use mercerized thread and a medium stitch of 12 to 15 to the inch, testing tension and pressure on a scrap of fabric before you begin. Keep seams stretched lightly as you stitch to prevent stitches from popping later. Use your zigzag machine for permanent stitching and for seam and hem finishes. You may also finish the hem edge by overcasting, or by pinking and edge-stitching with 2 rows of machine-stitching, then complete with a tailor's hem.

Stay shoulder seams and waistlines with woven seam binding to prevent stretching. For waistbands, use preshrunk grosgrain belting as interfacing in a band cut double on the lengthwise grain of the knit. Buttonholes may be bound or machine-made, and you will want to reinforce the area with organdy or muslin.

Lace

A lace garment is transparent and delicate and should be completely underlined. If you intend to make a special slip for the garment, then underline with net, organza or marquisette. If you want to build the slip into the garment, then taffeta the same color as the lace is a good choice. If the fabric is not underlined, use matching tulle or marquisette for facings. In cutting, try to keep the lace design intact. Select a simple pattern design without center seams or elaborate seamings, to avoid breaking up the lace design. Use machine or hand-appliqué to join lace sections; stitch lace over tissue. Transparent horsehair makes an excellent hem finish. When using a lace with a scalloped edge or border, let that be the hem.

Laminates

There are a variety of laminates available to the home-sewer; woven cottons, jersey and knitted laminates will be found most frequently. Your choice of a pattern will be determined by the fabric. The jersey or knitted laminates present no particular problem in pattern selection; however, if you choose a firmly woven cotton laminate, do not select any design calling for eased seams, such as princess lines or normal set-in sleeves, because with these laminates you cannot ease a long seam to a shorter one without forming gathers.

Smooth pattern flat and trim to the marked cutting line before using to prevent tearing of the tissue. Use sharp shears to cut these fabrics. Tailor's tacks, chalk or pins can be used to transfer pattern markings, but the tracing wheel and dressmaker's carbon do not mark successfully.

To stitch laminates, loosen pressure on presser foot; use a looser tension and longer stitch (10 to the inch). Because its foam underside prevents the fabric from feeding evenly, you must use tissue on each side of the fabric if you stitch on the wrong side. Tear tissue away after stitching.

Stay-stitch all bias and curved seams. To control stretching of bias seams, place tissue under fabric and seam binding on top of the seamline, and stitch the binding in with the seam. Grade all seam allowances to prevent bulk; trim wide darts to ⅝ inch and press open, forming a triangular pleat at the point. Faced edges should be top-stitched to keep them flat. Press laminates on the right side only with a steam iron and press cloth. Be careful not to touch the foam side with the iron.

Net

Net presents very little trouble. Seams on net garments may be trimmed without raveling. The number of stitches to use per inch on the machine depends on the size of the mesh, so test a scrap before doing any permanent stitching. Transparent horsehair provides a nice finish for the hem, but is not essential.

Nylon

The biggest problem in working with nylon and some of the other pure synthetics is seam puckering. Stitching tends to draw seamlines and ripple the fabric on either side. Bias or off-grain seams pucker less than straight lengthwise ones, so it's best to select a style with flared gores cut with bias seams. When stitching nylon, always use a fine machine needle, and either nylon or mercerized thread. Use a fairly small stitch (12 to 15 to the inch) and loosen both bottom and top tensions as much as you can to produce a good stitch. Avoid stitching over pins. As you stitch, use the same technique suggested for jersey, stretching the seam slightly but allowing the fabric to feed normally under the presser foot.

Pile Fabrics

Velvets, velveteens, corduroys and velours require special handling because of their napped surface. Follow layouts given for napped fabrics, being certain that all pattern pieces are laid in one direction. For a very rich color, let the nap run upward toward your face; for longer wear, run the nap toward the hem. Use fine pins and silk thread to prevent marring the surface. On velveteen, avoid the bulk of double thickness by using chiffon or taffeta for facings. Use a long machine-stitch (10 to 12 to the inch) and avoid top-stitching the garment. Press according to the instructions given in Chapter 8.

Sheer Fabrics

Treat all sheers as you would chiffon. Use full-skirted, classic shirtdresses or dressy evening designs. Sheers will have skirts of double layers of fabric, and often matching separate or built-in slips. Slips may be taffeta or cotton satin; interfacings are organdy, organza, or net. Add required yardage for double skirt and for deep hem; sheers must have a hem of at least 6-10″ on the outer skirt. Circle sheer skirts have a narrow, hand-rolled hem.

Stretch Fabrics

There are three types of stretch fabrics available to the home-sewer: warp or lengthwise stretch, generally used for ski pants or slacks; filling or crosswise stretch, generally used in jackets, skirts or dresses; two-way stretch used in ready-to-wear for bathing suits. Most of the stretch fabrics on the retail market for home-sewing are the warp type. The home-sewer should be careful to choose the type of stretch the pattern calls for.

Care should be taken to prevent stretching the fabric when cutting or marking. Use sharp shears to cut, and stay-stitch all curved and bias edges before beginning construction. Stitch with a small zigzag stitch to allow seams to stretch without thread breakage; avoid pulling the fabric in stitching. You may use synthetic or mercerized thread.

If stretch fabric ravels, you must use a secure seam finish: overcast edges, use your attachment or machine to zigzag near the seam edge, or turn under and edge-stitch.

If buttonholes are part of your design, place a small patch of interfacing under the buttonhole to prevent stretching. You may steam-press stretch fabrics, but don't use pressure.

Be sure to check the bolt of fabric for cleaning instructions. Fabrics made of rubber must be washed, since dry-cleaning will tend to stiffen and swell the rubber fiber. Nylon or Helanca stretch fabrics are both dry-cleanable and washable.

Sequin and Beaded Fabrics

The glamorous sequin and beaded fabrics are "cycle" fabrics which return to popularity at frequent intervals. Usually it is best for the home-sewer to sew these fabrics by hand, using a fine back-stitch. These fabrics will break machine needles, or often the machine needle will break the sequins or beads in the stitching. If you don't want to sew by hand, try a scrap of your fabric on the machine, always stitching on the wrong side of the fabric, using a regulation stitch (12 to 15 to the inch). These fabrics vary according to the number of sequins or beads sewn to the fabric so they may sometimes be successfully stitched on the machine.

Metallic Fabrics

Metal thread woven into other fibers adds a touch of glitter but presents a few problems. Metallic fabrics must be pressed with a moderately hot iron, or they may melt under high heat. Pin marks can mar the surface when the fabric has a high percentage of metal, so it's best to place all pins in the seam allowances. Most metallic fabrics tend to ravel badly so seams should be overcast and bound buttonholes should be avoided.

PRESSING

The final step in preparing your fabric is the pressing. Press the fabric on the wrong side, always pressing with the grain lines. Remove all wrinkles and creases, especially the folded crease lines. On crease-resistant fabrics the fold line may be difficult to remove, and a damp press cloth will be needed. If the crease cannot be pressed out, refold your fabric and avoid this line as you cut, otherwise the crease will show on the finished garment. For tips on what method to use in pressing various fabrics, see Chapter 8.

LAYING OUT THE PATTERN

Laying pattern pieces on fabric is anything but a haphazard affair. Easy sewing is possible only if you know exactly how to place patterns on fabric and cut them out accurately. If it is not done with care and skill, the garment simply will not go together easily and correctly, and it will never hang properly.

Prepare a Cutting Surface

The first thing to do is to find a large cutting area, large enough for the entire length of fabric if possible. A large table is best; just be sure to protect the surface if necessary. You may also wish to pad a very slippery surface such as formica. The cutting boards mentioned in Chapter 5 provide just the right padding. If you haven't a suitable table, then use the floor, protecting your fabric from soil by placing an old sheet or clean paper beneath it. Never use the bed for laying out and cutting fabric. You will find it does not give firm enough support for accurate cutting because the fabric and pattern pieces do not lie flat.

Circle the Correct Layout

If you have not circled the layout to be used, do it now. Find the correct layout diagram on the instruction sheet for the size pattern and the width of fabric you are using. Be sure to circle the layouts for lining, interfacing or contrasting fabrics if they are necessary for your design.

Sort Your Pattern

Open the envelope and sort through the pattern pieces, selecting only those you need for the version you are making. Check each piece with the layout diagram and the diagram of pattern pieces on the back of the pattern envelope. Be sure to select all the pieces you need, and check to see that all pieces are marked with the same size and pattern number. Put the other pieces back in the envelope; they only add confusion and are likely to get lost if left loose.

Press the Pattern

Press each pattern piece flat, using a very low temperature on a dry iron. Moisture or steam will shrink and pucker the tissue pattern, and it will no longer be the true size.

Fold Your Fabric

Fold the straightened and pressed fabric as illustrated on the layout diagram. Always fold on the straight grain of the fabric: lengthwise fold on a single lengthwise thread parallel to the selvage; a crosswise fold on a single crosswise thread with the selvages folded back on themselves. Fold the fabric with right sides together, unless it is necessary to match design motifs in the fabric which are only visible on the right side.

Pin Pattern to Fabric

Start laying the pattern on the fabric as shown in the diagram. You may be one who loves to devise her own layouts, but by and large it is wisest to use the ones shown in the instructions. Rest assured, pattern experts have worked to give you the most economical layout possible for your fabric width. The diagrams are drawn to scale and show the exact placement of each piece.

Always lay out the entire pattern on the fabric before you cut one snip of it. If your cutting area is not quite large enough, place a few pieces of the pattern on the fabric, secured with just a few pins, carefully roll this section up, and continue laying the pattern until it is completely laid out. You want to be sure there is ample yardage before you cut, not afterwards when it is too late.

Usually all the pattern pieces are placed on the wrong side of the fabric when the fabric is folded. When single thicknesses are cut, the pattern pieces are normally placed on the right side of the fabric. This insures that the right and left sides of the garment, if they are not identical, will be placed correctly on the right side of the fabric. McCall's patterns have an extra margin of tissue outside the double cutting lines. This is designed to make the printed pattern accurate and to help you cut more accurately. Remember you can overlap these margins to the cutting line when laying out the pieces. The margins fall away as you cut your fabric.

McCall's patterns are laid out with the printed side up unless the layout shows a shaded piece. The shading indicates that the piece should be placed with the printed side down on the fabric. This usually occurs when the same piece is used for a right and left section and the piece is placed printed side up one time; printed side down the other. If a piece is drawn with a dotted line, it means the piece is to be cut identically a second time. If a pattern piece has a single printed line, marked "place on fold," lay it face up with the printed line exactly along the straight grain fold of the fabric.

Check Grain Lines

Each pattern piece has a printed grain-line arrow-marking indicating the correct grain for that section of the garment. To lay the pattern piece on the correct grain easily, place the pattern on the fabric with the grain line parallel to the selvage for lengthwise grain or parallel to the crosswise fold. Measure with a yardstick or ruler from each end of the arrow to the selvage or fold, being sure that each point measured is an equal distance from the edge. Place pins at each end and center of the printed grain-line arrows before you attempt to pin the edges of the pattern. It is essential that the grain placement be secured so the piece does not slip out of position while the rest of it is pinned.

After the grain-line arrows are pinned, smooth the tissue out from the grain-line arrow until it lies flat and smooth on the fabric. Pin the corners and the long outside edges of the piece, placing pins parallel to the cutting edge within the seam allowance. Use just enough pins to keep the pattern in position while cutting; too many will distort the edges.

CUTTING THE FABRIC

Get out your well-sharpened, bent-handled dressmaking shears and start to cut. Keep the fabric flat on the cutting surface by placing one hand flat on the tissue and fabric as you cut. Cut with long, even strokes in the direction of the fabric grain. The fabric grain direction is indicated on each edge of the pattern by small directional arrows printed on the seam line. Cutting with the grain will produce a cleaner raw edge, one that is less likely to ravel.

When cutting a McCall's pattern, cut directly between the double line printed on the pattern. If you are accurate in your cutting, you will have the exact ⅝-inch seam allowance intended for the piece. If you use a pattern from another company, measure from their cutting line to the seamline to determine whether you should cut inside the cutting line or outside to maintain the correct ⅝-inch seam allowance.

Cut all notches outward when you cut, so they will be easily seen when you have to match them in construction. Remember to cut double or triple notches in one continuous strip across the top of the notches as indicated by the printed line.

Cut out all the pieces before going on to the next step of transferring the markings to the fabric. This will speed up both cutting and marking time.

If you own pinking shears, save them for finishing raw edges after seams are stitched. Do not use pinking shears to cut out your pattern and fabric. They tend to pull the fabric, easily distorting the pieces, and you will not have a clean cutting edge from which to measure the seam allowance.

USING McCALL'S SPECIAL FEATURE PATTERNS

The patterns with special features such as McCall's Instant and proportioned-to-height patterns require slightly different handling when laying them out and cutting them. This does not mean that they are more complicated to use; on the contrary, they are usually easier.

Instant Patterns

Instant Patterns are printed with all of the pattern pieces on one large piece of tissue paper so that the layout is already done for you. Each piece of pattern is positioned so it will be on the correct grain line of the fabric, which eliminates checking each piece for grain perfection. Again, the layout is designed for the most economical use of fabric.

When using an Instant Pattern, you have to buy the exact amount of fabric indicated on the yardage section of the pattern envelope. Check the width and length of the fabric needed for your size and purchase only that amount.

Straighten and press the fabric as you would any other material. Fold it as illustrated in the pattern guide sheet. Pin the pattern in place on the correct grain, fastening each piece securely to make cutting accurate, then cut it out. That is all there is to it.

One word of caution for those who find it necessary to alter their patterns before cutting. If alterations must be made, you will have to cut out the separate pieces of the pattern and alter them. Then lay them out again just as you would a regular pattern.

Proportioned Patterns

McCall's Proportioned Patterns are designed for the tall (5′ 8″), medium (5′ 6″) and short (5′ 3″) figures. All the darts, lengths and proportioning details of the design are clearly marked on the pattern for these three heights.

Some of the Proportioned Patterns have separate bodices and skirts for each individual height all packaged in one envelope. Each of these pieces is clearly marked "tall," "medium" or "short." Double-check to be sure you have selected the correct pieces for your height. Once a piece is cut the wrong height, there is little you can do to correct it.

Other Proportioned Patterns will have only one pattern piece for bodice and skirt with darts, pleats and other details specified for each height. These pattern pieces are actually proportioned for the tall figure, with instructions printed on the piece for shortening it to fit the medium or short figure. Remember to do any alterations necessary and cut the hemline along the appropriate printed marking before you lay the pattern on the fabric. Cut the adjusted pattern just as you would any other pattern.

FABRICS REQUIRING SPECIAL LAYOUTS

Some fabrics require special handling in pattern layouts. Remember, you should always use a pattern which is specifically designed for fabrics needing special handling such as napped, pile, one-way textures or designs, plaids, stripes, checks, prints, border prints and lace. If a pattern is suitable for one of these, the illustration on the front of the envelope will show this and the "Suggested Fabrics" section will list it. The time may come, however, when you want to use one of these fabrics and can't find a style you like specifically designed for the fabric. Another style can be selected as long as you know exactly how to work with the fabric you have selected. Check the following suggestions and instructions before you begin to cut.

"With Nap" Layout

When yardage requirements on the back of the pattern envelope list fabrics "With Nap," it means that a layout is given in which all the pieces are placed on the fabric in one lengthwise direction. This is necessary since napped or pile fabrics reflect light differently, depending on their direction or, in the case of some fabrics, the design may have a definite up-and-down direction.

If you use a pattern which does not give yardage for "With Nap" fabrics, and plan to use one, then read the instructions on page 22 for computing the exact yardage you will need when using napped fabrics. Fabrics which must be cut according to napped layout are:

Napped Fabrics

Short fibers are brushed and raised to the surface of the fabric; the fibers are usually brushed smoothly in one direction. Some napped fabrics have woven raised loops, as well. Commonly used napped fabrics are wool broadcloth, camel's hair, fleece, some flannels, doeskin, melton, cashmere and suede cloth. To test the direction of the nap, rub your finger over the lengthwise surface of the fabric. If the surface feels smooth, the direction is referred to as down; if it is rough, the direction is up. Most napped fabrics are cut with the nap running down toward the hem.

Pile Fabrics

These are woven with a third set of threads that form a looped or tufted surface on the fabric. Common pile fabrics are velvets, velveteens, corduroy, velour, fur fabrics and terry cloth. Test the direction of the pile as you do for napped fabrics. For a richer color and greater light reflection, cut velvets, velveteen and corduroy with the pile surface running toward the face. Fur fabrics and terry cloth should be cut with the pile surface running down.

One-Way Textures

Fabrics which reflect light differently when held up or down. These include satin, sateen, some brocades, damask, chino and some gabardine and flannels.

One-Way Designs

Any fabric which has a woven or printed design that has a definite up-and-down direction.

When using any of these fabrics, first determine the direction you wish the fabric to take in the garment. To place all the pattern pieces in one direction lengthwise, you may have to work with the fabric unfolded, if your pattern design has a definite right and left. Most of the time, however, you can work with a center lengthwise fold. If the pattern requires two full-width layers, cut it along the crosswise fold and reverse the under layer so that right sides of both layers are still face to face but with the nap going in the same direction.

Plaids, Stripes and Checks

If you select a pattern which is not specifically designed for these fabrics, problems will arise. These fabrics must be matched at seam and design lines if the garment is to be at all attractive. Try to find a pattern that has straight seams and little detailing. Eased seams, bias seams, or a large number of pattern pieces will add to your matching problem.

EVEN PLAIDS. On these the designs are balanced in both lengthwise and crosswise direction and are the easiest plaids to work with. Determine how you want the design lines placed on your figure. The vertical lines should be evenly arranged from the center front and back so that the right and left sides of the garment will be the same. Check, too, to see if you want a particular construction line placed on the horizontal design of the plaid. Straighten the fabric, if needed. Fold the fabric through the center of a plaid design, according to the diagram given for "Without Nap" fabric in the pattern layout. Be sure to match the lines of the plaid accurately when folding so that all corresponding lines are directly over one another.

Place the pattern pieces on the fabric so that the lines of the plaid will be correctly placed as previously determined on the figure. Put the center front and center back fold, seam lines or markings in the middle of

the desired plaid design. To match the design at all seams, place corresponding notches on the same line and color of the plaid. McCall's numbered notches will easily help you determine which notches match. When pockets or other detailing will be applied to the garment, be sure to match these with the lines of the plaid at the place on your garment they will be sewn.

Pin, cut and mark the sections carefully so that the garment will be identical on both sides. Slip-baste seams before machine-stitching to insure accurate matching.

UNEVEN PLAIDS. These plaids have an unbalanced design in both lengthwise and crosswise directions and are the most difficult plaids to work with. They should be avoided by the beginner, but for the experienced sewer with time and patience they present a challenge and are well worth the time and effort. The unbalanced design lends itself to more variety and interest in the plaid and makes up into a most attractive garment if the pattern is appropriate for the fabric. Remember to select a pattern with as few construction lines as possible. Plaid is most effective if it is not cut up by a lot of seams. For instance, never select a large plaid for a princess-line garment.

Uneven plaids should be cut on the bias forming a chevron at center front and center back seams. If you do not want the fabric cut bias, then the plaid is matched all in one direction going around the body with no center seams. Although there are directions available for cutting an uneven plaid half on the wrong side and half on the right side of the fabric in order to make the plaid match at a center front seam, it is best not to do this. There are very few fabrics that do not show a difference if the dress is cut half on the wrong side of the fabric.

UNEVEN STRIPES. Stripes of this type are more difficult to work with since there is not an even repeat. Any stripe with variety in color or width of the stripes is considered an uneven design and requires extra thought and care in matching. Place the predominant stripe in the center of the figure and cut the pattern according to a "With Nap" layout.

EVEN STRIPES. These are stripes in which the color and width of stripes are repeated consecutively either lengthwise or crosswise of the fabric. They are the easiest to work with. Fold the fabric so that the stripes are identical on each side of the fold. Lay the pattern on the fabric, following the "Without Nap" layout and placing the pieces so that the stripes will be properly positioned on the figure. Put corresponding notches on the same stripe design for correct matching.

Like uneven plaids, uneven stripes are matched all in one direction rather than trying to make the right and left sides of the garment symmetrical. Uneven stripes are also very effective if cut on the bias so that they form a chevron at center front and center back.

CHECKS. These are treated in the same way as an even plaid. The checks should be matched at all seamlines and centered on the figure.

Prints

First check to see if the print has a regular directional pattern. If so, then treat it as a napped fabric. If not, then you will merely want to space the print attractively on the figure.

Large prints and some medium-size prints should be spaced to give the most pleasing effect. Hold the fabric up to your figure and test the placement of the design. Usually the dominant motif is placed in the center front and back of the bodice and skirt and in the center of the sleeve. Match large designs at seam lines whenever possible. Place the pattern seam lines, not the cutting line, on the design lines you want to match. It is best to work with large prints folded right side out when you lay out the pattern so that you can more easily determine the proper spacing of the print.

Border Prints

A border print usually appears along one lengthwise edge of the fabric. Select a pattern with straight or nearly straight side seams in the skirt, if you really want to use the border effectively. Place the pieces on the crosswise grain, if you want the border at the hemline of the garment. Other details which can use borders effectively are straight sleeve edges, squared necklines or styles with fairly wide ruffled borders.

When placing pattern pieces on the fabric, arrange them so the border design will match at seam lines. If you make a bordered skirt, be sure to shorten or lengthen the pattern piece before cutting out the fabric, so that you do not have to cut away the border when you mark the hem.

Lace

If lace has a scalloped or finished edge, then treat it as a border print. When working with any lace, try to keep the motifs centered and intact as much as possible. Place the motifs properly on the figure, just as you would a large print. Always underline lace so that the pattern of the lace is not lost by the conflict of darts, seams and slip straps showing through.

MARKING THE FABRIC

Once all your pattern pieces are accurately cut, you will want to transfer all the pattern markings to the fabric. If you don't, you will have a very difficult time deciding where the different pieces go. No matter how experienced a seamstress you are, always mark each piece. It is the only way to avoid needless errors.

There are several methods of marking the fabric. It is wise to select the one most suitable for the fabric being used. One method cannot be employed for all types of material.

Tracing Wheel and Carbon

This method works on most fabrics. However, it cannot be used on sheers, which will show the markings on the right side, or on heavy or napped woolens on which the markings won't show. Buy the non-wax type of dressmaker's carbon in the color closest to your fabric color. Test a scrap of the fabric before marking the whole garment to see that the markings show clearly on the wrong side of the fabric but do not show through on the right side. Be particularly careful in using white and pastel fabrics to be certain that the marks disappear when washed or dry-cleaned. Also be sure that the tracing wheel does not mar the fabric.

To use the carbon, place the marking side of the paper next to the wrong side of the fabric. If the fabric was cut double, place a piece of carbon paper in each layer next to the wrong side of both pieces of fabric. In this way they will both be marked at the same time. You may have to remove a few pins in order to place the paper smoothly between the two thicknesses. Place the fabric piece on a smooth, hard surface. If you use a table top which is likely to be marred, place a fairly firm board beneath the fabric. Use a ruler as a guide and run the wheel along the side of the ruler. Do not use heavy pressure, just enough to make the markings visible. Transfer all markings. At the termination point of darts, tucks, pleats, etc., mark a short straight line across the point. Use two short crossed lines to indicate circle markings. The same method is used with the tailor tacker, which is used like a stylus.

Tailor's Tacks

This method can be used on any type of fabric, and is especially good for heavy or nubby woolens, fine silks and sheers. Once the garment is made, the thread markings are easily pulled out and will not mark the fabric in any way. Use darning cotton or embroidery floss for the tailor's tacks. They do not slip out as easily as other threads. Always use a contrasting thread so that the marks can be easily seen.

Using double thread, take a small stitch at the point

to be marked through the pattern and fabric. Leave an inch or more thread end. Take a second stitch in the same position leaving a small loop. Then take a stitch at the next marking, leaving the thread loose between the two markings. Continue in this manner until all markings have been made on the section. Cut the thread between markings. Unpin the pattern from the fabric and remove it carefully by pulling threads through the tissue. Spread the two layers of fabric apart; cut the threads between the layers, leaving thread tufts in each piece of fabric.

Tailor's Chalk or Chalk Pencil

This marks easily and can be removed usually by brushing or rubbing the surface of the fabric. A white chalk pencil is even better to use than the old-fashioned tailor's chalk. It can be sharpened to give a much more accurate, thin line. Chalk in either form is a quicker method of marking than the tailor's tacks, and is a good method to use if the fabric will not take carbon well. On nubby or heavy woolens, the chalk will not mark well. Always mark on the wrong side of fabric.

Place pins through the pattern and fabric at the positions to be marked, with the pins pointing toward the center of the garment. Remove the tissue pattern by slipping it off the marking pins, and mark the position of the pins with tailor's chalk. Both layers of the fabric can be marked without repinning, if the right sides of the fabric are together and the wrong sides out. Mark the top side and then turn the fabric over and mark position of pins on the underside.

Tailor's chalk markings are also used in fitting. When the garment is being fitted right side out, pin in any necessary alterations. Remove the garment, turn inside out and chalk mark the position of the pins on the wrong side of the fabric. Further instructions for fitting garments can be found in Chapter 8.

Clip Marking

This method is not recommended for beginners, since they are very likely to clip too far into the seam allowance. However, an experienced sewer may find the clip marks easy, since they can be done in the same operation with cutting the garment. Using sharp shears, take a small clip no longer than ⅛ inch in the seam allowance with the point of the shears. This marking is used to identify center front and back, top and bottom of pleats, tops of darts, tucks and fold lines.

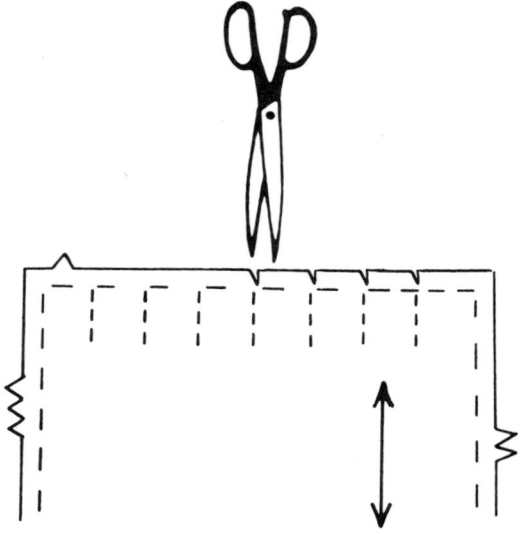

Basting

This is used for marking the center front and center back lines and the straight lengthwise and crosswise grains at the cap of a set-in sleeve to help in fitting the garment and seeing that proper grain lines are maintained.

BASTING STITCH ALONG FOLD

When it is necessary to transfer pattern markings from one side of the fabric to the other, use a machine- or hand-basting stitch. Buttonholes, placement of trimmings and pleats are often marked in this way. Test fabric first before machine-basting to be sure the stitching does not mark the fabric when basting is removed.

REMOVING THE PATTERN

After the fabric is completely marked, you are ready to put the parts of your garment together. Remember this is similar to doing a jig-saw puzzle. Unless the parts are joined correctly, the finished design will never appear as the artist or designer intended.

The thought and efficiency with which you work will influence the perfection of your garment and the satisfaction you receive from making it. Try to handle your materials as little as possible. Study the sewing guide and directions on pattern pieces carefully before the pattern is removed so that you know exactly what you are to do.

Some people prefer to leave the pattern pinned to each section until they are ready to work on it. Others like to remove all the pattern pieces before starting to sew, identifying each section of the garment by initialing it on the wrong side in tailor's chalk (SF for skirt front, BB for bodice back). If this method is used, be sure to identify the small facing pieces carefully since these tend to look alike. Mark the wrong side of your fabric if it is difficult to distinguish it from the right side.

The pattern should be removed carefully, folded neatly and returned to the pattern envelope. A pattern can be used several times if it is handled with care. Keep the envelope handy for ready reference in case a direction is not clear or a marking has become indistinct.

It will also be helpful if you keep all parts of a section together. Place them so that they may be joined without unfolding. This keeps the fabric in good condition. As soon as possible, hang up the various sections. Unnecessary wrinkles do not appear if this is done.

Some fabrics will tend to slip and shift when stitched. In this case it is best to stitch each fabric piece to tissue paper. Place the tissue paper next to the wrong side of the fabric. Stitch through the fabric and tissue paper. Leave the fabric stitched to the tissue until the construction sewing has been completed. Gently rip the tissue paper away when finished.

STAY-STITCHING

There is no need for stay-stitching seams on the new, stabilized fabrics. However, stay-stitching has a definite purpose as a reinforcement, and to be of any value, it must be placed on the seamline. This kind of reinforcement is found on a corner or a curved seam which requires clipping to complete the construction. Always stay-stitch before you clip or slash at a point. Adjust the machine for 15 stitches to the inch. Starting 1 inch from the point, stitch on the seamline to the point. Raise the presser foot, pivot the fabric, lower the presser foot, and continue stitching along the seamline for an inch beyond the point.

Always stay-stitch an inward curved seam that is to be attached to a straight seam (the curved seam of a princess bodice or the waistline seam of a circular

skirt). Stitch, using 15 stitches to the inch, on the seamline around the entire curved area. Clip the seam allowance to the line of stay-stitching at half inch intervals to release the curved seam allowance so that the two seams can be stitched together smoothly.

CHAPTER 8

BLUEPRINT FOR THE PROFESSIONAL

Throughout this book, you will find constant reference to the "professional"-looking garment . . . the kind you want to have. Defining the term, it means a garment that looks as if it came from the finest couturier house, even if it is a housedress.

There are many factors which contribute to the professional look. The way you work is one important aspect; the originality you add to the design; the way you fit the garment to your figure for a custom-made appearance; and the careful pressing of each detail so that by the time the last stitch is taken, the garment needs just a quick press to make it ready to wear.

This chapter is concerned with developing your professional aptitude and skills. Beginners take note. Start immediately to work like a pro. Veterans, check the suggestions. Many of them will simplify your work and help you turn out garments that completely satisfy your own desire for truly fine work.

To test your own professional skill, you may want to make a dress, following the chart in this chapter. This outlines each step that gives a garment the look of having been made by an expert craftsman. Once you've followed this method, you can apply the principles you learn to every other garment you make. Soon you will be working with the skill and speed of the finest dressmakers.

THE PROFESSIONAL APPROACH

Sewing habits vary with each personality. Some seamstresses practically refuse to make a garment unless they can finish it at one sitting. Others have temperaments which allow them to sew only an hour or two at a time. The latter group is more likely to have a better looking garment; the former will have more garments in a shorter time. You have to establish your own philosophy, whether you want fewer garments of good quality in your closet or many garments of lesser quality.

Sewing, like any skill or art, takes planning and organization if the results are to be satisfactory. Plan your sewing time, if possible. Always have all your equipment handy—pattern, fabric, notions, and, above all, have the ironing board, iron and all pressing equip-

ment set up right at hand. It's too much of a temptation to think you can forget pressing a detail simply because it means going into another room or filling the steam iron. Pressing is absolutely essential to a good-looking garment.

If you are inclined to become bored or nervous at the machine, then plan to spend no more than two hours at a time. Organize your work into planned sessions. Fit the pattern at the first session, cut and mark at the next, stay-stitch and stitch the darts and press at the next, construct each section at a time throughout the next few sessions, working only until that first feeling of impatience, frustration or case of "nerves" sets in.

It is best to plan sewing time after other essential household work is done, so you can devote your mind to your sewing and not sit there feeling guilty because the dinner isn't started or the dessert made. You're likely to start making mistakes and just waste your time. Dress comfortably, and stay as neat as possible.

ASSEMBLING YOUR GARMENT

For beginners, the easiest and least time-consuming method for assembling a garment is to complete each type of construction process wherever possible before proceeding to the next. This may not be the procedure outlined in the Easy Sewing Guide for your pattern, but for the beginner, this system has certain advantages:

□ Each construction process is a learning process and should be mastered before proceeding to the next.

□ There is less chance of error when following only one process at a time.

□ It is time-saving, since each process can be done with the same machine-stitch at the same spot. There is no running from the machine to the ironing board and back to the machine.

□ Short amounts of time can be used to advantage when each construction process is done at one time.

Place a flat surface, such as a table, next to the sewing machine so you can lay all the garment pieces flat when you are not working with them. Working carefully and neatly is one of the secrets of a well-finished garment. Treat the fabric as you would the finished garment. Don't overwork it. Ripping needless stitching caused by not stitching correctly the first time, unnecessary handling and trying on, can make a garment look worn out before it is even finished.

Complete each construction process wherever possible during the assembling of your garment by using the following outline as a guide.

□ Make all necessary pattern alterations.

□ Straighten the fabric.

□ Press the fabric.

□ Fold the fabric for correct layout following the diagram on the Easy Sewing Guide.

□ Lay all the pattern pieces on the fabric.

□ Pin all pattern pieces securely on the correct grain of the fabric.

□ Cut out all the garment pieces.

□ Transfer all markings.

□ Remove all tissue pattern pieces.

□ Stay-stitch all curved and bias edges of each piece.

□ Baste the construction details—darts, tucks, etc.—and the sections of the garment together and fit correctly before stitching permanently; chalk-mark corrections on wrong side of fabric.

□ Stitch all darts, dart tucks, and pleats, fastening thread ends securely wherever necessary and cutting thread ends close to the fabric.

□ Press lightly.

□ Stitch all plain seams that can be stitched before a collar, pockets, etc., are applied.

□ Finish seam allowances in appropriate manner.

□ Press seams.

□ Apply collars, sleeves, pockets and other garment details, studying the Easy Sewing Guide. There are some of these steps which must be completed before other seams are joined.

□ After completion of the garment, give it a final pressing, or for tailored garments, send them to be professionally pressed.

The Easy Sewing Guide will not follow this procedure, because these guides are designed for seamstresses with some skill and experience. Most of the pattern guide sheets are based on a unit method of construction in which the bodice is completed, the skirt completed, the two joined and small finishing details such as zipper application and hems done as the last process. After you know basic sewing constructions, you may find that working with your garment in units is a quicker way of assembling it. You should try both methods and find the one which works best for you and gives you the most satisfactory looking garment.

To illustrate the method of assembling a garment

by completing each construction process before proceeding to the next, in the professional way, this

Guide to Easy Sewing chart has been designed. This has been "use-tested" in schools throughout the coun-

STEP 1
DARTS

STEP 2
SEAMS

STEP 3
COLLAR

STEP 4
BOW

STEP 1 — DARTS

1. Remove pattern pieces from fabric.

2. To make darts in bodice front, bodice back and sleeves, fold fabric, right sides together, on center marking of dart. Match stitch-line markings accurately. Place pins at right angles to stitching line at each end of dart and then at center.

3. Stitch darts from wide end tapering to point. Remove pins as you stitch. Take three stitches along fold line at point. Reverse the stitching direction and stitch back three stitches on the original stitching line to fasten ends of thread. Clip threads at both ends of darts.

4. Press each dart. Use a tailor's ham and an iron regulated for your fabric. Press on each side of stitching, then press front darts toward center front; back darts toward center back; underarm darts toward waist; and sleeve darts toward wrist.

5. Finish by pressing on right side of fabric, using a press cloth. Always press with grain of fabric.

STEP 2 — SEAMS

1. Place two front bodice sections together at center front seam, right sides of fabric together, matching edges evenly. Place pin at lower edge at right angles to and directly on the seamline. Match and pin markings for end of center front opening. Pin notches together.

2. Stitch seam ⅝" from edge using 12 stitches to the inch and a seam guide. Stitch evenly and at a moderate speed from lower edge to marking for center front opening. Remove pins as you stitch. Stitch back three stitches to fasten ends of thread. Clip threads at both ends of seam.

3. Pin and stitch front and back bodice sections together at shoulders, right sides together, stitching from neck edge to armhole. Clip threads at both ends of seams.

4. Pin and stitch front sections of skirt together along center front seamline, right sides together, beginning at lower edge. Remove pins as you stitch. Clip threads at both ends of seam. Pin and stitch back sections of skirt together at center back seamline in same manner.

5. Pin front and back sections of skirt together at side seams, right sides together. Stitch left side seam from lower edge to marking for placket opening. Stitch back three stitches to fasten ends of thread. Stitch entire right side seam starting at lower edge. Remove pins as you stitch. Clip threads at ends of seams.

6. Edge Finishes:
Fabrics that do not ravel: Trim edges with pinking shears, ⅛" from edge.
Fabrics that ravel slightly: Stitch ¼" from edge and pink close to raw edge.
Fabrics that ravel:
(a) Finish with machine zigzagging.
(b) Stitch close to edge and hand overcast.

7. Press all seams open using an iron regulated for your fabric. Press on the wrong side using a steam iron or a dry iron and a damp press cloth.

STEP 3 — COLLAR

1. Trim diagonally across points of interfacing ¾" from edge to remove bulk from corners. Baste interfacing to wrong side of undercollar.

2. Pin undercollar to upper collar, right sides together. Match edges evenly. Stitch on seamline around outer edges, leaving neck edge open. Take a diagonal stitch across points.
3. To grade seam allowances: trim interfacing close to stitching; undercollar to ⅛"; and upper collar to ¼". Clip curve at ½" intervals to seamline and trim diagonally across points, ⅛" from stitching line.

4. Turn collar to right side. Press seam allowance toward undercollar.
5. Understitch edge, stitching undercollar to seam allowance close to seamline between points. Stitch into points as far as possible. Draw threads to inside and tie ends. Clip threads.

6. Press collar flat and baste neck edges together.
7. Pin collar to bodice at neck edge, right sides up, matching notches, centers and markings. Place pins at right angles to edge. Hand-baste in place.

8. Stitch back facing to front facing sections right sides together, at shoulders. Clip threads. Trim seam allowances to ¼". Press seams open.
9. Turn under ¼" on unnotched edge of facing and hand-baste. Machine-stitch close to edge. Remove basting and press.

10. Pin and hand-baste facing over collar, right sides together. Match notches, shoulder seams and centers. Stitch from center front opening around the neck edge. Tie ends of thread securely at front edges. Clip threads. To grade seam allowances: trim bodice to ⅜"; collar to ¼"; facing to ⅛". Clip curve at ½" intervals to line of stitching. Trim diagonally across corners at front neck edge.

11. Turn facing to inside. Press seam allowance toward facing. Understitch facing to seam allowance from facing side, stitching close to seamline and into corners as far as possible at center front. Draw threads to inside and tie ends. Clip threads.

12. Turn bodice to inside. Press facing flat. Match shoulder seams of facing to shoulder seams of bodice. Pin with pins at right angles to edge of facing. Catch-stitch edges of facing to bodice seam allowances.

STEP 4 — BOW

1. Close neck edge with hook and eye. Sew hook to inside right front edge with overhand stitches around the holes and three stitches across end of hook and through facing. Sew round eye to inside left front with eye extending beyond the edge. Use overhand stitches around holes and take three stitches across each side of eye and through facing.

2. Fold bow lengthwise, right sides together, matching notches and cut edges. Pin edges together with pins at right angles to and directly on the seamline.

3. Stitch around cut edges, leaving a 2" opening at center of bow for turning. Grade seam allowances and trim diagonally across points, ⅛" from stitching line.

4. Turn bow to right side through opening. Pull out the corners with a pin. Baste along seam edges. Turn in the edges of opening and slip-stitch together. Press.

5. Fold bow in half and bring ends together. Match dotted lines and pin at right angles to line. Stitch together along dotted lines.

6. Spread ends. Bring seam to center of bow. Gather ¼" from each side of center marking with a hand running stitch. Draw up gathers to 1¼" and fasten ends of threads.

7. With right side of fabric uppermost, make pleat in knot on lines indicated. Baste in place along folded edge. Press.
8. Fold knot, right sides together, and match notches. Stitch a ⅜" seam along notched edge. Press seam open.
9. Turn knot to right side. Place seam at center of knot and press flat.

10. With pleat on the outside, place knot over center of bow.

11. Bring ends of knot to back of bow. Sew one end to center of bow. Turn in other end ⅜" and lap over raw edges. Sew in place with a hemming stitch. Do not attach bow until dress is finished.

12. Pin front and back bodice sections together at underarm, right sides together. Stitch entire right underarm seam starting at armhole. Remove pins as you stitch. Stitch left underarm seam from armhole to marking for placket opening. Stitch back three stitches to fasten ends of threads. Clip ends of threads on both seams. Press seams open.

try, and has been proven to be of great help to students of sewing. Following the chart, you can hardly help turning out a garment that you'll be proud to wear anywhere.

STEP 5 SLEEVE

1. Stitch around top of sleeve on the seamline. Use 12 stitches to the inch from underarm to first notch; change to 6-8 stitches to the inch between notches; back to 12 stitches from notch to underarm seam.

2. Pin and stitch sleeve seam. Clip seam allowance to seamline at hemline marking. Press seam open using a sleeve board.
3. Turn up lower edge of sleeve on hemline and baste in place.

4. Pin sleeve into armscye, right sides together, matching underarm seams, notches, small dots and center point of sleeve to shoulder seam.
5. Starting at center point of sleeve, pull up bobbin thread until sleeve cap fits armscye. Pin and baste sleeve firmly in place.

6. Shrink out any fullness in sleeve cap by pressing sleeve and armhole seams together from the sleeve side.

7. Try on bodice and check the following places for fit. Make any necessary adjustments.

• Waistline seam at natural waist and parallel to floor.
• Center front seam and center back basting line in middle of figure and perpendicular to floor.
• Side seams halfway between front and back and perpendicular to floor.
• Shoulder seams straight on top of shoulder.
• Bodice darts pointing directly to fullest part of bust.
• Sleeve seamline falls across tip of shoulder.
• Sleeve length is becoming.
• Neckline fits smoothly.
• Sufficient ease throughout for movement.

8. Stitch sleeve into armhole with sleeve uppermost on machine. Seam allowance at top of sleeve is turned toward sleeve and left turned up at underarm. Finish sleeve and armhole seam allowances separately.

9. Turn under lower edge of sleeve ¼". Stitch close to folded edge.
10. Baste upper edge of hem to sleeve. Sew hem to sleeve with a tiny slip-stitch. Remove bastings. Press on a sleeve board.

STEP 6 WAISTLINE

1. In preparation for gathering the upper edge of the skirt, thread the top of the machine with regular sewing thread; bobbin with heavy duty thread. Adjust machine for 6-8 stitches per inch.

2. Stitch each of the four skirt sections separately. With right side of fabric uppermost, start at placket seamline and stitch along the seamline of upper edge of skirt to center back seam. Leave ends of thread 2" long. Place a second row of stitching ¼" above in the seam allowance. Leave ends of thread 2" long. Stitch each of the other three skirt sections in this manner.

3. Cut waistline stay from woven edge seam binding using the waistline stay pattern. Transfer all pattern markings to the seam binding with carbon and tracing wheel.

4. Pin center of waistline stay to seamline at upper inside edge of skirt. Place ends of stay even with placket edges. Match center fronts and center backs and place large circle at right side seam. The small circles are placed in line with notches on upper edge of skirt.

5. Pull up bobbin threads until gathers fit waistline stay. Adjust gathers evenly. At left front section of skirt, adjust gathers so that fullness starts ½" from placket seamline. Baste stay to skirt.

6. Pin skirt to bodice, right sides together. Match placket edges, centers, notches and right side seams. Baste in place, being careful to keep gathers flat in seamline.

7. Try on complete dress. Pin placket opening on seamline. Check fit of waistline. Seam should be at natural waistline and parallel to floor.

8. Thread bobbin with regular sewing thread. Adjust machine for 12 stitches to the inch. Stitch waistline seam with the waistline stay uppermost. Clip threads. Remove bastings. Press seam allowance toward bodice.

STEP 7 ZIPPER

1. Pin left side opening closed, right sides together, matching waistline seams.

2. Machine-baste placket opening using 6-8 stitches to the inch.
3. Press seam open.

4. Attach zipper foot to machine and adjust to right-hand side of needle. Change machine stitch to 12 stitches to the inch. Open the zipper. Place face down on back seam allowance. Match bottom of zipper chain to beginning of machine-basting with teeth on seamline. Stitch zipper to seam allowance close to teeth from bottom to top. Sew through zipper tape and back seam allowance only. Clip threads.

5. Adjust zipper foot to left-hand side of needle. Close zipper and turn face up. Press fabric away from zipper forming a fold in back seam allowance along zipper. Stitch from bottom up through seam allowance and tape close to zipper teeth.

6. Spread garment flat and turn zipper face down over front seam allowance. There will be a small pleat at top and bottom of placket. Starting at seamline, hand-baste across top of zipper, down the front side and across the bottom.

7. Turn dress to right side. Adjust zipper foot to right-hand side of needle. Using the basting as a guide, stitch across the bottom of the zipper. Raise presser foot, pivot fabric, lower presser foot and stitch an even distance from the seamline to top of zipper. Raise presser foot, pivot fabric, lower presser foot and stitch across top of zipper. The top-stitching on the front of the zipper application should be an even distance from the seamline, and will be stitched through front of dress, front seam allowance and zipper tape. Pull threads to wrong side and fasten securely at each end of zipper. Clip threads.

8. Press zipper application. Remove hand-basting and machine-basting from the seamline.

STEP 8 HEM

1. Put on the dress and the shoes to be worn with it. Stand in normal posture position with feet together. Have someone mark skirt at correct hem length for you, measuring an even distance from floor.

2. Take off the dress. Turn up hem on marked line. Baste close to folded edge. Press.
3. Mark width of hem using a ruler or hem gauge and trim hem allowance evenly.

4. The hem edge is finished according to the fabric.

   a. The turned and stitched hem is used on fabrics to be machine-washed.

   (1) Turn under the edge ¼". Stitch along folded edge, leaving just enough room to slip a needle through the fold when hemming the skirt.

   (2) Baste upper edge of hem to skirt. Slip-stitch hem in place.

   b. The dressmaker hem may be used on all other fabrics.

   (1) Stitch ¼" from the edge (8-10 stitches to the inch).

   (2) Pink the edge if fabric does not ravel. If fabric does ravel, zigzag or overcast the cut edges. (See edge finishes in Step 2.)

   (3) Baste hem in place ½" from the upper edge.

   (4) Turn hem back so that folded edge of skirt falls along line of stitching on hem.

   (5) Sew hem to skirt with a French hemming stitch. Working from right to left, pick up one thread of the skirt fabric, then take a small stitch in the hem diagonally above. Continue this stitch being careful not to pull the thread too tight. Press finished hem.

5. Sew bow to right front neck edge of dress with overhand stitches.

FITTING

The real reward of sewing your own is having a custom fit in every garment you own. You can spend hours and hours doing meticulously careful construction, but unless it is properly fitted, the garment will not look professional.

Most of the fitting should be done in the pattern before the garment is cut out. Actual fitting of the garment should include only minor changes such as repositioning darts, slight taking in or letting out of seams. Until you become really expert at altering your pattern, you may find you will have to do some fitting of the garment after it is cut and basted together.

To prepare a garment for fitting, be sure that all curved and bias edges are stay-stitched. Machine-baste the garment together before you do any permanent stitching. Use a non-matching color thread so that you can see the basting when it is to be removed. This will eliminate the possibility of forgetting to stitch permanently a construction detail that is only basted. Never hand-baste a garment for fitting. The basting pulls and stretches and does not give an accurate fit. The garment always ends up tighter after it is stitched.

Stitch all darts, tucks and construction details and press them lightly. Don't press hard, since the markings may be difficult to remove if refitting is necessary. Machine-baste shoulder seams, underarm seam, and front and back seams of the garment. Pin up the hem of the skirt, and join the skirt and bodice together at the waist by overlapping the seam allowances and pinning along the seam line.

Put the garment on, right side out, over the undergarments you will be wearing with the finished garment. Always fit a garment right side out. Because the left and right sides of the body are never identical, one side may need to be fitted while the other may not. If there are noticeable differences between the right and left sides of the body, be sure not to fit the garment too snugly or the differences will be more apparent. Try to make the figure appear as symmetrical as possible. Wear the correct shoes, and have the correct width of belt if one is part of the design. Pin in shoulder pads if they are to be used. Fit suits over blouses or sweaters, jumpers over blouses or sweaters, jackets over blouses and skirts, and coats over dresses or suits.

Determine the fit of your garment by checking the following points:

☐ Sufficient fullness at all points for movement, standing, bending and sitting. A garment is not worn by a

mannequin but by a moving figure and, therefore, must have ease allowance for this.

☐ Grain lines at bust, waist, hip and upper arm are parallel to the floor.

☐ Grain lines at side seams, center front and back are perpendicular to the floor.

☐ Center front and back seams are in the middle of the figure.

☐ Side seams are straight and placed halfway between the front and back.

☐ Shoulder seams lie straight across the top of the shoulder.

☐ Bodice length is correct above and below the waist and waistline seam fits snugly at natural waist. To find your natural waist, bend to the side and place your hand on bend. This is your natural waistline.

☐ Skirt is the most flattering length for your figure within the fashion range.

☐ Sleeve length is correct above and below the elbow, with center elbow dart pointing to the tip of the elbow when the arm is bent.

☐ Bodice darts point directly to the fullest part of the bust.

☐ Hip darts point to the fullest part of the hip and end just above this point.

☐ Sleeve seam line lies across the outer edge of shoulder.

☐ Neckline fits smoothly without pulling or gaping.

If any of these fitting points is not correct, the correction should be pinned in, removing the basting wherever necessary.

Fitting Shoulders

The area of fitting which is most important to the entire "hang" of a garment is the shoulder and neck area. Not only is it most important, it can cause the greatest difficulty in fitting. To help you fit the shoulders properly, here are suggested corrections for the most common fitting problems.

SLOPING SHOULDERS. Remove the basting at shoulder seam. Smooth up any wrinkles formed around armscye and pin in a new shoulder seam, tapering from neck edge to sleeve edge. This makes the seam at sleeve edge wider than at neck edge to take care of the slope. When the garment is removed, the underarm will have to be lowered the same amount as was removed from the shoulder seam. Rebaste the shoulder seam and check the alteration.

SQUARE SHOULDERS. Open the basted seam, smooth out the wrinkles and pin in a new shoulder seam, tapering out from neck edge to sleeve edge. The sleeve edge will be the narrower end of the tapered seam. If a sleeve is to be inserted, the sleeve seam will have to be tapered also to fit smoothly in the enlarged armhole.

NARROW SHOULDERS. Move the sleeve about ½ inch higher on the shoulder—taking a deeper seam allowance on the shoulder than in the sleeve. If this still doesn't take care of the extra width, then take small darts at mid-shoulder in both front and back bodice. For best results this alteration should be done in the pattern before the garment section is cut.

Fitting Necklines

Necklines are another area which cause some problems in fitting. Again, adjustments should be made in the pattern. If you failed to make adjustments, or the adjustments were not correct, you can do some fitting in the garment.

TIGHT NECKLINE. If the neckline is too tight, lightly chalk the correct depth on the garment and recut. Remember to recut the facing in the same way.

LOW NECKLINE. If the depth of the neckline is too low and the neckline is the jewel type, you might try adding a bias edging of the fabric to fill in around the neckline, or a shaped band or facing turned to the outside.

SCOOP NECKLINE. Scooped necklines which gap cannot be fitted very successfully once you have cut the garment. This alteration definitely should be made in the pattern. The shoulder seams can be raised about ¼ inch on each side of the neckline. If this doesn't correct the gaping, place a row of machine-basting around the neckline. Ease the fabric and shrink out the excess fullness until the neckline lies smoothly.

All scooped necklines fit better if the facing is cut slightly smaller than the neck edge, and the neck edge eased to the facing.

DEPTH OF NECKLINE. If in doubt about the depth of a neckline there is an easy way to test it before cutting your fabric. Cut the facing pieces from muslin or a scrap of fabric and stitch up the shoulder seams. Cut away the seam allowance on the facing neck edge. Put the facing on over your head and place the seams on the shoulder seams of the dress you are wearing. You will be able to see just where the neckline of the dress will come on you.

Final Alterations

After the correct fit has been achieved, remove the garment. Mark any corrections on the wrong side of the fabric by turning the garment inside out and marking the position of pins with tailor's chalk or white pencil. Remove the pins from the outside of the garment and repin along the markings on the inside. Baste the garment again, and check the fit. Keep checking until you are satisfied that you have a perfectly fitted garment.

Remove the basting wherever the construction seams meet or cross each other, or where it is necessary in order to stitch construction details. For example, the neckline may have to be finished before side seams are joined, so the side seam bastings will have to be removed.

For fitting slacks and shorts, check the section under Pants Alterations in Chapter 6. Complete instructions for pattern alteration and fitting procedure are outlined there.

PRESSING

Pressing is as important to the professional look as any sewing technique you will master. It is absolutely essential to the good looks of a garment. Keep your ironing board and iron as handy as your sewing machine, and as close to it as possible. Unless you are using wash-and-wear fabrics, you should press each construction detail completely after it has been stitched before proceeding to the next step. Unless you do this, you will not be able to stitch the next step smoothly and evenly, and your garment will have a homemade look. Don't expect to correct everything with a final pressing. It just isn't the same. Once you recognize and accept the fact that time spent in pressing as you work is the best investment a home-sewer can make, you are well on your way to becoming a professional.

However, if you are using wash-and-wear fabrics, finger-press a seam until you are sure the stitching line is in the correct place. Press marks are difficult to remove in this type of fabric.

Before you begin to press, read any pressing instructions given on the hang tag or on the bolt of fabric. Check the chart in Chapter 3 which gives special instructions for man-made fibers. Be sure you know the fiber content of the fabric. If you aren't sure what temperature will be best, or have neglected to find out the fiber content, then test a scrap of your fabric. Beginning with the lowest setting on iron, increase the temperature until you can iron the fabric smoothly and easily. Always use a press cloth to prevent shine when it is necessary to press on the right side of the garment.

To press successfully, raise and lower the iron as you move across the fabric, using a gentle up and down motion. This will keep the fabric grain in its original position. Pushing the iron across the fabric will tend to stretch it and distort the grain. When pressing any bias sections which are easily stretched, move the iron in the direction of the straight grain. For example, in pressing a bias skirt, pressing diagonally with the grain will keep the hem edge even. If you press straight up from hem to waistline, the most bias sections of the skirt will hang longer at the hem than the portions cut on straight of grain.

Steam-pressing is necessary on almost all fabrics to achieve a professional-looking garment. Test a scrap of your fabric first to be sure that it does not water-spot. If it does, use an extra dry press cloth next to the fabric to prevent spotting. Press with a steam iron or a dry iron and a damp press cloth. The steam iron may be satisfactory for some fabrics, but many materials require more steam than you get from the home steam iron. A damp press cloth in addition to the steam iron may be needed, particularly in tailoring.

There are many commercial press cloths on the market but a piece of closely woven cheesecloth makes an excellent one. The texture allows the steam to pass through but the weave protects the surface of the fabric from shine. Wet half of the cloth and squeeze out the excess moisture. Fold the dry and wet sections together and wring the cloth to dampen both sides evenly. Use one, two or three layers of the cheesecloth depending on the amount of moisture you need for the area being pressed, but never place a really wet press cloth on your garment.

The bottom of the iron must be kept clean at all times. Starch and sizing collect on the surface of the iron and will mark fabric. When the iron is cool it may be cleaned off with soap and water. If the iron is warm, sprinkle scouring powder on wax paper and slide the iron over it.

Press the fabric and the tissue pattern pieces before pinning the pattern to the fabric since it is impossible to cut accurately when fabric or pattern are wrinkled. Press the pattern pieces with a dry iron; steam will shrink the tissue.

Cotton and Linen

Use a high temperature and press on the wrong side wherever possible. On light-colored fabrics, you may be able to press directly on the right side. On dark colors, use a press cloth when pressing on the right side to prevent shine. To obtain flat smooth edges you will always need moisture and steam-pressing. Press all seams completely dry to avoid puckering.

Wool

Use a moderate temperature plus moisture—either a steam iron or a damp press cloth and a dry iron. Press on the wrong side as much as possible. Sometimes top pressing or pressing on the right side is necessary. To protect the right side of the fabric, use a dry wool press cloth under the damp press cloth. Press fabrics that shine easily over a needle board or cover the end of your ironing board with a piece of wool fabric. Moisture is very necessary in shrinking out fullness and shaping wool, but do not press a wool garment while it is wet. The garment will shrink and the elasticity of the fabric will be destroyed.

Silk

Use a medium temperature and press on the wrong side. Silk requires less moisture than other fabrics, and it water-spots easily. Always press with a dry press cloth or a piece of tissue paper next to the fabric to prevent water-spotting.

Synthetics

Use a low temperature setting since most synthetics melt or fuse at a high temperature. Repeated pressing of some white synthetics with too hot an iron will cause yellowing. Press on the wrong side as much as possible. If right-side pressing is necessary, protect the fabric with a press cloth. Test a scrap of your fabric for the correct temperature and for water-spotting before ironing your garment. If fabric water-spots, use a dry press cloth next to the fabric.

Blends

Press according to the directions for the most delicate fiber in the blend. Be sure to test a scrap of your fabric for the correct temperature setting and water-spotting before applying moisture or a steam iron to your garment.

Wash-and-Wear Fabrics

Use a steam iron or a dry iron and a damp press cloth. Be sure to try to press out the center fold crease before cutting out your garment. If the crease will not press out, as is the case with some fabrics, refold your fabric and cut garment sections to avoid this crease mark. Press darts and seams lightly for the first fitting. Pressed creases are difficult to remove from these fabrics if changes have to be made.

Pile Fabrics

Velvet, velveteen and corduroy should be steam-pressed on a needle board to keep from matting and flattening the pile. Place the fabric face down on the needle board with a damp press cloth on wrong side to steam-press. If you do not have a needle board, stand the iron on end and place a wet press cloth over it. Holding the fabric lightly, draw the wrong side of the velvet across the iron. Be careful not to hold the fabric tightly as it will finger-mark.

A pile fabric garment can have the wrinkles removed most easily by hanging it in a steaming room. Turn on the hot water, and when the room is filled with steam, hang the garment on the shower rod. After the wrinkles have disappeared, let the garment dry thoroughly before touching it. This steam-pressing in the shower is an excellent thing to remember when traveling. It takes the packing wrinkles out of most fabrics and saves having to carry a travel iron.

Laminated Fabrics

Press on the wrong side of the fabric with a press cloth. Never touch the foam side with the iron. Use steam-pressing during construction. To press on the right side, use a damp press cloth and a dry cloth under it if the fabric shines.

Lace and Embroidered Fabrics

Press on the wrong side. To keep from flattening the design, place the fabric face down over several layers of Turkish toweling. Do not press on the right side or you will flatten the design.

During the construction of a garment, the pressing of each detail after stitching is essential to the final appearance. It is so much easier and more accurate to press and shape small areas of the garment as you work. Press on the wrong side as much as possible and use a press cloth. There are different methods of pressing and it is important that you use the correct one for the construction detail being pressed.

Seams

Press along the stitching line before pressing the seam open. Place flat sections on the ironing board and curved sections over a tailor's ham. Always put the wrong side of the fabric uppermost. Hold the seam allowances open with the fingers and press with the point of the iron along the stitching line. Avoid seam imprints by pressing over a seam roll or by placing strips of brown paper between the seam allowance and the garment. Press two or three inches at a time on a curved seam to avoid stretching the seam out of shape. If the seam allowances are to be pressed to one side, press the seam open first and then to the side to give a smooth, clean line.

Before joining seams where one section has to be eased to the other, shrink out the fullness in the eased section. After placing a line of stitching along the area to be eased, draw up and distribute the fullness evenly. Place the section over a curved surface such as a tailor's ham with the wrong side of fabric up. Steam-press along the seam allowance to the line of stitching, shrinking out the fullness. Using the tip of the iron, press into the seam line over the ham to retain the curved shaping beyond the seam line. Press again after the seam has been stitched placing the curved area over the ham.

Darts

Press on both sides of the dart using the point of the iron along the line of stitching, then press the dart to one side over a tailor's ham. Press from the wide part of the dart to the point, shrinking out fullness at the point. If a ridge is formed by the fold of the dart on the right side of the fabric, slip a piece of heavy brown paper between the dart and the fabric. In bulky fabric, trim the dart ½ inch from the stitching. Place over a tailor's ham and press the dart open along the seam, using the tip of the iron. Fold a triangle at the point of the dart.

Vertical darts, such as at waistline and shoulder, are usually pressed toward the center front or center back. Horizontal darts such as bust and elbow darts are pressed down.

Tucks

Place flat on the ironing board, right side up. Press along line of stitching on both sides of tuck with the tip of the iron, using a press cloth. Then press the tuck to one side, again using the press cloth. Turn to the wrong side and press along the line of stitching.

Press released tucks in the same way as regular tucks but do not press flat beyond the line of stitching.

Dart Tucks

Place over a tailor's ham with wrong side of fabric up, and press along the line of stitching. Then press to one side as for a regular dart. Turn to the right side. Press along line of stitching, using a press cloth. Do not press flat beyond the line of stitching.

Pleats

Place the basted pleats flat on the ironing board, right side up. Using a press cloth and steam, press lengthwise along the pleat folds. Turn to the wrong side and press the pleats in the same way. If the pleated section has a hem, press the pleats only to the hemline until the hem has been turned up. After the garment is completed, remove the bastings and press the pleats again on both the right and wrong sides. Use steam and a press cloth to remove basting thread marks.

Gathers

Place the gathered section on the ironing board, wrong side up. Smooth the fabric flat below the gathered section and press into the gathers with the point of the iron. Lift the gathered edge as you press into the gathers to keep from forming creases. Never place the iron flat along the line of gathering or you will form creases and destroy the full effect of the gathers. When one edge is gathered, press the seam allowance away from the gathered edge. When two gathered edges are stitched together, use a seam roll to press seam allowance open for less bulk.

Faced Edges

After the facing has been stitched to the garment, press the seam open with the tip of the iron wherever possible. Use the point presser to open seams in corners. Curved areas will have to be clipped and seams graded before seam can be pressed open. Understitch when necessary and turn facing to inside. Press flat along the edge with a damp press cloth for best results. Pressing the seam open first, and then pressing both edges in one direction, gives a flatter finish. On collars and faced edges, where the seam line should not show along the edge, roll the seam lines slightly to the underside and press in this position. Edges of wool garments can be flattened further by pounding the edges with a wooden clapper while there is still steam in the fabric. See Chapter 14 for full tailoring instructions.

Plackets

A zipper application should be pressed over a tailor's ham to retain the curve of the hip seam. Close the zipper. Press from the right side with a press cloth. Slip a piece of brown paper between the chain and the fabric to keep the imprint of the zipper from pressing through to the right side. Press to within an inch of the top of the closed zipper. Do not try to press over the bulk of the pull tab; open the zipper to press the top of the application.

Sleeves

Press the armhole seam line from the sleeve side with the sleeve and armhole seam allowances together. Place the seam line on the edge of the sleeve board and press several inches at a time. Continue around the armhole, pressing from the cut edge to the stitching line. Press in the same way with the garment side uppermost. Then press the seam allowance at the top of the sleeve into the sleeve, leaving the underarm portion turned up.

Press the lower edge of sleeves on the right side with a press cloth to retain the circular shape. If pressed on the wrong side, the inner facing or hem may become stretched, causing the lower edge to ripple.

Hems

After marking the hemline, place the garment wrong side up on the ironing board. Turn the hem along the markings and press the fold lifting the iron with each stroke. Do not push the iron along the folded edge. This will stretch and ripple the edge. After the hem has been trimmed evenly, press again in position. If the skirt is straight, press the hem flat working from fold edge to hem edge. If the skirt hem has fullness, place a gathering thread ¼ inch from the edge. Match the seams, then draw up the thread and distribute the ease evenly from seam line to seam line, until the hem fits smoothly. Use a damp press cloth to shrink out the fullness in the hem allowance. A heavy piece of brown paper placed between the hem allowance and the garment will prevent a ridge on the right side. Press again after hem has been finished.

Final Pressing

If you have done a thorough job of pressing as you worked, the final pressing will be greatly simplified. This should be just a matter of pressing out wrinkles caused by working on the garment and touching up the edges to remove basting marks and any shiny spots.

Some people prefer to send their wool garments to the tailor for a final pressing, particularly with fabrics that are very difficult to press, since he has special steam and heavy pressing equipment. A tailor can flatten the seams and edges of your garment. However, he can never build in the shaping that you have lost by failing to press and shape as you work. He can improve an unpressed garment, but he can never give the garment a professional finished appearance unless you have done your work well.

CHAPTER 9

CONSTRUCTION DATA–STITCHES AND SEAMS

This chapter and the next few following contain complete instructions for all basic techniques of sewing. Beginners will find them helpful for describing in detail stitches or finishes which may be mentioned in a pattern guide sheet without specific directions. And even an experienced seamstress may discover that a brief "refresher course" will remind her of details she may have forgotten, or bring her up to date on techniques and methods that have been developed since she learned to sew. Remember that your success as a home-sewer depends on how well you master the very elementary techniques.

MACHINE STITCHES

Machine stitches are divided into two types—straight and zigzag. The straight-needle machine makes only straight stitches, unless a special attachment is used; whereas the zigzag machine can create both.

Regulation Stitch

This is the stitch used for permanent stitching such as seams, darts and tucks. The length and tension of the stitch may vary according to the fabric used. (See page 67. On most medium-weight fabrics, the regulation stitch is about 12 stitches to the inch; sheers require a finer stitch (16 to the inch); heavy or coarse fabrics generally take 8 to 10 stitches to the inch.

Basting Stitch

Basting stitches are used for temporary joining of sections or details which may require reworking when the garment is fitted or for marking. Use the longest stitch on the machine (6 to 8 per inch) and a contrasting thread so that the markings and bastings are easily seen and easily removed. Use the same tension on the machine as you do for permanent stitching on your fabric. To remove basting, clip the needle thread every few inches and pull out the bobbin thread using small, sharp-pointed scissors.

Stitching For Gathering

Sections which require easing or gathering should be stitched with a long stitch (6 to 10 to the inch) in matching color thread. Leave long threads at the ends of the stitching. Anchor threads at one end around a pin, then pick up the bobbin thread at the other end and gently draw it up to form the amount of easing or gathering needed. The shorter stitch (10 to the inch) will form finer easing or gathering; the longer (6 to the inch) will create fuller easing or gathering. Sometimes a heavier thread is used on the bobbin.

Stitching For Reinforcement

Areas where there is strain or a need for reinforcement, such as points of collars, cuffs, gussets, pointed faced openings of necklines, underarm seam of kimono sleeves, will need a finer, tighter stitch, usually 16 to 20 stitches to the inch.

Zigzag Stitch

Zigzag machines are capable of making the zigzag stitch but a straight-needle machine will require a special zigzag attachment. (See page 73.) The small zigzag stitch may be used to stitch seams in jersey and loosely woven fabric with bias seams, giving greater elasticity which helps prevent seam splitting. It can also be used as a seam finish for edges that ravel by

stitching close to the raw edge or by overcasting the edge.

HAND STITCHES

Permanent hand stitches are usually worked from right to left unless the directions state otherwise. If you are left-handed you may have to reverse the direction of the stitching. All the diagrams shown here are designed for a right-handed person. Begin and end any permanent hand stitches with tiny back-stitches on the wrong side of the garment to hold threads securely.

Running Stitch

This is the simplest form of hand stitch. It can be used for gathering, quilting, mending, tucking and seams that do not require much strain. For easing and gathering, take stitches $\frac{1}{16}$ to $\frac{1}{4}$ inch in length, pass the needle through the fabric several times and then pull the needle through. Continue across the work, gently easing the fullness. For a permanently stitched seam, use tiny stitches $\frac{1}{16}$ to $\frac{1}{8}$ inch in length. Do not draw the thread up; keep it flat and smooth in the work. On sheer fabrics use the tiny 1/16-inch stitch; on heavier woolens a $\frac{1}{8}$-inch stitch may be the smallest you can make.

Basting Stitch

A basting stitch is used to hold two or more pieces of fabric together temporarily, to transfer construction symbols from wrong to right side of fabric and to indicate guide lines. Use a contrasting thread so the basting stitch can be easily identified when permanent stitching is made and the basting is removed. The stitch is a larger version of the running stitch, about $\frac{1}{4}$ to $\frac{1}{2}$ inch in length, depending on the weight of the fabric and how securely the pieces of fabric should be held together.

EVEN BASTING. Used when there will be some strain on the seam. Make stitches about $\frac{1}{4}$ inch long, even on both sides of fabric.

UNEVEN BASTING. Used in seams where there is little or no strain or as a guide line for stitching. Take long stitches on one side of fabric and short stitches on other side.

DIAGONAL BASTING. Used to hold several layers of fabric securely together. Stitch through the fabric at right angles to the fabric edge. This gives a diagonal stitch on the upper side and a short horizontal stitch on the underside. It is used to hold interfacings, linings and facings in place during fittings.

SLIP-BASTING. Most often used when matching seams in plaids or stripes or to baste alterations made on the right side. Fold under the seam allowance on one side of the seam and press flat. Then place this over the other section of the seam, right sides up, matching accurately at the seam line and pin. Place the needle through the seam line on the underside and back through the seam line. Take stitches about $\frac{1}{4}$ inch in length. Place the needle through the seam line fold and out on the fold line. Continue in the same manner. No stitches will show on the right side, while on the wrong side, there is a regular basting stitch.

Back-Stitch

Back-stitching is used to stitch a seam securely or permanently. It looks like machine-stitching on the right side, but stitches overlap on the wrong side. Take a small running stitch ($\frac{1}{8}$ inch long) through the fabric on the underside. Take a stitch back, placing the needle in the fabric at the beginning of the first stitch and bringing it out a stitch ahead. Continue in this manner working across the fabric.

Half Back-Stitch

Used as a decorative stitch. The needle is carried back only half the length of the first stitch. This looks like a running stitch on the right side, but stitches overlap on the wrong side.

Prick Stitch

A variation of back-stitch and half back-stitch, the prick stitch is used for applying zippers by hand. The needle is carried back only one or two threads of fabric.

Slip-Stitch

The slip-stitch is used when stitching should not show, but it isn't very strong. It differs from the slip-basting stitch in the length of the stitches. Place a stitch through the fold of the fabric about ⅛ to ¼ inch in length. Pick up only one or two threads of the under fabric. Continue in this manner taking a stitch through the fold and then in the under fabric.

Hemming Stitch

A slanting stitch which shows on the wrong side and is stronger than the slip-stitch. Used for all types of hemming. Take up one thread of the garment fabric and then bring the needle through the fold of the hem edge. Stitches should not show on the right side.

Catch-Stitch

This is a fairly loose but secure stitch used to hold raw edges of facings and interfacings. Working from left to right, take a small stitch through the upper fabric from right to left, then pick up one or two threads in the under fabric from right to left. Do not pull the stitches tight. The threads will cross each other between stitches.

Invisible Stitch

Sometimes called the French hemming stitch. This stitch is used for hems and for attaching facings and interfacings in tailoring. Fold hem or facing back on garment. Working from right to left, pick up a thread of the garment, then pick up a thread of the hem or facing diagonally above. Do not pull the stitches tight.

Overhand Stitch

This is used when a strong, secure and invisible seam is needed. It is often used on table linens, to sew on lace, to patch and for hems. Fold and press back the two seam allowances and place the fabrics right sides together with seam lines matching. Place the needle straight through the back fold and then through the front fold, picking up only one or two threads each time. Bring the needle out straight toward you. This produces a straight stitch. The stitches are kept close together.

Whipping Stitch

This may be used in place of the overhand stitch, since it serves the same purpose, or in tailoring. The only difference between the two stitches is that the whipping stitch is done with slanting stitches, taking stitches over the edge with the needle in a slanted position. Again, take only one or two threads of the fabric.

Overcasting

This stitch may be used on raw edges, either single or double, to prevent their raveling. Take stitches over the edge with the needle held in a slanting position.

Stitches should be close together and an even distance apart. Keep the depth of the stitches uniform.

Pad Stitch

This stitch is very similar to the diagonal basting stitch. It is a shorter stitch, and the underside of the stitch is much shorter, catching only one or two threads. It should be almost invisible on the outside. It is used to tack interfacing to collars and lapels of tailored garments. (See page 253 for instructions on using this stitch in a tailored garment.)

SEAMS

Pinning

Although it is possible to stitch seams without pinning them, this requires a great deal of skill and control. Normally, seams are joined first with pins, then basted or permanently stitched. To pin plain seams correctly, place the two pieces to be joined together evenly on a flat surface. Insert pins at right angles to the seam line with the pin holding the two fabrics securely together along the seam line. This prevents the two fabrics from shifting on the seam line while you are basting or stitching. Place a pin at each end, matching edges, and then at the notches before pinning the remaining area.

If you are working with an eased seam, the pinning will be slightly different. Place the fabrics together with the section to be eased on top toward you. Place pins at right angles to the seam along the seam line. Put them very close together leaving slight fullness between pins in the eased section. This can be done easily and evenly if you roll the fabric over your finger as you join the two sections with the pins.

When you pin a crossed seam (where two or more seams cross each other), first be sure the stitched seams match. Place a pin through the middle of the stitched seams at the seam line and place pins on either side of seams on the seam line.

To pin a lapped seam, turn under the seam allowance on the section to be lapped and place it in position. Place pins at right angles to the fold edge close to the fold through all thicknesses.

Stitching

Usually a pinned seam is taken directly to the sewing machine and either machine-basted or permanently stitched. If it is a seam which will not require addi-

tional fitting such as a center front seam, or the joining of a facing to a neckline, it is permanently stitched. Seams which may need refitting should be machine-basted. In either case, you'll want to remove the pins as you stitch. Most machines are equipped with a traveling foot which rocks backward and forward over the pins, so an entire seam can be stitched and the pins removed after stitching. However, this is not the best method, since many fabrics may require slight easing of the top layer because the two thicknesses do not travel through the machine at exactly the same rate. When a seam is pinned such fabric is likely to bunch at the pins, unless it is carefully eased. It is better to stitch slowly, removing each pin with your right hand just before it reaches the edge of the machine foot. Keep a pin cushion handy on your wrist or at the right side of the sewing machine, and place the pin in it as soon as you remove it from the fabric.

DIRECTION OF STITCHING. Seams should always be stitched so that both ends and edges match accurately. Stitch on the exact seam line indicated by the pattern piece. Usually this is ⅝ inch unless otherwise noted. Stitch seams in the direction of fabric grain, just as you cut and stay-stitch with the grain.

SECURING ENDS. When stitching seams or darts permanently, the machine-stitches should be secured at each end. There are several ways to do this. At the end of a seam, the needle and bobbin threads can be clipped, leaving enough thread to tie the two together several times in a square knot.

When stitching does not reach an edge, the two threads can be pulled to one side of the fabric and tied securely in a square knot. To do this, gently pull the bobbin thread until the loop of needle thread is visible. Catch this with the end of a pin and pull it through, so that both threads are on the same side of the fabric.

Back-stitching is an excellent way to secure threads, but it does require a little practice at the machine.

Take several stitches back over the stitches in the seam by adjusting the machine for back-stitching. Since you must stitch directly back over the seam, it is easier to turn the machine wheel by hand to do these back-stitches.

Very skilled seamstresses may wish to try the lock-stitch. However, if this is not done accurately, the needle thread may jam in the bobbin case of the machine. Practice several times on a scrap of fabric before trying it on a garment. To do the lockstitch, leave the needle in the fabric at the end of stitching. Raise the presser bar very slightly (this is the tricky part—the presser bar must be raised just the slightest bit), hold the fabric securely, and take several stitches right over the last stitch.

After threads have been fastened securely, clip the ends close to the fabric, using very sharp scissors. Be careful not to clip the fabric. You may find the little thread clippers suggested in Chapter 5 very helpful for this operation. Do not neglect clipping these threads. The garment will look much neater, and further sewing will be easier, since there will be no loose threads to catch in other stitching or on the presser foot.

Trimming

In working with a pattern, you'll find that you will have to trim many seams. This simply means that you cut away both allowances to an even width. Seams are trimmed to reduce bulk, particularly at faced edges.

Grading

Grading a seam allowance means that the layers of fabric are cut to different widths, with the wider seam allowance next to the outside fabric. When there is an interfacing joined in a seam, trim this close to the line of stitching. Grading eliminates a ridge being formed by the bulk of several layers of fabric in a seam allowance.

Clipping

Most curved seams, such as necklines, princess seam lines, collars, kimono sleeves at the underarm, require clipping in order to make the seam lie flat. On an inward curve, grade seam allowances and clip to the stitching line about ¼ inch apart. On outward curves, grade seams and make notches to line of stitching about ¼ inch apart.

Types of Seams

In garment construction there are several types of seams. The type to use in a garment is determined by the fabric and the design of the garment. For example, if you are working with a sheer fabric, you'll use a French seam which won't show through the sheer fabric. When making a man's sport shirt, the flat-fell seam is used since it is stronger and will hold up under the stress given this sort of garment. You should know the various types of seams and how to construct them, as well as where they are commonly used in a garment.

PLAIN SEAM. The seam most frequently used to join two sections of fabric. Pin two pieces of fabric, right sides together, and stitch. Sometimes back-stitches are used for this joining. Press seam open and finish seam edges.

PLAIN EASED SEAM. When two pieces to be seamed together are slightly unequal in length, the longer piece must be eased to the shorter. Although this easing provides shaping for a curved area of the body, the seam should appear smooth. It is often found at the bust, elbow and shoulder seam of a garment. To construct the seam, place a row of long stitches (6 to 10 to the inch) on the seam line of the longer piece of fabric between the markings for easing. Pull up the bobbin thread of this row of stitches until the seam edge of the longer piece is the same length as the shorter one. Distribute the ease evenly and steam-press to shrink out any fullness at the seam line. Pin the two pieces together and stitch the seam, keeping the eased seam on top as you stitch.

PLAIN SEAM JOINING BIAS PIECE AND STRAIGHT PIECE. If one section of fabric to be joined at a seam is bias and the other on the straight grain, place the bias section on top; ease if necessary and stitch with the bias section up toward you. To control stretching of bias seams, place woven seam binding along the seam line and stitch the tape to the seam as you are stitching the seam.

PLAIN SEAM JOINING NAPPED FABRIC AND SMOOTH FABRIC. When one section to be joined in a seam is napped and one is smooth fabric, place the smooth section on top. Stitch with smooth fabric up toward you.

PLAIN SEAM, TOP-STITCHED. A top-stitched seam not only adds a decorative effect to a garment, it also provides a strong seam construction. It is similar in appearance to the lapped seam. Stitch a plain seam and press the seam open first, then press both seam allowances toward the section to be top-stitched. Place a row of stitching close to the seam line, stitching on the right side of the garment through both seam allowances.

PLAIN SEAM, DOUBLE TOP-STITCHED. This seam is mainly used for a decorative trim, although it does provide a strong

seam. Stitch a plain seam and press the seam open. Top-stitch on the right side an equal distance on both sides of the seam line.

LAPPED SEAM. This seam is most often used for yokes and applied pieces such as gussets. One section is lapped over the other and top-stitched. Fold under the seam allowance on the section to be lapped and press flat. Place the sections together, right sides up, matching the fold to the seam line accurately and baste in position. Stitch close to the folded edge through all thicknesses.

SINGLE LAPPED SEAM. This seam is used for joining seams in interfacings and interlinings because it gives the least possible bulk. Seam allowances are lapped one over the other, matching seam lines. Stitch on the seam line and trim both seam allowances close to stitching.

TUCKED SEAM. This is a decorative seam finish. The lapped seam is stitched back from the edge to form a tuck.

FLAT-FELL SEAM. This strong, sturdy seam construction is used for sportswear, men's sport shirts, children's clothes and pajamas. Garments which will receive a great deal of stress or must withstand repeated washing will be sturdier if constructed with flat-fell seams. However, avoid using the construction on bulky fabrics; the seam is thick and difficult to construct in a heavy, bulky fabric. Place the pieces to be joined wrong sides together, and stitch a plain seam. Press the seam to one side and trim the lower seam allowance to ⅛ inch. Turn under the raw edge of the other seam allowance and place over the trimmed edge. Stitch close to the folded edge through all thicknesses.

HEMMED-FELL SEAM. This seam is similar to the flat-fell seam and begins with a plain seam on the wrong side. The under layer is trimmed to ⅛ inch and the upper edge is turned under, pinned and slip-stitched by hand, catching only a single thread of fabric. This eliminates machine-stitching on the right side and gives an inconspicuous finished seam on the wrong side.

WELT SEAM. This seam is similar in appearance to the flat-fell seam on the right side. It is also good for heavy fabrics since it gives a smooth, flat finish without the bulk of a flat-fell seam. First stitch a plain seam, press it open, then press the seam allowances toward one side. Trim the underneath seam allowance to ¼ inch and press the other seam allowance over trimmed edge. Stitch close to the raw edge.

DOUBLE WELT SEAM. This seam construction for the double welt seam is the same as for the welt seam. It does give a sturdier seam construction, and gives the same appearance as the flat-fell seam. The only difference between this and the welt seam is an additional row of stitching placed close to the seam line through all thicknesses.

FRENCH SEAM. This is a particularly good seam for sheer fabrics and is used for infants' clothes because it leaves no unfinished seam edges. Place the fabrics, wrong sides together, and stitch a plain seam ⅜ inch from the edge. Trim the seam allowances to ⅛ inch or less. Turn the garment with right sides together and press flat at the seam line. Pin and stitch on the regular ⅝-inch seam line marking. In infants' clothing, this seam construction is often done by hand.

MOCK FRENCH SEAM. This seam is similar in appearance to the French seam and is often used in similar fabrics. It is easier to construct, especially in curved seams, such as those of set-in sleeves. First stitch a plain seam, with right sides of the fabric together. Turn in the raw edges of the seam allowance ¼ inch toward the center seam line. With the folded edges meeting, stitch them together close to the folded edge.

FRENCH SEAM WITH ONE EDGE HEMMED. This seam is used on bodices and areas of a dress made of sheer fabric that requires fitting. Make a plain seam. Trim one edge to ¼ inch. Turn under raw edge of other seam allowance and hem by hand along stitching line.

SLOT SEAM. This is primarily used as a decorative seam because of the tucked effect which results. The pattern may have slot seams as part of the design detail, or you may wish to devise your own, using the slot seam on yokes, side skirt seams, sleeves, pockets. A strip of fabric is placed under the seam. It may be the same fabric or a contrasting color or fabric, and may be cut on the straight of the goods or on the bias. To construct the seam, turn under the seam allowances on the seam line and press flat. Cut a strip of fabric on the desired grain, the length of the entire seam, and appproximately 1½ inches wide. Place a row of basting stitches down the center of the strip. With right

sides up toward you, place the seam line folds so they meet exactly at the center basting line. Baste in position close to the folded edges. Top-stitch through all thicknesses an even distance from each side of the center marking to produce the desired width tuck.

PIPED SEAM. This is a decorative seam often used in neckline seams with a facing and at the waistline. Use a folded bias strip of fabric, ribbon, bias tape or braid. Place it on the right side of one section of the fabric with the fold extending the desired amount beyond the seam line toward the main part of the garment. Baste. Place the other section in position, right sides together, and stitch seam. Press seam allowances to one side.

CORDED SEAM. This is also used as a decorative finish, and is similar to the piped seam. The corded seam has cording inside the bias strip. Encase the cording inside a bias strip, using the zipper-cording foot. (See page 233.) Place the cording on right side of one section of the fabric to be joined, with the stitching on the cording matching the seam line. The cording should face toward the main part of the garment. Baste. Then place the other section in position, right sides together, and stitch, again using the cording foot on the sewing machine. Press seam allowances to one side. If the seam is bulky, grade the seam allowances.

Special Problems

TAPING A SEAM. When a seam must be very sturdy, or when it must be prevented from stretching, the seam is usually taped. This is often necessary with waistline seams and shoulder seams, or when stitching bias seams in loosely woven fabrics. Place a strip of woven seam binding with the center of the binding on the seam line. Stitch in position at the same time you are stitching the seam.

SEAMS IN INTERFACING. Seams in interfacing are lapped, stitched and trimmed to eliminate bulk. See instructions for the Single Lapped Seam on page 130.

STITCHING SEAMS OVER TISSUE. In fabrics such as jersey, sheers, or smooth, slippery fabrics which tend to slip, stretch or pucker, or if the feed dog of the machine mars your fabric, you should stitch through tissue paper. Place a piece of tissue under the fabric, and another on top. After the stitching has been completed, tear the tissue away.

SEAMS WITH INWARD CORNERS. When applying a facing to a square neckline, or at any point where there will be an inward corner in the seam,

stitch to within ½ inch of the point, change the length of the stitch to a short stitch (14 to 16 to the inch) and stitch to the point. Raise the presser bar, pivot, lower presser bar and stitch for ½ inch. Change back to the normal stitch length and continue the seam. Grade the seam allowances and clip diagonally through seam allowance to point.

SEAMS WITH OUTWARD CORNERS. In collars which have outward points, or any part of the garment where two pieces are seamed together to form an outward corner, stitch to within ½ inch of point, shorten stitch to 14 to 16 to the inch and stitch to point. Raise presser bar, pivot, lower presser bar, take two stitches across point, raise presser bar, pivot, stitch for ½ inch, then adjust to normal stitch length. Grade seam allowances; clip diagonally across point close to stitching; clip diagonally on each side of point.

133

Seam Finishes

No garment is complete unless the raw edges of seams are finished. This prevents raveling, and gives the garment a neat appearance on the inside. The type of finish to use will vary according to the fabric and the design of the garment. For example, fabrics which hardly ravel at all can be finished merely by pinking the edges. Those which are very "ravely" and bulky, loosely woven fabrics need a more secure finish. Unlined jackets need a very neat finish since the inside of the jacket is often on display.

PINKED OR SCALLOPED EDGES. For fabrics that are firmly woven and do not ravel, a pinked or scalloped edge is sufficient. Using pinking or skalloping shears, cut along the raw edge. Hold the shears firmly and cut with long even strokes.

EDGE-STITCHED EDGES. To finish a seam for fabrics that ravel slightly, machine-stitch ⅛ inch from the raw edge. To give a more secure finish, machine-stitch ¼ inch from the edge, and then trim ⅛ inch from the edge with pinking or skalloping shears.

ZIGZAGGED EDGES. For fabrics that ravel and need a secure finish, zigzag stitch close to the raw edge, using an automatic machine or a zigzag attachment. The depth and width of the zigzag stitch is determined by the weight and closeness of the weave of the fabric. Use a smaller stitch on firmly woven fabrics and a wider stitch on loosely woven fabrics.

OVERCAST EDGES. A hand finish similar to the zigzag is made by the overcast stitch. Take small, even stitches over the raw edge and be careful not to pull the stitches tight. If the seam has been stitched with both seam allowances to one side, overcast both edges together. A row of machine-stitching close to the raw edge serves as a guide for keeping overcasting stitches even.

TURNED AND STITCHED EDGES. The turned and stitched edge finish is used for non-bulky fabrics. Fold under the raw edges ¼ inch and machine-stitch ⅛ inch from the edge.

BOUND EDGES. For heavy or bulky fabrics, the edges are bound with woven or bias seam binding depending on whether seam is straight or curved. Fold and press the tape so that the under section is $\frac{1}{16}$ inch wider than the upper section. Having the under edge just slightly wider will help insure stitching through both edges of the binding. Place the binding over the edge and machine-stitch close to the edge.

ROLLED EDGES. On sheer fabrics, a trim finish is the rolled edge. Stitch a plain seam, press both seam allowances together and trim to ⅜ inch. Roll both seam allowances together, using your thumb and forefinger, to the line of stitching. Sew over the edge close to the line of stitching with a whipping stitch. Keep stitches evenly spaced and do not pull tight.

CHAPTER 10

CONSTRUCTION DATA

In garment construction you work in three dimensions. You not only join sections, but you shape them to fit the curves of the body. There are various ways that garments are shaped, depending on the amount of curve needed in the garment and the design of the garment. Shaping is formed by curved seams, darts, tucks, pleats and gathers. Then, to help your garments hold their shape, you apply facings, interfacings and linings.

DARTS

Darts are the most frequently used shaping construction. In fact, you'll seldom make a garment that doesn't have some sort of dart shaping in it. Darts are placed on the garment so that the rounded fullness they produce is at the fullest part of a body curve. For example, bust darts should point to the fullest part of the bust; waistline darts in a bodice should also point toward the fullest part of the bust and end about 1½ inches below; hip darts should end just above the fullest part of the hip; elbow darts should point toward tip of the elbow when the arm is bent; shoulder darts should point toward the shoulder blades.

It is best to machine-baste darts in your garment before you stitch them permanently. Since the placement of the darts may vary according to the contours of your individual figure, adjustments may be necessary when fitting the garment.

Darts should always be pressed over a curved press mitt or ham to give the proper curve to the garment. Waistline darts and shoulder darts are pressed toward the center front or center back. Bust and elbow darts are pressed down. When pressing any dart, place the dart over the curved cushion, wrong side up. Press along each side of the stitching, in the direction of the stitching, then press the dart to one side. Reverse the garment and press it on the right side. Be sure your garment will take the direct heat of an iron, if not, use a press cloth. Additional tips on pressing can be found in Chapter 8.

Dart constructions, like seam constructions, vary according to the area they are to shape and the design of the garment. The most frequently used dart constructions are:

Standard Dart

Fold the dart on the fold-line marking, right sides of fabric together, matching stitching line markings accurately. Pin in position, placing pins on the stitching line at right angles to it. Baste, if you wish. Stitch, beginning at the wider edge, to the point taking the last two or three stitches directly on the fold. This is extremely important in order to eliminate a tuck at the point. Fasten thread ends. Press the dart flat to one side.

Double-Pointed Dart

Begin stitching at either point, taking several stitches directly on the fold at both points. Fasten thread ends. Cut several small clips to the line of stitching in the center section of the dart to allow it to spread and lie flat. Press dart flat to one side.

Decorative Dart

When darts are used decoratively they are stitched on the right side of the fabric and, therefore, should be stitched without any thread ends at the point. To do this, the machine must be threaded with the bobbin thread. Remove the spool thread from the needle and thread the needle with the bobbin, going through the eye in a reverse direction from normal threading. Tie the bobbin thread to the spool thread and wind the thread on the spool until sufficient bobbin thread, twice the length of the dart, has been threaded on the upper section on the machine. Mark the dart as for the standard dart but fold with wrong sides of the fabric together. Start stitching exactly at the point and continue to wider edge. Rethread the machine for each dart.

The Dart Tuck

This is often referred to as a "released dart" because fullness is released at the wider end. It is often used in blouses to give shaping at the waistline and fullness at the lower edge. On the wrong side of the fabric, mark the stitching and fold lines and also a short straight line at each end of dart tuck. Fold right sides of fabric together on the center marking, matching stitching lines accurately. Pin or baste in position. Starting at point, take several stitches on the fold and then stitch to wide edge, pivot, stitch straight across the fold edge. Fasten thread ends at both ends and press.

Slash-Gathered Dart

This dart gives added fullness and shaping. Mark on the wrong side of the fabric. Reinforce the point by stitching with a short machine-stitch (14 to 16 stitches to the inch) on the seam line marking, approximately ½ inch each side of point; then slash to point. Place a row of medium-length machine-stitches (9 to 10 stitches to the inch) on the longer or lower side of dart between the markings for ease or gathering. Pull up these stitches until the two edges are the same length. Distribute the fullness evenly. Pin with right

sides together and stitch as for standard dart. Press to one side away from fullness. If it is an eased dart, steam-pressing into fullness will shrink out the fullness at the line of stitching. If it is a gathered dart, press into gathers with point of iron being careful not to flatten gathers. For added reinforcement and decoration, top-stitch through all thicknesses close to seam edge.

TUCKS

Tucks can be used to hold fullness in place or for a decorative effect. If tucks are part of a pattern design, the pattern will indicate the width and spacing between the tucks. If you are designing your own tucking as a decorative part of a design, you'll have to determine the width you want and space them yourself. First decide where the tucks should be placed on the figure, then how wide and how far apart you want them. They can be used in groups or clusters and in graduated widths. Tucks may be made by hand or machine, using the tucker attachment. Tucking the fabric before cutting the garment section may prove easier since you can work with a straight piece of fabric.

To make tucks, use a tracing wheel and dressmaker's carbon or chalk pencil for marking. Tailor's chalk or tacks do not provide as accurate, sharp lines. Make a gauge by cutting a heavy piece of cardboard several inches longer than the width of the tucks. Mark the width of each tuck by cutting a notch in the cardboard; cut another notch the distance between tucks. Crease or press fabric along the fold lines of

the tucks, using the gauge as a guide. Keep the creases on grain. Hand-sew with a fine running stitch if you do not plan to machine-stitch the tucks. Sometimes the fold line of a tuck may be marked by pulling a thread from the fabric.

There are several methods of tucking, depending on the effect desired:

Pin Tucks

Small fine tucks usually found in dainty infants' clothing or sheer blouses. After marking and creasing on a single thread, stitch very close to the fold edge. On sheer, firmly woven fabrics such as organdy, you can pull out a single thread and crease on this line.

Corded Tucks

Give additional decoration to a garment since they have the added dimension of thickness. The width of the tuck is determined by the thickness of the cord used. The tuck must be wide enough to encase the cord securely. Measure and mark for tucks. Place cording on the wrong side of the fabric at center of tuck and form tuck over cord. Sew close to cording with fine running stitches or use the cording foot on the sewing machine.

Shell or Scalloped Tucks

A very decorative tuck made by hand. Mark and crease for a straight tuck. On the line of stitching, mark the position for the shell tucks at even distances. Sew the tuck with small running stitches to the first dot. Take an overhand stitch at the dot and pull the thread tightly. Continue across in this manner.

Cross Tucking

This type of tucking is done on the fabric piece before the garment is cut. Measure, mark and stitch all tucks on the lengthwise grain of the fabric. Press all tucks to the side in one direction. Measure, mark and stitch tucks on the crosswise grain. Press all crosswise tucks in one direction.

Group Tucking with Scalloped Effect

Should be done on the fabric before the garment is cut. Measure, mark and stitch the tucks, placing them close together. Press to one side. Mark the fabric at even intervals in the opposite direction for the crosswise stitching. Stitch across the tucks in the direction they were pressed. Then stitch in the opposite direction, stitching tucks down away from the direction in which they were pressed. Continue stitching, alternating the direction of the tucks in each row. The quilting guide will help to keep the rows of stitching straight and an even distance apart.

Released Tucks

Often used to give shaping to a garment, as well as for decorative effects. Usually they are folded and pinned on the marking lines with the right side of the fabric together. Starting at the bottom of the tuck, stitch to the top. For reinforcement, pivot at the top of the stitching and stitch straight out to the fold line. Backstitch and clip threads.

PLEATS

Pleats form folds in the fabric and give fullness and shape to a garment. Unpressed pleats are those which do not have the pleat crease line pressed in place and are used to create a rather soft effect. Pressed pleats have the crease line firmly pressed in position the entire length of the pleat. This gives the garment a crisp, tailored look. Usually the pattern will indicate the type of pleat to use, but sometimes it may be left to your discretion. Your choice should depend on the effect you wish and the fabric you're using. For example, a soft drapable fabric which does not retain a crease will be best with unpressed pleats, while a very crisp fabric with little drape to it should have the pleats pressed flat in position. If you select pressed pleats, test your fabric to see how well it will hold a crisp, pressed crease line.

Mark the wrong side of the fabric for pleats with pin and chalk pencil method. Draw solid and broken lines as indicated on pattern on the wrong side of the fabric. Pleating from wrong side saves time because you do not have to transfer the pleat markings to right side of fabric with basting.

Match and pin solid line to broken line of each pleat with right sides of fabric together. Place a pin at each end of pleat and at center, then pin every two inches between. Baste from lower edge of pleat to top of skirt along chalk line. Remove pins as you baste. The basting on inside will not mark the fabric when pleats are pressed. Various effects are created by the direction pleats are turned.

Side or Knife Pleats

This type of pleat is the simplest pleat to form. The folded edges either face in one direction around the garment or the direction is reversed only at the center front and center back pleat.

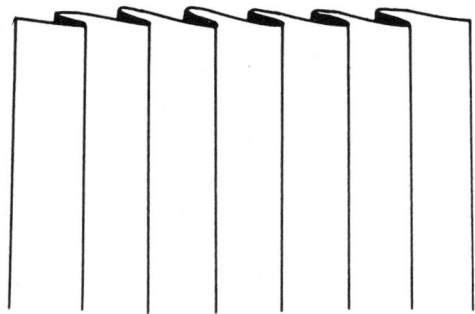

Box Pleats

A box pleat is formed by two side pleats which turn toward each other on the wrong side forming a panel on the right side of the fabric. McCall's patterns will clearly mark in which direction each fold of the pleat is to go. Follow these guide arrows carefully.

Inverted Pleats

A pleat formed by two side pleats which turn toward each other on the right side forming a panel on the wrong side of the fabric.

Unpressed Pleats

Match markings and baste with wrong side of skirt uppermost. Turn each pleat in correct direction and pin fold edge of pleat to skirt at upper edge. Pin at right angles to cut edge. Baste ½ inch from edge.

Pressed Pleats

Press a sharp crease on inside fold line of each pleat on the wrong side of fabric and then turn each pleat in correct direction. Pin fold edge of pleat to skirt at upper edge. Baste ½ inch from edge. Place skirt on ironing board. Press each pleat from right side of fabric to establish crease on outside edge of pleat.

Edge-Stitched Pleats

A special finish used to retain a perfect crease. It is particularly necessary if the pleating is done on the bias grain of a flared skirt. Simply form the pleats as directed. Top-stitch close to the folded edge beginning at the bottom and stitching to the top. Put in the hem before pleats are edge-stitched.

Inside Stitched-Down Pleats

Stitching gives a smooth, flat fit over hipline. Measure down from waistline to fullest part of hip. Mark this position on each pleat on inside of skirt. Baste pleats in place, then stitch from inside of skirt along basting line, from hipline to waistline. Fasten threads securely. Press pleats in desired direction.

Outside Stitched-Down Pleats

This gives a more tailored look than the inside stitching. Baste and press pleats in desired direction. Turn skirt to right side. Measure down from waistline to hipline and mark this point on each pleat on outside of skirt. Top-stitch the pleats close to the fold edge, from hipline to waistline. Fasten threads securely.

Stitched-Down Edge-Stitched Pleats

This is a combination of the stitched-down pleat and the edge-stitched pleat. Baste and press pleat in position. Top-stitch close to fold edge from hem to hipline marking where pleat is to be stitched to skirt. Lift presser foot, pull fabric out slightly and cut bobbin thread only. Rearrange pleat over garment, rewind spool of thread to take up slack and continue stitching along fold edge of pleat up to waistline.

Accordion Pleats

Accordion pleats are tiny pleats made on straight lengthwise grain of fabric. These can only be done successfully by a commercial pleating process. Hem skirt before having pleating done.

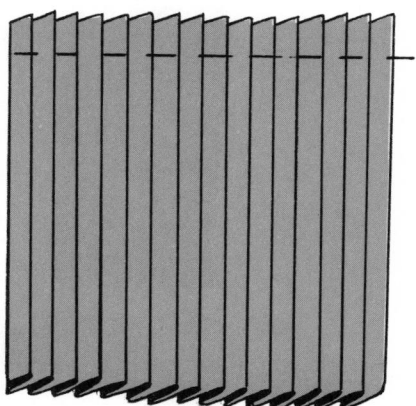

Commercially Pleated Fabric

Pleating can often be purchased in skirt lengths, and is usually priced by the inch. Buy enough to fit over hip (with pleats lying flat) plus seam allowances. Place a row of machine-basting across top of pleats. Pull up bobbin thread, easing it to fit waistline. You may also have your own fabric commercially pleated. Allow three times hip measurement. Join all seams but one, and hem skirt before sending it to be pleated.

Cartridge Pleats

Cartridge pleats are round pleats used for decoration. A large section of fabric is stitched to a smaller section. The undersection is marked into even spaces. The upper section is marked with the same number of spaces but they are wider. Baste and stitch the upper section to the lower section, matching the marking lines exactly. Do not press.

Hemming a Pleat with Seam

After the pleat has been made, turn up the hem and mark position of hem at seam allowance. At that point, clip the seam allowance to the line of stitching. Press seam allowance open in hem. Turn up and hem skirt. Press pleat in position.

Inverted Pleat with Underlay in a Seam

Stitch seam to marking for pleat and machine-baste below marking. Press the seam open. Pin underlay in position, right sides together, matching edges and seam lines. Stitch the side seams of the skirt and underlay. Press flat. Baste underlay to garment along top seam line. Stitch through all thicknesses. Remove basting. Hem using the method for hemming a pleat with seam.

Inset with Inverted Pleat

Stay-stitch on seam line of opening for inset. Clip to the seam line at each point. Turn the seam allowance to inside, using stay-stitching as guide. Baste close to

the edge. Fold and baste the pleat in the inset piece. Place in position on garment matching edges and seam line accurately. Baste in position through all thicknesses. Turn garment to right side and top-stitch close to the edge. Press. Remove bastings.

GODETS

Godets are flared or pleated inserts used for decorative effect or to give added width to the bottom of a skirt.

Inserting a Godet

Stay-stitch along the seam edges of the godet piece. Reinforce the opening of the garment by stitching on the seam line where the inset is to be joined, taking one stitch across the point. Use a regular machine-stitch for your fabric and matching thread. Slash through the center of the opening as far as the stitched point. Pin the godet inset to the opening, right sides together, matching the seam lines accurately. The seam allowances on the opening taper from a normal seam allowance width at the bottom edge to almost nothing at the point. Baste together along the seam line. Stitch the seam taking only one stitch across the point. Press the seam allowances to one side toward the main part of the garment.

Inserting a Godet with Top-Stitching

Stay-stitch the godet inset section and reinforce the opening as described above. Turn under the seam allowance of the opening along the seam line, using the reinforcement stitching as a guide. Baste close to the edge and press flat. Pin the godet section in position, right sides up, matching the seam lines of the inset to the folded seam line edge of the garment. Baste the inset in position close to the folded edge. Top-stitch in position through the garment and seam allowances close to the folded edge. Remove the bastings. Press.

GATHERING AND SHIRRING

Gathering and shirring are perhaps the most popular methods of controlling fullness in a garment. Gathering is one or two rows of stitching drawn up to form very tiny pleats in the fabric. Shirring is three or more rows of gathers.

When either gathering or shirring, it is important that the fullness be distributed evenly throughout the entire area. When pressing, press with the tip of the iron directly into the fullness. Pressing on top will flatten the fullness and spoil the effect.

By Machine

Gathering or shirring by machine is the easiest and quickest method. Adjust the machine to the longest stitch and loosen the top tension slightly if bobbin thread does not pull easily. Place a row of machine-stitching on the seam line for gathering with another line close to it. For shirring, place several rows of stitching under each other about ⅛ inch apart. Pull the top threads through to the wrong side of the fabric and anchor the threads at one end securely around a pin. Distribute the fullness evenly by pulling bobbin thread from the other end.

By Hand

You can gather or shirr by hand, if you prefer. To gather, fasten the thread securely with several tiny back-stitches. Sew on the gathering line with small evenly spaced running stitches. Pull up the thread and distribute the fullness until the section measures the desired length.

Shirring by hand is done the same way, except there are several rows of stitches. Be sure stitches are placed directly under one another. After all rows have been stitched, the threads are drawn up at the same time until the section measures the desired length. Anchor the threads around a pin at each end of the stitching and distribute the fullness evenly.

On a Large Area

When large sections are to be gathered or shirred, as in a full gathered skirt, divide the section to be gathered into quarters or eighths and mark each with a pin or small clip marking. If the sections will later be attached to a smaller section such as a bodice, also divide the bodice into quarters or eighths. Place two rows of machine-stitches along the top of the section

to be gathered, about ¼ inch apart. Use the longest stitch on the machine and loosened tension. Break the stitching at the end of each quarter or eighth section, leaving long thread ends. Pin the section to be gathered to the smaller section, matching the quarter or eighth markings on each. Pull up threads until the two sections measure the same. Fasten threads securely by winding them around a pin. Distribute fullness within each section evenly. If you use heavy-duty thread for the bobbin thread, the construction will be easier because the thread will not break so readily.

With Machine Attachments

The ruffler attachment is also capable of gathering large sections of fabric. Test it on a scrap of fabric; adjust the length of the stitch and tension until you obtain the desired amount of fullness. The longer the stitch, the greater the fullness; the shorter the stitch, the less fullness.

For shirring large sections, you may wish to use the gathering foot. This distributes fullness evenly and locks it in position as it stitches.

With a Stay

Staying the shirring acts as a reinforcement to hold the fullness permanently in position. Cut a piece of sheer fabric, on the lengthwise grain, the length and width of shirred area plus ⅜-inch seam allowance on all sides. Turn under the seam allowances and press. Pin the reinforcement strip to the wrong side of the fabric over the shirred area. Hem in position with a tiny stitch. Instead of cutting a strip of fabric for a stay, you may use woven seam binding. This construction is used for waistline stays in many garments with gathered or pleated skirts.

With Elastic Thread

Elastic thread is often used for gathered effects, and can be used on the machine. Wind elastic thread on the bobbin by hand. Be sure not to stretch the elastic. Use regular thread as the upper thread. Test on a scrap of your fabric, adjusting the length of stitch and tension until you obtain the desired fullness.

With Cording

Shirring can be made with cording, and the cording used as a drawstring type closing. Cut a strip of fabric the length of the fabric to be gathered and the width of the cording plus ¼-inch seam allowances on all edges. Turn under the seam allowances and press. Place the strip of fabric on the wrong side of the material in the proper position. Stitch one edge of the strip close to the fold edge. Run the cording between the strip and fabric. Stitch close to the cording, using the cording foot. Draw up the cord, pushing the fabric back on the cord for the desired length. Distribute the fullness evenly along the cord.

Gauging

Gauging is another decorative method of handling fullness. It is done by hand. Fasten thread with tiny back-stitches and taking long stitches on the right side of the fabric and short stitches on the wrong side, place several rows of stitching underneath each other in identical patterns—long stitches under long, short under short. Draw up the fullness and folds will form. Distribute the fullness evenly.

FACINGS

Facings are used to provide neat finishes to raw edges in a garment and to support the shape of necklines, armholes, front closings, cuffs, collars, etc. They may be cut in one piece with the garment section or applied separately.

Usually a facing piece is cut on the same grain as the edge it is to finish. For example, if the facing is used to finish and support a front closing which is on the lengthwise grain, the facing should also be cut on the lengthwise grain of the fabric. On a curved edge such as a rounded neckline, the facing should be cut on the same curved grain as the neckline edge of the garment section.

Remember, when cutting facings, if you altered the garment section to which the facing is attached, you'll have to alter the facing, too, in exactly the same manner.

There are several types of facings, each requiring slightly different methods of construction. The type of facing needed will either be indicated by a separate pattern piece or the pattern piece will indicate the cut line of the facing, if it is cut in one with the garment section. If a garment piece such as a collar is to be faced, you often use the same pattern piece for collar and facing. This will also be indicated on the pattern piece.

Below are listed the most commonly used facings with more detailed instructions for construction than you usually find in pattern instructions.

Facing Cut in One with the Garment Piece

This is found when the edge to be faced is a straight edge. Some coat and jacket patterns are made this way, since a heavy fabric is often used. This type of facing eliminates bulky seams at the front edges of the garment. The facing is simply folded back on the fold line indicated on the pattern and the fold line pressed.

Fitted or Shaped Neck Facing

All neck edges should be interfaced to give body and prevent stretching. Use facing pattern to cut interfacing if no interfacing pattern is given. Baste interfacing to wrong side of bodice front and back. Stitch shoulder seams. Trim interfacing close to stitching. Press seams open.

To construct facing, pin the right sides of the facing pieces together at shoulder seams, matching notches and edges. Stitch and press seams open.

Select a method of finishing the lower edge of the facing that is suitable for the fabric and that will give a flat finish. Pink fabrics that do not ravel or ravel only slightly. For the pinked finish, first edge-stitch ¼ inch from the outer edge, then pink ⅛ inch from the edge.

Zigzag or overcast ravely fabrics. For this finish, first edge-stitch ⅛ inch from the outer edge, then machine-zigzag or hand-overcast the edge. The edges of non-bulky fabrics may be turned and stitched. For the turned and stitched edge, machine stitch ¼ inch from the outer edge. Turn the fabric to the wrong side along the row of machine stitching and crease. Stitch close to the folded edge. Press the finished edge of the facing.

Pin facing to neck edge, right sides together. Match notches, seams and edges. Stitch facing to neck edge on seamline, removing pins as you stitch. Grade this seam to reduce bulk. Clip the curved edge at ½ inch intervals to the line of stitching. Press the seam toward the facing, using a steam iron or dry iron and damp press cloth. Press over a tailor's ham. Next understitch the facing to prevent it from rolling to the outside.

Turn facing to inside and baste ½ inch from neck edge. Press facing from the inside over a tailor's ham. Catch-stitch facing to carefully matched shoulders seams. Prick stitch facing to interfacing along the row of machine stitching at the lower edge. Trim the interfacing even with the finished edge of the facing. Press the finished facing from the outside. Remove basting.

Fitted or Shaped Armhole Facing

The fitted armhole facing is applied in the same manner as the fitted neck facing, only the area being faced differs. The sleeveless armhole area should be interfaced before applying the facing. Refer to directions given for the fitted neck facing. Begin and end understitching at underarm seam. Catch-stitch facing to both shoulder and underarm seams.

One-Piece Neck and Armhole Facing

Since this type of facing is usually used on a sleeveless garment with a scooped or open neckline, it is important that an interfacing be used to prevent stretching and gapping. Pin and baste interfacing to wrong side of bodice front and bodice back at neck, shoulder, armhole and underarm edges.

Pin bodice front to bodice back at shoulder and underarm seams, right sides of fabric together. Stitch shoulder and underarm seams. Trim interfacing close to line of stitching. Press seams open.

To make facing, pin front and back facing pieces at shoulder and underarm seams, right sides together. Stitch and press seams open. Finish the lower edge of facing by one of the methods discussed under "Shaped or Fitted Neck Facing."

To attach facing to neck edge, pin facing to neck edge, right sides together. Match notches, center markings and seams. Begin at shoulder seam and stitch facing to neck edge. Grade seams. Clip curved seam at ½ inch intervals to line of stitching. Press seam toward facing and understitch. Turn facing to inside of garment and baste close to neck edge. Press facing flat over tailor's ham.

To attach facing to armhole edges, pin facing to bodice along armhole edges with wrong sides together, seams matched. Facing edge will extend beyond bodice armhole. Trim facing to match bodice so that edges are exactly even and facing fits perfectly flat. Remove pins from armhole edges and bastings from neck edge. Place garment in front of you with wrong side upper-

most. Turn the underarm area of the facing to the right side of the bodice and match underarm seams, right sides together. Working from underarm to shoulder seam, on bodice back, match notches and pin back facing to back armhole. Roll the facing back and pull the seam to the outside as you pin. Baste with even stitches ½ inch from edge. Begin machine stitching at underarm seam and continue to shoulder seam. Grade seams and clip curved edges at ½ inch intervals. Press seam toward facing.

Repeat procedure for front section. Pin, baste and stitch front facing from underarm to shoulder seam at front armhole. Grade seams and clip curve of front armhole at ½ inch intervals. Press seam toward facing.

Understitch the facing at back armhole seam, starting at underarm seam and stitching to shoulder seam. Repeat procedure for front. Overlap stitching at both ends of seam to secure threads.

Catch-stitch facing to underarm seam allowances. After facing has been applied to other armhole, attach facing to interfacing with prick stitch along lower edge of facing on row of machine stitching. Trim interfacing even with finished facing. Remove basting threads and press.

To simplify this procedure when there is a center back opening, the side seams and center back seams may be left open so the facing may be applied to the garment while it is still flat. Stitch facing at neck and armhole edges. Turn by pulling the back sections through shoulder openings. After facing has been applied, join bodice at the side seams. Pull facing out at underarm so that right sides of facing are together. Pin, baste and stitch from waist to outer edge of facing. Press seam open. Turn facing to inside of bodice and catch-stitch to underarm seam. Stitch center back seam.

For methods of finishing facing at placket, refer to section on zipper application.

Facing Slashed V-Neckline

Stitch along each side of slash marking and across point. Stitch facing shoulder seams, right sides together. Press seams open and trim allowance. Finish outer edge of facing appropriately. Pin the facing to the garment, right sides together along the slash line markings. Stitch neckline seam and along each side of slash line marking. Taper stitching at slash line; taper from ¼ inch at neck to point, take one stitch across point and taper other side. Grade seam allowances, then slash along marking to stitching at point. Clip curved neck edge at ½ inch intervals. Turn facing to inside, press and understitch. Baste close to folded edge, press and sew facing to shoulder seam allowances with catch-stitches.

Decorative Facings

These facings are finished on the outside of the garment for decorative detailing. Stay-stitch neck edges of bodice and stay-stitch inner and outer edges of facing. Stitch shoulder seams of facing, press seams open, and trim seam allowances. On the garment, the shoulder seams must be reversed under facing to keep the raw edges of seam allowances from showing. Mark position for edge of facing on garment and make a second mark, ½ inch from this, toward neckline. Pin bodice shoulder seams, right sides together, and stitch from armscye to second marking. Fasten thread ends.

Clip seam allowance to stitching. Press seams open. Turn bodice to right side and stitch remainder of shoulder seams. Press seams open. Pin and stitch facing to neck edge, right side of facing to wrong side of garment. Grade and clip seam allowances. Turn facing to right side. Baste close to fold and press. Turn under seam allowance on facing edge, using stay-stitching as a guide, and baste in position. Stitch in position by hand with slip-stitch or top-stitch by machine close to the edge.

Bias-Strip Facing

Stay-stitch edge of garment to be faced. Cut strip of true bias fabric (see page 229) the desired width plus seam allowances and desired length. Baste strip to garment edge, right sides together, beginning at a seam. Ease bias on inward curves and stretch on outward curves so it will lie flat at inner edge. Stitch the bias together at seam line where bias began and ended. Press seam open. Grade seam allowances and clip at curves. Turn facing to inside and baste close to fold edge. Turn under raw edge and hem to garment.

Bias-Strip Facing on V-Neckline

Follow same procedure as for Bias-Strip Facing above. However, begin and end strip at point of V, allowing sufficient fabric to join the bias in a seam at the point.

Facing with Seam Binding

If the edge to be faced is straight, woven seam binding can be used. Stitch the seam binding, right side up, to the raw edge beginning at a seam. Turn under on seamline, press and hem seam binding to the garment.

Mitering a Corner

There are two methods of folding a miter, depending upon the seam finish.

MITERED CORNER WITH SEAM FINISHED ON RIGHT SIDE. At the point, fold the fabric with a straight crease from the point even with the edge, and the fabric folded back on itself. Then fold a diagonal crease line from the point to

inner edge of facing. Slip-stitch the miter fold together along the diagonal fold.

MITERED CORNER WITH SEAM FINISHED ON WRONG SIDE. At the point, fold the fabric with a diagonal crease from the point so that the grainlines are at right angles. Then form a straight crease from the point even with the edge. Stitch the facing together along the diagonal crease line. Trim ¼ inch from the seamline and press the seam open.

Facing an Outward Corner

Cut a continuous facing strip on the straight grain of fabric. Pin facing to the garment, right sides together, as far as the corner point. Fold and finish miter as described under "folding mitered corner with seam finished on the wrong side." Continue pinning facing to the garment. Stitch the seam and grade seam allowances, cut seam allowance diagonally across the point. Turn facing to inside and baste close to the fold edge. Turn under raw edge and hem to garment.

Facing an Inward Corner

Pin facing to the garment as far as the corner point. Fold the facing in a diagonal crease from the point and then fold a straight crease even with the edge of the facing. Stitch facings together along the diagonal crease marking. Trim to ¼ inch from stitching line and press seam open. Continue applying facing on other side of corner.

HEMS

A hem is a finish for a raw edge. It may be made in various widths, depending on its placement. In garment construction, it is usually the final step.

Hem in Garment

After finishing all other detailing, allow the garment to hang for at least twenty-four hours before attempting to mark the hem. By letting it hang, the weight of the fabric will cause bias edges to stretch into their normal position, and will prevent unsightly, uneven hems.

MARKING HEM. It is far easier and more accurate to have someone mark the hem for you. Be sure to wear the undergarments and shoes you will wear with the garment. Pin up the front portion of the garment first to find the length which is most flattering for your own figure, within the limits of current fashion. Stand in your normal posture while the person marking the hem moves around you. A chalk marker, pin marker, or yardstick may be used. Make pin or chalk markings approximately every three inches around the entire skirt, keeping measuring tool straight and an even distance from the figure for each marking.

To mark a hem yourself, you can use a chalk marker. This is not as accurate as pin marking, but it is much better than trying to turn up the hem by eye or measuring from the top down. Place the marker on the floor and then move slowly around it trying not to twist or pull the garment out of line as you turn. Be

sure to try the chalk on a scrap of the fabric first. Chalk leaves marks on some fabrics that will not come off even with dry-cleaning.

Once the hem has been marked, remove the garment carefully so markings are not distorted. Turn the hem to the inside along the markings and pin in position close to the hemline edge. Baste ½ inch from the fold edge, removing the pins as you baste. Press the hem lightly in position. Measure the hem allowance using a ruler or hem gauge, an even distance from the lower edge, approximately 2 to 3 inches for a straight skirt and 1 to 2 inches for a full bias skirt. Trim the hem allowance evenly along marking. Pin the hem in position matching seam lines first, and placing pins at right angles to the edge.

EASING HEM FULLNESS. When the hem has been turned up, the edge is often fuller than the skirt at the point where it is to be sewn. In order to make the hemline edge even, this fullness should be distributed evenly. Fold back the hem allowance and stitch (approximately 10 stitches to the inch) close to the raw edge from seam to seam. Pin the hem in position at each seam. Draw up the bobbin thread until the hem edge fits the skirt smoothly. Distribute the fullness evenly, then steam-press the hem to shrink out fullness. Press with the grain of the fabric from folded hemline edge up, never across the hem as this will stretch the fabric. Inserting heavy brown paper between the hem and skirt will keep from making an imprint of hem edge on the right side of the skirt.

Types of Hems

The hem finish to use on a garment depends upon the fabric and the style of the garment. Analyze the weight of the fabric. Test its raveling quality. Become familiar with the types of hems normally used for specific styles.

STITCHED AND TURNED HEM. Use on light-weight, firmly woven fabrics that are not bulky and do not ravel easily. After trimming the hem to an even width, turn under the edge ¼ inch. Stitch along folded edge, leaving just enough width to slip a needle through the fold when hemming the skirt. Baste upper edge of hem to garment. Use hemming stitch or slip-stitch to hold hem in place.

HEM FINISHED WITH SEAM BINDING. Used for fabrics that ravel. After trimming hem evenly, put a row of stitching along edge. Draw up thread the necessary amount and distribute ease. Stitch seam binding to raw edge. Use woven seam binding on a straight skirt and bias seam binding on a flared skirt. Be sure not to put the binding on too tightly or it will pull and make the hem show on the right side. Slip-stitch hem to garment.

TAILOR'S HEM. Used on bulky and heavy fabrics that do not ravel. After trimming the hem to an even width, stitch ¼ inch from the edge. Pin the hem in the garment at the seams and pull up bobbin thread to ease out any fullness. Shrink out any fullness and pink the upper edge. Baste hem in place ½ inch from the upper edge. Fold upper edge back and sew hem to garment with invisible stitching being careful not to pull the stitches too tight. When the hem is pressed down, the stitches lie between the hem and the garment and are completely invisible. This hem shows less than any other on the right side of the garment.

DRESSMAKER'S HEM. Similar to the tailor's hem but can be used on almost any type of fabric except sheers or a garment that is to be machine laundered. After trimming hem to an even width, stitch along edge. Draw up the bobbin thread and shrink out the fullness. Hand overcast or zigzag the raw edge if the fabric ravels. If the fabric does not ravel, pink the edge. Baste and sew in position with invisible stitching same as the tailor's hem.

CATCH-STITCHED HEM. Used on wool fabrics or velvet when no seam binding is used. This stitch protects the raw edge and holds the hem more firmly than the tailor's hem. However, the more firmly stitched hem may press through to the right side of the garment and show a ridge at the upper edge of the hem. The heavier the fabric, the more it will show. After trimming the hem to an even width, shrink out any fullness at the upper edge so that the hem lies flat, and baste in place. Working from left to right attach the hem to the garment with a catch-stitch. See page 125 for detailed description of stitch.

NARROW MACHINE-STITCHED HEM. Used on blouses and men's shirts. Stitch ⅛ inch from raw edge to serve as a stay and guide. Turn under the

raw edge on line of stitching and then turn under again the same width. Baste and stitch in place. This type of hem may be made with a narrow hemming machine attachment which double-folds and stitches the hem at the same time. Follow the instructions provided with the attachment.

NARROW HAND-SEWN HEM. Used on blouses and on sheer or fine fabrics. Turn under the edge ⅛ inch and stitch close to the edge. Turn under the fold edge the same width and baste. Slip-stitch hem edge to garment.

HAND-ROLLED HEM. A fine hand-finished hem used on sheer fabric, scarves, sashes, lingerie, etc. Machine-stitch ⅛ inch from edge. Trim close to stitching. Roll fabric between the thumb and forefinger of the left hand, several inches at a time, and then hem in position with a hemming stitch or slipstitch or a fine whipping stitch. Do not baste.

QUICK HAND-ROLLED HEM. With this method the hem is rolled by pulling up stitches placed at the upper and lower edges of the hem instead of rolling it between the thumb and forefinger. Machine-stitch ⅛ inch from edge and trim close to stitching. Turn edge just beyond the stitching. Insert the needle in the turned edge and take a ⅛-inch stitch along the fold of hem. Pick up a single thread of the garment fabric directly below this stitch. Carry the needle over the fabric for ⅛ inch and pick up another single thread of the garment. Take another stitch directly above in the fold of the hem. Continue taking several stitches in hem and garment and then pull up the stitches. The hem will roll into place and the stitches will be encased in the hem. Note that the stitches must be perpendicular to the edge of the hem and not slanting.

NAPERY HEM. This is used for hemming table linens. Napkins have a ⅛-inch hem and tablecloths about a ½-inch hem. Turn under the raw edge ⅛ inch and then make a second turn. Baste in place and press flat. Fold the hem back against the right side of the fabric at the upper edge of the hem. With a fine needle, overhand the hem to the fabric, taking the stitches close together. See page 126 for instructions for the overhand stitch.

HEM STIFFENED WITH WIDE HORSE-HAIR BRAID. Measure and trim hem off evenly, allowing a ¼-inch hem allowance at the edge of skirt. Pin two-inch-wide horsehair braid to the lower edge of the skirt, right sides up, overlapping ¼ inch. Stitch braid in position. Turn hem to inside along edge of braid, placing pins at right angles to edge. Then pin top edge of braid at seams. Draw up the thread on the top edge until horsehair fits smoothly and distribute ease evenly. Pin and baste edge. Attach edge with hemming stitch.

HORSEHAIR BRAID FINISH FOR LACE SKIRT. Measure and trim hem evenly, allowing a ⅝-inch hem allowance at edge. Turn under hem allowance and baste close to fold edge. Pin narrow horsehair braid along hem edge on inside of skirt. Baste through center of braid. Stitch along each edge of braid through hem allowance and skirt. Remove bastings. Trim off hem edge of lace close to edge of braid.

FACED HEM. The faced-hem finish is used when the skirt is not long enough for a normal hem allowance or when you want to lengthen a skirt that is too short. Cut a strip of true bias fabric the desired width and length plus seam allowances. Or you can buy a commercial facing especially for this purpose. Measure an even hem on the garment allowing at least ½ inch. Pin bias fabric to edge of hem, right sides together and join ends with plain seam. Press seam open. Stitch facing to hem. Turn facing and edge of hem to inside using width of seam allowance for turning line. Baste along fold edge. Pin hem facing to skirt at seams. Ease fullness if necessary and baste in position. Sew hem facing to skirt with hemming stitch or slip-stitch.

Hems with Special Finishing Details

HEM WITH SEAMED PLEAT. After trimming the hem to an even width, clip the seam allowances at the top of pleat to the seamline. Trim the seam allowances in hem section to ⅜ inch. Press the seam open inside hem. Finish hemming the skirt. Press pleat in position.

HEM WITH FACED OPENING. This finish is used at the bottom of jackets, coats and vents. Hem the lower edge before finishing facing edge. Turn the hem up and finish edge. Stitch hem in position the entire length at the lower edge of facing. If the fabric is bulky, trim facing and the hem allowance inside of facing to ½ inch. Sew the remaining hem in position. Turn facing to inside. Baste close to edge. Slip-stitch lower folded edges together and catch-stitch inner edge of facing to hem using very small stitches.

HEM WITH STITCHED MITERED COR-NER. This finish is sometimes used on dresses but more often on aprons or home furnishing items. Turn the hem allowances to the right side of the garment along marked hemlines. Fold the miter diagonally from edge point to inner point where edges of hem meet. Stitch hems together along diagonal fold. Trim ¼ to ½ inch from line of stitching. Press seam open forming diagonal fold at the point. Turn hem to inside. Turn under raw edges of hems and sew to garment with hemming stitch or slip-stitch.

HEM WITH HAND-FINISHED MI-TERED CORNER. Fold hems to wrong side along hemline. Fold miter at corner from outer point diagonally to edges of hems. Place fabric flat and trim off corner diagonally ¼ inch from miter fold line and point. Turn under edge ¼ inch on diagonal line and ¼ inch on raw hem edges. Turn hems to inside again. Baste edges of miter in position. Stitch edges of miter together with tiny whipping stitch. Slip-stitch hem to garment.

UNDERLININGS

The many uses of underlining are listed in Chapter 3 under "Shaping Materials." Briefly, underlining will help retain the shape of a garment, add to its life expectancy, create fashion effects and provide greater crease resistance.

It is often better to underline dresses, skirts and slacks rather than use a lining. The construction is easier, and the underlining provides a firmer foundation for the garment. For help in selecting the right underlinings for your garment, see page 39.

Directions for Underlining

Underlining fabric is cut from the same pattern pieces as the garment sections it will back, and should be cut on the same grain as the garment pieces. Cut the underlining so that the right side of the underlining fabric will show on the inside of the garment.

PREPARING. Trim the underlining along the hemline markings to eliminate bulk at the hem. Transfer the pattern markings to the underlining fabric only, not the garment sections. Pin the two sections together matching notches, seam lines and any construction details. Baste the two pieces together, stitching directionally with the grain. Machine-baste through the center of darts, tucks and pleats. This will eliminate shifting of the two sections during construction.

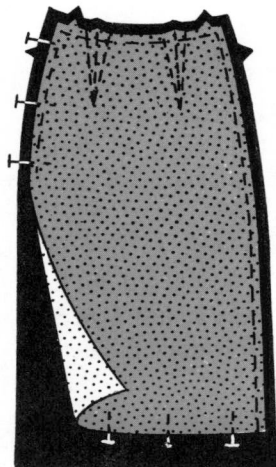

MAKING UNDERLINED GARMENT. Assemble the garment, treating the two layers as one fabric. Turn the garment hem allowance over the underlining, and attach hem to underlining only. After the garment is completed, remove the construction bastings.

The bodice front and back are underlined in garments, but the sleeve underlining is sometimes omitted for a set-in sleeve. In bulky fabrics, the armscye seam will be too thick if underlining is used.

LININGS

If you wish the inside of your garments to look as nice as the outside, you may wish to line the entire garment instead of using underlining. Sometimes a skirt section is lined to control stretching.

Linings are also cut from the same pattern pieces as the garment for skirts, dresses and slacks. However, jacket and coat linings are cut slightly different from the garment itself. See Chapter 14 on tailoring for details in cutting a jacket or coat lining.

Again, as for underlinings, cut the lining fabric so that the right side of the lining will show on the inside of the garment. Transfer the pattern markings to both the lining and the garment fabric, since the lining and garment are constructed separately. Follow the sewing instructions given for the garment when constructing

the lining. Pin the lining to the inside of the garment, wrong sides together, matching construction details. Join the lining to the garment along at least one major seam. In skirts and slacks, the lining is basted to the waistline of the garment before the waistband is applied. The seam allowance on the lining is turned under along the placket opening and slip-stitched to the zipper tape. Slack linings are attached at the hemline the same as the lower edge of a jacket. (See Chapter 14 on tailoring.) Skirt linings are hemmed separately from the garment and are made slightly shorter than the skirt.

If the entire dress is lined, the bodice and sleeve lining can be attached by hand in the same way as for a jacket (see Chapter 14 on tailoring) or the sleeve lining can be machine-stitched to the bodice lining. If the latter method is used, tack the lining to the inside of the bodice at the underarm and shoulder seams with a long loose stitch. When a dress bodice is lined, the neck facing is applied last to give a clean finish to the neckline. Baste the finished lining to the bodice at the neckline and then apply the facing.

The sleeve lining is slip-stitched over the hem of the sleeve. Turn in the seam allowances and slip-stitch bodice lining over the waistline seam and zipper tape to give a clean finish. If the lower edge of the bodice is gathered, then it is best to baste the lining and bodice together at the lower edge. Treating it as one fabric, stitch the waistline seam.

INTERFACINGS

Interfacings are used to give added body to an edge or a construction detail. Instructions for applying interfacings are included with the instructions for the various sections where interfacings are used. See Collars, Cuffs, Waistbands and Tailoring sections.

INTERLININGS

Interlinings are used to provide additional warmth in a garment and are usually found only in coats. We have included instructions for constructing interlining in the section on tailoring in Chapter 14.

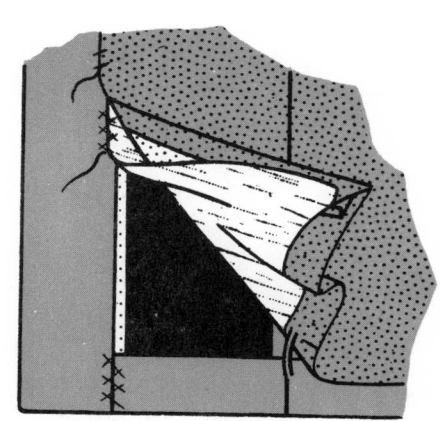

DESIGN DETAILS—SLEEVES AND CUFFS, COLLARS AND POCKETS

Working with the smaller design details can be frustrating but interesting. The pieces are usually smaller, the seaming more difficult to handle, and the work must be done with a great deal of precision. However, if you have mastered the basic techniques of sewing, don't hesitate to tackle a set-in sleeve, a French cuff or any style of collar. These details are often what give your garment its individuality.

SLEEVES

A smoothly fitted sleeve is one of the marks of an expert seamstress. A sleeve with unsightly gathers and puckers or one which twists because proper grain lines were not maintained is the sign of the inexperienced and careless.

There are two basic types of sleeves—the set-in or mounted sleeve and the sleeve cut in one with the bodice or unmounted sleeve. The one-piece sleeve, the two-piece sleeve and the puffed sleeve are set into a normal armhole. The shirt sleeve, the dolman sleeve and the raglan sleeve are variations of the set-in sleeve but fit into a deeper or an irregularly shaped armhole. The kimono sleeve is cut in one with the bodice. It can be made without a gusset or with a one- or a two-piece gusset.

All set-in sleeves are cut with a sleeve cap that is larger than the armhole section into which it must fit. This extra fulless or "ease" is necessary for the sleeve to fit over the arm and hang correctly. The home-sewer must learn to distribute this fullness evenly across the sleeve cap so that it is eased and not gathered. On a McCall pattern special markings make this task easy to do.

One-Piece Set-In Sleeve

PREPARING SLEEVE CAP AND MAKING SLEEVE. Stitch around top of sleeve on the seam line. Use a regulation machine-stitch from underarm to first notch, change to machine-basting stitch between notches and then back to regulation stitch from notch to underarm seam. Stitch the darts or ease in elbow fullness, then stitch sleeve seam.

With wash-and-wear and some cottons it is difficult to shrink and ease in fullness. When using a set-in sleeve on such fabrics, mark the ⅝-inch seam allowance around top of sleeve on the wrong side of fabric with white pencil or carbon. Stitch with regulation and machine-basting as outlined above, but place stitching ⅛ inch inside seam-line marking around front and back curve of sleeve cap between notches and center of sleeve cap, tapering from original seam line at notches and back to original seam line at center of sleeve cap. This reduces the ease but does not change the length of the sleeve cap.

INSERTING SLEEVE IN GARMENT. Pin sleeve into armscye, matching underarm seams, notches and center point of sleeve to shoulder seam. Starting at center of sleeve, pull up bobbin thread until sleeve cap fits armscye. This gives a more even distribution of fullness and avoids ends of thread wrapped around pins. Pin and baste sleeve firmly in place. Shrink out

the fullness in the sleeve cap by pressing the sleeve and armhole seams together from the sleeve side. This shrinks the sleeve cap to the exact size and shape of the armscye. If you take the sleeve out of the armhole and try to shrink out the fullness, there is nothing to stay the shape of the armhole and the fullness may shift with the result that there is too much fullness shrunk out of one-half of the sleeve cap and not enough out of the other half.

Stitch the sleeve into the armhole with the sleeve uppermost on the machine. The seam allowance is turned toward the sleeve at the top and left turned up at the underarm.

FINISHING LOWER EDGE OF SLEEVE.

The elbow darts or fullness can be measured and adjusted before the garment is cut but the sleeve length should be determined after the sleeve is stitched in the armhole. Never hem the lower edge of a sleeve first, any more than you would hem a skirt before attaching it to waistband or bodice. Turn up the lower edge of the sleeve on the finish line indicated on the pattern and baste in place. Try the garment on and look at yourself in a full-length mirror. If the sleeve is not a becoming length, adjust it to suit the proportions of your figure. After correct length has been determined, finish the lower edge with a hem or cuff, depending on the design of the garment.

Two-Piece Set-In Sleeve

This sleeve is found mostly in suits and coats. Both sections of the sleeve are shaped to produce a fitted sleeve. The parts should be joined with a plain seam and pressed. After the sleeve is made it is sewed into the armhole in the same way as the one-piece sleeve, and the lower edge finished in an appropriate manner.

Puffed Sleeve

Stitch the underarm seam and finish hem edge of the sleeve. Place two rows of machine-basting between markings on sleeve cap. Place one row on the seam line and the other ⅛ inch into the seam allowance. Pin sleeve into the armscye, right sides together, matching seams, notches and markings. Draw up the bobbin threads evenly until the sleeve fits the armscye smoothly, and distribute the gathers evenly. Holding the sleeve toward you, baste the sleeve in place. Then stitch. Press the seam at the top of the puffed sleeve away from the gathers and toward the neckline. Press only to the seam line to keep from flattening the gathers.

Shirt Sleeve

The construction of this type of sleeve is quite different from that of the regular set-in sleeve. The cap of a shirt sleeve is more shallow and has much less fullness. A flat-fell seam is used instead of a plain one.

First join the shoulder seams or yoke of the shirt and finish the seams as instructed on the pattern, but do not sew side seams. Pin the sleeve into the armscye, wrong sides together, matching notches and markings and keeping seam lines even at underarm. Ease in the fullness across the cap of the sleeve. There will not be enough fullness to require a gathering thread. Press the seam open and then toward the sleeve. Trim sleeve seam allowance to ⅛ inch. Turn under the raw edge of the shirt seam allowance ¼ inch and stitch it over the trimmed seam allowance. Pin underarm seam of shirt and sleeve, wrong sides together. Make flat-fell seam. Finish lower edge of sleeve with a cuff or hem as directed on the pattern.

Dolman Sleeve

This sleeve is attached to the bodice before the underarm is stitched because of the deep armhole. There will be very little ease in the cap of the sleeve. Pin the sleeve into the armhole, right sides together, matching notches, markings and keeping seam lines even at underarm. Ease in fullness of sleeve cap so that it fits smoothly. Baste and stitch the sleeve in place. Press the seam open, clipping curve at intervals so that the seam will lie flat. Pin underarm seam of bodice and sleeve, right sides together. Stitch the seam and press it open. Finish lower edge of sleeve as directed on the pattern.

Kimono Sleeve without a Gusset

This is the easiest sleeve, so if you are a beginner, look for styles with this sort of sleeve if it is flattering to your figure.

Join the bodice front and back at the shoulder with a plain seam. Press this curved seam open over a tailor's ham to retain the curve. Join bodice front to back at the underarm seam, right sides together, matching notches. Stitch seam and clip curve at intervals. Press seam open. This seam will need reinforcement under the arm, since it will be subject to a great deal of stress in normal body movement. Reinforce it by basting a piece of woven seam binding about 1½ inches long to the inside of the bodice along the curve of the underarm seam. Turn bodice right side out. Stitch ⅛ inch from the seam, through bodice, seam allowance and seam binding, along both sides and ends. Or if you do not wish the stitching to show on the right side, baste the seam binding to the seam line on the inside and stitch it only to the seam allowance on both sides of the seam.

Raglan Sleeve

Stitch the shoulder dart of the sleeve and press the dart open. Pin sleeve to bodice front and back, right sides together, matching notches and edges. The sleeve section will require easing when it is joined to the bodice but not enough to require a gathering thread. Stitch the seam and clip curve at intervals. Press seam open. Pin the underarm seam of bodice and sleeve, and stitch in a continuous seam. Press seam open. Finish lower edge of sleeve as directed on the pattern.

Kimono Sleeve with a One-Piece Gusset

The gusset construction is a rather difficult one but the fit of the sleeve is so much better that you should learn how to make it. On the pattern there will be a slash marking at the curve of the underarm. Mark this on the wrong side of the garment section. Cut strips of fabric to face this slash, approximately 2 inches wide and 1 inch longer than the marking. Pin and baste facing strip along slash marking, right sides together. Stitch, beginning at edge ⅛ inch from slash marking and taper to the point. Take one extra stitch across point and stitch down other side. Slash on marking to stitching at point. Turn facing to inside

and press flat. Pin and stitch underarm seams of bodice and sleeve, matching notches and faced edges accurately. Press seam open. Turn bodice to right side. Pin and baste gusset inside opening, right sides up. Lap faced edges of opening to seam line of gusset. Stitch gusset in position by top-stitching close to faced edge of opening.

Kimono Sleeve with a Two-Piece Gusset

Cut facing strips. Face slash markings in the same way as for the one-piece gusset. Pin and baste front and back gusset pieces to bodice front and back. Place faced edges of bodice over each gusset piece, right sides up, lapping the faced edges to seam line. Top-stitch close to edge. Turn bodice to wrong side. Pin underarm seam, matching notches, seam lines for gusset sections and edges accurately. Stitch underarm seam of bodice and sleeve in a continuous seam. Press seam open.

Kimono Sleeve without a Gusset Pattern

If you select a pattern with a kimono sleeve and it does not have a gusset, you may want to add one to give you more ease. Simply mark a diagonal slash line 4 inches long at the highest point of the underarm curve of bodice front and back. Cut two facing strips 2 inches wide and 1 inch longer than the slash marking and a 5¼ inch square on the straight grain of your garment fabric. Follow the instructions given for inserting a one-piece gusset.

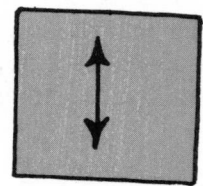

CUFFS

Sleeves are often given interest by the use of cuffs. There are many different types, each one creating a definite fashion effect. They may be straight or shaped, closed or open, applied or cut in one with the sleeve.

Turnback cuffs may be applied as separate pieces or are sometimes cut in one with the sleeve and faced. Applied cuffs are either straight or shaped and can be closed or open at the ends. The straight cuff has a fold at the upper edge and fits close to the sleeve. The shaped cuff has a seam at the upper edge and can be curved so that it will flare away from the sleeve. The cuff cut in one with the sleeve can be made with or without an opening. When an opening is used, it may be in the seam.

Cuffs are often interfaced to give them body and firmness. For a straight cuff, cut the interfacing half the width of the cuff or to the fold line; for a shaped cuff, use cuff pattern; for a cuff cut in one with the sleeve, the sleeve facing piece.

Cuffs are applied with a bias facing, a shaped facing or a self-finish.

Straight Cuff Closed at Ends

Join the seam edges of the interfacing with a lapped seam. Stitch seam of cuff and press it open. Baste the interfacing to the inside of cuff with one edge along fold line. Slip-stitch to fold line. Fold cuff, wrong sides together, and baste one inch from open edge to hold sections of cuff together until it has been attached to the sleeve.

Straight Cuff with Open Ends

Baste the interfacing to the inside of cuff with one edge along fold line. Slip-stitch interfacing to fold line. Fold cuff, right sides together, and stitch ends. Trim interfacing close to stitching and grade the seams so that the widest seam is on the edge without the interfacing. This keeps seam edges from pressing through

to the right side of cuff. Turn cuff to right side and press thoroughly while it is flat. Slip-stitch the open ends of the cuff together for ¾ inch up from the open edge. Baste layers of fabric together, one inch from the open edge.

Shaped Cuff Closed at Ends

Join the ends of the interfacing with a lapped seam. Stitch end seams of each cuff section and press open.

Baste the interfacing to the inside of the under-cuff section. Stitch the under-cuff section to the top cuff section at the unnotched edge, right sides together and seams matched. Trim interfacing close to stitching and

grade seam allowances. Turn cuff to right side and baste seamed edge rolling seam slightly to the inside, Baste cuff one inch from open edge.

Shaped Cuff with Open Ends

Baste the interfacing to the under section of the cuff. Place right sides of cuff sections together and stitch at unnotched edges. Grade the seams and turn cuff to right side. Baste close to edge, rolling seam slightly

to the inside. Slip-stitch the open ends of the cuff together for ¾ inch up from the open edge. Baste cuff 1 inch from the open edge.

Cuff Applied with Bias Facing

Roll the lower edge of cuff slightly toward the side with the interfacing to get the amount of ease necessary to allow the cuff to turn back, and baste the cut edges together. Note that the cut edges will not be even. Baste the cuff to the right side of the sleeve. Cut a strip of bias fabric the length of the lower edge of the sleeve plus a seam allowance. Place the bias on top of

cuff, right sides together, and baste. Join ends with a plain seam. Stitch around the lower edge of sleeve through all thicknesses of fabric. Grade seam allowances and press seam toward sleeve. Turn under free edge of bias and hem to inside of sleeve. Turn cuff to right side of sleeve.

Cuff Applied with Shaped Facing

Roll the lower edge of cuff toward the side with the interfacing and baste cut edges same as above. Baste the cuff to the right side of the sleeve. Join facing, right sides together, with a plain seam, and press seam open. Finish unnotched edge of facing with edge-stitching or a finish suitable for fabric. Put facing over sleeve and cuff, right sides together, and baste. Stitch around the lower edge of sleeve through all thicknesses of fabric. Grade the seam allowances and press seam toward sleeve. Turn facing to inside of sleeve and press flat. Hem free edge of facing to sleeve. Turn cuff to right side of sleeve.

one-inch basting line to keep it free from stitching line. Baste the right side of top cuff section and the interfacing to the inside of the sleeve and stitch the seam. Grade the seam allowance and press the seam

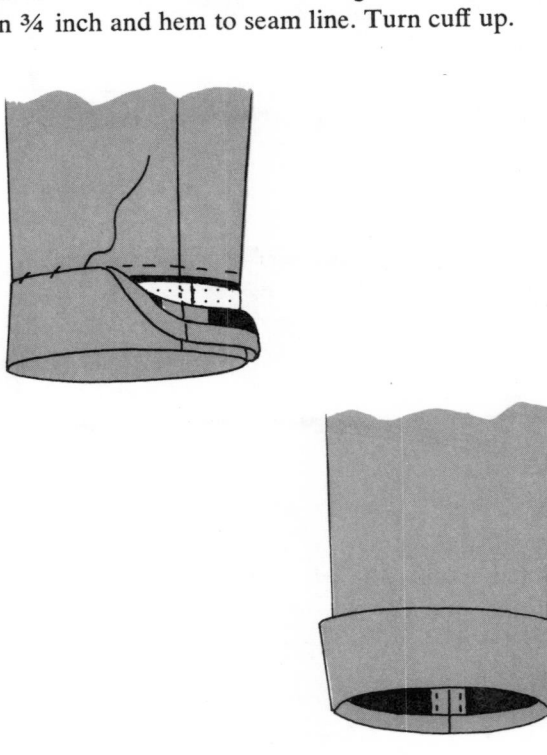

toward the cuff. Turn under free edges of under-cuff section ¾ inch and hem to seam line. Turn cuff up.

Cuff Applied with Self-Finish

Edge-stitch the sleeve seam several inches up from the lower edge. Turn back the under-cuff section at the

Sleeve and Cuff Cut in One with No Opening

Trim off ¾ inch from the unnotched edge of the interfacing. Join the interfacing with a lapped seam. Baste the interfacing to the inside of the lower edge of the sleeve and attach the unnotched edge to the sleeve with invisible stitching. Stitch facing seam and press it

open. Edge-stitch the unnotched edge of the facing. Baste and stitch the facing to the lower edge of the sleeve, right sides together. Trim interfacing close to stitching and grade the seam allowances. Turn facing

to inside and baste the edge, rolling the facing seam slightly to the outside. Turn the cuff up and pin it in place. Turn the sleeve to the wrong side and slip-stitch top facing edge to the sleeve.

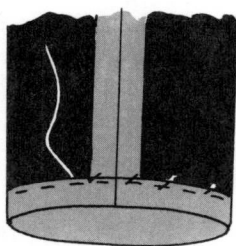

Sleeve and Cuff Cut in One with a Slash Opening

Follow the same procedure as for the cuff cut in one with no opening. Stitch the facing to the lower edge of the sleeve, right sides together, taking an extra stitch at point of slash to insure a sharp corner when turned. Slash opening, trim interfacing close to stitching and grade seam allowances. Turn facing to inside and finish same as facing with no opening.

Sleeve and Cuff Cut in One with Opening at Seam

Trim off ¾ inch from the unnotched edge of the interfacing. Baste the interfacing to the lower edge of the sleeve and attach the unnotched edge to the sleeve with invisible stitching. Stitch sleeve seam, leaving open below marking. Clip to marking and trim interfacing close to stitching. Press seam open. Stitch the

facing seam above the marking, clip to marking and press seam open. Edge-stitch the unnotched edge of facing. Baste and stitch the facing to the lower edge of sleeve, being careful to match notches and markings at the clip. Trim interfacing close to stitching and grade seams. Turn facing to inside and finish same as facing with no opening.

Roll-up Sleeve

The true roll-up sleeve has the underarm seam finished with a flat-fell seam and must be made of fabric with no right and wrong side. The lower edge of this straight shirt sleeve is finished in a narrow hem and then the sleeve is turned up twice to give the appearance of a cuff. If the fabric has a right and wrong side, you must cut the sleeve long enough to make a very deep hem. This makes it possible to turn up the lower edge of the sleeve without the wrong side of the fabric showing. Edge-stitch the lower edge of the sleeve. Turn the deep hem to the inside and slip-stitch in place, then roll up the sleeve.

Sleeves with Plackets

The full sleeve is finished with a band or shirt cuff which extends down from the lower edge of the sleeve instead of turning back. The French cuff is a double-width shirt cuff folded back and fastened with cuff links.

The interfacing for the band cuff is cut half the width of the cuff to the fold line. The shirt cuff and French cuff interfacing are cut from the cuff pattern. Plackets are part of the cuff construction in these instances, so instructions are included for their application also.

Sleeve with Faced Opening

Apply the facing to opening before stitching underarm seam of sleeve. Turn under and edge-stitch the side and upper edges of the facing piece. Pin and baste facing to lower edge of sleeve, right sides together, with center of facing along slash marking for opening. Stitch along both sides of marking, starting ¼ inch from edge and tapering to point. Take an extra stitch across point to insure a sharp corner when turned. Double-stitch at point and slash between stitching to point. Turn facing to inside and tack corners of facing to sleeve.

Sleeve with Continuous Lap Placket

Apply placket before stitching underarm seam of sleeve. Reinforce slash marking with a row of stay-stitching, starting ¼ inch from edge and tapering to point. Slash on marking to point of stitching. Cut a lengthwise strip of fabric twice the length of the slash and 2 inches wide. Open the slash and spread until line of stitching is straight. Pin fabric strip to opening, right sides together. Stitch ¼ inch from edge, tapering to end of slash. Press seam away from sleeve. Turn

under the free edge of strip and hem it to the seam line. Turn placket to inside along front edge, baste at lower edge and lap over back placket.

Sleeve with Faced Lap Placket

Apply placket before stitching underarm seam of sleeve. Cut a facing 3½ inches wide and an inch longer than the placket. Turn in the long edges ¼ inch and press. Pin center of facing to slash marking, right sides together. Stitch along both sides of marking, starting ¼ inch from edge and tapering to point. Take one extra stitch across point. Slash between stitching to point. Turn facing to inside and press seam away from sleeve. Hem the turned-in edges over the seam.

Stitch upper edges together. Turn in front lap at seam and baste at lower edge.

Band Cuff

The band cuff can be used with any one of the above placket finishes. Stitch the sleeve seam and press it open. Make two rows of machine-gathering at lower

edge of sleeve. Baste interfacing to inside of cuff at notched edge with one edge at fold line. Slip-stitch interfacing along fold line. Fold cuff and stitch ends. Trim interfacing close to stitching and grade seams.

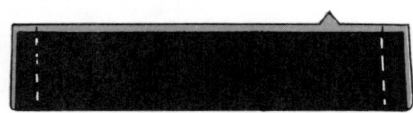

Turn cuff to right side and press. Pull up gathering stitches on sleeve edge to fit cuff. Pin notched edge of cuff to sleeve, right sides together, and adjust gathers evenly. Stitch and grade seam. Press seam toward the cuff. On the inside, turn under the free edge and hem over seam. Finish cuff with button and buttonhole. (See Chapter 12.)

Shirt Sleeve Placket

Make placket before stitching underarm seam of sleeve. Reinforce slash marking with a row of stay-stitching same as continuous lap placket. Slash to point of stitching. Stay-stitch edges of overlap and underlap. Turn under seam allowances on outer edges using stay-stitching as a guide. Pin underlap to inside of back edge of opening and overlap to inside of front edge of opening. Match stay-stitching line of opening to seam lines of overlap and underlap, and stitch

seams. Press seams toward facings. Turn underlap to right side and stitch turned-in edge over seam. Turn overlap to right side and crease at fold line. Baste turned-in edge over seam. Lap placket and baste together at upper edge. Starting at lower edge of sleeve stitch turned-in edge over seam, around point and across top of placket, catching the top edge of the underlap. Join sleeve seam with a flat-fell seam. Gather and pleat lower edge of sleeve to fit cuff.

Shirt Cuff

Baste interfacing to cuff facing. Trim away interfacing seam allowance at upper edge. Stitch cuff to cuff facing, right sides together, leaving upper edge open. Trim interfacing close to stitching and grade seam allowances. Turn to right side and press. Baste and stitch cuff facing to inside of lower edge of sleeve, adjusting gathers evenly. Press seam toward cuff facing. Turn under free edge of cuff and top-stitch over seam on right side. Continue top-stitching around entire cuff. Close cuff with button and buttonhole. (See Chapter 12.)

French Cuff

The French cuff is made the same as the shirt cuff. Before applying the cuff to the sleeve edge turn underlap of placket to the inside and baste at lower edge. Apply the French cuff to the lower edge of sleeve same as the shirt cuff. Make buttonholes in both edges of cuff. (See Chapter 12.) Fold the finished cuff in half and fasten with cuff links or linked buttons.

Long Tight Sleeve

The long tight sleeve usually has no cuff and the placket opening is closed with snaps, loops and buttons or a zipper. The lower edge of the sleeve is finished with seam binding or a narrow self-facing.

SLEEVE WITH SNAP CLOSING. Cut two strips of woven seam binding one inch longer than opening. Turn under upper edge of one piece of seam binding and stitch to seam allowance of front edge of opening ⅛ inch from seam line, right sides up. Turn seam allowance to inside along seam line and press. Hem edge of seam binding to sleeve. Turn under upper edge of other piece of seam binding and stitch to seam allowance at back edge of opening ⅛ inch from edge, right sides up. Clip to seam at top of seam binding of back seam allowance. Turn seam binding back along inside edge and press flat. Hem edge to inside of seam allowance. Cut a strip of seam binding ¾ inch longer than lower edge of sleeve. Turn under ⅜ inch on each end of binding and stitch seam binding to right side of lower edge of sleeve. Turn seam binding to inside and press flat. Hem edge to sleeve, mitering at corners. Overlap edges of opening to seam line. Sew snaps along opening.

SLEEVE WITH THREAD LOOP AND BUTTON CLOSING.

Finish opening and lower edge of sleeve as described above for snap closing. Work thread loops along front edge of opening. (See page 223.) Overlap opening to seam line and mark position for buttons on back edge of sleeve through center of each loop. Sew buttons at markings.

SLEEVE WITH FABRIC LOOP AND BUTTON CLOSING.

Make fabric tubing or cording and cut in lengths to fit over buttons. (See page 223.) Baste loops to front edge of opening along seam

line on right side. Cut a bias strip of fabric 1⅜ inches wide and long enough to face both sides of the opening and the lower edge of the sleeve plus seam allowances. Turn under ends of strip. Baste to front edge of opening over loops, right sides together, around lower edge of sleeve and along back edge of opening. Miter at corners and stitch. Trim seam allowances and turn facing to inside. Turn under edges of facing and hem

to sleeve. Overlap opening to seam line and mark position for buttons along back edge through center of loops. Sew buttons at markings.

SLEEVE WITH ZIPPER CLOSING. Insert zipper by the slot-seam method given on page 197. To

finish the lower edge of the sleeve, cut a strip of woven seam binding ¾ inch longer than the measurement of the sleeve and turn under ⅜ inch on each end. Baste and stitch seam binding to right side of lower edge of sleeve. Turn seam binding to inside and press flat. Hem edge to sleeve, mitering at corners.

SLEEVE WITH VENT CLOSING. Normally vent sleeve closings do not unbutton. Sometimes a bound or worked buttonhole is made for decorative purposes but the buttonhole is never cut through on the facing side. Stitch the sleeve seams leaving extension edge open below marking. Clip seam allowances

to marking at top of extension of undersleeve. Press seams open. Turn up lower edge of sleeve at hemline and baste. Attach hem to sleeve with invisible stitch-

ing. Turn under extension of upper sleeve along seam fold line and press. Catch-stitch edge to hem allowance. Lap upper sleeve extension over undersleeve,

matching edge markings for opening. Catch-stitch in place along hem allowance and baste permanently to undersleeve extension above hem. Turn sleeve to right side and sew buttons in position on upper sleeve through all thicknesses.

COLLARS

The collar is about the most important part of any garment, and must fit well. Although there is a variety of collar designs and shapes, construction-wise they all fit into one of three groups—round, pointed, or collar and undercollar cut in one.

All collars except the detachable ones are normally interfaced to give them needed body and shaping. The type of interfacing to select will depend upon the design of the collar and the fabric used. For help in selecting the proper interfacing, consult Chapter 3 on shaping materials.

Flat collars, or those which have only a slight roll, normally have the upper and undercollar cut from the same pattern piece. The interfacing is also cut from this piece and on the same grain as the collar sections. When interfacing small flat collars in a smooth, light- or medium-weight fabric, you may wish to try iron-on interfacing. This is placed face down on the wrong side of the collar and pressed in position until it is bonded to the fabric. This eliminates the need to stitch interfacing to the collar, but is not really successful for use on coarse, heavy fabrics or for tailored garments.

Collars which have a decided roll need two separate pattern pieces—one for the top and one for the undercollar. The undercollar is slightly smaller than the top section, to allow the top collar to roll properly. The interfacing is cut from the undercollar piece.

When the top and undercollar are cut in one piece, to be folded in half to form the collar, the interfacing is cut only half the width of the collar pattern piece or to the fold line.

If you are using sheer fabric, cut the interfacing from the top collar pattern piece and baste the interfacing to the top collar section. This prevents the seam from showing through the sheer collar when it is finished.

In some patterns, especially suits and coats, there is a separate pattern piece for the interfacing. This interfacing is cut on the bias with a seam at the center back so that both sides of the collar are cut on the same grain and will roll the same. This type of collar is discussed in detail in the chapter on tailoring.

Round Collar

Baste interfacing to wrong side of undercollar. Stitch two sections of collar, right sides together, leaving neck edge open. Trim interfacing close to stitching and grade seam allowances so that the widest seam is on the edge without the interfacing. This will keep the seam edges from pressing through to the right side. Clip small notches to seam line in outward curve. Press seam open, using the tip of the iron. Turn collar to right side. Understitch the seam allowance to the undercollar section. Press collar flat and baste around the outer edge.

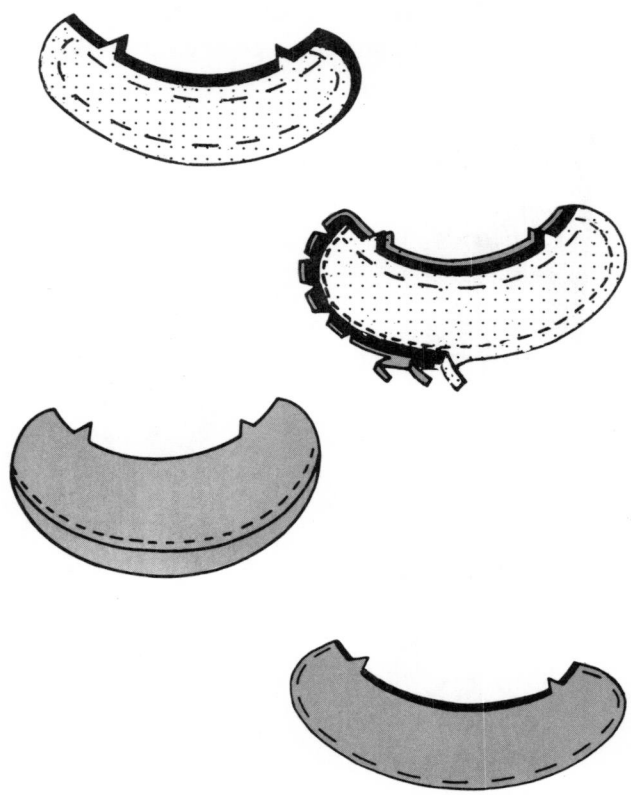

Pointed Collar

Baste interfacing to wrong side of undercollar. Stitch two sections of collar, right sides together, leaving neck edge open. Start at neck edge, stitch to point, take one diagonal stitch at point and continue stitching. Grade seam allowances same as for round collar. Cut diagonally across points. Press seam open. If you have a point presser, slip collar over board to press seam

open. Turn collar to right side and pull out the corners, using fine needle. Understitch the seam allowance to undercollar, stitching as far into the points as possible. Press collar flat and baste around the outer edge.

Collar and Undercollar Cut in One

Baste interfacing to wrong side of undercollar with one edge on fold line. Slip-stitch interfacing to collar on fold line. Fold collar in half, right sides together, and stitch side edges. Trim interfacing and grade seam allowances same as for round collar, trim diagonally across points at fold edge. Turn to right side, pull out corners and press. Baste around outer edges.

It is best to attach the collar as soon as possible so that neckline does not become stretched while working on the garment. Collars are applied with a bias facing, a back and front facing, or without a back facing. There are special instructions for applying the collar when the facing has a slash opening, fits on a V neckline, or if collar is two-piece. All of these methods are described in detail below.

Collar Applied with a Bias Facing

Pin and baste collar to neck edge of bodice, right sides

up, matching notches, centers and markings. Finish outside edge of facing in manner appropriate for the

fabric. Turn facing to outside at fold line and baste at neck edge. The facing will overlap the ends of the collar. Cut a bias strip ½ inch wide and baste to neck edge over collar, lapping bias about ½ inch over facings. Stitch entire neck edge. Grade seam allowances and clip curve at intervals. Turn facings to inside.

Press seam allowances toward bodice. Turn in free edge of bias facing and hem to bodice.

Collar Applied with Front and Back Facing

Pin and baste collar to neck edge of bodice, right sides up, matching notches, centers and markings. Join back and front facings, right sides together, with a plain seam. Press seams open. Finish outer edge of

Collar Applied without a Back Facing

Finish shoulder and outer edge of facing in manner appropriate for the fabric. Pin and baste collar in position, right sides up, from front edge to shoulder seam, match notches and markings. Clip top collar seam allowance at shoulder seam. Pin the undercollar only to the back bodice neck edge between the shoulder seams, leaving the top collar free. Baste in position. Stitch the entire neck edge as basted, leaving the top collar free across the back. Grade seam allow-

facing in manner appropriate for the fabric. Pin neck edge of facing to neck edge of bodice, matching notches and centers. Stitch entire neck edge. Grade seam allowances and clip curve at intervals. Press seam allowance toward facing and understitch to facing. Turn facing to inside and press. Tack facing at shoulder seams of bodice.

ances and clip curve at intervals. Turn facing to inside and press, pressing back neck seam allowance up toward collar and front seam allowance down. Turn under seam allowance of top collar and slip-stitch to back seam line. Slip-stitch shoulder edge of front facing to shoulder seam allowance of bodice.

Collar Applied to a V-Neckline without Center Front Seam

Reinforce point of neckline with a row of stitching along seam line. Slash seam allowance at point to stitching. Baste collar to right side of neck edge, matching notches, centers and markings. The ends of the collar must meet at the exact center front. Note that when the seam line at the front edge of the collar is matched to the center front of the bodice, the ends of the collar seam allowance extend over the seam line on the other side of the V neckline. The slash at the point of the V makes it possible to separate the V enough to attach the collar without catching the end of the collar in the seam line. Stitch front and back

facings at shoulder seams and press seams open. Finish outer edge of facing in a manner suitable for the fabric. Reinforce the point of the neckline with a row of stitching and clip to stitching line. Baste facing over collar, right sides together, matching notches and centers, and keeping ends of collar free. Stitch entire neck seam and grade seam allowance. Press seam toward facing. Understitch facing to seam allowance. Turn facing to inside and tack facing at shoulder seams.

Collar Applied to a V-Neckline with a Center Front Seam

Stitch center front seam of bodice to seam line marking at neck edge. Clip to seam line at end of stitching. Stitch bodice back to bodice front at shoulder seams. Press seams open. Baste collar to right side of neck edge, matching notches, centers and markings. The ends of the collar seam allowance extend over the seam line on the other side of the V neckline, the same as in the V-neckline without center front seam. The open seam above the clip at the point of the V makes it possible to separate the V enough to attach the collar without catching the ends of the collar in the seam line. Stitch center front seam of facing to seam-line marking at neck edge. Clip to seam line at end of stitching. Stitch front and back facings at shoulder seams and press seams open. Finish outer edge of facing in a manner suitable for the fabric. Baste facing over collar, right sides together, matching notches and centers, and keeping ends of collar free. Stitch entire neck seam and grade seam allowances. Turn facing to inside and press seam toward facing. Understitch facing to seam allowance. Tack facing at all seams.

Collar Applied with a Slash Opening

Pin and baste collar to neck edge of bodice, right sides up, matching notches, centers and markings. Place the front seam line edge of the collar at the stitching line for the slash opening. The ends of the collar seam may overlap at neck edge, depending on the width of the slash opening at the top, but this will not interfere with stitching the seam. Stitch back fac-

ing to front facing at shoulder seams. Press seams open. Finish outer edge of facing in a manner appropriate for the fabric. Baste facing in place, right sides together, matching notches, seams and slash markings. Stitch entire neck edge and along both sides of slash markings, tapering at point. Take an extra stitch at point. Slash opening to stitching, grade seam allowances and clip curve at intervals. Press seam toward facing. Understitch facing to seam allowance, stitching as far into corners as possible. Turn facing to inside and press. Tack facing to shoulder seams.

Applying a Two-Piece Collar

Construct same as a one-piece collar. Tack ends together at seam line at center front, to hold in place while collar is being attached. Note that ends of collar overlap above seam line. Baste collar to neck edge, right sides up, matching notches, centers and markings. This kind of collar can be attached with a bias facing or a back and front facing, depending on the pattern and the design.

This general information can be applied to these specific types of collars:

Peter Pan Collar

This is a round flat collar, and can be one- or two-piece. It is attached to the neck edge with a bias or fitted facing.

Convertible Collar

Any collar that can be worn open or closed at the neck. It can have a seam at the outer edge, or can be cut all in one with a fold at the outer edge. It can be attached to the neck edge with or without a back facing. The back facing is used when the neckline stands away from the neck.

Sailor Collar

This is a wide, square collar in back, and comes to a V in front. It can be applied to a V-neckline with or without a center front seam.

Shirt Collar

Construct collar section same as pointed collar. Top-stitch around outside edges of collar ¼ inch from

edge. Cut interfacing for collar band from collar band pattern. Baste interfacing to inside of undercollar band section. Turn in lower edge of outer collar band section at seam line and baste. Trim seam allowance to ¼ inch. Baste one section of collar band on each side of collar, right sides together, matching notches and markings. Stitch seam continuing to ends of collar band. Grade seam allowances and clip curve at in-

tervals. Turn collar band down and press. Stitch interfaced section of collar band to inside neck edge of shirt. Grade and clip seam allowance, and press seam toward collar band. Baste turned-in edge of collar band over seam and top-stitch, continuing to stitch around collar band close to edges.

Shawl Collar

Mark seam allowance on wrong side of fabric where neck and shoulder seams meet on bodice back. Use a chalk or pencil and mark several inches on either side

of point. Stitch center back seam of collar, right sides together, and press seam open. Lap and stitch center back seam of interfacing, and trim close to stitching. Baste interfacing to inside of bodice front and collar. Reinforce corner at neck and shoulder on bodice front with a row of machine-stitching on seam line through interfacing. Slash a stitching line at corner. Pin front

and back together at neck and shoulder seams, match centers and reinforced corners to marked point on bodice back. Trim interfacing close to stitching and grade neckline seam. Clip curve at intervals and press seam toward collar. Press shoulder seams open. Stitch

ing in a manner suitable for the fabric. Stitch collar and facing to bodice, matching centers and notches. Grade seams and trim interfacing close to stitching. Clip curve at intervals and turn facing to inside. Baste outer edges, rolling seam slightly to the underside on collar and to the inside on front edge. Press. Baste and slip-stitch over back neck seam line. Slip-stitch shoulder edge of facing to shoulder seam allowance of bodice.

center back seam of collar and facing. Press seam open. Reinforce corner at neck and shoulder with a row of machine stitching on seam line. Slash to point of stitching. Turn under neck and shoulder edge of facing at seam line and baste. Finish outer edge of fac-

Tie Collar

A narrow straight collar that stands up from the neck edge and ties at center front. It is used on a round neck with a lapped front closing. Finish the edge of the front facing in a manner suitable for the fabric. Turn the facing to the right side and stitch neck edge from fold to center front or marking for end of collar. Clip neck seam at end of stitching and trim seam allowance. Turn facing to inside and baste facing to neck edge beyond clip. Baste interfacing to inside of tie

collar with one edge on fold line. Slip-stitch interfacing to collar at fold line. Interface the full length of the collar and tie section for a tailored bow. For a soft bow, omit interfacing in the tie section. Interface collar section to center front marking. Baste interfacing edge of tie collar to neck edge, right sides together, matching center backs, notches and markings. Stitch neck edge between clips. Fold ends in half lengthwise with right sides together and stitch along edge and across ends. Trim interfacing close to stitching and grade seams. Turn to right side. Turn under free edge of tie collar between clips and slip-stitch to neck edge.

Band Collar

A narrow straight collar that stands up from the neck edge same as the tie collar, but stops at the center front and has no tie ends. When the collar fits close to the neck it is applied the same as the tie collar. If the band collar is used on an open neckline, it is applied with a front and back facing.

Turtle-Neck Collar

A wide true bias band that stands up from the neck edge and then rolls back over the neckline seam. If the collar is stretched as it is applied to the neckline, the collar will roll higher and fit close to the neck. If the collar is eased as it is applied to the neckline, it will roll less and stand away from the neck. Baste interfacing to inside of collar with one edge along fold line. Slip-stitch interfacing to fold line. Fold collar lengthwise, right sides together and stitch ends. Trim interfacing close to stitching and grade seams; turn and press. Baste interfaced edge of collar to right side of neck edge, matching centers and notches. Stitch seam. Clip curve at intervals. Press seam toward the collar. Turn under free edge of collar and hem over neckline seam.

Detachable Collar

The detachable collar is never interfaced. Stitch two sections of collar together, leaving neck edge open. Trim seams, clip curve at intervals and turn to right side. Press and baste outer edge. Use commercial cotton bias tape or cut a bias binding 1 inch wide and stitch to neck edge of collar in a narrow seam. Turn in the ends and free edge of binding and hem along seam line. Collar can be basted to neck edge, or attached with snap fasteners.

Top Collar Applied to Attached Collar

This would be used when applying a velvet collar to a coat or suit. Turn under all seam allowances of the top collar and baste. Baste top collar over the attached collar matching neck edges and centers. Slip-stitch all edges of top collar in place.

POCKETS

Pockets are functional and often decorative as well. There are three types—the patch pocket which is stitched to the surface of the garment, the set-in pocket for which a special opening is made in the garment, and the pocket set into a seam in the garment. Follow the directions on your Easy Sewing Guide sheet for specific directions as to when the pocket should be applied and for any special construction details for that pattern design.

Transfer the pattern markings for the exact placement of the pocket to the wrong side of the fabric. Pin-mark the pocket location and try on the garment to be sure that this is the correct and most flattering placement for your figure.

Patch Pockets

For pockets that are to be applied to the right side of the garment, baste-mark the location of the pocket on the right side of the garment.

If a patch pocket is applied in a fabric that should be matched, such as printed, checked, or plaid fabric, be sure to cut the pocket so it will match the fabric design on the garment exactly at the place the pocket is to be applied.

UNLINED PATCH POCKETS. Turn under the raw edge ¼ inch at the top of the pocket. Edge-stitch close to the folded edge. Turn down the top of the pocket on the right side along the fold-line marking. Beginning at hem fold, stitch around three sides of pocket along the seamline. Fasten thread ends at the tops of pocket. Trim the seam allowance from ¼ to ⅜ inch and clip points diagonally at top corners. For square-corner and pointed pockets, cut diagonally across the corners in order to miter the seam allowances. For rounded pockets, cut small notches in the seam allowance on curved edge. Turn the top hem allowance to the wrong side. Press in position. Turn under the seam allowances along the line of stitching.

On square-corner and pointed pockets, fold miters in the seam allowances at the corner points. Press seam allowances flat. Baste around the pocket close to the edge. If you wish the hem allowance to be top-stitched in position, turn pocket to wrong side and stitch close to the folded hem edge. Fasten thread ends by tying them on the wrong side of pocket. Pin the pocket, right side up, to the right side of the garment, matching corners of pocket to markings accurately. Baste in position. Top-stitch pocket in position close to edge, starting at upper edge of pocket. The top corners may be reinforced by stitching a tiny triangle of fabric at the corner on wrong side. Fasten thread ends securely. Remove bastings and press. If the pocket is to be used mainly for decoration and you do not wish the stitching to show, slip-stitch the pocket in position with tiny, fine stitches.

LINED PATCH POCKET. Stitch the right side of the lining to the right side of the pocket at the upper edge, leaving an opening at the center of the seam. Press seam toward lining. Fold pocket at seam line, right sides together. Baste and stitch lining to pocket around outer edges. Grade seam allowances and turn pocket to right side through opening. Baste close to edges rolling seam slightly toward the lining. Slip-stitch the opening and press pocket flat. Pin and baste the pocket to the right side of garment matching edges of pockets to markings accurately. Top-stitch or slip-stitch in position in the same manner as for unlined patch pocket.

lining. Press flap. Pin and baste right side of flap to right side of garment about ¾ inch above pocket or at markings. Stitch in place and fasten ends of thread securely. Trim seam allowance of flap section to ⅛ inch. Turn in edge of lining section and ends diagonally so they do not show when flap is pressed down. Stitch turned-in edges of lining and press flap down.

PATCH POCKET WITH FLAP. Construct and apply pocket same as lined patch pocket. Stitch lining to flap, right sides together, leaving upper edge open. Grade seam allowance and turn to right side. Baste close to edges, rolling seam slightly toward the

Set-In Pockets

The set-in pocket is made by cutting an opening in the garment, and the construction is similar to that of a bound buttonhole. There are three types of set-in pockets—welt, flap and bound. The welt pocket has the extension covering the opening extending above the pocket. The flap pocket has the extension turned down over the opening. The bound pocket has an even width binding on either side of the opening. The bound pocket can be made of one or two pieces, and sometimes the binding is corded.

Pockets are cut of self-fabric in light-weight materials. In heavy fabrics, the pocket is cut of lining material and the area near the opening is faced with self-fabric.

WELT POCKET. Baste-mark position of the pocket on the right side of the garment. Fold the fabric strip for welt in half lengthwise, right sides together, and stitch ends. Trim seam allowance, turn to right side and press flat. Pin welt to right side of garment, with fold edge down and raw edge along bottom of marking for opening. Baste along seam line. Pin

welt section up over opening. On wrong side, baste second section of pocket over the first section. Stitch pocket section together around all outside edges. On the right side, slip-stitch the seamed edges of welt to the garment with tiny, invisible stitches or top-stitch close to edge of welt.

one pocket section to garment, right sides together matching markings for opening accurately. Baste in position. Turn garment to wrong side. Stitch all around slash on seam line. Slash between stitching and clip diagonally into corners. Draw pocket piece through slash to wrong side and baste around opening. Press

FLAP POCKET. Baste-mark the position for pocket opening on the right side of the garment. Stitch facing to flap section leaving upper straight edge open. Grade seam allowances and turn flap to right side. Baste close to edge, rolling seam slightly to facing side. Top-stitch close to finished edges if desired. Pin flap to right side of garment, with raw edge along top of marking for opening. Baste along seam line. If pocket sec-

tions are cut of lining fabric, cut two pieces of garment fabric about 2½ inches wide to fit the top of the pocket sections. Turn in the lower edge and stitch fabric piece over lining with upper edges matched. Trim away the lining fabric under the applied fabric

pieces. Transfer markings for slash opening to one of these applied fabric pieces. Place this section over pocket opening, right sides together, and markings matched. Turn the garment to the wrong side and stitch around slash on seam line. Note that corners are not square; lower ends taper slightly so that they do not show when flap is pressed down. Slash between stitching lines and clip diagonally into corners. Draw

pocket piece through slash to wrong side. Fold up the lower section of pocket, forming a welt at bottom edge of opening wide enough to fill the space and marking pleats at ends on inside. Stitch welt in position close to seam line at lower edge of opening. On inside, stitch ends of welt, catching small triangles and pleats. On the right side, press the flap section down over the

welt. Turn garment to wrong side and baste second section of pocket over the first section. Trim off lower edge of second section so that edges are even. Stitch together all edges of pocket. For a simulated patch pocket, stitch garment to pocket on right side. Add another row of stitching ½ inch outside the first row and across the top of the flap.

ONE-PIECE BOUND POCKET. Baste-mark the position for pocket opening on the right side of the garment. Be sure the marking is exactly on a single yarn of the fabric if the pocket opening is to be straight. Cut a piece of fabric 1 inch wider than the opening and twice the depth of the finished pocket plus 1 inch to allow for the binding. Measure 1 inch down from the center of the piece and mark the line for the opening the same width as pocket opening. Place the pocket section on the garment, right sides together, with the shorter pocket section below opening. Match markings accurately and baste together along opening. Stitch ¼ inch from each side of opening and across ends. Slash through center of marking and cut diag-

onally into corners to line of stitching. Draw the pocket through the slash to the wrong side. Bring folded edges together forming an even binding on each side of opening on right side and inverted pleats at ends on pocket. Cut strips 1 inch wide and 1 inch longer than the opening. For bound opening, fold the strips of binding in half lengthwise, wrong sides together and press. If pocket opening is to be corded, fold the strip of binding over the cording and stitch close to cording with special foot on sewing machine. Baste the binding strips to the right side of the garment with the raw edges exactly along the marking for the opening. If the pocket sections are cut from lining fabric, cut a strip of garment fabric 2 inches wide and the length of the top of the pocket. Turn under lower edge and baste over one lining piece with upper edges even.

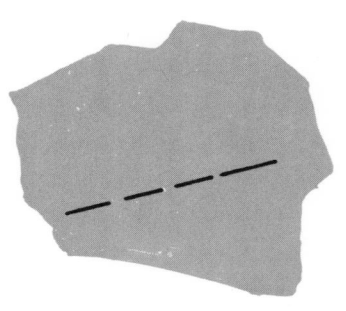

wrong side. Catch-stitch the center folds of bindings together on the right side and stitch around pocket opening close to binding. On the inside, press the upper section of pocket down and stitch the pocket sections together around outer edges. Remove catch-stitching and press the finished pocket.

TWO-PIECE BOUND OR CORDED POCKET. Baste-mark position for pocket opening on the right side of fabric. If pocket opening is on straight grain, be sure marking is along a single yarn of the fabric. Cut two strips for binding on straight grain of fabric. If fabric is plaid or check, the strips can be cut on the bias to give a decorative effect to the

Stitch lower edge of strip to pocket section and trim away lining under self-fabric. Baste the pocket sections over the binding, right sides together and raw edges meeting at marking for opening. The pocket section with the self-fabric facing is placed above the opening.

Turn garment to wrong side. Stitch ¼ inch above and below the marking for opening, keeping both lines of stitching exactly the same length. Fasten ends of thread securely. Slash through the center on marking and cut diagonally to the ends of stitching. Draw pocket sections through the slash opening to the wrong

side. Press binding strips toward center of opening and catch-stitch edges together. On the wrong side of garment, press the upper section of the pocket down over the lower section. Stitch the pocket together at outer edges being sure to catch the binding and triangular pieces at ends of opening. Remove catch-stitching and press.

POCKETS SET INTO A SEAM. The pocket set into a seam can be any pocket in which the opening falls along a seam line of the garment. In heavy fabrics, this pocket is cut of lining fabric and faced with self-fabric same as the set-in pocket.

SIDE-SEAM POCKET. Stitch side seam, leaving it open between markings for pocket. Fasten threads securely at ends of stitching. Machine-baste seam between markings. Press entire seam open. Pin one section of pocket to garment front seam allowance, right side together. Stitch ⅜ inch from edge between markings and grade seams. Press seam open from edge. Clip back seam allowance at top and bottom of pocket to stitching line and press pocket section toward front. Baste and stitch outer edges of pocket together. Remove machine-basting at seam-line opening.

and understitch seam to pocket section. Press pocket section toward the front of garment. Pin other pocket section to back seam allowance and stitch ⅜ inch

FRONT HIP POCKET. Apply the pocket before side seams of the skirt are joined. This type of pocket should be interfaced to give the proper shape and support to the upper edge of the pocket. Cut the interfacing from the pattern piece for the pocket facing. Baste interfacing to inside of skirt front. Baste and

stitch pocket facing to right side of skirt front. Trim interfacing close to stitching, grade seams and clip curve at intervals. Turn facing to inside, press and understitch seam to facing. Lap front over side and pocket section to markings and pin in place. Note that

the pocket stands away. On the inside, stitch side and pocket section to facing along curved edge to form the pocket. Baste pocket to skirt front at side seam and waistline. Continue constructing skirt.

CHAPTER 12

IMPORTANT CLOSINGS

One of the most vital steps in garment construction is closing the gaps —joining bodices to skirts, inserting zippers, making buttonholes. Give these areas the same attention and care as you do the rest. A badly inserted zipper, a messy buttonhole, even an insecurely sewn button can almost ruin the look of the garment.

The method you use to close up gaps depends on the garment design. There may even be times when you want to change the closing suggested by the pattern. On very bulky or pile fabrics, you may decide to substitute another type of closing for bound buttonholes, which are difficult to manipulate in these fabrics. Machine-worked buttonholes or perhaps heavy hooks and eyes will suffice. If you are in a hurry and wish to avoid making long rows of buttonholes for the back closing of a garment, you may recut the back opening a bit and insert a zipper without ruining the looks of the garment. As you sew, you'll find the methods which you like best, both in appearance and ease of application. The pattern will show the best type to use, but you should be familiar enough with all types to be able to substitute when feasible.

JOINING BODICES AND SKIRTS

The most common gap you'll close is that between the bodice and skirt. The waistline is usually the joining point.

Waistlines

In fashion, waistlines wander from just below the bust to the hip. However, the waistline of most garments fits smoothly and comfortably at the natural waistline. There is usually from ¼ to ⅜ inch ease allowance in the normal bodice length to allow for movement and comfort. A bloused bodice will have more length.

To test for the correct bodice length and fit, put the bodice on over the undergarments you will be wearing. Pin the side opening with wrong sides of fabric together. Tie a heavy string around your natural waistline, adjusting it until it feels comfortable. If there is too much fullness in the bodice, or the side opening will not close, you need to adjust the fit of the waistline. To determine the correct length, move slightly until the bodice does not pull. Chalk-mark the waistline of the bodice along the bottom edge of the string.

Be sure the waistline of the skirt is the same size as

the waistline of the bodice and that darts are in corresponding positions with seam lines matching. Pin the bodice and skirt, right sides together, at the waistline. Match notches, center fronts and backs, side seams and construction darts, pleats, or gathers accurately. Baste. Try on the garment and check the fit and comfort of the waistline.

All waistlines should be stayed to prevent stretching. In most garments, a piece of woven seam binding stitched into the seam is sufficient. Woven seam binding is also used in the waistline of a lined jacket. Some garments require a firmer stay or an inside belt of grosgrain ribbon. This kind of stay is used to support a very full or heavy skirt as well as to hold a blouson top in place.

WOVEN SEAM BINDING STAY. Cut a piece of woven seam binding the length of your waist measurement plus seam allowances. Baste center of seam binding over waistline seam of the skirt side. Stitch seam through all thicknesses. Press seam toward bodice. If skirt is gathered, apply the waistline stay to the skirt before it is attached to the bodice. Press the seam toward the bodice. If bodice is gathered, apply stay to bodice and press waistline seam toward skirt.

INSIDE BELT OF GROSGRAIN RIBBON. Cut a piece of grosgrain ribbon 2 inches longer than your waist measurement. Be sure to take a snug waist measurement. Turn under the ends ¼ inch; make a ½-inch hem on one end and a 1-inch hem on the other. Sew a hook in the center of the 1-inch hem and an eye on the end of the ½-inch hem. Sew the grosgrain ribbon through the middle to the waistline seam of the garment, easing the seam to the ribbon if necessary. Place the hook and eye directly under the placket opening and leave the ribbon free for an inch on either side of the placket.

An inside grosgrain ribbon belt is also used to stay the waistline of a princess dress or any garment without a waistline seam. Sew the ribbon at all seams. Place the hook and eye closing directly under the placket opening.

WAISTLINE FINISHES

Waistbands

The waistband should fit snugly at the natural waistline and lap front over back at the side closing. If closing is at center back then the band laps left over right or the same direction as the lapped zipper application. Close waistband with hooks and eyes or a worked button hole and button.

The upper edge of the skirt should be ½ or ¾ inch larger than the waistband. This fullness is eased in to allow for the curve of the hip. The waistband is usually cut on the lengthwise grain of the fabric. For wool fabric, place the seamline of the inner edge of the waistband on the selvage and eliminate the seam allowance. The selvage finish on the inside of the hand is less bulky than a turned-in seam.

If you are cutting your own waistband without a pattern, cut a piece of fabric the length of your waist

measurement plus about 3 inches for seam allowances and overlap and twice the finished width plus seam allowances.

Waistbands are interfaced to give body and prevent stretching. Cut the interfacing half the width of the waistband pattern or to the fold line. Baste the interfacing to the inside of the edge of waistband to be stitched to skirt with other edge along lengthwise fold. Sew interfacing on fold line with a hemming-type stitch.

When applying a waistband, it may be slip-stitched

on the inside so that no stitching shows, or it may be top-stitch. Waistbands of double knit can be cut of single thickness of fabric and backed with elastic for a snug fit. In a very heavy fabric, the waistband can be cut of a single thickness of wool and backed with grosgrain ribbon to reduce bulk.

SLIP-STITCHED WAISTBAND. Fold waistband, right sides together. Pin ends and extension edge on back waistband. Stitch front end of band from seamline to fold. Stitch back extension to marking. Clip diagonally to end of stitching and grade seams. Press seam allowances open using a point presser to get into corners. Turn in edge of waistband without interfacing on seamline and baste. Clip diagonally across turned corner at front end of waistband to reduce bulk of seam allowance. Turn waistband to right side. Pull out corners and press waistband.

Pin notched edge of waistband to outside of skirt, right sides together. Match notches, center markings, front end of waistband to front edge of placket and extension edge to back placket edge. Ease skirt to waistband. Stitch on seamline with waistband uppermost. Trim interfacing close to stitching. Grade seam and press seam toward waistband.

On inside, lap free edge of waistband over waistline seam. Hem folded edge of waistband to seamline. Press.

TOP-STITCHED WAISTBAND. Finish ends of band and edge without interfacing same as for slip-stitched band. Pin right side of waistband to *inside* of skirt, matching notches, centers and markings. Ease skirt to band and stitch. Trim interfacing close to stitching and grade seam. Press seam toward band. Lap free edge of band over seam on right side of skirt and baste. Top-stitch through all thicknesses and continue top-stitching around all edges of waistband, if desired.

WAISTBAND BACKED WITH ELASTIC. With double knits, waistbands should be interfaced and backed with elastic to fit smooth and snug. First, cut the band singly, allowing for a seam allowance beyond the fold line. Cut a strip of lightweight hair canvas interfacing, half the width of the pattern or to the fold line. Baste the interfacing to the inside of the band. Turn down the seam allowance at the upper edge of the waistband and press.

Apply the band to the skirt, right sides together, and press the band up. Cut a strip of elastic, the width of the finished band and ½ inch shorter than the length of the band. Stitch the elastic to the ends of the band with right sides together.

Grade seams and turn the band to the right side. Stretch and pin elastic to band. Top-stitch through fabric and elastic around all four sides of the waistband.

WAISTBAND BACKED WITH GROS-GRAIN RIBBON. Allow only a seam allowance beyond the fold line at the upper edge of the waistband pattern when cutting the fabric waistband. Cut the interfacing half the width of the waistband pattern. Trim off the ⅝-inch seam allowance at the ends and lower edge of the interfacing. Baste interfacing to inside of waistband. Turn in the seam allowance on all edges of the waistband and baste over the interfacing. Lap waistband over upper edge of skirt to seamline and baste, matching centers, notches and markings. Ease skirt to waistband. Top-stitch band to skirt and continue stitching around all edges of band. Baste grosgrain ribbon to inside of waistband turning in ends of ribbon to match ends of waistband. Slip-stitch ribbon to inside of band.

Faced Waistline

This waistline is interfaced to prevent stretching. Interfacing is basted to skirt pieces and then skirt seams are stitched. Apply shaped facing to upper edge of skirt same as a neckline facing. For details see page 146.

PLACKETS

Plackets are openings in a garment usually put there for the purely practical purpose of allowing one to get in and out of a garment. Most plackets are closed with zippers, but there are some designs and garments that require a placket finished with buttons, hooks and eyes or snaps. Nylon tape is the newest closure on the market.

Zippers

Zippers are made with metal or nylon chains. The nylon chain is lighter-weight and more flexible than the metal chain. The automatic locking slider locks at any point on the chain. There are six basic types of zippers and it is important that you select the one designed for your particular purpose.

SKIRT ZIPPER. Open at the top; comes in 7- or 9-inch lengths to take care of any skirt opening.

DRESS ZIPPER. Closed at the upper edge with a bridge top stop; comes in 10-, 12- and 14- inch lengths. Use the longest length in tight-fitting dresses.

NECKLINE ZIPPER. Open at the top; used for necklines, sleeves, housecoats or underarm blouse plackets. It is made in lengths every inch from 4 through 10 inches, every two inches from 10 through 24 inches, 30-inch and 36-inch.

SEPARATING ZIPPER. Open at both ends; designed for use in coats and jackets that have to open down the front. This type is available in a light-weight chain in lengths every two inches from 10 through 20 inches and a heavy-weight chain in lengths every two inches from 14 through 24 inches.

TROUSER ZIPPER. Comes in just one length —11 inches. This is the only zipper that can be cut to fit the placket. The zipper is cut after it is inserted in the garment so be sure to read the directions carefully before cutting. The extra-wide tape allows for the double stitching necessary in the application. The slider is specially made to withstand frequent commercial pressings.

SLIPCOVER ZIPPER. Has a heavier chain and is put on a stronger, wider tape for use in slipcovers and pillows. It is made in 24-inch, 27-inch, 30-inch and 36-inch.

Zipper applications sometimes prove a bit difficult for beginners. They are really easy if the correct procedures are followed, and the zipper or cording foot is used on the machine. Never try to insert a zipper without this attachment. You'll risk breaking the machine needle, perhaps damage the machine, and it's doubtful that the zipper will look trim once it is in the garment.

There are various zipper applications depending on the placement of the zipper in the garment, and the type of garment. Excellent directions for various applications are usually furnished with any packaged zipper you purchase. However, there may be times when you will wish to change the type of application or you may purchase zippers with no accompanying instructions. Generally zippers are centered in a slot seam or hidden in a lapped seam.

Most zippers are inserted into seams. The placket or seam opening for the zipper should be ¼ to ⅜ inch longer than the metal teeth or nylon coils of the zipper. Don't include the top seam allowance, if there is one, in this measurement. Stitch the placket opening closed with a machine-basting stitch (8 to 10 stitches to the inch) on the seam line. Stay-stitch the seam allowances of the placket ¼ inch from the seam line in the direction of the grain. If the seam allowance is less than ⅝ inch, stitch woven seam binding to the edges, right sides up.

SLOT SEAM APPLICATION. This type of application is used at necklines, sleeves, center back or center front seams and under inverted or box pleats. Machine-baste seam for placket and press seam open.

Attach zipper foot to the sewing machine. Adjust to right-hand side of needle. Open zipper, keeping the pull tab up. Place face down on pressed open seam with bottom stop of zipper at start of basting for opening. With the teeth of one side of zipper on the seam line, stitch to the seam allowance close to the teeth from bottom to top of zipper. Sew through tape and seam allowance only. Adjust zipper foot to left-hand

side of needle. Match the other side of teeth to seam line and stitch zipper tape to the other seam allowance in same manner, beginning at turned-up pull tab. Sew through zipper tape and seam allowance only. Close the zipper by pulling up the pull tab. Spread the garment flat and stitch the zipper to the garment, starting at top of zipper, down one side, across the bottom, and up the other side. Sew through zipper tape, seam allowance and garment. Be sure to stitch an even distance from the teeth so that the stitching on the right side will be even from the seam. Some people prefer

to do this final top-stitching from the right side of the garment on the slot seam application. They feel that it is easier to get the two sides exactly even. Either way is correct, so choose the one which gives you the best results. Press and remove machine-basting.

If facing has been applied before the zipper, machine-baste seam together with facing turned up so as not to catch it in the seam. Apply zipper as described above. Trim zipper tape off at neckline seam. Remove basting. Press facing down over zipper tape. Turn under raw edges of facing and slip-stitch over zipper tape. Sew a hook and eye above zipper.

Finish outer edge of facing in appropriate manner. Stitch facing to neck or sleeve edge of garment, grade seam and clip curve at intervals. Understitch seam allowances to facing. Press facing down over zipper tape. Turn under raw edges of facing and slip-stitch over zipper tape. Sew a hook and eye above zipper.

LAPPED SEAM APPLICATION FOR DRESS PLACKET. This type of application is used primarily in the side seam of a dress or in any placket that falls in the middle of a seam. Baste the seam for placket by machine and press open. Attach zipper foot to machine and adjust to right-hand side of

needle. Open zipper and place face down on back seam allowance. Match the bottom of zipper to beginning of machine basting with teeth on seam line. Stitch zipper to seam allowance close to teeth from bottom to top. Sew through zipper tape and back seam allowance only. Adjust zipper foot to left-hand side

of needle. Close zipper and turn face up. Press fabric away from zipper forming a fold in back seam allowance along zipper. Stitch from bottom up through seam allowance and tape close to zipper. Spread gar-

ment flat and turn zipper face down over front seam allowance. Note the small pleat in seam allowance at top and bottom of placket. Starting at seam line, stitch across bottom of zipper, up the front side and across the top. Stitch an even distance from the teeth, sewing through zipper tape, seam allowance and front of

garment. The stitching line should be as close to folded edge as possible. Press and remove machine-basting.

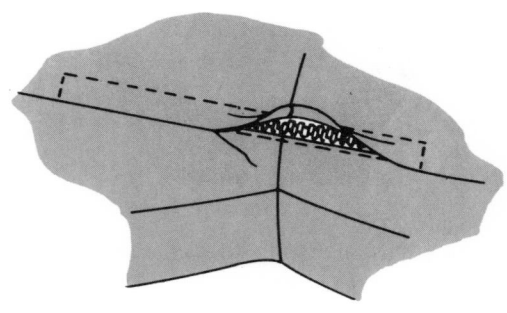

LAPPED SEAM APPLICATION FOR PLACKET OPEN AT ONE END. This type of application is used in skirts, necklines, center back or center front seams. Fashion-wise, the lapped application is more popular than the slot seam for back neckline or the long back zippers. The lapped application conceals the zipper better than the slot seam during normal movement of the body. Use the same method as the lapped application for dress placket but eliminate stitching across the top of the zipper.

Waistband Finish

Stitch waistband over ends of zipper tape to finish upper edge of a skirt.

Neckline Finish

Method of finishing back edges of facing depends on when zipper is inserted.

For a facing applied after the zipper, stitch neckline facing over ends of zipper tape at neck edge. Grade seams, clip curve at intervals and understitch facing. Press facing down over zipper tape.

On narrow side of zipper, turn in the end of facing and hem over double-stitched side of zipper tape. On lapped side of zipper, trim off seam allowance on end of facing to within ½ inch of neck edge. Turn facing down over zipper. Mark the corner of the top stop of the zipper on the facing with a dot. Clip diagonally from back edge of facing toward neck edge ending at marking for top stop.

Turn in edges of facing to clear zipper chain and hem facing to zipper tape. Finish with hook and eye sewed above zipper.

For a facing applied before the zipper, turn under end of facing on lapped side of zipper application 1⅛ inch and press. Trim facing to ½ inch. Turn under end of facing on narrow side of zipper application ½ inch and press. Pin facing to neck edge, markings matched, with end of facing 1⅛ inch from left back edge of garment and other end ½ inch from right back edge of garment.

Stitch neckline seam; grade seam allowances. Understitch, ending ½ inch from end of facing on lapped side of application. Turn under seam allowances of neck edge beyond ends of facing and press.

Turn facing up. Machine-baste placket opening. Insert zipper by lapped application. Trim off ends of zipper tape at neckline seam. Turn facing down over zipper application. Hem edges of facing over zipper tape. Slip-stitch neck edge of lapped side of application from zipper stitching to fold line. Sew hook and eye above zipper.

HAND-FINISHED APPLICATION OF A ZIPPER. The finest couturier garments have hand-finished zippers. This application gives a nice custom-finished appearance to the garment. It is preferable for many fabrics, such as velvet, velveteen, fleece, lace or sheer fabrics, when top-stitching is either difficult or unsightly. It is quite simple to do, and you should try it on your finer garments. It can be used with either the slot or lapped application. Complete all machine-stitching on the inside seam allowances of the garment. Spread garment flat with zipper face down and baste to garment instead of the usual top-stitching in the last step. Turn garment to right side. Sew zipper in place by hand with a half-back or prick stitch using basting as a guide line.

APPLICATION IN A KNIFE-PLEATED SKIRT.

Plan pleats so that seam falls on the inner edge of a pleat. Insert zipper before skirt is pleated. Stitch seam to marking for placket opening and fasten threads securely. Baste the seam for placket by machine and press open. Attach zipper foot to machine

and adjust to right-hand side of needle. Open zipper and place face down on back seam allowance. Match the bottom of zipper to beginning of machine-basting with teeth on seam line. Stitch zipper to seam allowance close to teeth from bottom to top. Sew through zipper tape and back seam allowance only. Adjust zipper foot to left-hand side of needle. Close zipper and turn face up. Press fabric away from zipper, forming a

fold in back seam allowance along zipper. Stitch from bottom up through seam allowance and tape close to

zipper. Turn zipper face down over front seam allowance. There will be a small pleat at lower end of placket. Starting at seamline, stitch across bottom of zipper and up the front side. Sew through zipper tape and front seam allowance only. Make pleats in skirt

and press. Baste pleats at upper edge leaving pleat over placket opening free. Remove machine-basting from placket opening.

APPLICATION IN A BOX-PLEATED SKIRT.

Plan pleats so that the seam with placket opening falls between two box pleats. Stitch seam to marking for placket opening and fasten thread securely. Machine-baste placket opening and press seam open. Insert zipper in seam by either the slot or lapped

application before skirt is pleated. The application you choose is a matter of personal preference since both are used in ready-to-wear. After the zipper application is completed, make the pleats in the skirt. The zipper will be concealed under the folds between two pleats.

APPLICATION IN A WELT SEAM.

Apply the zipper before completing the welt seam. Make a plain seam to marking for placket opening and fasten thread securely. Machine-baste seam for placket opening and press seam open. Apply zipper as directed for lapped seam application normally done in a skirt placket. To complete the welt seam, trim the front seam allowance to ¼ inch. Clip the back seam allowance to the seam line at bottom of zipper and press seam allowance toward the front over the trimmed seam allowance. Stitch close to the raw edge in line with stitching line for zipper.

APPLICATION IN A FLAT-FELL SEAM.

Before seam is stitched, cut a facing of self-fabric on the lengthwise grain 1 inch wide and the length of the placket opening. Pin the facing to the front seam allowance, right sides together, along placket opening. Place end of facing in line with marking for placket opening. Stitch in a ¼-inch seam. Turn facing to inside and press. Stitch the flat-fell seam to the marking for placket opening, wrong sides together. Press seam toward back. Clip the back seam allowance to marking for placket opening and trim back seam allowance below placket to ⅛ inch. Turn under front

seam allowance in line with facing and top-stitch to garment close to folded edge. Fasten thread securely at end of placket. Turn garment to wrong side and continue clipping the back across the flat-fell seam to

the last row of stitching. Machine-baste placket opening together along seamline of facing and press seam open. Apply zipper as directed for lapped seam appli-

cation. Remove machine-basting and open zipper. Top-stitch the front edge of the placket to meet top-stitching on flat-fell seam.

APPLICATION IN PERMANENT PRESS FABRIC. Special handling of zipper is needed to prevent puckering after laundering. Pre-shrink closed zipper by immersing it in hot water a few minutes and allowing it to air dry. Repeat shrinking operation twice and lightly press zipper before application. The lapped application is preferred because only one row of outside stitching is visible. Insert zipper according to di-

rections for lapped application with these exceptions. After machine-basting placket opening, clip basting at 2 inch intervals before pressing seam open. Pin or baste zipper in position, easing zipper tape to placket seams. Stitch zipper in place, using 10-12 stitches per inch.

APPLICATION IN A SKIRT OF REVERSIBLE FABRIC. The flat-fell seam application can be used if your fabric is light-weight. However, most reversible fabrics are too bulky for that extra facing piece. For heavy reversible fabrics it is important to note that the flat-fell seams must be made on the inside of the fabric so that the zipper can be inserted without the extra facing. Stitch the flat-fell seam to the marking for placket opening, right sides together. Press seam toward front. Clip the seam allowances to marking for placket opening and trim front seam allowance below placket to ⅛ inch. Turn under back seam allowance and top-stitch to garment close to folded edge. Fasten thread securely at end of placket. Machine-baste placket opening together along seam line. Apply zipper as directed for lapped seam application. Trim off seam allowances on both sides even with edge of zipper tape. Sew the zipper tape to the back of the garment with a very fine slip-stitch, being careful that it does not show on the right side.

When the skirt is worn on the reverse side, the zipper application will be on the right hip instead of the left. It is necessary to make a self-fabric shield to hide the zipper tape when the skirt is worn on this side. Cut a piece of skirt fabric 2½ inches wide and the entire length of the zipper tape plus a ¼-inch seam allowance. Fold in half lengthwise with reverse side of fabric together and stitch in a ¼-inch seam. Press seam open and match to center of piece. Stitch across one end in a ¼-inch seam. Turn to outside and press.

Center the piece over zipper tape. Sew to garment along bottom and front edge of zipper tape with a very fine slip-stitch. Press.

APPLICATION IN A REVERSIBLE SKIRT OF TWO FABRICS. Stitch seams of one skirt fabric, leaving open above marking for placket on left side. Stitch seams of second skirt fabric, leaving open above marking for placket on right side. Press seams open and fasten thread securely at ends of openings. Machine-baste placket openings in both skirts. Attach zipper foot and adjust to right-hand side of needle. Open zipper, keeping pull tab up. Place face down on placket seam allowance of first skirt with bottom stop of zipper at end of opening. With the teeth of one side of zipper on the seamline, stitch to the seam allowance, close to teeth, from bottom to top of zipper. Sew through tape and seam allowance only.

Adjust zipper foot to left-hand side of needle. Match the other side of teeth to seamline and stitch zipper tape to the other seam allowance in same manner beginning at turned-up pull tab. Sew through zipper tape and seam allowance only. Close the zipper.

Remove all machine-basting and press.

Spread the skirt flat and machine-baste the zipper to the garment starting at top of zipper, down one side, across the bottom and up the other side. Sew through zipper tape, seam allowance and skirt. Match seams

APPLICATION IN A KNIFE-PLEATED SKIRT OF REVERSIBLE FABRIC.

Plan your pleats so that all the seams fall in the center of the upper underfold of a pleat. The pleats must be at least 1 inch deep to conceal the zipper tape. The flat-fell seams must be made on the inside of the fabric because of the zipper application. Insert the zipper before making the pleats. Stitch the flat-fell seam to the marking for placket opening, right sides together. Press seam toward front. Clip the seam allowance to marking for placket opening and trim front seam allowance below placket to ⅛ inch. Turn under back

of both skirts at placket opening with wrong sides of skirts together and baste. Using regular machine-stitching, stitch along machine-basting down one side, across the bottom and up the other side of zipper.

seam allowance and top-stitch to front, close to folded edge. Fasten thread securely at end of placket. Machine-baste placket opening together along seam

When the skirt is worn on the reverse side, you will be able to look into the pleat containing the placket, so it is necessary to make a self-fabric shield to hide the zipper tape. Cut a piece of skirt fabric 2½ inches wide and the length of the zipper tape extending below the waistline seam plus a ¼-inch seam allowance. Fold in half lengthwise with reverse side of fabric together and stitch in a ¼-inch seam. Press seam open and match to center of piece. Stitch across one end in a ¼-inch seam. Turn to outside and press. Turn in ¼-inch seam at open end and slip-stitch together.

line. Apply zipper as directed for slot seam application. Trim off seam allowances on both sides even with edge of zipper tape. Make pleats in skirt and press; baste pleats at upper edge.

Center piece over zipper tape. Sew to garment along bottom and front edge of zipper tape with a very fine slip-stitch. Upper edge of shield will remain free. On a 1-inch pleat, the shield will be even with the folded edge of the pleat, while on a deeper pleat the shield will not reach to the edge of the pleat. Remove machine-basting from placket opening.

APPLICATION IN FLY FRONT OF SKIRT. Turn under right skirt front along fold line for overlap and baste close to edge. Press. Reinforce lower corner of placket opening on left skirt front with a row of stitching along seamline. Clip seam allowance diagonally to seam line at corner. Turn under seam allowance along side and lower edge of placket

and baste. Press. Place left skirt front over zipper with side edge of placket along zipper chain and lower edge of placket at bottom of zipper. Baste and then stitch close to edge, using zipper foot. Working from

right side of garment, lap right skirt front over left skirt front, matching center front markings accurately and baste. Baste to zipper tape above placket opening. Top-stitch entire length of fly front through all thicknesses, using zipper foot. Fold underlap piece in

half lengthwise, wrong sides together, and press. Baste underlap to left side of placket behind zipper, matching seam edges on wrong side. Turn to right side of garment and fold back front overlap. Using zipper foot, stitch across bottom and left side of zipper through all thicknesses over first row of stitching.

APPLICATION IN FLY FRONT OF PANTS. Be sure you are using the specially constructed trouser zipper. Face the left side of fly placket. Clip curve at intervals and press seam. Make the right fly shield and press it. Attach zipper foot to machine and adjust to right-hand side of needle. Place closed zipper face down on opened-out facing with right edge of tape matched to facing seam and bottom stop at seam allowance of facing. Allow any extra length of the zipper to extend above the waistline edge. Double-

stitch the left side of tape to the facing. Turn left fly facing to inside at seam line and baste. Stitch inner edge of facing to front, keeping end of unstitched, right zipper tape free. Clip right front seam allowance

to stitching. Open zipper. Turn in right side of fly placket at seam line and baste. Clip curve at intervals and to seam line at lower end of placket opening and press. Lap placket edge over right zipper tape and baste. Baste fly shield behind zipper, matching seam edges on wrong side. Stitch from right side close to zipper teeth through all thicknesses. Join crotch seam.

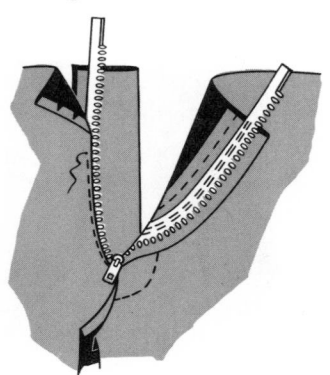

Clip curve at intervals and press seam open. Make a bar tack at bottom of fly. Open zipper. Attach waistband to garment. The waistband acts as a top stop for

the zipper. Now it is safe to cut off the excess tape extending above the waistband seam allowance. Cut between the metal teeth at edge of seam allowance.

APPLICATION OF SEPARATING ZIP-PER. Finish outer edge of facing in manner suitable for fabric. Make a chalk line on outside of front edge facing ¼ inch inside of seam line. Place open zipper face up on outside of facing with edge of teeth at chalk line. Stitch close to teeth, using zipper foot. Attach other side of zipper to other side of facing in same manner. If garment has a collar, baste the collar to the right side of neck edge. Stitch facing to garment at neck and lower edge, right sides together. Note that zipper tape is not stitched in with the neckline seam. Separate the zipper. Grade seam allowances and clip curve at intervals. Turn facing to inside and press zipper toward center front. Turn in seam allowance on front and press. On the inside, match edge of zipper teeth to front edge of garment and baste in place.

Stitch along edge of facing through all thicknesses, using zipper foot. Stitch other side of zipper to the other side of front in same manner. Close the zipper and press the application.

APPLICATION OF SEPARATING ZIPPER REPLACING BUTTONHOLE CLOSING.

It is easy to convert buttonholes on back of overblouse to a zipper closing. Mark the center back on right and left back pieces with a basting line. Turn facing under on left back along fold line and press a crease. The adjustment for the zipper is made on the right back. Using a plastic ruler and chalk pencil, lightly mark a line ¼ inch to the right of center back line on right back of garment. Turn facing under on this marked line and press a crease. Measure, mark and trim off right back facing so that it is the same width as left back facing. Finish edges of both back facings in a manner suitable for the fabric.

Turn facings to right side at the crease lines pressed in right and left back. Trim interfacing at crease lines. Apply neck facing, lapping it over back facings ½ inch. Mark and trim off extra length on back edges of neck facing. Stitch neck edge along seamline. Trim interfacing close to stitching. Grade seams. Clip curve at intervals. Understitch as far into corners as possible.

Turn facing to inside and press. Hem back facing to neck facing. Sew facing to shoulder seams with a catch-stitch. Sew edge of facing to interfacing with a prick stitch. Trim interfacing close to finished edge.

See Chapter 16 for application of slipcover zippers.

Turn up hem and finish lower edge. Open back facing and continue hem across lower edge. Turn facing back and slip-stitch lower edges together. Sew side edge of facing to hem with a hemming stitch. Lap and baste right back edge of overblouse over right zipper tape. Leave same amount of space above and below zipper. Turn under end of tape at top of zipper. Adjust zipper foot to left side of needle. Starting at hem edge, stitch entire length of right back, close to zipper. Lap left back over zipper. Baste center back marking on left back along left side of zipper chain, keeping neck and hem edges even. Turn under end of tape at top of zipper. Open separating zipper and stitch entire length of left back along center back marking with zipper foot on left side of needle. Hem upper ends of zipper tape securely to facing. Sew a hook and eye at neck and hem edge.

Plackets without Zippers

The placket without a zipper must always be faced, bound or hemmed to finish the edges. This type of placket is usually found either on infants' and children's clothes or in a sleeve opening.

CONTINUOUS LAP PLACKET IN A SEAM. Stitch the seam to marking for placket opening and fasten thread securely. Clip seam allowance to stitching line at end of placket. Cut a lengthwise piece of fabric 2½ inches wide and twice the length of the opening. Stitch one edge of piece to edges of opening, right sides together, in a ⅝-inch seam. Trim

seam and press toward facing. Turn under free edge of facing and hem over seam. Turn placket to inside along front edge and baste at upper edge. Lap over back placket.

HEMMED PLACKET IN A PLEAT. Slash garment on the straight grain of fabric the desired length of placket. Clip diagonally ¼ inch on both sides of point of slash. Turn in ¼ inch on each side of slash

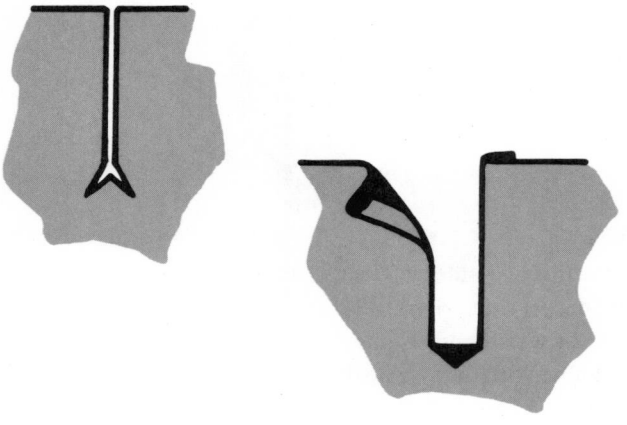

and press to wrong side. Turn under a ½-inch hem on each side of slash and stitch. Lap the hems forming

pleats. Stitch across lower end of placket through all thicknesses to hold pleats in place.

See page 168 for description of placket finishes used in sleeves.

Nylon Tape Closure

Nylon tape closure is excellent for fastening buckleless belts, waistbands in wrapped or adjustable-waist garments, jacket fronts, slipcovers and valances. Once you start using it, you will find numerous other uses for it. It is, however, too bulky to use in place of a zipper in a dress or skirt placket or in light-weight garments.

The tape comes in 1-inch widths, and you may purchase it by the yard or in packaged lengths. When preparing the tape for application, close it and cut to the desired length, press flat with a warm iron. It doesn't really matter which side of the tape is sewn to the underlap or overlap, but usually the fleece side is put on the section that comes in contact with the body. It is softer than the burr side and less apt to cause irritation.

APPLICATION WITH TOP-STITCHING. Separate the two sides of tape. Pin the fleece side, right side up, to facing side of overlap. Place ⅛ inch in from the folded edge. Machine-stitch around outside edges of tape through all thicknesses. Lap closing, centers and markings matched. Center the burr side of the tape, right side up, directly under the fleece side of tape. Pin the burr side of tape to the underlap and stitch around outside edges of tape through all thicknesses.

For a fly-front effect, make one row of stitching through all thicknesses along inner edge of tape.

APPLICATION ON A WAISTBAND. Separate the two sides of tape. Before making waistband, pin fleece side, right side up, to facing side of front edge of waistband. Center tape between seam line and fold line. Stitch to waistband facing around all sides of tape. Apply waistband to skirt. Lap waistband and pin burr side of tape to back underlap, right side up, directly under fleece side of tape. Stitch burr side to back edge of waistband through all thicknesses.

APPLICATION WITHOUT TOP-STITCHING. Separate the two sides of tape. Before facing is attached to the garment, pin fleece side of tape, right side up, to right side of facing. Stitch around all sides of tape. Apply facing to garment. Lap

closing, centers and markings matched. Center the burr side of the tape, right side up, directly under the fleece side of tape. Stitch the burr side to the underlap through all thicknesses.

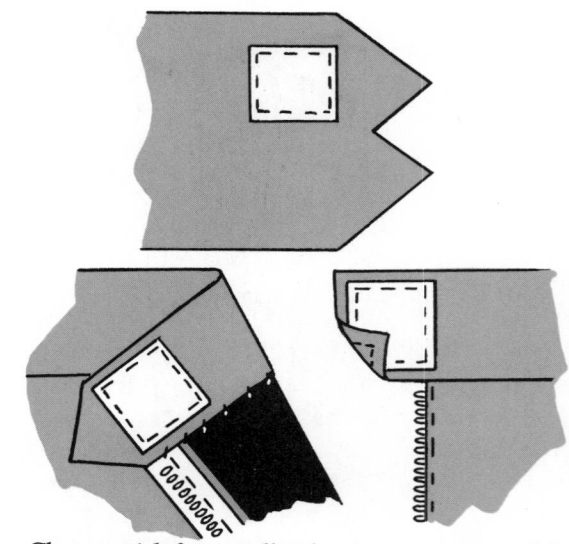

See Chapter 16 for application on slipcovers and valances.

BUTTONHOLES

Buttonholes can "make" or "break" a garment. There is nothing more discouraging than a well-made garment with unsightly buttonholes. Before making the buttonholes on your garment, practice. Make a test on a scrap of the same fabric. In this way you can decide whether you are using the correct method to obtain the effect you want.

The size and spacing of the buttonholes is indicated on patterns requiring buttonholes, but you may have to change the spacing if you use a size button other than the one suggested in the pattern, or if you alter the section in which the buttonholes are placed. If you use a bigger button, you may want to make fewer buttonholes and space them farther apart. The reverse is true if you use smaller buttons. When you change the size of the buttons, be sure to check the width of extension beyond the center marking of your garment. The extension should be one-half the diameter of the button plus ¼ to ½ inch. Increase or decrease the width of your extension accordingly, if you change the size of the buttons. If you alter the length of the garment, respace the buttonholes evenly, retaining the placement of the first and last buttonhole markings on the pattern.

and worked. Bound buttonholes have the edges finished with fabric while worked buttonholes have the edges finished with thread. All areas containing buttonholes should be interfaced. Bound buttonholes are made through the garment and interfacing before the facing is applied. Worked buttonholes are made through garment, interfacing and facing after garment is finished.

Mark horizontal buttonholes on the crosswise grain of fabric, vertical ones on the lengthwise grain. Each buttonhole should be the same length and an even distance from the center marking. Transfer buttonhole markings from pattern to wrong side of garment; then hand- or machine-baste through fabric so markings appear on the right side. Mark the length of buttonholes with a row of vertical basting at each end. Mark the position of buttonholes with basting between these two lines.

Buttonholes must be at least ⅛ inch longer than the diameter of the button. When the button is thick and bulky, the buttonhole must be even larger. Some buttons are difficult to measure because of their shape. The simplest way to determine the correct size buttonhole for a specific button is to cut a slit in a scrap of fabric and adjust the length until the button slips through easily and smoothly.

There are two general types of buttonholes—bound

The type of buttonhole to be used on your garment will usually be indicated on your pattern. Bound buttonholes are generally used on garments which are dry-cleaned and worked buttonholes on man-tailored or washable garments. The various kinds of bound and worked buttonholes which you may wish to use are outlined here.

Bound Buttonholes

Bound buttonholes require some practice before they are fully mastered. You should try all of the following methods and select the one you like best and find easiest to do. If you are making a number of buttonholes, prepare a long strip of fabric and then cut in pieces 1 inch longer than the finished buttonhole.

ONE-PIECE BOUND BUTTONHOLE. Cut a piece of fabric on lengthwise grain, 1 inch wide and 1 inch longer than the finished buttonhole. Mark the center of the piece. Bring the long edges to the center marking, wrong sides together, and press. Place

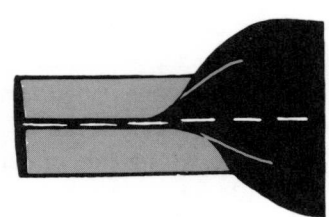

folded piece over buttonhole marking on right side of garment. Baste center of piece to buttonhole marking with cut edges up. Adjust machine to approximately

12 stitches to the inch and stitch around buttonhole ⅛ inch from center on each side and across ends. Start the stitching at the middle of one side and end by overlapping several stitches. Count the number of stitches across the ends to keep all buttonholes a uniform size. Cut along marking at center for ¼ inch and then slash diagonally to the corners. Turn piece to

wrong side through opening. The folded edges will form even bindings along each side and meet at the

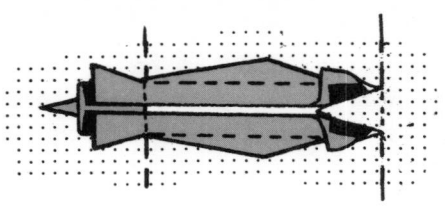

center of the opening. On outside, fold garment back over buttonhole and stitch triangular ends to ends of binding to form strong, square corners. Catch-stitch edges of binding together and press.

After facing has been attached to garment, baste around buttonhole in order to hold facing firmly in place. Insert a pin at each corner of buttonhole and center, from the right side through the facing, to serve as a guide for cutting buttonholes. Cut facing as you did for buttonhole opening, making a horizontal slash at center pin marking. Cut diagonally from slash to corner pin markings. Turn in edges of facing and sew to stitching line with tiny hemming stitches. Remove the basting and catch-stitching. Press finished buttonhole. The back of the buttonhole should look exactly the same as the front—corners square and edges even.

To finish buttonholes on loosely woven or very bulky fabric, the opening in the facing can in turn be faced with a light-weight fabric. Cut a piece of this fabric 1 inch wide and 1 inch longer than buttonhole. Mark exact position of buttonhole on the facing. Open out facing and baste piece to facing only, right sides together, with center of piece over buttonhole marking. Stitch ⅛ inch from marking and across ends forming a rectangle the size of the buttonhole. Slash along center of buttonhole marking and clip diagonally into

corners. Turn piece to wrong side of facing and press flat. Fold facing back on garment and baste around buttonhole. Hem finished edges of facing to buttonhole binding along the stitching. Remove basting and press.

TUCKED ONE-PIECE BUTTONHOLE.

This buttonhole is very similar to the regular one-piece buttonhole but the extra fabric beyond the tucks allows for blending of seams. In the one-piece buttonhole the seams are all the same width and may make a ridge when pressed in a heavy fabric.

Cut a piece of fabric 1½ inches wide and 1 inch longer than the buttonhole marking. Mark the center of the piece with a basting thread. Fold one edge of the piece ¼ inch from the center basting and stitch a ⅛-inch tuck. Fold and stitch the same kind of tuck on the other edge of the piece. The tuck stitching lines

will be ¼ inch apart. If you are making a number of buttonholes, prepare a long strip and then cut in pieces 1 inch longer than the finished buttonhole. Baste tucked piece to right side of garment with center basting matched to buttonhole marking. Stitch along lines of tucking between vertical bastings. Fasten threads securely at ends of buttonholes. Cut along

marking at center for ¼ inch and then slash diagonally to the corners. Turn piece to wrong side through

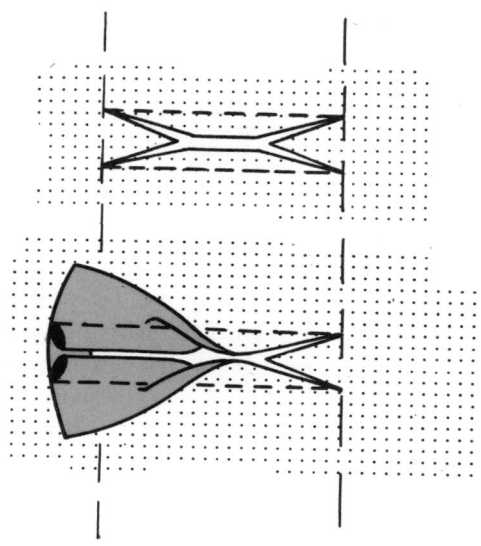

opening. Stitch triangular ends to ends of binding. Catch-stitch edges of binding together and press. Cut buttonhole through facing and finish by one of the methods described under the one-piece bound buttonhole.

TWO-PIECE BOUND BUTTONHOLE. Cut two pieces of fabric on lengthwise grain for each buttonhole ½ inch wide and 1 inch longer than finished buttonhole. Fold the pieces in half lengthwise, wrong sides together, and press. Stitch close to raw edges. Place the two pieces on right side of garment, with raw edges on the buttonhole marking. Stitch ⅛ inch from raw edges between vertical bastings the length of the buttonhole. Don't stitch across the ends.

Fasten threads securely at ends of buttonhole. Cut along marking at center for ¼ inch and then slash diagonally to the corners. Turn pieces to wrong side through opening. Stitch triangular ends to ends of binding to form strong, square corners. Catch-stitch edges of binding together and press. Cut buttonhole through facing and finish by one of two methods described under the one-piece bound buttonhole.

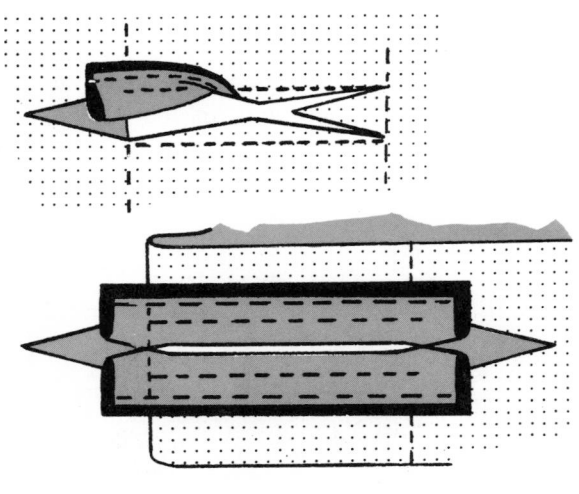

CORDED BUTTONHOLE. Place additional basting-line markings ⅛ inch above and below the buttonhole marking line. Extend the basting lines 1 inch beyond the buttonhole marking. Cut a strip of fabric 1¼ inches wide. Fold fabric over fine cording or soft string. Stitch close to cording, using the cording foot attachment on the machine. Cut the cording in pieces 1 inch longer than the length of

the finished buttonhole. Pin one piece to right side of garment with stitching line of cording matched to upper basting line. Baste in place with seam allowance toward center. Stitch the length of the buttonhole, using extended basting lines as a guide. Baste and

stitch other piece of cording to lower basting mark with seam allowance toward center. Fasten threads securely at ends of buttonhole. Cut along markings at center for ¼ inch and then slash diagonally to the corners. Turn pieces to wrong side through opening. Stitch triangular ends to ends of cording to form strong, square corners. Catch-stitch edges of cording together and press. Cut buttonholes facing and finish by one of two methods described under the one-piece bound buttonhole.

The tucked one-piece buttonhole can also be corded. Thread a darning needle with wool yarn and draw two strands of yarn through each tuck before cutting and finishing the buttonhole.

BUTTONHOLE IN A SEAM. Mark position for buttonholes on the seamline. Stitch seam, leaving openings between buttonhole markings. Fasten threads securely at each end of buttonholes. If the facing has a corresponding seamline, stitch facing section in

the same manner. Match the two openings and slip-stitch the folded edges together around the buttonhole opening. If the facing section does not have a seam, cut the buttonhole through facing and finish by one of two methods described under the one-piece bound buttonhole.

FIVE-LINE BOUND BUTTONHOLE. Cut strip 1½ inches wide and 1 inch longer than the desired buttonhole length. Center the strip, right side down, on the buttonhole marking on the right side of garment. Machine-baste the strip in place on center marking. Machine-baste through garment and strip ¼ inch above and below center basting.

Press down one free edge of the strip making a fold on the outer basting line. Turn to the wrong side. On the pressed side of the strip, permanently machine stitch exactly between the center and outer machine-bastings, the length of the buttonhole. Fasten thread ends.

Turn to the right side and press up the other free edge of the strip, making a fold on the outer basting line. Turn to the wrong side and permanently stitch between the center and outer machine-bastings, the length of the buttonhole. Fasten thread ends. Remove all machine-bastings.

If a corded effect is desired, thread darning needle with wool yarn and draw two strands of yarn through each tuck. Cut along marking at center for ¼ inch, then cut diagonally to corners.

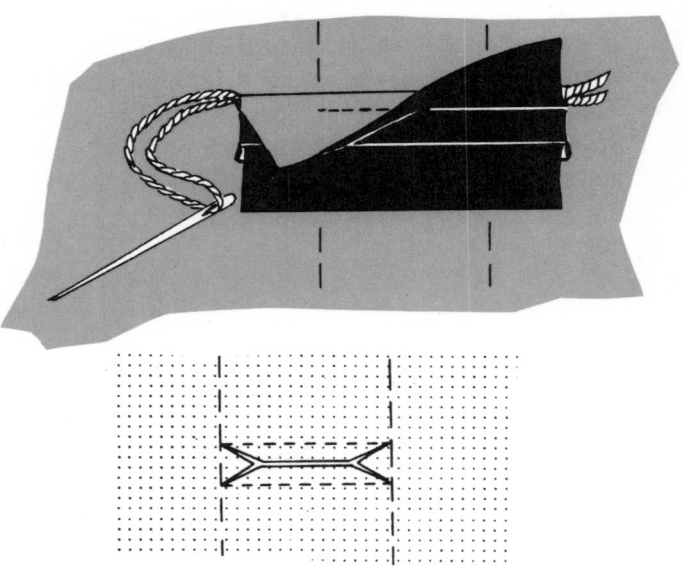

Turn the strip to the wrong side through the opening and press. On outside, fold garment back over buttonhole and stitch triangular ends to ends of tucks to form strong, square corners. Catch-stitch edges of buttonholes together and press. This buttonhole should not be used on fabrics that will be marked by machine-basting.

Worked Buttonholes

MACHINE-WORKED BUTTONHOLE.

Machine-made buttonholes save many hours of work and give satisfactory results for many garments. The swing-needle machines make buttonholes without an attachment, but for the standard machine it is necesary to use a buttonhole attachment. Follow the manual with your machine or attachment for specific instructions. Always test the buttonhole first on a scrap of your fabric.

HAND-WORKED BUTTONHOLE.

The tailored, worked buttonhole has an eyelet at the end of the buttonhole and is used on men's clothing and top coats. Mark buttonhole and punch a hole at the outer end with a stiletto. Cut on line for buttonhole and overcase edges of buttonhole and eyelet.

Work the buttonhole stitches from right to left over a cord and finish inner end with a bar tack. The cord makes a very strong buttonhole which will wear better than the regular buttonhole.

EYELETS.

Mark a small circle on the fabric the size of eyelet. Baste on the marking to serve as a reinforcement and guide. Punch a hole in the center, using a stiletto. Work over the edge with blanket stitches or buttonhole stitches, keeping them close together and even. If you insert the stiletto from the right side every few stitches, it will keep the fabric edge turned under and help shape the eyelet. Eyelets may also be made with buttonhole attachment, using a special template.

BUTTONS

Buttons may be used for decorative effect on a garment, as well as to serve a functional purpose. Select buttons which are suitable to the garment design and the color and texture of fabric. If the garment design is quite intricate, select a fairly simple button. If the garment is quite plain, then perhaps a decorative button would provide just the right touch. Also, you must consider the figure size when selecting buttons. A very large figure can take fairly large buttons, but the petite figure would be overpowered by big 3-inch buttons.

Buttons come in two different types—the sew-through type with holes, or the shank type which is attached to the garment from the underside of the button. These can have metal, cloth or self shanks.

Buttons are made of various materials—fabric, leather, bone, shell, jet, glass, metals and plastics. There are also inexpensive button forms which can be covered quickly and easily in the garment fabric. These are available at any notions counter, and complete instructions for covering are included in the package. Select the size which is right for your garment, and use the pattern in the package to cut the fabric covering.

To determine the placement for buttons, overlap the closing to the correct position and pin closed. Place a pin through each buttonhole at center front marking. Slip the pin through each buttonhole as you separate the closure. The center of the button is placed at the point marked by the pin.

Buttons are sewed to the garment with heavy-duty thread or buttonhole twist. If you cannot match your fabric with one of these, wax regular thread with beeswax to make it stronger. Use a double thread and a small knot. Buttons used for decorative purposes can be sewn close to the garment, but all other buttons need a thread or metal shank to allow the button to ride smoothly in the buttonhole. The thread shank holds the button away from the garment enough to allow for the thickness of fabric at the buttonhole. The bulkier or heavier the fabric, the longer the shank needs to be.

If the underside of your garment will not show, sew the button through all thicknesses of fabric. On coats and suits or any other garment that might be worn open, sew the buttons through fabric and interfacing but not through the facing.

Sew-Through Buttons

Take several small stitches on right side of garment to secure thread at point where button is to be placed. Bring needle through button and back into fabric, inserting a heavy pin, toothpick or matchstick over the button under the first stitch to allow for a thread shank. Continue sewing through fabric and button until button is secure. Remove the pin and pull button to top of threads evenly. Bring thread to right side of fabric and wind tightly around the stitches under button to form a shank. Fasten thread securely on underside with several stitches.

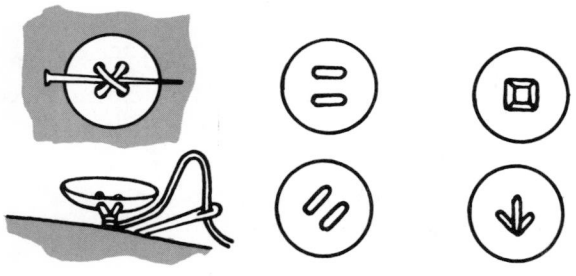

Shank Buttons

Buttons with a thin metal shank do not need a thread shank. Bring needle through fabric and shank then back through fabric. Make small stitches at right angles to buttonhole so that metal shank will line up with buttonhole rather than spread open the end of the buttonhole. Continue sewing through fabric and shank

until button is secure. Fasten thread on underside with several stitches.

Buttons with a cloth or self-shank will need to be sewn on with an additional thread shank. These shanks are bulky and will spread the buttonhole and are usually not long enough to allow the garment to button without pulling. Take several stitches on right side of garment at point where button is to be placed. Holding your forefinger between the button and the garment, bring the thread through the shank and back into the fabric. The forefinger holds the button away from the fabric as you continue sewing through fabric and shank until the button is secure. On the last stitch, bring the thread out of the button and wind thread tightly around the stitches to form the thread shank. Fasten thread securely on underside with several stitches.

Removable shank buttons are used on uniforms. Mark position for the button and make a small eyelet in the garment. Place metal shank through eyelet and fasten on underside with a special shank pin made for attaching these buttons or a small safety pin.

Stayed Buttons

When buttons are sewed to a single thickness of fabric or where there is a great deal of strain on the button, a reinforcement or stay is needed. A small patch of fabric or woven seam binding is used under a single thickness of fabric. A small button is used to stay the underside of buttons where there is great strain. Place square of fabric or small button on inside of garment under button and sew in place through button, garment and stay using the same method as for the sew-through button.

Link Buttons

These are used on French cuffs. Determine the length needed between the buttons. Holding the two buttons apart the desired distance, insert thread through both buttons several times. Fasten securely. Form a bar tack between buttons by making blanket stitches over the threads. Keep stitches close together.

OTHER FASTENINGS

Snaps

Snap fasteners range in size from 4/0, the smallest, used on sheer fabrics, to number 4, the largest, used on coarse heavy fabrics. Snaps are used to hold fabrics together where there is little strain on the garment. They give a neat flat closure. Place them close enough together to prevent the opening from gaping. Mark position for snaps on the overlap. The ball part is generally sewed to the overlap and the socket part to the underlap of the closure. Fasten thread on marking for snap and sew the ball section on with overhand stitches through each hole. Carry thread under snap from one hole to the next. Sew snap through facing and interfacing being careful not to have any stitches

show on the right side of the garment. After stitching ball section securely in place, lap the closure. Place pin through center hole of ball section and mark position for socket section. Then place a pin through center hole of socket section to hold it in position while sewing it on. Attach in the same manner as the ball section.

Hammer-on snaps are used on children's clothes and sportswear. These are easily and quickly applied according to the instructions on the package.

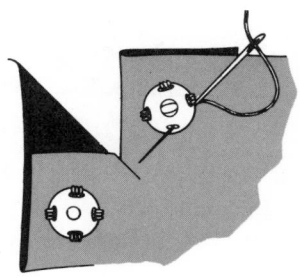

Hooks and Eyes

These range in size from 00, the smallest, for sheers to 12, the largest, for coarse heavy fabrics. They give a more secure fastening than snaps, and are often combined with snaps. Use a straight bar eye section when the edges of the closure overlap or a round eye section when the edges just meet. In place of either of the eye sections, a thread loop may be used. It gives a less conspicuous closing on a garment to be worn open at times or above a zipper.

Mark the position of the hook and eye. The hook is sewed to the overlap or to the right-hand side of the closure if edges just meet. Take several small stitches in the fabric at the marking for the hook to secure the thread. Place the hook about ⅛ inch from the edge of the closure and sew to the underside of the overlap with overhand or buttonhole stitches around the holes. Stitches should not show on the right side of the garment. Take several stitches across under the end of the hook and through the facing to hold it securely.

The bar eye should come just under the bend of the hook section when the garment is lapped and the curve of the bar eye should face toward the outer edge of the closing. Sew in position with an overhand or buttonhole stitch around the holes.

The round eye must extend beyond the edge of the garment. Sew in position with an overhand or buttonhole stitch around the holes. Take several stitches across the sides of the eye and through the facing to hold it securely. Round eyes are sometimes inserted in the seam between the facing and garment so that only the metal eye extends beyond the seam.

Thread eyes are made of matching thread so that they are inconspicuous. Sew two strands of thread on the underlap at the point where the eye is to be placed. Work over these strands with a blanket-stitch, using needle eye first. Bring the needle under the strands and through the loop formed by the stitch.

Lingerie Strap Holders

Use narrow tape or ribbon, about 2 inches long. The opening should always be placed toward the neck edge.

Turn under one end of tape and sew to inside of shoulder seam allowance. Turn under free end of tape and sew one part of snap to it. Sew other part of snap to shoulder seam allowance.

French Tack

This is used to hold two parts of a garment together loosely, as at the lower edge of a coat to hold the lining to the hem. Fasten the thread in one section of the garment and take a stitch in the other section. Take several stitches between the two sections, holding the fabric apart the desired amount. Work over the threads with a blanket stitch keeping them even and close together.

Chain Tack

This could be substituted for the French tack. Using a double thread, fasten the thread securely in one section. Take a short stitch to form thread loop. Hold needle with right hand. Slip thumb and first two fingers of left hand through loop and pick up needle thread. Pull thread through first loop forming a new loop. Continue in this manner keeping chain loops an even size until the chain is the desired length. Place needle through last loop and pull thread through to form knot. Fasten thread in other section of fabric with tiny back-stitches.

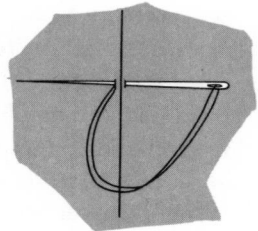

Thread Loops

This type of fastening is most often found at the neck edge of a convertible neckline so that the closing will be inconspicuous when the collar is left open. Use buttonhole twist, silk thread or elastic thread. The button size determines the length of the loop. They are worked the same as thread eyes. Lap closing and sew button under thread loop.

Fabric Loops

Cut a strip of bias fabric the desired width of loop plus seam allowances. Fold in half lengthwise, right sides together, and stitch, leaving ends open. Do not trim seam allowance. This seam allowance forms the filler for the tubing. Attach a strong thread to one end of tube at the seam. Draw the thread through the tubing with a bodkin or heavy needle inserted eye first. Continue pulling end of tube through tubing to turn to right side. Determine the length of loops needed to slip over the button smoothly.

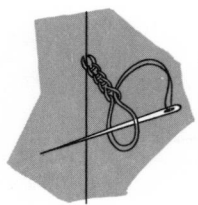

To apply loops in seam, cut loops to correct length plus seam allowance. Mark spacing and size of loops on brown paper and sew loops to paper. Stitch loops and paper to right side of garment along opening. Tear paper away. Apply facing and sew buttons to other side of closure. To apply loops to a finished edge, use a long strip of tubing. Mark position for loops on garment. Determine size of loop needed for button and mark off even lengths on tubing for the loops. Sew to garment between loops with an overhand stitch. Sew buttons to other side of closure.

Corded Loops

Cut a bias strip the necessary width to cover cording plus seam allowances and the desired length. Cut a piece of cording twice the length of the bias. Sew end of bias strip to center of cording. Fold right side of fabric over cording and stitch, using a cording foot. Trim seam allowance and draw enclosed cording out of tubing. This will turn bias inside out and pull free cording into tubing. Use the covered cording for your loops. They can be applied in a seam or to a finished edge in the same way as the fabric loops.

Corded Frogs

These may be made from cording or braid trim. Draw design for frog on brown paper with button loop long enough to slip over button smoothly. Pin and baste cording face down to paper, following pattern. Sew cording securely together where cording meets or crosses. Remove frog from paper and place face up on garment so that loop extends beyond front edge. Slip-stitch frog securely to garment from underside. Overlap edges of garment, centers matched and mark position for button. Sew button under loop.

BELTS

Belts can add a professional finished look to many garments, so select belts with care. Choose the type which is best suited to your garment and your figure. Remember, the wider and more conspicuous the belt, the more attention you will draw to your waistline. This is fine if you have a tiny waist, and don't mind looking a little shorter and wider. If your waist is anything but waspish, a narrow belt of the garment fabric is your best choice. You should investigate the kits available for making belts. Kits are available for various widths, both straight and contour, and usually have buckles with them which can also be easily covered with the garment fabric. They are quite simple to use, and excellent instructions for making the belt and buckle accompany each kit.

All self belts should have stiffening to keep them neat and in shape. The commercial beltings are the best stiffening to use for straight belts, since they are cut to standard widths and can be purchased by the yard. If you cannot find a commercial belting in the width you need, use a heavy interfacing or canvas. For a softer backing, you may wish to try grosgrain ribbon. Be sure to shrink the ribbon before using it in the belt, since it shrinks about 3 inches to the yard.

To determine the proper width belt for a garment, you may want to cut a sample belt of brown paper and try it to see the effect on the garment. Cut several in various widths to find the one which is most flattering.

When a buckle is used on a belt, the belt should be about ⅛ inch narrower than the inside measurement of the buckle. The belt should be cut about 6 inches longer than the waistline measurement to allow for overlap, attaching the buckle and seam allowances. Wide belts must be made longer than the waist measurement. For any belt over 1 inch wide, add ½ inch in length for every additional inch in width.

The popular tie belts are quite easy to make. You may want to make one for a dress which doesn't include one in the pattern. To determine the length, tie a string or ribbon around your waist, and cut it the length you think best. Use this as a guide for the length of your tie belt.

Belt with Belting

Commercial belting gives the most professional-looking belt and never loses its shape even after repeated laundering or dry-cleaning. Cut fabric on lengthwise grain 6 inches longer than waistline measurement and twice the width of the finished belt plus ½-inch seam allowances. Cut the belting the same length as the fabric minus seam allowances at the ends. Cut one end to a point. Fold belt fabric lengthwise, wrong sides together, and press a crease through the middle. Mark a ½-inch seam allowance along the lower edge

of the belt fabric. Baste the belting to the wrong side of the fabric seam allowance with one edge of belting along the marking and a seam allowance extending on each end. Turn in the upper edge of the belt fabric

⅝ inch. Baste and press. Place the belt right side up. Fold up the edge with the ⅝-inch seam allowance on the center crease line and fold the edge with the belting down over it so that the belting covers the belt. Stitch around point. Do not catch the belting in this line of stitching. Trim seam allowances and cut across

point. Turn to right side, encasing the belting in the belt. Note that the folded edge does not come to the lower edge of the belt on the inside. This keeps both edges of the belt the same thickness. Slip-stitch the folded edge to the belt. Do not try to top-stitch a belt with commercial belting. It is difficult to do, and there is danger of breaking the machine needle. On very heavy fabrics, the selvage edge can be used instead of the ⅝-inch turn-under as a finish on the wrong side.

Attach the buckle to the straight end of the belt. Pierce holes and work eyelets in the pointed end of the belt if the buckle has a prong.

Belt with Interfacing

Interfacing makes a much softer belt than belting. Cut fabric on lengthwise grain 6 inches longer than waistline measurement and twice the width of the finished belt plus seam allowances. Cut the interfacing half the width of the belt. Baste interfacing to inside of belt with one edge along center of belt. Tack interfacing to belt fabric along center marking. Fold belt in half

lengthwise, right sides together. Stitch, leaving an opening for turning. Trim interfacing close to stitching and grade seam allowances. Turn to right side and slip-stitch opening edges together. Baste around edges and press. Top-stitch all edges if desired. Attach buckle to straight end and work eyelets in pointed end if buckle has a prong.

Belt with Grosgrain Ribbon Backing

Grosgrain ribbon is used with very heavy fabric to reduce bulk, to finish the back of novelty braid and ribbon belts or to face the back of any fabric belt if you are short of material. Cut pre-shrunk grosgrain ribbon 6 inches longer than your waistline measurement. For fabric belts cut a piece of interfacing the same length as ribbon and ¼ inch wider. Omit interfacing on ribbon or braid belts. Cut fabric on lengthwise grain the same size as the interfacing with ⅜-inch seam allowances. Cut a point at one end of the fabric and interfacing. Baste interfacing to inside of fabric. Turn all edges of the fabric belt over interfacing and baste. Press. Top-stitch around belt, close to edges. Cut one end of the ribbon in the same shaped point as the fabric belt. Turn in ends of ribbon and baste. Baste the ribbon to the inside of fabric belt, wrong sides together. Ribbon will be narrower than belt so edges cannot show. Slip-stitch ribbon to inside of belt. Attach buckle to straight end of belt and work eyelets in pointed end if buckle has a prong.

Tie Belt

A tie belt, without stiffening, becomes a string in no time. Stiffening in the waistline section keeps it smooth and leaves the ends soft for a tie or bow. Cut fabric on lengthwise grain, the waistline measurement plus the desired length for tie ends and twice the width of the finished belt plus seam allowances. Cut a piece of commercial belting 1 inch shorter than the waistline measurement and shape both ends. The belting cut shorter than the waistline measurement allows space to tie the knot and the curved ends allow the fabric

to crush at the knot. Fold fabric in half lengthwise, right sides together. Stitch, leaving an opening at center back. Trim seam, turn and press. Insert belting through opening, matching center of belting to center

of belt. Slip-stitch opening edges together. It is not necessary to tack the belting. It will not shift if the belt has been made exactly the same width as the belting.

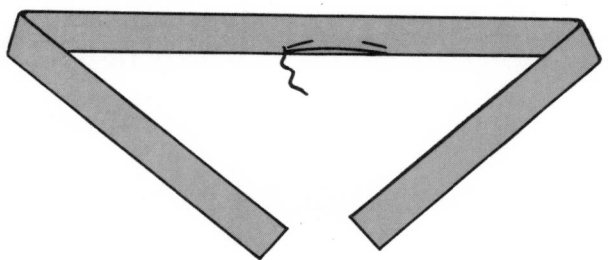

Cummerbund

In order for a cummerbund to fit smoothly to the body and conform to its shape, it should be cut on the bias. Cut a bias piece 10 inches in width and the necessary length, plus 1 inch for seam allowances and overlap. Turn under the lengthwise edges ¼ inch and stitch. Turn under a ¾-inch hem on lengthwise edges and press. Fold the cummerbund crosswise to find the center and then mark a line 1 inch from the center on the back section. The back section of the cummerbund must be smaller than the front to fit the figure

properly. Open out hem. Make three rows of machine basting ¼ inch apart at marking and three rows ½ inch from each end between hem folds. Draw up

gathers to desired width and fasten ends of thread securely. Cut two pieces of featherboning the length of the pulled-up gathers plus seam allowances. Push back the tape covering the boning and cut off the seam allowance from the boning. Fold tape over ends of boning and sew in place. Sew boning to inside of cummerbund over gathers in middle and at back edge. Fold hem back in place covering ends of boning. Tack hem to featherboning but leave rest of hem loose to allow bias to stretch as the cummerbund fits snugly around

the waistline. Stitch woven seam binding to ends. Turn seam binding to inside, turn in ends and slip-stitch in place. Lap front over back and fasten with hooks on the front and bar eyes on the back.

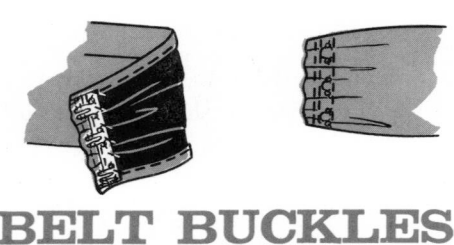

BELT BUCKLES

Buckles are decorative as well as functional and should be correct in color and style for the design and fabric of the garment. They are made from bone, metal, plastic or fabric. There are several types of buckle forms you can have covered or cover yourself with fabric to match your garment. These are very easy to do and the instructions come with the buckle form. Buy the correct size buckle for your belt. The inside of the buckle should be slightly wider than the finished belt width.

  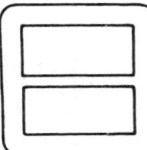

A plain buckle is attached by folding the straight end of the belt over the bar section of the buckle. Turn the straight end to the inside of the belt and stitch in place either by hand or machine.

A buckle with a prong requires an oblong opening at the straight end of the belt. Using a stiletto, punch two holes about ¼ inch apart near the straight end of the belt. Cut between the holes to form the oblong opening. Finish edges of opening same as eyelet. (See page 219.) Insert prong through opening and turn the straight end to the inside of the belt. Stitch end of belt in place by hand or machine.

All buckles with a prong require eyelets at the pointed end of the belt. Thread eyelets can be worked in the fabric or metal eyelets may be used. The metal eyelets come with all covered belt kits, and instructions for applying them are included. However, the metal eyelets are too thick and clumsy for use in fine fabrics.

BELT CARRIERS

Belt carriers are used to hold belts in position at the waistline. They may be made from narrow tubes of fabric or from thread. Make them ⅛ to ¼ inch longer than the width of the belt so that the belt can slip through easily.

Fabric Belt Carriers

Make a length of tubing as for fabric loops, page 223. Cut pieces the desired length plus a small seam allowance at each end. Turn under at the ends and pin in position on garment, centering over waistline seam. Stitch ends to garment and fasten thread securely.

Thread Loop Belt Carrier

Mark position for ends of thread loops on garment. Fasten thread on underside of garment, bring to right side, and take a small stitch at marked position on right side. Loops are worked the same as thread loops for buttons.

Chain Stitch Belt Carrier

This is worked the same as a chain tack, page 222.

CHAPTER 13

THE CUSTOM LOOK

You can be your own designer and give an air of individuality to an outfit, changing a plain one into something distinctive, by adding a touch of trimming to your costume. Browse through magazines and study ready-to-wear and then develop your own ideas.

However, before you begin the actual trimming, a word of caution. There is a general tendency to overdo trimming, so keep your trimmed design simple and make it look like a part of the original garment design. Use it to call attention to only one part of the garment instead of trimming collar, cuffs, hem and belt, so that the effect is confusing and you look shorter and, in turn, broader. Trim the neckline if you want to emphasize a pretty face; the belt if you are proud of a tiny waistline; the hem if you possess shapely legs.

There are a myriad of ways to trim a garment. Bindings, braids and embroidery are just a few. Select the one which is appropriate for the style of the costume and the fabric and be sure it enhances the design. If it doesn't, the trimming should be removed immediately. A plain costume is in better taste than an overly ornate one.

BINDING

Binding used in construction to finish and strengthen a raw edge may also add a decorative trim to a garment. In some cases, it may replace a facing at neckline and armhole edges, or be used to finish front closings, collars, cuffs and seams. Binding may be cut by hand and applied as single or double binding, or it may be purchased as commercial bias tape or binding.

The commercial bias binding is already folded for application, either in single-fold, which is a straight strip with the lengthwise edges folded under and pressed, or double-fold, which is a single-fold strip with an additional center fold pressed in it.

Preparing Binding

CUTTING BIAS STRIPS. Straighten the fabric on both the lengthwise and crosswise grains. Fold the fabric diagonally with the lengthwise grain parallel to the crosswise grain. The diagonal line of the fold is the true bias. Cut along this diagonal fold. Measure and mark the desired width of the strips, evenly spaced, parallel to the diagonal. Cut on these marked lines. The gauge mentioned on page 62 will make the cutting of bias strips easier.

JOINING BIAS STRIPS. To join strips, place two strips right sides together and at right angles to each other so that a diagonal seam will be on the straight grain of the fabric. Overlap the corners of the strips so that the edges are exactly even at the seam line. Stitch seam and press open. Cut off points that extend beyond the edge of strip.

JOINING AND CUTTING CONTINUOUS BIAS STRIPS. If you have a great amount of bias to cut into strips, you will find this method less time consuming. Take a long rectangular piece of fabric. Fold the fabric diagonally at both ends and from opposite corners for true bias. Cut along both diagonal folds. The center strip, shaped as a parallelogram, will be a long strip of true bias fabric. Mark the desired width of the strips on this piece of true bias fabric, beginning at one diagonal end. Join ends of fabric, right sides together with one strip width extending beyond edge at each side. Stitch seam and press open. Begin cutting on marking line at one end and continue in a circular manner.

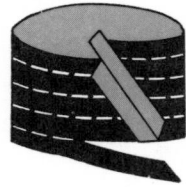

Applying Bias Binding

SINGLE BIAS BINDING. Determine the desired width of the finished binding. Cut a true bias strip of fabric that is twice the desired finished width plus the two seam allowances. Pin binding to garment right sides together, so center of binding will fold over edge of garment and ends. Join at a seam of the garment. Stretch the bias on inside curved edges and ease the bias on outside curves. Stitch the ends of the binding, right sides together, with a plain seam. Press seam open. Stitch binding to seam line of garment. Fold binding over edge of garment, turn under raw edge of binding and hem to stitching line.

To finish binding on the right side, stitch binding to inside of garment. Fold binding to right side and slip-stitch or top-stitch in place.

DOUBLE BIAS BINDING. If the fabric is sheer, it is best to use double bias binding so that raw edges will not show through the binding. Cut a true bias strip of fabric that is six times the desired finished width. Fold it in half, wrong sides together. Press. Stitch raw edges of binding over seam and hem fold to stitching line.

COMMERCIAL BIAS BINDING. The single-fold binding is applied in the same manner as the single bias binding. Double-fold binding is folded with one edge slightly narrower than the other. The double-fold binding can be slipped over the edge of the garment with the fold line directly on the edge of the section to be bound. Place the narrower side on the right side of the garment so that you will be sure to catch the binding on wrong side as it is stitched. Baste the binding in position. Join the binding by overlapping the ends at a seam and slip-stitch the ends together. Machine-stitch from the right side, close to the edge of the binding.

MACHINE BINDER ATTACHMENT. The binder can be adjusted to various widths of binding. Follow the instructions given in your manual which accompanies the attachment. When using the attachment, top-stitching will show on the right side of the binding.

Special Problems in Applying Binding

In working with binding there are certain areas which can cause a little difficulty if the binding application is not handled correctly. Corners need special attention.

BINDING OUTWARD CORNER. On an outward corner, such as the point of a collar, or the corner of a jacket, stitch the binding to the point; allow enough binding at corner to miter. Do not catch fold allowed for the miter in stitching the binding. Sew binding to rest of the edge. Turn bias to inside. At the corner, turn the binding over the edge forming a miter to the point on both sides of binding. Turn in the edge and slip-stitch binding in position on the wrong side of the garment.

BINDING INWARD CORNER. Apply the binding to the edge, drawing bias tight at corner. Leave needle in the fabric at point, raise presser foot and pivot to turn corner. Continue stitching binding to rest of edge. Turn binding to inside and form a miter at the corner on both sides of binding. Slip-stitch along the fold of miter to hold it permanently. Turn in the edge and slip-stitch binding in position on wrong side of garment.

BINDING SCALLOPS. Cut bias strip as for double binding. Fold in half, right sides out, and sew edges of binding to scalloped edge, right sides together. Ease in binding around curves and stretch at inner points. Clip points. Turn binding to inside, mitering binding at points. Hem folded edge to stitching line.

BANDS

Bias Bands

Make a paper pattern the exact shape of the band to be applied. Cut a crinoline stay from this pattern. The stay keeps the bias band an even width and makes it much easier to apply. Cut a bias strip of fabric twice the finished width of the band. Working on the ironing board, center the crinoline stay on the wrong side of the fabric band. Hold in place with a row of pins through the center of the stay, shaping the bias band to fit the stay as you work. Turn the raw edges of the bias band over the stay and steam-press in place. Baste the raw edges of the band over the center of the stay with diagonal stitches. Baste the band in position. From the wrong side of the garment, sew both edges of the band in place with a tiny back-stitch. Check as you work to be sure stitches are not showing on the right side.

RUFFLING

Ruffling is a strip of fabric or lace gathered or pleated at one edge. It may be purchased commercially or you may make your own.

Making Ruffle

To make ruffling, cut a strip of fabric on lengthwise grain the desired length and width plus hem allowance and seam allowance. To determine the desired length of the strip for the ruffle, first measure the exact length of the edge of the garment to which the ruffle is to be attached. Next determine the amount of fullness you desire in the ruffle. Usually a ruffle is 2 or 3 times fuller than the edge to which it is applied. A wide ruffle should have more fullness than a narrow one to keep it from looking skimpy.

Turn under and hem the lower edges of the ruffle by hand or machine. Make two rows of machine-basting along upper edge, one on the seam line and one ⅛ inch inside seam allowance. Use heavy-duty thread or buttonhole twist on the bobbin thread to keep the thread from breaking when the gathers are pulled up.

If you have a large area to gather it also helps to gather the piece in sections rather than on one continuous thread. Do not pull up the gathering threads until you are ready to apply the ruffle to the garment.

The ruffler attachment on the sewing machine can be used to gather or pleat the upper edge. Test on a scrap of fabric, adjusting the attachment according to the directions in the manual, until you obtain the desired fullness. The ruffler attachment will stitch the ruffling to the section of the garment at the same time the fullness is being gathered or pleated.

Although a ruffle is usually made of a single thickness of fabric, it can be made double. Cut a strip of fabric twice as wide as the width of the ruffle plus the seam allowance. Fold the fabric strip in half and treat as a single thickness.

Ruffle Applied in a Seam

Pin the ruffle to one of the pieces to be joined in the seam, right sides up, matching seam lines. Pull up the gathering threads and adjust the fullness evenly to fit the space. Baste in place. Pin the second section over the ruffle, right sides together, matching seam lines. Stitch the seam and grade the seam allowances. Press seam allowances away from the ruffle.

Ruffle Extending from an Edge

This occurs in collars, cuffs and edges of facings. Pin the ruffle to the garment or one section of the collar or cuff, right sides together, matching seam lines. Pull up the gathering threads and adjust the fullness, allowing a little extra fullness at corners. Baste in place, tapering ruffle at ends. Pin the facing or second section over the ruffle. Stitch seam and grade seam allowances. Turn facing to wrong side, leaving ruffle free.

Ruffle Applied with Bias Strip

Pin ruffle to garment, right sides together, matching seam lines. Pull up the gathering threads and adjust the fullness evenly. Baste bias strip over the ruffle and stitch the seam. Grade seam allowance. Press seam allowance and bias strip toward garment and away from ruffle. Turn in edge of bias strip and hem to garment.

Ruffle Applied with Heading

Turn under the upper edge of ruffle the desired width of heading plus a seam allowance. Make two rows of gathering, one along seam line, the other just above. Pin ruffle to under fabric, right sides up, matching seam lines. Pull up gathering threads and adjust gathers evenly. Baste and stitch seam with ruffle side up through all thicknesses.

Circular Ruffle

Cut ruffle in circular form the desired width plus hem and seam allowance. The smaller the inner circle the fuller the ruffle will be. Seam ruffle pieces together for desired length with a flat-fell, French or plain seam. Stay-stitch the inner edge of the seam line. Turn under and hem the lower edge by hand or machine. Clip to the stay-stitching on upper edge so it will lie flat. Pin and sew in position.

Double Ruffle

Cut ruffle the desired width plus hem allowances on both edges. Finish both edges with a narrow hand or machine hem. Place a gathering thread through the center of the ruffle. Pin center of ruffle to stitching line for ruffle on the garment, right sides up. Pull up gathering thread and adjust gathers evenly. Top-stitch ruffle to garment along line of gathering stitches.

CORDING

Cording is made by covering cord with bias fabric. It can be set into a seam or used as a surface trim. The bias fabric for covering the cord is cut and joined in the same way as for binding.

Cording in a Seam

Encase cord in a bias strip of fabric and stitch close to cord with a cording foot. Baste cording to right side of garment with stitching line along seam line of unfinished edge. Baste facing over cording and stitch seam with a cording foot. Grade seam allowances and press seam away from cording.

Turned Cording

This type of cording is used for buttonhole loops, ties and other surface trims. Cut a piece of cord twice the length of the strip of bias fabric. Attach one end of the bias strip to center of the cord. Fold right side of bias strip over cord and stitch, using a cording foot.

Trim seam. Pull the encased cord out of the tubing. This will automatically turn the bias to the right side and pull the free cord into the bias tubing. Cut off the extra cord.

BRAID

There is a wide variety of novelty braid on the market but all can be applied by one of these methods.

Narrow Bias Braid

Soutache and other narrow bias braid can be used to outline the lines of a design. It is applied by hand or by machine using a braiding foot. Follow directions given in machine manual. If braid pulls up, place paper under fabric and sew through it. Tear paper away after stitching is completed.

Flat Braid

These braids come in a number of widths and are used mostly as a border trim. They are applied with hand- or machine-stitching along both edges of the braid.

READY-FOLDED BRAID. These braids are of a woven bias construction so that they can be shaped to fit around a curved edge. The braid is already folded so that it can be easily applied as an edge finish. The top edge is always folded slightly narrower so that the underside is sure to catch when stitching. Shape the braid with a steam iron before basting it to a curved edge. Stretch the folded edge to fit around an outward curve and stretch the open edge for an inward curve. Stitch in place by hand or machine.

RICK RACK. Rick rack braid can be used as a piping, an edging or to outline a design. When used as a piping, the edge of the garment is lapped and stitched over the rick rack so that just half of the rick rack shows, forming a point design. As an edging, the rick rack is lapped and stitched over the edge of the

garment so that both pointed edges of the rick rack are visible. If used to outline a design, the rick rack is placed over the pencil or chalk marking for the design and stitched through the center.

FRINGE

Fringe is an edge trim made from threads of the fabric or from yarn. The kind of fringe used depends on the effect you wish to create. The fringe made by drawing threads of the fabric is very fine while fringe made from yarn can be heavy and bulky, depending on the weight of yarn used. Ready-made fringe can also be purchased by the yard.

Self Fringe

Be sure edge of fabric to be fringed is cut on a single thread of the straight fabric grain. Mark the depth of fringe on the fabric and stay-stitch this line with zig-zag or straight machine-stitching. Ravel the threads of the fabric to the line of stay-stitching.

Knotted Fringe

Cut a piece of cardboard the desired depth of fringe. Wind yarn around it. Cut at one edge. Count the number of yarns depending on the weight of fringe you wish to make. Insert a crochet hook through fabric and pull yarn through forming a loop. Draw yarn ends through loop and pull tight. Continue pulling groups of yarn through fabric, keeping each group the same size and an even distance from the edge.

Ready-Made Fringe

This comes with a heading and can be applied to a shaped edge, while fringe made by drawing a thread must always be on a straight edge. The ready-made

fringe can be top-stitched to the garment as a border or edging, or it can also be applied with a facing. When a facing is used, baste the fringe to the edge of the garment, right sides together, with seam line of fringe along seam line of garment. Baste facing over fringe and stitch seam. Grade seam allowance and turn facing to inside.

TASSELS

The tassel is used as a finish for the end of a tie or a cord. Cut a piece of cardboard the desired depth. Place a piece of yarn across top of cardboard and then wind yarn around cardboard to desired fullness. Tie the top firmly with the piece of yarn placed at the top of the cardboard. Wrap yarn around the top end several times and tie to hold strands together. Trim cut ends evenly.

POMPONS

The pompon is similar in construction to the tassel but has many more yarns and is very compact. The tassel hangs down while the pompon sticks up from the surface of the garment. The pompon can be used just as an ornament or can be substituted for a button trim. Cut a square of cardboard. Place a piece of yarn along the top and wind yarn around the cardboard. The more yarn on the cardboard the fuller the pompon will be. Tie securely at one end and cut yarn at other end. Shake to fluff up the yarn and then trim ends of yarn evenly to form a ball.

BEADING

Beading is a very effective trim but tedious to do. It should be done after the garment is completed. Mark the outline for design on the right side of the fabric with chalk. Wax the thread with beeswax to prevent the thread from twisting and breaking.

Beads Applied Singly

Working from right to left, sew each bead on individually with a back-stitch following along the line of the design. Be sure to fasten all ends of thread securely.

Beads Applied on a Thread

Tiny beads can be strung on a heavy thread. The thread holding the beads is then whip-stitched to the garment along the line of the design. A whip-stitch must be taken between each bead.

SEQUINS

Sequins, like beads, are applied after the garment is finished. Machine-stitching will break the sequins near the seam. Mark the design on the right side of the fabric with chalk.

Sequins Applied Singly

Sequins sewed on singly are usually applied with a small bead in the center. Fasten the thread on the wrong side of the fabric. Bring the needle through center of sequin and bead and back down through the center of the sequin. Fasten thread in the fabric.

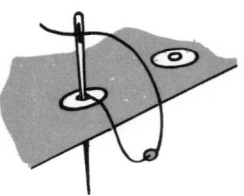

Sequins Applied in a Row

Working from right to left, bring needle through the fabric and the center of the sequin. Take a back-stitch in the fabric and draw up thread until sequin is flat against the fabric. Continue sewing on the sequins in this manner so that the edges of the sequins are overlapped.

APPLIQUÉ

Appliqué is the method of applying a design of one fabric to a second fabric. A motif may be selected from a printed fabric or the design can be traced on the fabric. It may be applied by hand or machine.

Hand Appliqué

Machine-stitch around the outside of the design. Cut out the design to be appliquéd, allowing a ⅛-inch seam allowance beyond the row of machine-stitching. Turn under the edges of the piece along the line of stitching and baste. Press the piece so that it lies perfectly flat before it is basted in position. The design may be applied with a blanket or buttonhole stitch or by slip-stitching.

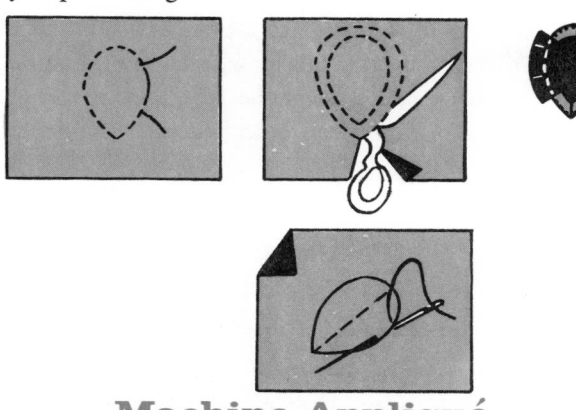

Machine Appliqué

Cut out the design of the appliqué, leaving a ¼-inch margin around edges. Pin the design to the fabric to which it is to be applied and machine-stitch in place along the seam line. Trim close to stitching. Cover raw edge and machine-stitching with a very close zigzag or satin stitch.

Bias Tape Appliqué

This is particularly suited to making monograms. Transfer the design markings to the fabric. Turn under the cut edge of the tape and pin single-fold bias tape along the markings. Stretch tape around outside curves, ease around inside curves and miter corners.

Turn in end of tape and slip-stitch or machine-stitch tape in position.

LACE

Lace can be used as an edging, as insertion or to make an entire garment. Due to the delicate, open construction of lace, special construction techniques are required.

Lace Edging

Lace edging has one straight edge which is applied to fabric or insertion. All edging should be gathered slightly before it is attached.

GATHERING LACE EDGING. Draw up heavy thread in upper edge of lace, gathering to desired fullness. Secure ends of thread by winding around pins. Adjust fullness evenly.

LACE EDGING APPLIED TO HEMMED EDGE. Gather edging the desired amount. Place lace on right side of finished hem. Working from right to left, sew lace to fabric with a close whip-stitch.

LACE EDGING APPLIED TO ROLLED EDGE. Gather edging the desired amount. Hold fabric toward you; roll edge of fabric and join edge of lace in one operation. Sew from right to left with a small, even whip-stitch.

LACE EDGING APPLIED TO INSERTION. Gather edging the desired amount. Place lace over insertion, right sides together. Working from right to left, whip-stitch the straight edges together.

LACE EDGING APPLIED BY MACHINE. Gather edging slightly. Lap the straight side of the edging over the edge of the fabric, right sides up. Join with a machine zigzag stitch.

LACE EDGING WITH A MITERED CORNER. Pin edging around corner of fabric allowing enough for mitering. Fold the edging at corner, forming a miter. Cut away excess lace and whip edges together by hand or with a machine zigzag stitch.

Lace Insertion

Lace insertion has both edges finished the same. They can be either straight or scalloped. The straight insertion is usually set into fabric or between fabric and lace edging. The scalloped insertion can also be used as a flat edge finish.

LACE INSERTION APPLIED BY HAND. Baste insertion to right side of fabric. Sew both edges of the insertion to the fabric with a fine hemming stitch. Cut away fabric under the lace, leaving enough so that edges of fabric can be rolled and whipped in place.

LACE INSERTION APPLIED BY MACHINE. Baste insertion to right side of fabric. Sew both edges of the insertion to the fabric with a machine zigzag stitch. Cut away the fabric under the lace, and trim close to stitching.

SCALLOPED INSERTION USED AS FLAT EDGE FINISH. Lap and baste insertion over unfinished edge of fabric, right sides up. Sew edge of insertion to fabric with a zigzag stitch. On the wrong side, trim fabric close to stitching.

DECORATIVE STITCHES

Decorative stitches or stitching should add to the finished appearance of a garment. Such trimming usually carries the eye to the one area and makes it the center of interest.

Hand Edge-Stitching

Saddle, glove and prick stitches are all decorative hand top-stitching used to outline the edges of a garment. These are usually done with several strands of embroidery floss or buttonhole twist in a matching or contrasting color.

SADDLE STITCHING. Take short stitches through the garment and facing an even distance from the edge. The stitches on the top side are longer than the stitches on the underside.

GLOVE STITCHING. This is done in the same manner as the saddle stitch but the stitches on the top and underside are equal in length.

PRICK STITCHING. Take short half-back-stitches in which only two or three threads of the fabric are picked up. Insert the needle diagonally through the fabric and pull each stitch tight.

Machine Edge-Stitching

Machine-stitching used to trim the edges of a garment can be placed close to the edge or as much as 1½ inches from the edge, depending on the effect you wish to create. You may use a single row of stitching or a number of rows. Keep stitching an even distance from the edge and the rows an even distance apart if there is to be more than one row of stitching. This top stitching must be straight or it will spoil the appearance of your garment.

Tacks

Tacks are decorative thread reinforcements used on the right side of the fabric at ends of pockets, seams and pleats. They can be made of buttonhole twist or embroidery floss. The bar tack is the least conspicuous and is used mostly on tailored garments or men's clothes. The arrowhead and crow's-foot tack are more decorative and very attractive when well made.

BAR TACK. Take several long stitches through fabric, across ends of opening. Cover these strands with overhand stitches close together, picking up a few threads of the fabric at the same time. Finish ends of bar tack with small bar tacks at right angles to it.

ARROWHEAD TACK. Mark the triangular outline for the tack on the right side of the fabric with chalk or basting stitches. Start by bringing needle out at lower left-hand corner and take a small stitch across upper corner from right to left. Insert the needle at lower right-hand corner and bring needle out at left corner just inside first stitch. Continue placing stitches close to each other in this pattern around the triangle until the entire area is filled in.

CROW'S-FOOT TACK. Mark outline of tack with chalk or basting stitches on the right side of the fabric. Bring needle out at lower left-hand corner and take a small horizontal stitch across upper corner from right to left. Insert the needle at lower right-hand corner and take a small diagonal stitch across the point from left to right. Insert the needle at lower left-hand corner and take a small diagonal stitch across the point from left to right. Continue placing stitches close to each other in this pattern around the triangle until the area is filled in.

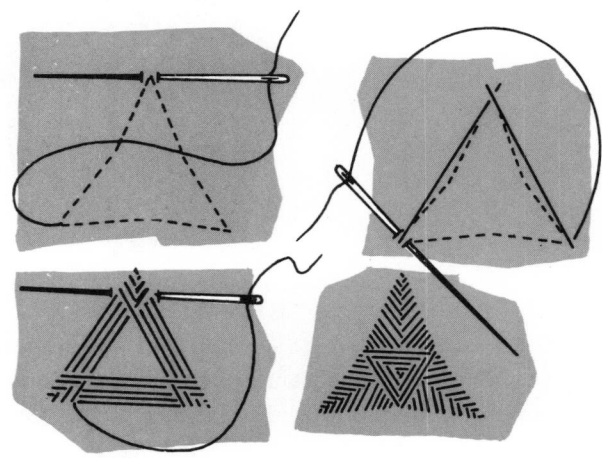

Hemstitching

Hemstitching is made by drawing out threads of the fabric. It must always be done in straight lines following the grain of the material. The different kinds of hemstitching are formed by grouping the threads of the fabric in various ways.

Mark the hem width and then draw out the required number of threads above the hem marking. Turn up the hem and baste it along the line where the first thread was drawn. Use regular mercerized sewing thread for hemstitching.

SINGLE HEMSTITCHING Work from left to right with wrong side of fabric uppermost. Bring needle out at the edge of hem. Pick up the desired number of threads on needle, passing needle from right to left.

Take a tiny stitch in the hem just to the right of the threads you have encircled. Pull the sewing thread tight around the drawn threads. Continue in this manner.

DOUBLE HEMSTITCHING. Make single hemstitching along the hem edge. Turn the work around and repeat the same stitch taking a tiny stitch through the fabric along the inner edge. Pick up the same groups of threads with each stitch to form straight bars between the edges.

DIAGONAL HEMSTITCHING. Make single hemstitching along the hem edge, picking up an even number of threads with each stitch. Turn work around. Pass the needle around half of the first group of threads and half of the second group of threads and then through fabric making a zigzag line of bars.

Fagoting

Fagoting is a decorative joining of two finished edges with buttonhole twist or heavy embroidery floss. This open-work stitch can be used on curved or shaped areas.

Turn under the raw edges of the two pieces of fabric to be joined. Press. Draw two parallel lines on a piece of brown paper, the desired distance apart. Baste the edge of the fabric to the paper along the lines marked, right side up. Work from the top of the design down.

CRISS-CROSS FAGOTING. Bring the needle to the right side of the material through the fold at the upper-left corner. Take a diagonal stitch across to the other side bringing the needle up through the fabric. Pass the needle under the thread and take a diagonal stitch on the other side. Continue stitching in this manner. Remove the paper when fagoting is completed.

LADDER OR BAR FAGOTING. Take stitches from left side to right side straight across. Wrap thread around needle several times and bring needle out at left again. Slip needle between fold along edge and bring out to start next stitch. Continue making stitches in this way. Remove the paper when completed.

Smocking

Smocking is a decorative way of holding fullness in even folds. It should be done on the fabric before the garment is constructed. There are two methods of smocking—regular and English smocking.

In regular smocking the transfer is stamped on the right side of the fabric, and the pleats and gathers are made as the dots of the smocking pattern are picked up. English smocking has rows of gathering thread run through rows of evenly spaced dots stamped on the wrong side of the fabric. These dots are pulled up to gather the material into evenly spaced pleats. The decorative smocking stitches are then worked on the right side of the fabric on top of the pleats. Gathering threads are removed after smocking is done. The same smocking stitches can be used in both types of smocking. Use six-strand embroidery floss for all smocking.

OUTLINE STITCH. Work from left to right. Bring the needle to right side of fabric at dot 1. Place thread above needle. Insert needle in fabric under dot 2. Pull up the thread so that fold is made. Continue in this way making one stitch at each dot.

CABLE STITCH. Working from left to right, bring the needle to right side of fabric at dot 1. Put thread above needle. Insert needle in the fabric under dot 2 and bring it out. Draw up the thread. For second stitch, hold the thread below needle and make a stitch at dot 3. Hold the thread above needle for stitch at dot 4. Continue across the row in this manner.

DOUBLE CABLE STITCH. Work a second row of cable stitches under the first, placing thread above and below the needle in opposite directions.

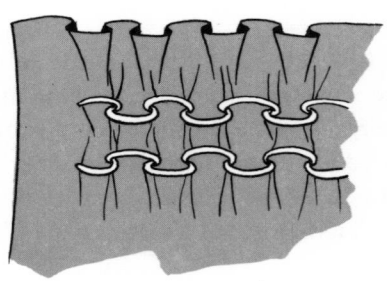

HONEYCOMB OR SEED STITCH. Work from left to right on two alternating rows of dots. Bring the needle up to right side of fabric through first dot on top row. With thread above needle, take a small stitch at dot 2 and another at dot 1. Draw together tightly. Insert needle at dot 2, carry thread under fabric and bring it out at dot 3 on the row below. Keeping thread below needle, pick up dot 4 and dot 3 in the same manner as dot 2 and dot 1. Insert needle at dot 4, carry thread under fabric and bring out at dot 5 on the top row. Continue working in this manner, alternating the stitch from one row to the other until completed.

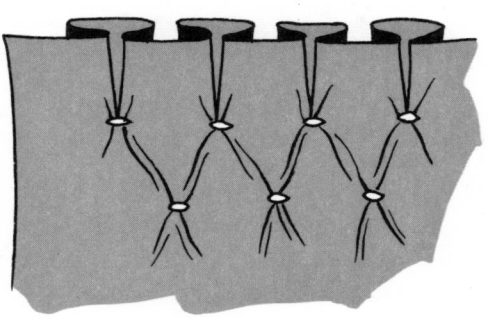

TWO-STEP WAVE STITCH. This is done with six dots in each wave group. Working from left to right, bring the needle up at left of dot 1. Take a stitch through dot 1 with thread above needle. Pull down, drawing thread tight. Take a stitch through dots 2 and 3 with thread above needle and pull down after each stitch. Take a stitch through dot 4 with thread below needle and pull up. Take a stitch through dots 5 and 6 with thread below needle and pull up after each stitch. Pick up dot 1 of next group with thread above needle and pull down. Continue in this manner until design is completed.

DIAMOND OR CHEVRON STITCH. This looks like the honeycomb stitch except that the thread between the rows is carried on top of the fabric instead of under the fabric. Work from left to right on two alternating rows of dots. Bring the needle up to right side of fabric through first dot on top row. With thread above needle, take a small stitch at dot 2. Draw together tightly. Take a stitch at dot 3. With thread below needle, take a stitch at dot 4 and pull the thread tight. Take a stitch at dot 5. With thread above needle, take a stitch at dot 6. Draw together tightly. Continue in this manner alternating from one row to the other.

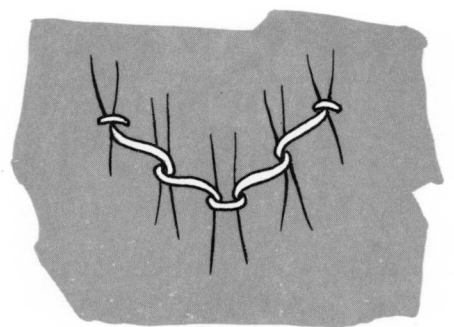

THREE-STEP WAVE STITCH. This is done with eight dots in each wave group. Working from left to right, bring the needle up at left of dot 1. Take a stitch through dot 1 with thread above needle. Pull down, drawing thread tight. Take a stitch through dots 2, 3 and 4 with thread above needle and pull down after each stitch. Take a stitch through dot 5 with the thread below needle and pull up. Take a stitch through dots 6, 7 and 8 with thread below needle and pull up after each stitch. Pick up dot 1 of next group with thread above needle and pull down. Continue in this manner until design is completed.

Hand Embroidery

There are a great variety of hand-embroidery stitches. These stitches may be used individually or combined with other stitches to form a more elaborate design.

When doing hand embroidery, mark the design on the right side of the fabric. Always use embroidery hoops to hold the fabric firm and keep it from puckering as stitches are pulled tight. Fasten the threads with tiny back-stitches instead of using knots.

RUNNING STITCH. Working from right to left, pick up several small stitches on the needle. Draw the thread through the fabric. Continue in this manner, keeping the stitches an even size and length.

TWISTED RUNNING STITCH. After completing the running stitch, working from left to right, overcast the stitches with thread of matching or contrasting color and weight. Use a blunt-end needle and run it under each stitch but do not catch any of the fabric. This gives the effect of a twisted cord.

STEM OR OUTLINE STITCH. Working from left to right, bring thread through to right side of fabric. Take a back stitch ¼ inch away. Take a second back-stitch, bringing needle out close to last stitch. Continue in this manner, keeping stitches even. For the stem stitch the thread is placed below the needle; for the outline stitch the thread is placed above the needle.

STRAIGHT OR SPOKE STITCH. This is a single flat stitch used to form flowers, stems, leaves.

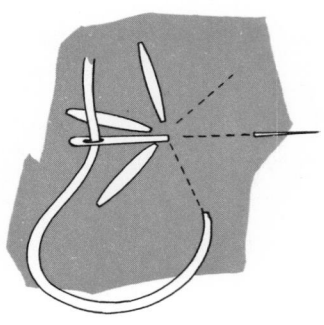

SATIN STITCH. This makes a smooth covering for regular- or irregular-shaped spaces. Carry the thread across the design and take a stitch under the fabric, bringing the needle out at the starting point. Keep the stitches even and very close together. For a more raised effect, the design should be padded with tiny running stitches in the opposite direction from the satin stitch to be applied over it.

HERRINGBONE STITCH. This is the same as the catch-stitch used in sewing. Work from left to right along two parallel lines. Bring the needle out at lower left corner. Take a stitch through fabric from right to left on top line. Then take a stitch through fabric from right to left on bottom line so that the thread between the two parallel lines is slanted. Keep stitches an even length and an even distance apart.

CROSS STITCH. Work from left to right along two parallel lines. Make first half of crosses by taking diagonal stitches with needle straight and point down. Complete entire row forming half of the cross stitch. Then work from right to left, filling in the second half of the cross in the same manner. Keep stitches even.

BLANKET STITCH. Working from left to right, bring needle out on marked line or at edge of the fabric. Hold thread down and take a stitch, pointing needle toward you with thread under needle. Draw needle through loop that has been formed. Stitches may be even length and distance apart or grouped and spaced according to the desired effect. Keep stitches or groupings even.

SCALLOPED EDGE. Outline the scallops with small running stitches. Working from left to right and holding lower edge of scallops toward you, work blanket stitches between the outline stitches. Keep stitches very close together and even. Trim fabric away close to scallops after embroidery is completed.

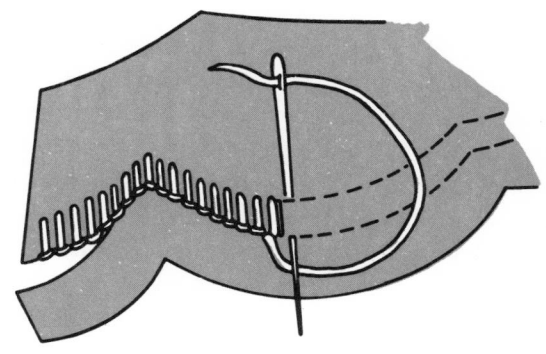

FEATHER STITCH. This is a blanket stitch made at an angle. Working from top to bottom, bring needle out at beginning of marking. Hold thread down and take a slanting stitch to the right, and a little below this spot. The needle will be pointing to the left. Pull the needle through the fabric and over the thread. Carry thread to the left and make a similar stitch with needle pointed to the right. Continue alternating the stitches from right to left, keeping them evenly spaced. This stitch can be varied by marking several blanket stitches on each side.

CHAIN STITCH. Work from right to left. Bring needle to right side of fabric. Insert needle in fabric at almost the same point and take a stitch, looping thread under the point of needle. Pull up the thread, forming a loop. Put needle back into fabric inside loop, close to emerging thread. Take another stitch with thread around and under point of needle. Continue, keeping stitches and loops even.

LADDER STITCH. A double row of dots is used to mark the ladder stitch. Working from top to bottom, bring needle out at top left-hand dot. Hold thread down. Take a slanting stitch from top right-hand dot to second left-hand dot, passing needle over the thread. Pull up thread forming a loop. Take another slanting stitch from second right-hand dot to third left-hand dot. Pass needle over the thread and form the next loop by pulling up the thread. Continue in this manner, working down the dots from right to left.

FLY STITCH. This is an open chain stitch made in the shape of a V. Working from left to right, bring needle to right side of fabric at a point which will be the top of the left side of the V. Hold thread down, insert needle at the top of the right side of the V and bring it out at the base of the V. Pull the needle through the fabric and insert the needle below the base of the V to hold the loop in place.

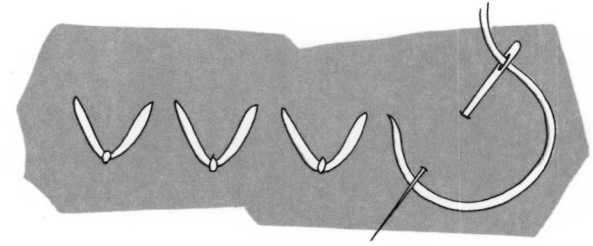

LAZY DAISY STITCH. This is a detached chain stitch radiating from a center point to form petals of a flower. Bring needle to right side of fabric at center of flower. Holding thread down, insert needle as close as possible to the starting point. Take a long stitch the length of the petal to form a loop. Pull the needle through the fabric and take a short stitch to hold the end of the loop in place. Bring needle back to center to start the next petal.

SEED STITCH. This is a very tiny chain stitch tightly drawn and scattered in all directions to fill an open area.

FRENCH KNOT. Bring needle to right side of fabric at point knot is to be placed. Wind thread around needle two or three times. Holding thread firmly around needle, insert needle in fabric as close as possible to the point it came out. Pull thread to wrong side. The more times the thread is wrapped around the needle the heavier the French knot will be.

BULLION STITCH. This stitch is similar to the French knot in construction. The thread is wrapped around the needle four or five times and the needle is inserted a short distance from the point it emerged. It is used mainly for embroidering roses.

COUCHING STITCH. Use a single or double cord of either matching or contrasting color to follow the line of the design. Working from right to left, catch the cord down firmly by bringing thread over cord and through fabric with evenly spaced stitches.

Machine Embroidery

Machine embroidery can be done with attachments on your straight-stitch machine or by a zigzag machine. Follow the directions in the booklet supplied with the sewing machine. Always make a test sample first on your fabric. Test thread, pressure on the presser foot and tension. Practice using the machine until you are adept at handling the machine for decorative stitching.

You can follow designs provided with the pattern or make your own designs. Transfer markings for the design to the right side of the fabric and do the embroidery on the right side of the material.

To embroider designs on sheer fabric you may need to baste a piece of tissue or organdy to the wrong side of the fabric under the design to keep the fabric from slipping and pulling. If tissue is used, tear it away after embroidery is completed. If organdy is used, trim it close to stitching after embroidery is completed.

CHAPTER 14

TAILORING TALK

One of the biggest events in the life of a seamstress is the day she appears in a beautifully tailored suit or coat of her own making. She has a perfect right to be proud. Tailoring is not a hard task, but it is an exacting one. It takes time and attention to detail to tailor well, but the extra effort is rewarded by the overwhelming sense of pride one takes in turning out a truly high quality garment.

Before you attempt any tailoring, you should have an ideal in mind. You should know what constitutes a good coat or suit. If you are going to spend the extra time it takes to tailor, you want the garment to have a professional appearance.

Examine better ready-to-wear tailored garments. If possible, visit a custom tailor's shop and examine the garments he makes. Note how thin the edges of the garments are, even where you would expect to find thick, bulky seams. Notice, too, how the edges of the lapels curl toward the body, never outward. Seams are flat and straight with no crooks or puckers. Linings are loosely tacked to the seams so they don't interfere with the drape of the garment. Buttons are carefully sewed on with an ample shank so they won't pull on the buttonholes. The collars and lapels roll smoothly. Only by recognizing good tailoring in a garment, can you attempt to become an expert tailor.

TAILORING EQUIPMENT

Tailoring requires some additional equipment besides that needed for dressmaking. You will need a tailor's ham, wooden clapper, point presser, needle board and a seam roll. (See page 61.) If you plan to do quite a bit of tailoring, you may want to invest in one of the heavy tailor's flatirons. The extra weight of the iron helps produce the sharp tailored edges you want.

The secret of fine tailoring is actually in the pressing and molding of the garment, so keep your pressing equipment handy. You will use it just as often as your machine.

FABRICS FOR TAILORING

Tailoring is a building and molding process. It is best to select a fabric which can be easily molded through steaming, shrinking and pressing over shaping mate-

rials. Wool is the best selection since it shapes and shrinks so beautifully. A medium-weight wool with a spongy texture and an unfinished or napped surface such as tweed or flannel will be best for your first tailored garment. They are easier to shrink and shape and will not shine readily when pressed. Avoid the worsteds such as covert, gabardine or anything with a hard finish. These are difficult to shrink and press. Save plaids, checks, stripes and very heavy coatings until you have had some experience in tailoring. The patterned materials create problems in matching and very heavy coatings tend to slip under the presser foot of the machine when stitching several thicknesses of fabric.

Linings

Linings are subject to more wear and stress than the actual garment fabric. Select a lining fabric that is durable, opaque, colorfast to perspiration, capable of being dry-cleaned and in a color which harmonizes with the color of the garment. Select a smooth-finished fabric which is easy to slip in and out of. Fabrics most frequently used are silk crepe, soft satin, silk taffeta, surah, rayons or synthetics of similar construction.

Aluminum-backed lining fabrics will provide additional warmth without weight. These are available in crepes and satins and a few have both the aluminum and a laminated backing which gives greater warmth to the garment than those without the laminated backing.

Interfacing

For any tailoring, you will need interfacing fabric to give firmness and shaping to the garment and to reinforce collar, cuffs, buttonholes, buttons and hems. For tailoring woolen garments, use a weight of hair canvas that is suitable for the weight of your fabric. This same hair canvas or pre-shrunk muslin is used to interface sleeve and jacket hems. For tips on selecting the proper interfacing, check the chart in Chapter 3.

Interlining

For heavy coats which need additional warmth, you will want a lining plus an interlining. Make it of special interlining material. There are several good commercial interlining fabrics on the market, and these are listed in the shaping materials chart.

Patterns will give the proper yardages for garment fabric, interfacing, interlining and lining. Most suits will have lining fabric listed only for jackets. If you wish to line the skirt also, purchase additional yardage equal to the yardage needed for the skirt. If skirt yardages are not listed separately on the pattern, then measure the length of the skirt and buy lining yardage equal to two skirt lengths.

Pre-Shrunk and Grain Perfect

Be sure that all fabrics you use are pre-shrunk and that they are grain perfect. Check our suggestions in Chapter 7 for fabric preparation. In tailoring it is even more essential to the good looks of the garment than it is in dressmaking for grain lines to be perfectly straight. The garment simply will not mold and shape correctly if grain lines are not maintained on all fabrics.

Notions

Select all the notions needed for the garment before you begin any construction. Usually you will need seam binding, zipper, silk or mercerized sewing thread, buttonhole twist, ¼-inch twill tape, buttons, hooks and eyes and snaps. Check pattern envelope carefully for special items such as cording, braid or weights which may be needed for your garment. Shoulder pads are optional.

THE PATTERN

Your first suit or coat should be an important item in your wardrobe for years to come. After all, if you are going to spend the time and effort required to tailor well, you will want a garment you can wear for more than the current season. Select a basic suit in classic style. Avoid the extreme styles which may become dated. Select the suit design which is most flattering. Buy the pattern in your correct figure type and size.

Suit and coat patterns are both purchased in the same figure type and size as your dress patterns. DO NOT buy a larger size. The correct amount of ease for proper fit has been included in the pattern and it is not necessary to allow extra.

Adjust the suit pattern, just as you do your dress pattern. If you need to narrow the shoulders, then do so using the same method as outlined for narrow shoulders in a dress, page 80. It is never necessary to allow extra for pads. Shoulder pads today are used to correct figure faults such as one low shoulder or sloping shoulders. Adding extra pad allowance to your pattern only creates a worse alteration problem.

If you are in doubt about your alterations, then make the suit in muslin, just as you made your basic pattern. Remember that muslin will not drape the same as wool fabric. Additional minor alterations will have to be made in the wool fabric but the muslin will be very helpful if you have a number of major alterations. Be sure to allow sufficient ease in the muslin for the weight of the fabric, interfacing and lining.

TAILORING A SUIT

Cutting and Marking

After all necessary pattern alterations have been made, lay out the pattern following the diagrams on the pattern guide sheet. If the fabric has a nap, cut it with the nap running down and place all pattern pieces in the same direction. Material with a pile is usually cut with the pile running up for a rich effect. Plaids should be matched both crosswise and lengthwise. Use the same line of the plaid for center front and center back. Diagonal-weave fabrics should be cut with the diagonal running from the left side toward the right in the front and from the right to the left in the back.

Cut and mark the fabric following the same procedure as suggested for dressmaking on page 103. Be careful to cut and mark accurately. You may find when cutting a double section that the under fabric is cut slightly larger than the upper section of fabric, because shears slip slightly due to the thickness of the material. Check each section, and trim so that the two are identical in size with the pattern.

If the wool is a very soft or stretchy one, you may wish to underline each section with china silk or the lightest weights of commercial underlining. Cut from the same pattern pieces used for the suit, and mark these carefully. If an underlining is used, you will not have to mark the suit fabric, except for placement of trims, center front and back and grain-line positions. These markings are best done by hand-bastings.

The pattern usually has separate pattern pieces for interfacing sections. If for some reason these pieces do not accompany the pattern, then cut them from the jacket pieces. Mark the cutting lines on the pattern. On the pattern front, mark the width of the facing from hemline along the front edge. Then mark a short line 3 inches below the armscye. Draw a curved line from the underarm marking to ½ inch wider than the facing width at the front edge. On the back, mark a line from

3 inches below the underarm curving up to 4 to 5 inches below the center back neckline. Cut the interfacing on the same grain as the suit fabric, using the marked pattern pieces.

Be sure to make all the alterations on the lining pattern pieces that you made on the jacket pattern. If you wish to line a suit, and no lining pattern is given, you can make a lining pattern by using your jacket pieces. On the front pattern piece, extend the cutting line 1¼ inches beyond the marking for front facing. The lining overlaps the front facing ⅝ inch and the other ⅝ inch gives seam allowance for turning under

the raw edge. On the back pattern piece, extend the cutting line 1¼ inches beyond the marking for the back facing. The back of the lining section has a pleat at the center back to keep the lining from pulling during wear. Fold the fabric and place the center back marking ¾ to 1 inch beyond the fold to allow for the back pleat. Cut lining along the hemline marking at the bottom of the jacket. The sleeve is cut the same as the suit sleeve except that it is cut off at the hemline marking.

If you plan to line the skirt completely, use the skirt pattern pieces, and cut the lining fabric identical to the skirt sections. For underlinings, use the skirt pattern and cut off at the hemline marking. For partial lining or underlining over the hip area in front and back, use the skirt pattern pieces and cut about 18 inches in length or to the top of the back pleat.

Be sure to mark all fabric pieces accurately. Transfer all markings to the wrong side of the suit fabric, interfacing and lining fabric; when underlining is used the right side of the fabric is marked.

If the garment is underlined, pin the two sections—fabric and underlining—wrong sides together. Stay-stitch together at each seam allowance. Baste together through center of darts, other construction details and along hemline edge.

Darts

Stitch all darts and construction details, following the pattern guide sheet. Do not baste and press the darts expecting to stitch them later. It is next to impossible to do a good job of stitching a dart point after it has been basted and pressed even lightly. If darts are wide,

trim them to ⅝ inch, or in bulky fabrics, narrow darts can be slashed open through the center to within ½ inch of point. On curved darts, such as waistline darts, clip to stitching line at center of dart but only after jacket has been fitted and all alterations are complete.

Pressing of darts should be done over the tailor's ham. Use the wide part of the ham for shaping and molding the bustline and hip, carefully shrinking the areas at the ends of the darts. Place heavy brown paper between the dart and the body of the suit to eliminate the impression of the dart showing on the right side. Press front darts toward center front, underarm darts down, back darts toward center back, sleeve darts down. If the darts were trimmed or slashed through the center, press open forming triangle folds at the points.

Press on the wrong side of the fabric, using a damp cloth. The home steam iron does not give enough steam for tailoring—an additional damp press cloth is needed. A dry wool press cloth under a damp cheesecloth is helpful for problem materials that shine.

Make all darts in the interfacing by slashing darts along the center marking and overlapping the edges of the slash to the dart stitching line. Stitch along the dart seam markings with a straight machine-stitch or small catch-stitch. Trim the seam allowances on each side of the dart, close to the line of stitching. Press the darts, placing interfacing over tailor's ham to retain the shaping.

Seams

Mark the seam allowance on the neck and front edges of the interfacing with chalk or pencil. Baste the interfacing to the jacket front and jacket back pieces.

Machine-baste the shoulder and underarm seams for an accurate fit. Hand-basting will stretch, and many times the garment will be too tight after the seams are stitched. Press seams open lightly. Join the sleeve seams following the guide sheet directions. Press the seams lightly on the wrong side and hand-baste the sleeves in the armhole. Stitch the undercollar at center back seam. Join the seam in the undercollar interfacing by overlapping the seam allowances and matching the seam lines. Stitch along seam line with straight stitch or small catch-stitch through both thicknesses of fabric. Trim seam allowance close to stitching.

Mark seam allowances on the undercollar interfacing with chalk or pencil. Baste the interfacing to the undercollar and then baste the undercollar to the neck

edge. If shoulder pads are to be used, pin them in position.

First Fitting

Try the jacket on, right side out over the undergarments, completed skirt and blouse or sweater you will be wearing with the suit. Also, put on the shoes you plan to wear with the garment. Overlap the jacket closing, matching the center front basting markings. Pin together at buttonhole markings.

Check the fit and the grain lines of the jacket carefully. In adjusting the fit of the jacket, be sure to allow sufficient ease over and above the normal ease for the lining.

Check the following places for the correct fit and make any necessary adjustments.

☐ Center front and back markings should be in the middle of the figure and perpendicular to the floor.

☐ Grain line markings across the chest and sleeve cap should be straight and parallel to the floor.

☐ Grain line marking in center of sleeves should be straight and perpendicular to the floor.

☐ The front darts should be straight and pointed toward the fullest part of the bust.

☐ The back darts should be straight and pointed toward the shoulder blades.

☐ Underarm seams should be straight and in the middle of the figure.

☐ Shoulder seams should be straight and lie smoothly across the top of the shoulder.

☐ Sleeve armhole should fit smoothly and comfortably and lie across the end of the shoulder point.

☐ The center sleeve dart should fall at the tip of the elbow.

☐ The widest part of the waistline dart should fall at the natural waistline.

☐ The collar should fit smoothly and hug the neck.

Check the length of the sleeves and jacket and mark the correct length.

Pin in any necessary adjustments on the right side of the jacket. Remove the bastings and make the necessary adjustments. Try the jacket on again, and recheck until all necessary alterations have been made. Make only one adjustment at a time, as correction of one may affect the fit of another.

Construction Details

Once the jacket is correctly fitted, check the position of the *buttonholes*. The waistline buttonhole is usually at the natural waistline and the buttonholes equally spaced. Mark the roll line on the undercollar and lapel. Check the length of the sleeves and length of the jacket again. Adjust length to suit your particular figure.

If there are any *decorative details,* such as pockets or trim, check to be sure these will be in the correct and most flattering position of the figure.

Make bound or corded buttonholes through the suit fabric and interfacing, following the procedure given on page   Follow guide sheet for construction of pockets or other trim.

Stitch the seams and trim interfacing close to stitching on shoulder and underarm seams. Press straight seams open over seam roll or flat on the board. Curved seams should be placed over the tailor's ham and pressed.

Pressing the garment as you sew is essential to the final appearance of the suit. Don't depend on one final pressing by a tailor to give a professional look to your suit—it won't. Press each seam before crossing it with another seam.

Now you are ready to *shape the roll of the lapel.* Baste the interfacing to the jacket front along the roll line and remove the bastings at the outer edge of the lapel. Roll the lapel over your hand with the interfacing on top. This makes the underpart of the lapel a little smaller than the interfacing and keeps the corners of the lapel from rolling up. Starting just inside the roll line, work parallel rows of padding stitches ½ inch apart through the interfacing and fabric. Use matching silk thread and be sure to catch only one thread of the suit fabric each time. Pad-stitch only to the seam line. Shape both lapels in the same manner.

Always *stay the front edge* of the jacket with ¼-inch pre-shrunk twill tape to prevent stretching. Trim away the seam allowance of the interfacing at front and neck edge to the center front. Baste tape to front edge of the jacket along the seam line and across the neck edge to the center front. Slip-stitch outer edge of tape to seam line and inner edge to interfacing only.

Baste interfacing to *undercollar* along roll line, remove basting at outer edges of undercollar. Holding undercollar over the hand to create desired slight roll, pad-stitch from roll line to neck edge and then from roll line to outer edge of undercollar. End pad-stitching at seam line. Trim away the seam allowance of interfacing on all edges except the neck edge.

Attaching the collar is ·one of the most important steps in the construction of a suit. Be very accurate in matching all notches, centers and any other markings. Pin and stitch undercollar to neck edge of jacket, right sides together. Trim interfacing seam allowances at neck edge close to stitching. Trim fabric seam allowance and clip along neckline curve to stitching. Press

seam open, placing neck edge on the tailor's ham to retain shape of neckline.

Join back facing to front *facing* at the shoulder seams and stitch top collar to the facing. Trim seam allowance and clip to stitching line. Press seams open.

Turn jacket right side out. Pin facing and top collar to jacket, right sides together. Ease top collar to undercollar and front facing to lapel to allow collar and lapel to roll and lie smoothly. Baste together, being very careful to have seams match at the point where collar and lapel join. Stitch across hemline at lower edge of front facing, up front edge, around the lapel and to center back of collar. Stitch the other side of the jacket in the same manner, overlapping stitches at center back of collar for about ½ inch. This keeps roll of lapel and collar the same on both sides. Do not catch tape in the seams.

Trim across lower edge of jacket to within 1 inch of inner edge of front facing. Grade the seam allowances. Trim seam allowance of front facing narrower than suit fabric as far as roll line on lapel. Then reverse, trimming suit fabric closest to stitching. This will place the wider seam allowance nearest to the outside and prevent ridges from showing. Clip to point where collar and lapel meet, and trim diagonally across outside corners of hem, lapel and collar.

Press seams open first in order to form flat, smooth edges. Use the point presser to open seams in corners and areas difficult to reach. Turn the facing and collar

to the inside of jacket. Roll the seam edge very slightly to the inside below the roll line on the front edge. Turn the seam edge above roll line and around collar slightly to the underside. Using silk thread, baste in this position so that seam edges will not show.

For the first time, it is necessary to press on the right side of the garment. This is known as *top-pressing*. For best results, use a damp cheesecloth over a dry wool press cloth. Top-press from the underside of the lapel and collar. From the end of the roll line to the hem, turn and top-press from the facing side. Start with a rather damp press cloth to produce steam. Remove press cloth immediately and pound seam edge with a wooden clapper to flatten the seam. It may be necessary to repeat this several times, depending on the fabric. After the crease line on the edge has been firmly established, remove the silk basting threads and give the edges a final pressing on the needle board to remove the basting marks. Use the damp cheesecloth and the dry wool press cloth with the needle board to protect both sides of the fabric.

Slip-stitch the *back neckline* seam allowances together. Baste the facing to the interfacing. Tack facing to interfacing with invisible stitching to within 5 inches of the lower edge. *Finish bound buttonholes* on facing side of front.

Stitch around top of *sleeve* on seam line to ease in fullness. Use a regulation machine-stitch from underarm to first notch, change to machine-basting between notches and then change back to regulation stitch from notch to underarm seam. Ease and shrink out fullness at the elbow. If darted at elbow, press darts down. Stitch the sleeve seam and make any changes necessary. Press seams open.

Set sleeve in armhole, right sides together, holding wrong side of jacket up toward you and looking into armhole. Pin sleeve in position, matching notches, seams and other markings. Starting at center point of sleeve, pull up bobbin thread until sleeve cap fits armhole. Distribute ease evenly. Pin every half inch and baste firmly. Press the sleeve and armhole seams together from the sleeve side, shrinking out any fullness in the sleeve cap. This shrinks the sleeve to fit the armhole without distorting the shape of the sleeve cap.

Second Fitting

Fit the jacket for the second time. Pin in shoulder pads if they are to be used. Recheck all the points checked in the first fitting. Also check the sleeves carefully to be sure the shoulder line is correct and that there is enough ease to allow for moving and raising the arms. Make any necessary alterations, rebaste and try the jacket on again. Recheck the sleeve length to be sure that it has not changed.

Stitch the sleeve into the armhole with the sleeve uppermost under the machine. Press the seam lines together from the sleeve side the same as when shrinking out fullness. Turn the seam allowance at the top of the sleeve into the sleeve; the underarm seam is left turned up. For heavy fabrics, clip seam allowance at notches and press seam open over cap of sleeve.

Turn the sleeve and jacket *hems* up along the marked lines. If the hem is an uneven width, trim hem allowances evenly. Baste close to the edge. Press the hems up and shrink out any fullness. Remove the basting. Cut strips of true bias interfacing fabric or muslin for the jacket and sleeve hems. Cut ½ inch wider than the hem allowances and the length of the lower edges plus seam allowance. Baste interfacing inside hems with one edge at lower edge of hem and other extending ½ inch beyond hem edge. On jacket front, overlap end of bias strip at interfacing and tack. Use invisible stitching to attach bias strip to jacket. Attach hem to bias strip with the same stitch. Fasten the raw edge of the front facing to the hem with a very fine catch-stitch.

Lead *weights* may be used at the seams to give a better hang to the garment. Encase the weight in a small piece of lining fabric and attach to the top of the hem at the seams.

If *shoulder pads* are to be used, try on the jacket and adjust the pad to the proper position. Pin the pads securely from the right side of the garment. On the inside the pads must go under the facing. Clip the stitches holding the facing in place, slip the pad under the facing. Attach the pad loosely but firmly to the shoulder seam and to the armhole seam at each side. Tack facing to the pad.

A *waistline stay* of woven seam binding will keep the waistline from stretching. Pin the seam binding in position along the waistline of the jacket, beginning and ending at the facing edge. Catch-stitch the seam binding to the jacket at facing edges, darts and seam allowances.

When the design of a jacket calls for *edge finishing* such as saddle stitching, glove stitching, prick stitching or machine top-stitching, it is done at this time. Reverse the top and bottom stitches at the roll line of the lapels and around the collar.

Press the jacket completely before the lining is attached. Remove all bastings except the one marking the center front. Allow the garment to dry thoroughly. If you wish to have the garment professionally pressed, have it done before applying the lining.

The *buttons* are attached after the final pressing. Heavy thread or buttonhole twist is the most satisfactory thread for sewing on buttons. If these are not available in a matching color, mercerized or silk thread can be substituted by first waxing it with beeswax. Follow the procedure on page 219 for marking the position and attaching the buttons.

Tailoring Collar and Lapels by Hand

The person who has had some experience in tailoring may wish to try constructing the collar and lapels by hand. This is not as difficult as it sounds at first. It takes a little longer, but the professional appearance of your finished garment makes it well worth the extra time. Once you have mastered the technique, you will never want to go back to the machine method.

After the lapel has been pad-stitched, stay-stitch the front and entire neck edge on the seam line. Trim off the interfacing at the stay-stitching. Tape the front and neck edge to the center front as directed on page 253.

Clip front seam allowance to stay-stitching at beginning of roll line. Trim the fabric seam allowance above clip on lapel and neck edge to ¼ inch. Turn in the seam allowance on the line of stay-stitching and baste. Clip curved areas, miter and trim out corners so that seam lies flat. Catch-stitch the seam allowance to the interfacing. Press thoroughly—the edge should be completely flat with no thick spots at the corners.

Follow the directions on page 253 for pad-stitching the undercollar. Stay-stitch all edges and finish same as the lapel and neck edges. Press the undercollar and let it dry thoroughly.

Pin the undercollar to neck edge of jacket—right sides together. Whip-stitch the two finished edges together catching the rows of stay-stitching in your stitches. Keep stitches close and pull them tight. Press seam over tailor's ham.

Stitch back facing to front facing at the shoulder seams. Stay-stitch on seam line of the lapel and neck edge above the roll line. Clip at roll line; trim seam above clip to ⅜ inch. Turn in the seam allowance just beyond the stay-stitching, clipping at curved edges, and baste with silk thread. Press, being sure that the crease line on the edge is well established. Stay-stitch

and top-press. Pin the top collar over the undercollar and lapels, wrong sides together. The top collar and lapel should extend beyond the undercollar, then the seam edge will never be able to roll up and show on

all edges of top collar on seam line. Trim seam to ⅜ inch. Turn in the seam allowance just beyond the stay-stitching, miter at corners and trim out excess fabric. Baste in place and press.

the right side. Baste and slip-stitch the edges together with a very fine stitch. Remove bastings and top-press with a damp cheesecloth and a dry wool press cloth over a needle board.

Pin top collar to neck edge of facing, right sides together. Use a small, tight whip-stitch to sew the two finished edges together and press over the tailor's ham.

This method leaves the corners of the collar and lapel much flatter and thinner than it is possible to get with the machine application.

LINING A JACKET

Turn jacket right side out. Stitch facing to jacket, right sides together below the roll line. Grade seam allowances and press seam open. Turn facing to inside and roll seam slightly to the inside. Baste in position

If the garment to be lined was altered in any way, make the corresponding changes on the lining, but never make the lining smaller than the garment. Stay-stitch the armholes and back neck on the seam line. Machine-stitch waistline and back neck darts. Press waistline and back darts toward center. Clip darts to stitching if necessary to make them lie flat. Stitch the underarm seams and press them open. Baste the pleat in the center back of the lining, press to the right.

Turn lining to right side. Lap front shoulder darts to stitching line and catch-stitch halfway down from the top. Catch-stitch the back pleat for about 1½ inches at the neckline, waistline and at the hemline. Press entire lining.

Open the jacket and place flat on a table with the wrong side up. Pin lining to the jacket down the center back, wrong sides together. Match the underarm seams of the lining to the corresponding seams of the jacket; tack together with a long, loose stitch to within 3 inches from the hem.

Turn under the seam allowance along the front of the lining. Lap and pin the lining over the front facing, easing slightly over the bustline. Baste and slip-stitch to within 3 inches of the hemline. Baste front shoulder seam allowance of lining to back shoulder seam allow-

ance of jacket. Turn under the seam allowances of the back lining section at neckline and shoulder seams. Clip the seam allowance to the stay-stitching at the neckline to make it lie flat. Lap and baste the neck edge of back lining over the lower edge of the back facing and the shoulder along shoulder seam line of front lining. Slip-stitch in place. Baste the lining to the jacket around the armholes, just outside the seam, close to stay-stitching.

The lining of a jacket is always attached to the hemline. Baste the lining to the jacket about 5 inches above the hem. Turn under a seam allowance at the lower edge of the lining and lap over hem of jacket about ½ inch. Pin and slip-stitch in position. The extra length in the lining forms a fold at the hem and prevents drawing. After the hem is finished, press the fold down and finish slip-stitching front edges to the facing.

Stitch sleeve seams same as for the jacket. Press seams open. Stay-stitch on seam line of the underarm section between the notches and place one row of machine-gathering on the cap of the sleeve. Turn under the seam allowance at top of sleeve, clip underarm section to seam line to allow it to lie flat.

To attach the sleeve lining, turn sleeve and lining inside out. Match corresponding seams and tack together with a long, loose stitch. Leave 2 inches free at the armhole and 3 inches free at the lower edge. To turn the lining over the sleeve, place your hand inside the lining, catch the lining and sleeve at the bottom and pull through.

Lap the lining over the armhole seam allowance to stay-stitching, ease the fullness and pin and baste in place. Slip-stitch the lining in the armhole with a very small stitch. Finish lower edge of sleeve lining same as lower edge of jacket lining.

TAILORING A COAT

A coat is tailored in the same way as a suit with one exception—the lower edges of the coat and lining are finished separately.

If no lining pattern is given and you are using the coat pattern pieces to cut the lining, follow directions for the jacket on page 250 but DO NOT cut off the hem allowance on the coat lining.

A coat may need to be lengthened, so it is unwise to trim off the fabric at the lower front facing as is done on a suit. Open the facing and continue the hem across the lower edge. Pink the upper edge of the hem on materials that do not fray, overcast or zigzag edges of materials that fray. Attach the hem and interfacing with invisible stitching same as the jacket. The interfacing may or may not extend above the hem. If the interfacing extends above the hem, the hemline will show less on the right side.

Turn facing back, slip-stitch the lower edges together and catch-stitch the inner edge to the hem. The lining is hemmed separately and should be about ¾ inch shorter than the coat. Finish slip-stitching front edges to the facing, and fasten lining to hem with 1-inch French tacks at seams.

Some expensive ready-to-wear slim coats have the entire back underlined with a light-weight hair canvas. This helps the coat keep its shape and gives added warmth to a mid-season coat. Cut the hair canvas the same as the coat back pattern, but cut off at the hemline. Make darts in underlining same as darts in interfacing. Stitch and press darts in coat back. Baste underlining to wrong side of coat back, stay-stitching seam allowances together and baste along hemline edge. Treat as one fabric and construct coat same as usual.

Construct and insert body of the lining same as jacket except for the lower edge. Hem the lining over the lower edge of the interlining. Finish slip-stitching front edges to the facing and fasten lining to hem with 1-inch French tacks at seams.

An interlining is used in most winter coats for added warmth. Cut interlining from lining pattern, making any alterations that were made on the coat. Trim off the interlining at the hemline of the coat and sleeve. Interline the entire one-piece sleeve but only the upper section of a two-piece sleeve. Omit pleat in back of interlining.

There are two ways of attaching an interlining. The interlining can be stitched in with the lining seams, but this may be bulky. The other method is to apply the interlining before the lining.

Slash, lap and stitch the darts same as the interfacing. Lap and stitch the shoulder and underarm seams same as the darts. Trim seams to remove bulk. Trim off seam allowance at front and back neck edge. Pin interlining to inside of coat. Baste side seams loosely together to within 3 inches of hem. Baste the armhole seam allowances together. Catch-stitch interlining to facings to within 3 inches of hem.

Stay-stitch interlining to sleeve section of lining along sides and across sleeve cap. Trim away interfacing seam allowances close to stay-stitching. Treat as one fabric and insert the sleeve lining in the usual manner.

CHAPTER 15

THE THREE R'S–REPAIRING, REMODELING, REMAKING

Even though you may not be interested in making all or some of your own clothes, there are certain techniques of sewing that you should learn in order to keep yourself well groomed. And there are many things you can do to make ready-to-wear fit better. We no longer mend and darn the way our grandmothers did; the emphasis on what we mend has changed. It is no longer practical to darn socks; in fact the new stretch socks cannot be darned. However, there are a variety of repairs that are necessary to good grooming. Modern living has still found no escape from the loose button, the pulled-out hem, the broken strap or the cigarette burn in a new garment. That "stitch in time" does wonders for one's personal appearance.

LOOSE FASTENERS

Buttons

Taking the time to sew on a loose button will save losing the button and having to replace a whole set. Regular sewing thread is not strong enough to hold buttons. Heavy-duty thread or buttonhole twist is best, but if these are not available in a matching color, then wax your sewing thread with beeswax to make it stronger. If the button has dropped off, be sure to remove all the old threads from the fabric before restitching the button. See page 220 for detailed directions for sewing on the different kinds of buttons.

Snaps

A loose snap can be sewed firmly in place by taking a few stitches over the edge of each hole. Carry the thread under the snap from one hole to the next. If the snap has come off completely, remember that the ball section is sewed to the upper part of the closing and the socket section to the under part. See page 221.

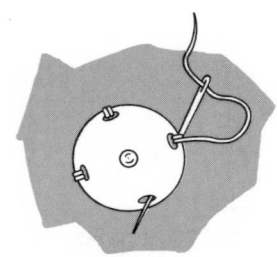

Hooks and Eyes

Take several small stitches under the hook to secure the thread. Take small overhand stitches around each hole being careful that the stitches do not show on the right side of the garment. Carry the needle to the hook end and take several stitches across the end of the hook to hold it securely. The eye is sewed in position by taking overhand stitches around each hole. If it is a round eye, take several stitches across the sides of the eye to hold it securely. A round eye is used when the closing just meets and the bar eye is used when the closing is lapped.

RIPPED SEAMS

In Garments

When the thread of a machine-stitched seam in a garment breaks, it can be repaired by hand or machine. Hand-stitches are usually used if the ripped seam is in an area difficult to reach by machine or if a machine is not available. Turn the garment to the wrong side and clip the loose threads close to the fabric. To repair by hand, begin about ½ inch from the opening and take tiny back-stitches along the original seam line. Continue about ½ inch beyond the opening. To repair

by machine, adjust the length of stitch to correspond with that used on the rest of the seam. Follow the original seam line and let the new stitching overlap the old about ½ inch on either side of the opening. Pull threads to one side and tie ends in a double knot before clipping. Press the seam.

In Gloves

Gloves are made with a wide variety of seams. When repairing a glove seam, duplicate the original stitching as accurately as possible, using a matching thread. Gloves that are stitched on the inside should be turned to the wrong side for mending. Try to follow the original seam line and use the same needle holes. The new stitches should overlap the old ones at both ends of the opening. Fabric gloves are frequently made with the seams showing on the right side. If the seam is made with small running stitches, then the same kind of hand-stitches should be used to repair the seam.

PULLED HEMS

The hems of all garments are under constant strain and are subject to catching. The thread in hand-sewn hems can break very easily. Remove a few stitches from each end of the ripped area so that the ends can be fastened. Either knot the threads or take a few back-stitches to fasten the ends. Replace the hem in the ripped area with the same kind of stitch used in the original hem. Press the hem after it has been repaired.

RIPPED PLEATS

It is a very common problem to have the stitching break at the top of a pleat in a narrow skirt. When this happens, clip the broken threads close to the fabric and restitch. Sometimes, if there is fabric under the pleat it is wise to raise the pleat to allow more room for walking. To raise the pleat, turn the skirt to the wrong side and pull out the stitches the desired distance above the end of the original pleat. Tie the ends in a double knot and then thread them into a needle and take a few back-stitches along the seam to secure the ends. Press the pleat to remove the old stitching marks.

If the fabric has been pulled or torn at the end of the pleat, it will have to be reinforced. Restitch the pleat from the inside of the skirt, as directed above. On the right side, embroider an arrowhead or a crow's-foot tack at the end of the pleat. See page 240 for detailed directions for making these tacks.

LINGERIE REPAIRS

Broken Shoulder Strap

If the top of the garment is made of a double thickness of fabric, the shoulder strap should be placed between the two layers of material. Insert the strap deeply enough that it cannot pull out easily again. Sew along the original stitching line with a tiny back-stitch extending beyond the strap on both sides. If the strap has been attached to lace or a single thickness of fabric, take tiny hemming stitches along the turned-in end of the strap and along the top edge of the lace or fabric so the strap will be secured in two places.

Broken Fagoted Seams

Remove several stitches from either end of the break and fasten the ends with several tiny stitches on the wrong side of the garment. Baste a strip of brown paper under the section that is to be refagoted. With buttonhole twist, working from the top down, replace the broken stitches. See page 241 for detailed directions for making the various fagoting stitches. Use the stitch which matches the fagoted seam in your garment.

Replacing an Elastic Waistband

Remove the old elastic, noting the way in which it was applied so that you can replace it the same way. Cut a piece of elastic the measurement of your waistline plus ½ inch for lap or joining. Divide the waistline of the garment into halves, quarters and then eighths and mark each division with a pin. Divide the piece of elastic to be applied in halves, quarters and then eighths and mark the same way. Match the markings on the elastic to the markings on the garment. Lap the ends of the elastic and stitch securely. Distribute the fullness evenly between the pins. Stretch the elastic as you stitch so that the fabric passes under the presser foot of the machine without any gathers or puckers. As the elastic springs back into place, it gathers the fabric. Regular machine-stitching can be used but a zigzag stitch will be stronger on elastic fabrics because it has more give. Apply the elastic with the same number of rows of stitching as was used on the original elastic.

Replacing Elastic in a Casing

Look for an opening in the casing. If there is none, rip the stitching enough to remove the old elastic. Cut a new piece of elastic the desired length plus ½ inch for lapping. Run the elastic through the casing with a bodkin or a safety pin. Sew the ends of elastic securely and replace the stitching in the casing.

Replacing a Garter

Old garters should be removed by opening the seam line at the lower edge of the garment. Slip the new garter in place and sew with two rows of machine-stitching. Bring the facing down over the garter and sew it in place with machine-stitching or small zigzag stitches.

REWEAVING

This is a job that requires great skill and patience. If it is done well, there is no visible sign of mending. Study the weave of the fabric carefully so that you will be able to duplicate it exactly. Working under a magnifying glass is most helpful. Use an embroidery hoop to hold the fabric taut. You can only use threads raveled from the fabric for reweaving. Working from the right side of the fabric, fill in all the lengthwise threads weaving them several stitches into the body of the fabric to hold them. Weave in the crosswise threads to match the original weave of the fabric. Steam-press the area after you finish, and the mend should be completely invisible.

INVISIBLE PATCHING

This is an easy way to mend a hole in a loosely woven fabric and is not quite as tedious as reweaving. Determine the size of the patch needed. Cut a piece of fabric from the hem or some part of the inside of the garment, 1 inch larger all around than the desired patch. The lengthwise threads of the patch and the garment must be matched as well as any design in the fabric. Ravel out the threads on all sides of the patch until it is the

 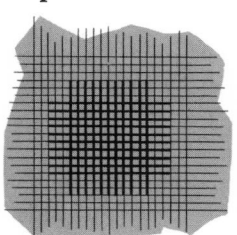

exact size needed. Place the fabric in an embroidery hoop and lay the patch right side up over the hole. Baste the patch in place. Beginning at one corner, pull the raveled threads through to the wrong side with a crochet hook. Follow the weave of the fabric in drawing the threads through. If the fabric is a plain weave, the edges of the patch will be even, otherwise the edges

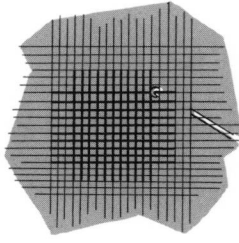

of the patch will be uneven. After all threads have been pulled through, turn the garment to the wrong side. Take tiny hemming stitches close to the spot where each raveled thread was pulled through. These stitches should not show on the right side. Clip the ends of the raveled threads about ¼ inch from the fabric. Steam-press the area after the patch is finished.

REPLACING A BROKEN ZIPPER

When the chain of a zipper is broken or damaged, there is no way to repair it other than to replace the entire zipper. Examine the application carefully before removing the broken zipper. It is important that the new zipper be put in the same way. Remove the old zipper and all the threads. In a skirt, open waistband about 1 inch on either side of the placket. Baste the opening together along the original seam line and press the seam open. Insert the new zipper according to detailed directions given in Chapter 12, depending upon the type of application used in your garment.

REPLACING A LINING

Occasionally a lining will become worn or damaged while the outside of the garment is still in good condition. It is practical to replace a lining if there is at least another season's wear in the garment. The original lining can be removed and used as a pattern. Before ripping the old lining apart, mark key construction points on it so that it will be easier to assemble the new lining. With chalk or a pencil, mark a horizontal line across the seam at the following places: underarm seam about 4″ below the armscye, midpoint of the armscye front and back, point where shoulder seam joins cap of sleeve, and point where front dart joins back shoulder seam. Rip the lining apart and press all the pieces out flat. Pin the pieces on the new fabric, placing the center back on a fold. With chalk or a pencil, mark accurate ⅝-inch seam allowances on all pieces, make notches at the key construction points marked with the horizontal lines and mark the center back pleat and front shoulder dart. Cut out the lining. Assemble the lining pieces and attach the lining to the garment according to the directions given in Chapter 14.

ALTERATIONS ON READY-TO-WEAR

Most of us cannot walk into a store and buy clothes without needing some alteration to attain a perfect fit. If a garment requires major alterations, it is not wise to buy it. Shoulder and neckline alterations are difficult to make and should be avoided. However, lengthening and shortening or adjusting a waistline or hipline are simple alterations and do much to improve the appearance of a garment.

Shortening or Lengthening a Skirt or Dress

Rip out the original hem. If seam binding has been used, remove it and pick out all the threads. Working from the wrong side, press out the crease mark of the hem. (See Chapter 8 for suggestions on how to press various fabrics.) Press out the seam binding.

Try on the garment with the shoes and foundation garment you intend to wear with it. Decide how far from the floor the finished skirt should be. With a yardstick or hem marker, have someone pin an even line parallel to the floor at this point. Turn hem up on marked line and baste about ½ inch from the folded edge. A hem should be 2½ to 3 inches wide. Mark the width of the hem by measuring up from the folded edge with a ruler or hem gauge. Cut along the marking.

Finish the cut edge of the hem the same as it was finished before. If there is excess fullness at the upper edge of the hem, place a row of machine basting ¼ inch from the cut edge. Pin the hem at the seams of the skirt and pull up the bobbin thread to ease in the full-ness until the hem fits flat on the skirt. Adjust fullness evenly and shrink out the excess.

After the cut edge has been properly finished, baste the hem in place and stitch by hand. See Chapter 10 for detailed directions on various hem finishes.

Facing a Skirt

When a skirt has to be lengthened and there is not sufficient fabric to turn up a new hem, the skirt will have to be faced. Rip out the hem and pick out all the threads. Press the hem thoroughly so that there is no crease line showing. Skirt facings must be bias. If you have matching fabric, cut a true bias strip the length of the lower edge of the skirt plus seam allowances. When matching fabric is not available, commercially packaged skirt facing can be purchased in cotton or taffeta in a variety of colors. Start at a seam and pin facing to lower edge of skirt, right sides together. Join bias on the straight grain. Press seam open. Stitch facing to lower edge of skirt and press

seam open. Understitch the seam allowance to the facing. Turn facing to inside using the seam allowance width as the turning line. Baste along folded edge. Turn under the upper edge of facing and stitch close to edge. Slip-stitch facing to skirt.

Adjusting Back Pleat When Skirt Is Shortened

A pleat in the back of a skirt must be open at least 4 inches to be of any value. Be sure to check this when shortening a skirt. If there is fabric under the pleat, it is very easy to rip the pleat up the desired amount and tie the threads on the wrong side to finish the end of the pleat. If it is impossible to raise the pleat, it is best to stitch the pleat shut entirely. Your skirt will look look better without a pleat than with a skimpy useless one. Mark a ⅝-inch seam allowance beyond the stitching line and trim off the extra fabric. Press the seam in the same direction as the other seams of the skirt.

Shortening or Lengthening a Coat

If the fabric is trimmed out under the facing at the front corner, it will be impossible ever to lengthen the coat. If it has not been trimmed, rip out the hem in the coat and the lining. Pick out all the threads and press out the crease line in coat and lining. See Chapter 8 for pressing directions for various fabrics.

Try on the coat with the shoes you intend to wear with it. Attach the coat to the lining with a row of pins placed about 12 inches from the lower edge of the coat. This allows room to hem the coat and the lining and still holds the two layers together so that you won't end up with the lining hanging longer than the coat. Decide on the proper length for the coat and have someone pin a line parallel to the floor at this point with a yardstick or hem marker. A coat should be hemmed about 1 inch longer than you wear your dresses. Remember that a very heavy, bulky fabric will always be a little shorter than it was marked after the hem has been turned.

The lower edge of a coat and lining are finished separately. Hem coat first. Rip the lining from the front facing for 6 to 8 inches to allow room to turn the hem on the front facing. Turn up the hem and facing on the new line and baste close to folded edge. Coat

hem is 2 to 2½ inches; the lining hem is 2 inches. Lap and button the coat and check the lower edge to be sure that one front corner does not hang longer than the other. It is easier to adjust this now than to discover it after the hem has been finished. Using a ruler or hem gauge, mark the width of the hem. Cut on this marking. Continue the hem the same width on coat and facing. If the hem does not fit smoothly, place a row of machine-basting ½ inch from the cut edge. Pin the hem at the seams and pull up the bobbin thread to ease in any fullness. Steam-press to shrink out the extra fullness. Finish the upper edge of hem the same as it was finished before. Baste the hem in place and stitch by hand. See Chapter 10 for details on hem finishes. Turn the front facing back, slip-stitch the lower edges together and fasten the raw edge to the hem with a very fine catch-stitch.

The lining should be about ¾ inch shorter than the coat. Turn up the lower edge and baste along the fold. Mark and trim hem and even width. Turn under the edge ¼ inch and stitch. Baste hem and slip-stitch in place. Slip-stitch front edges of the lining to the facing and fasten lining to coat hem with 1-inch French tacks at seams.

Adjusting Sleeve Length

Sleeves can be shortened without too much trouble. Take out the hem or remove the cuff, depending on how the sleeve was finished. Remove all the threads and press the lower edge flat. Decide on the correct sleeve length, then measure up from the lower edge and mark a line around the sleeve. Cut the sleeve off a seam or hem allowance below the marking, depending on the way your sleeve is to be finished. Finish the lower edge of the sleeve in the same way that it was finished originally.

A sleeve with a hem can always be lengthened by letting down the hem or even facing it if necessary. However, if the sleeve is finished with a cuff, it is usually not possible to lengthen it.

Shortening a Coat Sleeve

Baste around the sleeve below the elbow to hold the sleeve and lining together. Turn the sleeve wrong side out and open the lining at the lower edge. Rip out the hem of the sleeve and press the crease marks out of the lining and the sleeve. Mark the new sleeve length. Turn up the hem on the marking and baste close to lower edge. Mark the width of the new hem same as the original one and cut along the marking. Press, then remove basting. Baste interfacing inside hem with one edge at lower edge of hem. Use an invisible stitch to attach hem edge to interfacing. Attach interfacing to sleeve with the same stitch.

Turn sleeve lining up so that it is about ¾ inch shorter than the sleeve. Cut the lining off, leaving a seam allowance beyond the fold line. Lap the lining over the sleeve hem and slip-stitch the lining in place.

Lengthening a Coat Sleeve

Baste around the sleeve below the elbow to hold the sleeve and lining together. Turn the sleeve wrong side out; open lining and remove sleeve hem. Press the old crease line out of the sleeve and lining. The hem can be let down or faced, depending on the amount of length needed. If a facing is to be used, apply it same as for a skirt. Baste interfacing to inside of hem or facing with one edge at lower edge of hem. Attach hem to interfacing and then sew interfacing to sleeve with the same invisible stitch. If lining is not long enough to reach the top of the hem, then it is necessary to add a strip of fabric to the lower edge of the sleeve

lining. Turn up the lower edge of lining so that it is about ¾ inch shorter than the sleeve. Lap lining over the upper edge of the sleeve hem and slip-stitch in place.

Shortening a Belt

When a belt is too long, never shorten it by punching an extra eyelet. This only leaves a long ungainly end, and the new eyelet will never match the original ones exactly. Take your waist measurement over the garment to be belted. Remember that a belt for a bulky fabric suit or coat always has to be a little longer than the belt for a soft silk dress. Remove the buckle. Measure the belt from the center eyelet to the buckle end and mark waistline measurement. Punch two holes about ¼ inch apart on either side of marking. Cut an oblong opening between the two holes for the prong of the buckle. Insert prong through the opening and turn end of belt to inside. Cut off extra length and stitch end of the belt in place. On leather belts or other fabric that is difficult to stitch, use a thumbtack to punch holes for the needle.

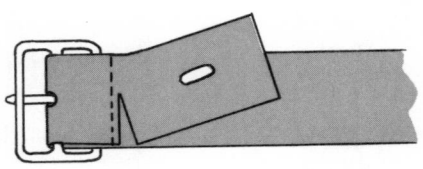

Shortening a Slip

If a slip needs to be shortened only a slight amount, you can do it by taking several small pin tucks around the lower edge or just above the lace or ruffle. This adds a decorative touch and can be done by hand or machine. Any large adjustment in length will have to be made by cutting off the lower edge. Be sure to allow enough for a narrow hem finish. A tailored slip is usually finished with just a narrow hem. If the slip is finished with lace or a ruffle, this has to be removed and restitched to the lower edge.

Lengthening a Slip

A band of lace or a ruffle can be stitched to the lower edge of a slip to give added length. Lace is lapped over the lower edge finish on the slip and stitched in place.

The finished lower edge of the slip should be lapped and stitched over the binding on purchased ruffling.

Shortening a Skirt from the Waistline

A skirt that is too tight in the hipline or has some decorative detail at the lower edge can be shortened by raising from the waistline. Pin a tuck just below the waistband, raising the skirt the necessary amount. The width of the tuck tells you how much the skirt should be shortened. Rip off the waistband, remove the zipper and cut off the top of the skirt the amount to be short-

ened. Try on the skirt and pin in the darts and side seams until the skirt fits smoothly. Restitch the darts and seams, tapering the new stitching into the old. Remove the old stitching and press seams open and darts toward the center. Replace zipper according to

directions given in Chapter 12. Replace the waistband, duplicating the original method of application, and sew on the hooks and eyes.

Shortening a Bodice

Short-waisted people very often find that the waistline seam of a dress falls below their natural waistline. When this happens, take out the zipper and rip the waistline seam. Try on the bodice and pin placket closed. Tie a cord or tape around your waistline and mark a new waistline seam with pins or chalk along the lower edge of the cord. Pin and baste the skirt to the bodice along the markings for the new waistline seam, matching centers, seams and darts. Stitch the new waistline seam and trim off the extra fabric after you have tried on the dress and are sure the seam is in the correct place. Replace the zipper according to directions given in Chapter 12.

or let out. Remove the zipper and open the waistline seam. Divide the total amount of the adjustment by the number of darts and seams. Make the same amount of alteration on each seam and dart on the skirt and bodice. Taper the new lines of stitching into the original stitching, then remove the old threads. Press seams open and darts toward the center. When a garment is let out, be sure that the marks of the original seam line are pressed out completely. Baste skirt to bodice, matching centers, seams and darts. Try on the dress again to check the fit above and below the waistline. Stitch the waistline seam and replace the zipper according to directions in Chapter 12.

Taking In or Letting Out a Waistline

A waistline can usually be nipped in without too much trouble. However, if the waistline is tight, before buying the garment check to be sure there is enough fabric in seams and darts to let out. Try on the garment and determine how much should be taken in

Taking In the Hipline

The curve of the hipline varies with each individual, so it is a very common problem to need slight adjustments at this point. It is not usually necessary to take off the waistband or open the waistline seam, but the zipper will have to be removed if it falls in the side seam. If you have very straight hips, the seam line on most skirts will have too great a curve over the hip. Try on the garment and pin out the extra curve or bulge in the seam. Make the same adjustment on both sides of the skirt to keep it balanced. Restitch the seam line, tapering into the old stitching. Remove the original stitching and press seam open. Replace the zipper according to directions in Chapter 12.

Letting Out the Hipline

When a skirt is tight in the hipline, the adjustment becomes a greater problem. First, before buying the garment, check to see that there is enough fabric in the seams to let out. Remove the zipper and open the hem. Press side seams together so that they will be easier to restitch accurately. Determine the amount of extra fullness needed and let out each side seam half this amount. Restitch the side seams, tapering from the original seam line near the waist to the hipline, and then continue stitching down the side to the lower edge. Letting the skirt out the same amount from the hipline to the lower edge retains the original shaping and proportions of the skirt. Press seams open, replace the zipper and hem.

Sometimes fabric is left under a wide center-back pleat. If there is not enough fabric to let out the side seams, this wide pleat can be opened. Restitch the center back seam tapering from the original stitching line near the waist to the amount needed at the hipline. Continue stitching parallel to the center back seam from hipline to the top of the pleat. Never let the back pleat out just in the hip area. This gives a very unattractive line and the skirt will always have a seat even if it is lined. Machine-baste from top of pleat to lower edge, parallel to the old crease line. Remove the original stitching and press out the marks of the orig-

inal seam and pleat. Press the pleat in the same direction as before and remove the machine-basting. Tie the threads at the end of the pleat and take a few back-stitches in the fabric to secure the threads. Turn up the hem and stitch it in place again.

Adjusting for Sway-Back

Wrinkles across the back of the skirt just below the waistline indicate that the skirt should be raised across the back. This is a very common alteration for people with a sway-back. Rip the waistline seam across the back. Raise center back of skirt ½ to ¾ inch and taper to side seams. Baste back waistline seam and try garment on to check fit. Side seams should hang straight and back of skirt should fit smoothly without wrinkles. Restitch and press back waistline seam.

Adding a Gusset to a Kimono Sleeve

A tight kimono sleeve can be eased by adding a gusset, if extra fabric is available. Measurements and complete directions for doing this without a pattern are given on page 163.

CHAPTER 16

THE DECORATOR'S TOUCH

Decorating a home can be fun, and it is especially so when one knows how to sew. A pillow, a bedspread, a slipcover can transform the mood, the personality, and even the seasonal fitness of a room. You can make your home the right background for the new you. Browse through magazines to get ideas. Shop the stores for interesting fabrics. Use your sewing know-how to give your home the custom look.

DECORATIVE PILLOWS

Pillows are so easy to make, and so effective as a decorating tool, that everyone should know how to make them. They can provide wonderful color accents to "spark" room decor, giving the room a completely new look. Variations on the pillow theme are limitless. Let your imagination soar. Put all of those designer hopes to work. Combine unusual fabrics and trimmings in a variety of shapes. Seams may be trimmed with cording, ruffling, lace or fringe. Tassels, buttons or embroidery can be used to give a decorative touch to the pillow top. Recently, hand-smocked pillows have been extremely popular. Notice how many different effects can be produced by a few simple smocking stitches.

Inner Pillow Form

When planning your pillows, consider the inner construction. Special forms can be purchased or made. If you wish to buy a form, you should do so before you make the covering so it will be the correct size. Forms of solid foam rubber, synthetic foam or ticking filled with down or kapok are easy to use. It is also possible to buy foam by the yard which you can shape as you wish.

If you decide to make your own form, cut fabric in the desired size and shape. Muslin can be used for the inner pillow covering but ticking or a downproof fabric must be used if the pillow is to be stuffed with feathers. Use a ½-inch plain seam to sew pieces together and leave a 3-inch opening in one seam. Stuff to desired fullness with synthetic stuffing, kapok, nylon stockings, clippings or down. Turn in raw edges of opening and sew together with close overhand stitches. If down

from an old pillow is used, open one corner of the covering and pour water on the feathers. The damp feathers can be transferred to the new covering without filling the room with down. Be sure that the opening is securely stitched shut and then place the new pillow in the automatic dryer to fluff-dry the feathers. Remove the pillow as soon as it is dry. Do not let the dryer run a full cycle.

Pillows without Boxing

Pillows can be made with or without an insertion of cording or trimming between pieces. If cording is to be used, this should be made before pieces are put together according to directions on page 233. Also, if applied decoration is being used, such as smocking, quilting, or appliqué, it should be done before construction begins.

Measure pillow from seam to seam. The cover should be snug but not tight. Add ½-inch seam allowance to each edge. Join the two pieces with a plain seam. If cording or trimming is to be used as an edge finish, stitch it to one section before making the plain seam. Leave an opening wide enough to insert the pillow form. Slip-stitch the edges of the opening together after the pillow has been put in place. Or, if fabric will need to be laundered or dry-cleaned frequently, it is wise to close the opening with a zipper so that the cover can be removed easily.

Pillows with Boxing

Solid foam forms are easiest to use for box pillows. Measure the cushion, length and width, as well as the depth of the boxing and its circumference. Cut two identical pieces for the top and bottom and a strip of fabric for the boxing. To each edge, add ½-inch seam allowance. Pin-fit the covering fabric over the cushion and stitch as for a seat cushion, described on page 297.

If a soft filling is used, the inner pillow should be packed very tightly.

CURTAINS AND DRAPERIES

In choosing fabric and style for curtains and draperies consider first your needs for light, air and privacy. Do you want to frame the view or hide it? Then appraise the windows in relation to the room. Should the windows appear higher or wider to make the room seem to be in good proportion? Perhaps two windows should be treated as one. Sometimes curving folds will do more to enhance a room than straight ones. Should there be a valance? Check outside effect. How will the style and fabric appear in relation to the exterior architecture? Will your home look friendly and inviting? Browse through magazines for information about new style trends. After you have done a thorough research job, select the style and fabrics that you like best, that are suited to your needs and flatter your decor.

Window Hardware

After you have decided upon the style of curtains and draperies which will best suit your rooms, your next step is to find the correct hardware to support them. There are two basic kinds of rods for curtains and draperies: *stationary rods,* which hold draperies in one

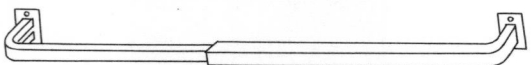

place; and *traverse rods,* which allow draperies to be opened and closed. In both types, you can buy single

or double extension rods, rods to fit around curves and corners, and rods to swing into the room. All are available in plain and decorative finishes. Many variations provide solutions for every window problem.

Extension rods and brackets increase the width and height of curtains beyond the actual size of the window. Special brackets attach rods to window frames, inside casings of windows, walls, or ceilings. Special screws are available for use on different wall finishes.

You will also discover many new types of rings and hooks for attaching curtains to their rods. You will have many new ideas after shopping for drapery hardware.

Attach rods to the wall or window frame, and you are ready to begin.

Window Measurements

Before you can begin to make your curtains, you have to decide how long and how wide they should be. The finished length is the distance from the rod to the lower edge of the finished curtain. Curtains and draperies should begin and end with a structural part of the window or wall. They begin at the ceiling, window top or beneath a cornice and end at the sill, apron, baseboard or floor. The finished width encompasses the length of the curtain rod, including the part that curves into the wall (the return) plus the amount of the center overlap.

Fabric Measurement

To figure the total length of one panel, take the measurement you have decided on for the finished length of the curtain and add to it the allowance for heading and hem. If patterned fabric is used, one extra pattern repeat must be added for matching.

For total fabric width you must decide on the amount of fullness you want. For very full, sheer curtains, multiply the finished width by three. When using medium- or heavy-weight fabrics, reduce the amount of fullness by multiplying the finished width by two or two and a half. To this amount, add allowance for seams or side hems on each panel.

HEM ALLOWANCES. Before the final yardage can be figured, you must make some decisions about hem width. Hem allowances will vary with the fabric used. Average hem measures are given here. For further information, check specific instructions for the type of curtain and heading you decide to make.

Top Hem Allowances

Straight hems (used with clip-on rings or loops):	1¼ to 4 inches
Casing with heading	3 inches
4-Cord shirring	4¼ inches
Ready-made 4-cord shirring	¾ inch
Pleating	4 to 5 inches
Ready-made pleater tape	½ inch
Scallop	4¼ inches (or depth of scallop plus 1¼ inches)

Bottom Hem Allowances

	Single Hem	Double Hem
Glass Curtains	3¼ in.	6 in.
Café Curtains	2¼ to 3¼ in.	4 to 6 in.
Drapery	4 to 5 in.	7 to 9 in.
Ruffled Curtains	¼ inch (first, subtract width of ruffle from finished length; then, allow ¼ inch hem)	

Before you decide on the exact yardage to buy, consider the advantages of a double hem. In sheer fabrics, the turned-under raw edge will not show when light shines through the curtain. The extra weight of the double hem will make draperies hang better. Extra fabric is available to let down if shrinkage occurs, or if draperies are moved to another window. With these decisions made, take out paper and pencil and figure the yardage you need. Remember the width of your fabric will influence the amount needed.

Cutting the Fabric

Accuracy is extremely important when cutting out curtains. Press the fabric to remove wrinkles and crease marks. Lay fabric on a large smooth surface with right side up. Check grain line carefully. It is as important to have the grain line perfect in curtains and draperies as it is in clothes. They will not hang properly unless it is.

Decide in which direction the pattern or pile should go. All fabric lengths should run in the same direction.

PATTERNED FABRIC. It is important that the design be properly placed so that the effect will be pleasing. On long curtains, an unbroken pattern repeat should be at the finished top of the curtain since a broken repeat will be less noticeable at the floor. On short curtains, the bottom repeat is more noticeable and so should not be broken.

MEASURING. Mark finished top edge. Mark top hem allowance above this line. Draw a thread to make a straight line, and cut on this line.

Measuring from the finished top edge, mark the length of the finished curtain. From this line, add hem allowance. Draw out a thread to make a straight line for cutting. After cutting, check grain line. Straighten fabric if necessary, following directions on page 97.

Cutting Additional Panels

Place fabric right side up on cutting surface. Then put cut panel right side down on fabric. Match design carefully. Be sure the designs run in the same direction, using the cut panel as a pattern for cutting the other lengths.

After cutting, follow directions for specific types of curtains. You will find headings treated separately, since most types of headings may be used on all types of curtains and draperies.

Glass Curtains

This type of curtain hangs straight from the rod, against the window. If used alone, decorative headings may be applied. If another curtain or drapery is used over the glass curtain, the top finish is a simple casing and heading.

After determining the finished length, add 3¼ inches for bottom hem (6 inches, if double) and 2¾ inches for top heading and casing (5 inches, if double.) The width of the curtain is decided by the fabric. If the material is not too sheer, 2½ times the finished width will be attractive. However, on sheer fabrics, 3 times the finished width will create a more pleasing effect. Allow ½ inch for seam allowances and 2 inches for each double side hem.

After cutting the panels, join them with tiny French seams. Turn double hems in the sides, 1 inch deep. Press and machine-stitch using 8 to 10 stitches to the inch.

For top hem, follow directions on page 281 for plain casing with heading. Many fabrics used for glass curtains tend to stretch with hanging. To overcome this, hang curtains on rod for several days. Then make a 3-inch hem, preferably double. To make a 3-inch double hem, turn 3-inch fold to underside. Press. Turn another 3-inch fold, making the hem double. It may be stitched by machine or hemmed by hand.

Ruffled Curtains

Curtains with ruffled edges are the favorite of all informal window treatments. They are generally made of crisp light-weight or sheer fabrics and are tied back to the edge of the window frame. More formal ruffled curtains are also possible. The formal types hang straight from the curtain rod and are made of softer fabrics, such as pongee, ninon and silks.

In determining the finished length of the curtain, subtract the width of the ruffle that falls below the bottom edge of curtain body but add 3 inches for top casing and heading and ¼ inch for lower edge. For width, allow 2½ to 3 times the finished width, adding ½ inch for seam allowance joinings, 1 inch for double hems for outer side edges, and ¼ inch for center side hems or seams.

A ruffling strip should be cut 2 to 3 times the finished length and width of the curtain. A fuller ruffle gives a more luxurious, expensive look. Although the ruffling strip can be cut on the lengthwise or crosswise grain, the lengthwise grain is preferred. If necessary, the strips should be joined with a tiny French seam. A small hem is used to finish the raw edges. When the ruffle is attached to the body of the curtain with a heading, both edges are hemmed, but when the ruffle is attached to the curtain with a seam only one edge must be hemmed. Using the narrow hemmer attachment will simplify this task a great deal.

It is also easier to use the ruffler attachment when making ruffles. Directions for making ruffles are found on page 232.

RUFFLE WITH HEADING. On the body of the curtain, measure 3 inches down from top edge. Do not apply ruffles above this point. Make a ⅛-inch double hem on bottom and center-side edges of curtain body. With right sides up, pin gathering stitches on ruffle to stitches on hem. At corners, allow enough extra fullness to make ruffle fall gracefully around corner. Stitch on gathering line. Be careful not to catch in folds of the fabric.

RUFFLE WITHOUT HEADING. Place ruffle on top of curtain body, wrong sides together and stitch ¼ inch from edge. Press seam toward curtain. Turn ruffle back over curtain, right sides together. Press fold formed along edge of seam allowance. Stitch along first row of stitching, enclosing the raw edges as in a French seam.

To finish curtain body, make a ½-inch double hem on outer edge. Begin at top of curtain body and continue to lower edge of ruffle. At top edge, make a casing and heading as shown on page 281.

RUFFLE VALANCE. Sometimes a ruffle valance is used with ruffled curtains. The finished length of the ruffle valance is the same as the finished width of the curtain body. Finish both edges of the ruffling strip with ⅛-inch double hems. After making the ruffle, pin line of gathering stitches to top row of stitching for casing. Stitch on this line.

RUFFLED TIE-BACKS. To determine size of tie-back, hang curtains on rod. Put tape measure around curtain, as if it were the tie-back, to get the desired effect. Add 1 inch to this measurement for seam allowance.

TIE-BACK WITH ONE RUFFLE. Cut 2½-inch-wide band the necessary length. Stitch the ruffle to the band with a plain seam along one long edge beginning and ending ½ inch from ends. With right sides together, stitch ends of band together with ½-inch plain seam. Turn band to right side. Turn in free edge of band and pin to ruffles along gathering line. Top-stitch along folded edge.

TIE-BACK WITH RUFFLE ON BOTH SIDES OF BAND. Cut two bands, each 1½ inches wide. To one of the bands, pin ruffle along one edge, right sides together. Pin second band in place along ruffle, right side down. Stitch across ends and down length of band. Turn band right side out and press. Second ruffle is applied as for one ruffle tie-back.

Café Curtains

Café curtains may be made in many variations. You may use two or more tiers in the same or varying lengths. You may use a café curtain on the bottom half of the window only and combine it with a valance of full-length over-curtains. Almost any heading may be used.

First, attach café rods and brackets to window frame, or rod and sockets to inside of window frame. If there are horizontal wood strips between the panes of glass in the window, the rod (or rods) should be mounted even with one of the strips.

Check the measurement for each tier carefully. For the bottom tier, measure from top of rod to sill or apron. Add 2½ to 3 inches for bottom hem (6 inches for double hem on sheers). Add the necessary amount, depending upon heading used, for the top hem allowance. For upper tiers, measure from rod which will hold tier to rod directly below it. Add 3 inches for overlap, 2½ to 3 inches for lower hem (6 inches if double hem is used) and the necessary amount for top hem allowance, depending on heading used.

TWO TIERED CAFÉ
THREE TIERED CAFÉ

In order for the curtains to fall in pleasing folds, allow at least two times the finished width of the curtains. Add 1½ inches for each side hem (2 inches for double hem) and ½-inch seam allowances if joining seams are necessary.

Finish the side and lower edges with appropriate hems. Use special heading for top of each tier. Various types are described on page 281.

Draperies

Draperies may be lined or unlined. Unlined draperies are used in informal treatments. They are made of light- or medium-weight fabrics which are attractive on both sides. Loosely woven fabrics are very effective when unlined, when the sun shines through, casting shadow within the room.

Lined Draperies

Lined draperies are made of medium- to heavy-weight fabrics. The lining provides additional weight, causing the fabric to hang in deeper, more formal folds. Linings also protect drapery fabrics from dust and from sun-fading, presenting a more attractive appearance from the outside of the house.

Before cutting out the draperies determine the length and width of each piece. To finished *length,* add:

- 1 inch for heading or the amount that will extend above the rod,
- Plus 4 inches for the top hem,
- Plus bottom hem: single—5 inches; or double—9 inches.

If pleater tape is to be used, no top hem is needed. Allow only ½-inch seam allowance for attaching the pleater tape.

For *width:*

- Allow 2 to 2½ times the finished width for regular drapery fabrics, and 3 to 4 times the finished width for very sheer fabrics.
- Add 1½ inches for each side hem (1 inch for hem and ½ inch for seam allowance).
- Add ½ inch for seam allowances to join lengths of fabric for multiple-width draperies.

Cut out draperies according to instructions on page 275.

To join fabric lengths, clip or cut off selvages and press. Pin fabric lengths together, carefully matching patterns. It is often best to slip-stitch edges together for perfect matching. Stitch and press seams open.

FINISHING UPPER EDGE OF LINED DRAPERY. Place stiffening on inside of drapery fabric with upper edges even and ends 1½ inches from side edges of drapery. Stitch along lower edge of stiffening.

Turn top hem to inside along edge of stiffening.

When pleater tape is used, lap the tape ½ inch over the top edge of the drapery, right sides up. Top-stitch

in place. Then turn the pleater tape to the inside and stitch along lower edge of tape through all thicknesses.

Preparation of Lining

LINING WIDTH. For multiple-width draperies, lining fabric must be the same width as the fabric. Draperies made of a single fabric width may use a lining fabric 4 inches narrower than fabric width.

CUTTING. Cut lining 4 inches narrower than drapery. For multiple-width draperies cut 2 inches off each side edge so that fabric and lining seams will match.

Cut lining 1½ inches shorter than the finished length of the drapery. This allows 2½ inches at the bottom (2 inches for hem and ½-inch turn-in) and ½-inch seam allowances on top and both side edges.

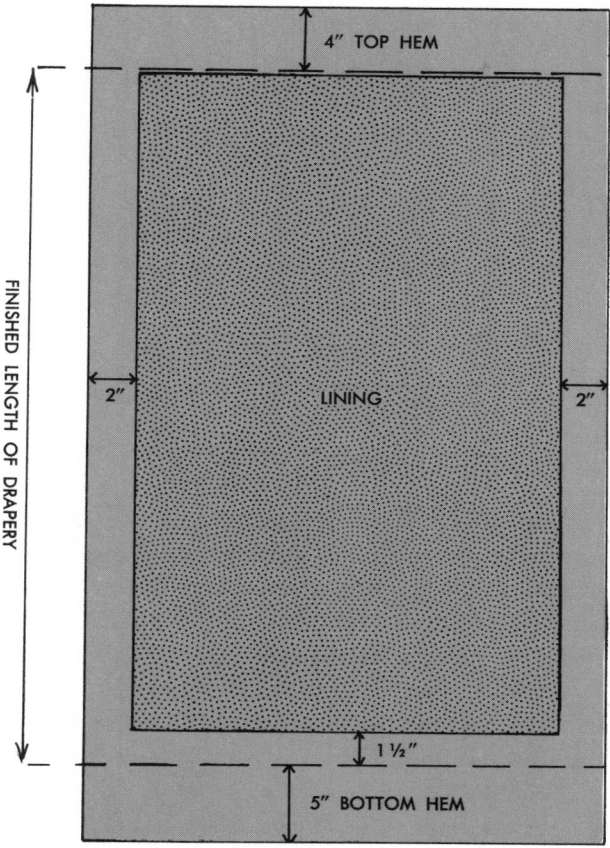

JOINING LINING LENGTHS. Match width of lining lengths to corresponding widths of drapery lengths. Lining and drapery seams will be matched together. Stitch lining seams. Trim seam allowances to ½ inch. Press open.

Turn in ½ inch at upper and lower edge of lining and press.

Turn up and stitch a 2-inch hem at lower edge of lining.

JOINING LINING TO DRAPERY. Place lining over drapery, right sides together. Pin both side edges of lining and drapery together. Start folded top edge of lining 3½ inches down from the top of the drapery. Stitch in a ½-inch seam. Clip seams every 3 to 4 inches and press open.

Turn to right side and center lining over drapery. Pin seams of lining and drapery fabric together on multiple-width draperies. Press. There will be a 1-inch side hem of drapery fabric showing on either side of the lining. Turn in the edge of the side hem above the lining. Miter the top corner and slip-stitch the side hem in place. Pin the top edge of the lining over the lower edge of the top hem or pleater tape. Slip-stitch the lining to the top hem or pleater tape.

If pleater tape is not being used, make pleats according to directions on page 282.

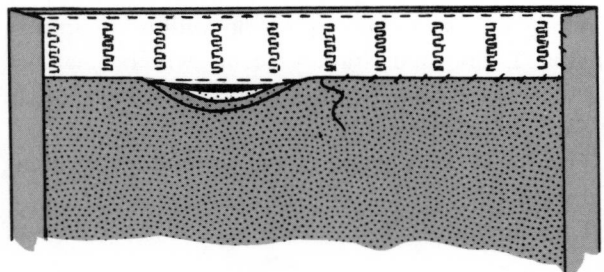

FINISHING LOWER EDGE OF LINED DRAPERY. Allow drapery to hang for several days before finishing lower edge. It is much more accurate to turn and adjust the hem after the drapery has been hung. The fabric of your drapery will affect the finished length. Heavy fabrics will hang straight and some may stretch longer, while crisp, light-weight fabric will billow out and may require slightly more length.

Finish the lower edge in a single or double hem according to the allowance planned. For a single hem, turn in the edge and turn hem up the correct width.

For a double hem, turn up the edge one-half the amount allowed and then turn the same width a second time. Slip-stitch hem in place.

Turn in the edge of the side hem below the lining. Miter lower corner and slip-stitch the side hem in place.

The lining hem hangs free from the drapery hem and overlaps the top edge by about 2 inches. The lining hem is held to the drapery hem with a French tack every 12 to 14 inches.

Unlined Draperies

To Measure:
- To finished *length,* add 1 inch for heading or the amount that will extend above the rod,
- Plus 4½ inches for the top hem,
- Plus bottom hem: single—5 inches; or double—9 inches.

If pleater tape is to be used, no top hem is needed. Allow only ½-inch seam allowance for attaching to the pleater tape.

For *width:*

Allow 2 to 2½ times the finished width for regular drapery fabric and 3 to 4 times the finished width for very sheer fabrics. Add 1½ inches for each side hem (1 inch for hem and ½ inch for turn-in). Add ⅝-inch seam allowances to join lengths of fabric for multiple-width draperies.

Follow cutting directions on page 275.

TO JOIN FABRIC LENGTHS. Clip or cut off selvages and press. Pin fabric lengths together, carefully matching patterns. Stitch and press seams open. Pinking seams is a satisfactory finish for most fabrics but sheer fabrics that ravel may need to be French-seamed. Extensive seam finishing on these long seams will cause puckering.

TO FINISH UPPER EDGE OF UNLINED DRAPERY. Place stiffening on inside of drapery fabric ½ inch from upper edge with ends 1½ inches from side edges of drapery. Stitch along lower edge of stiffening. Turn top edge of drapery over stiffening and press. Turn top hem to inside along upper edge of stiffening. Stitch along lower edge of stiffening through all thicknesses.

When pleater tape is used, finish same as for lined drapery, page 279.

TO FINISH SIDE EDGES OF UNLINED DRAPERY. Turn in side edges ½ inch and press. Turn in 1 inch for a hem and miter upper corners. Pin in place. Slip-stitch or machine-stitch hem to within 6 inches of finished length.

If pleater tape is not being used, make pleats according to directions on page 282.

TO FINISH LOWER EDGE OF UNLINED DRAPERY. Finish lower edge in a single or double hem same as for lined draperies, page 280. After hem is turned up, continue side hems to the lower edge. Miter corners at lower edge and stitch in place.

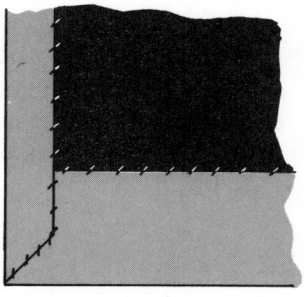

Headings

Headings give an attractive finish to the top of curtains and draperies. There are many different types which can be used in a variety of ways. Some are straight, while others may be pleated and scalloped.

PLAIN CASING WITH HEADING. A hem is placed in the top edge of the curtain. After the rod casing has been stitched, the part above the rod is called a heading. In deciding on the width of the hem, determine the width of the heading. To this add one-half the distance around the rod, ¼-inch ease, and ¼-inch seam allowance.

After the hem has been made, place rod inside hem along stitching line. Put a few pins above the rod to mark the width of the casing. Remove rod. Stitch along marked line. When the finished curtain is slipped on the rod, you will have the effect of a small ruffle above the rod.

LOOPED TOPS. Straight or shaped bands of fabric, decorative tape or braid can be used for making loops. Sew loops to top of straight hem or attach with facing to seam at top edge. If you wish, sew only one end of loop and attach other end in a decorative way, using a button and buttonhole.

READY-MADE CAFÉ CURTAIN HEADING. This is a decorative cotton braid with loops woven into it. It is available in different styles and colors. The braid is stitched flat to the top hem and inserted through the loops.

CLIP-ON RINGS. The top edge of the curtain is finished with a hem. The rings are clipped to the hem, at even intervals, and the rod slipped through the rings.

FOUR-CORD SHIRRING. When this heading is used, the total fabric width should be 3 times the finished width. At top edge, turn down fabric 4¼ inches to the wrong side and press. Turn under the raw edge ¼ inch and press.

Mark lines for cording beginning at stitching line. Place a mark ¼ inch from stitching for the first cord, then marks at 1 inch and 1¼ inches for second cord; at 2 inches and 2¼ inches for third; 3 inches and 3¼ inches for fourth. A ¾-inch space is left between each cord.

Use cable cord of ⅛-inch diameter. Buy four times the total fabric width plus four feet. Insert the cord in hem against the stitching. Stitch on marked line using cording and zipper foot. Stitch on the second marked line. Insert cord and stitch on third line which is just above cording. Continue in this manner until the four rows of cording have been inserted.

Stitch down one side edge, across cords, to hold them securely in place. Pull up cords from opposite end to desired length, distributing fullness evenly. Stitch across ends to hold cording securely.

READY-MADE SHIRRING TAPE. Two- and four-cord widths are available. Turn down ¾-inch fold at top. Stitch tape flat to wrong side of fabric above the top cord and below the bottom one. Stitch along one side edge to hold cords in place. Draw up fullness from other side and stitch.

PLEATED HEADINGS. This is the type of heading used on draperies. To keep the pleats standing upright, a stiffening fabric such as crinoline or buckram must be used. A 4- to 5-inch top hem is pressed into place with the raw edge turned under ½ inch.

Cut stiffening the same width as the top hem. Open hem and place edge of stiffening inside the tuck-under fold of the hem. Stitch along edge of fold. Turn hem back into place with stiffening inside. Pin hem into place. Press and stitch.

To determine the size and placement of pleats, you must first know the amount of fabric you have for pleating. To get this figure, subtract from the total fabric width the finished width of the drapery. There should be an uneven number of pleats on each panel and each pleat should fall in graceful folds. Try pleating a piece of fabric to see how deep the pleats should be.

Here is an example of how this is done:

You have 40 inches to pleat. You want each pleat to be about 5 inches deep. Divide 5 inches into 40 inches. You will have eight pleats. But, you want an uneven number of pleats. And so you divide seven pleats into 40 inches. Each pleat will be almost 5¾ inches deep. You decide that your pleat will be too bulky.

Therefore, you try dividing nine pleats into 40 inches. Each pleat will be a little less than 4½ inches. You try making a 4½-inch pleat. This looks better than the 5¾-inch pleat. And so nine 4½-inch pleats is your selection.

To mark the place for the pleats along the top of the drapery, measure in, from the outer side edge of the drapery, the distance that the rod curves into the wall. This is where the outermost pleat will be. Mark the 4½-inch width of the pleat.

The innermost pleat will be 2 inches in from the center side edge of the drapery; again mark the 4½-inch width of the pleat.

The third pleat is centered between the two outside pleats. The rest of the pleats are evenly spaced between the center pleat and each side edge pleat. Be sure to mark the width of each pleat.

Form the pleat by pinning the markings for each pleat together with the folded width of the pleat on the right side. Stitch the markings together on the right side, from the top edge to ¾ inch below the heading.

You are now ready to make the type of pleat you desire.

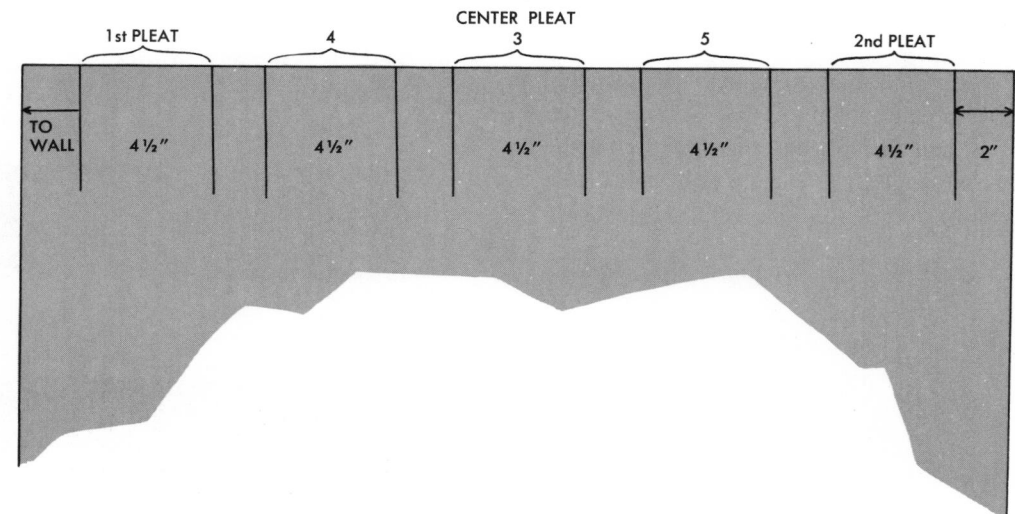

FOLDED PLEATS. Leave pleats as they are. Press and attach to rod with rings or loops. These are not suitable for heavy fabrics.

BOX PLEATS. Find center of pleat fold. Pin to stitching that holds fold in place. Now, there are folds of equal width on either side of the stitching line. Press. Sew pleats into place, tacking from wrong side.

If the rod will show, use rings or loops at the top center of each pleat. If the rod is to be covered, attach hooks to wrong side of pleat.

PINCH PLEATS. Divide fullness of pleat fold into three equal, smaller folds. Baste top and front edges of folds together. Press. Machine-stitch across the folds at the bottom of the heading.

FRENCH PLEATS. Divide fullness of pleat fold into three equal, smaller folds. At the bottom of the heading, sew by hand through the three pleats on the right side of the fabric. Pull thread up tight and fasten securely. Top edge of heading is not pressed into pleats.

PLEATER TAPE. Stiffening in the top hem is not necessary when pleater tapes are used. Leave only ½-inch allowance above the finished top edge. Place top of tape across top edge of fabric, right sides up, with tape overlapping about ½ inch of fabric. Pin and stitch. Turn tape to wrong side and press. Turn under raw edges of tape at side hems and pin lower edge of tape to fabric. Stitch only along the bottom edge of tape. Insert hooks in pockets. Pleats are made automatically. For sheer fabrics, make double hem on top, the width of the tape, to prevent tape from showing through.

PLEATER TAPE WITHOUT HOOKS. This tape is made with spaced slots. It is stitched flat to the top of the curtain or drapery. Pleats are made as the rod is run through tape casing and slots.

SCALLOPED HEADINGS. The width of top hem and interfacing depends upon depth of scallop used. There should be an even number of scallops on each panel. For a 3-inch scallop, allow 4¼ inches for top hem. Make hems on side and bottom edges of curtain. Fold top edge down 4¼ inches on the right side of the fabric. Pin and press in place.

Draw scallop pattern on interfacing strip. Be sure the number of scallops, the size and the space between them, form a pleasing look in proportion to the curtains. Pin interfacing to wrong side of the fabric along folded top edge. Then pin along lower edge of interfacing. Using a small stitch, stitch along scallop markings on interfacing. Cut scallops out, ¼ inch from stitching. Clip seam allowance. Turn hem to wrong side. Press scallops evenly along seam. Turn edge of hem under ¼ inch. Press and stitch.

Other decorative shapes can be made in the same manner. Attach loops or rings to points of scallops.

SCALLOPS WITH PINCH PLEATS. A special pleater tape is available for this purpose. Apply tape to right side of fabric. Cut out scallops and turn tape to underside. Stitch lower edge of tape to fabric. Insert pleater pins for pleats.

Weights

Weighting will make your curtains and draperies hang more evenly. Weighted tapes and lead weights are available in many sizes.

SMALL SHOT INSIDE FABRIC CASING. This type of weighting is sold by the yard. It is most satisfactory when used on medium- to light-weight fabrics. Cut weighting strip as long as the width of the curtain. Lay inside the bottom fold of the hem. Turn under the raw edges at the ends of the casing, forcing out the last piece of shot if necessary. Tack inside each side corner of the hem. Further tacking is unnecessary, as its own weight will hold it in place as the curtain is hanging. Remove before washing.

INDIVIDUAL LEAD WEIGHTS. Individual weights are used on heavier fabrics. You may buy sew-on or pin-on weights. For lined draperies, cover weight with lining fabric. Attach at top of fabric hem on the wrong side, underneath lining hem. Place one weight near each side hem. For longer, heavier draperies, use one weight opposite each fixture which attaches drapery to rod. For unlined draperies, cover weight with drapery fabric and fasten to lower hem on the wrong side.

TO COVER WEIGHTS. Cut two pieces of fabric in the shape of the weight, leaving ¼-inch seam allowance on each side. With right sides facing, stitch around three sides, with scant ¼-inch seam. Trim seam close to stitching. Turn right side out. Drop weight into pocket. Finish last side, turning edges in and stitching by hand.

Another very satisfactory method is to cut one piece of fabric the size of the weight, with ¼-inch turn-under on each side. Turn under edges a scant ¼ inch and press. Place patch on drapery and sew by hand around three sides. Drop weight into pocket. Sew fourth side.

Anchoring Draperies

At the outside edge of the drapery, sew plastic rings to the top and bottom corners. Screw a cup hook into the wall where each corner of drapery should meet the wall. Hook rings on drapery into cup hooks. This will hold curtains and draperies in place.

VALANCES

Valances should blend in style and fabric with the draperies or curtains and with the room decor. They conceal drapery hardware and also help to balance the proportions of a window or to connect several windows treated as one.

The depth of the valance depends upon the height of the window. Generally, the deepest part of the valance should be from one-sixth to one-ninth the length of the curtain. You should experiment to find the best length for your window.

Shaped Valances

Permette, a special, firm buckram, is made especially for this purpose. It holds the valance stiff and straight, as it hangs from a regular curtain rod. Cotton flannel is often used for interlining.

Tape a piece of heavy paper to the curtain rod. Determine the depth and shape of valance desired. Using the paper as a pattern, cut the buckram to the measurements of the finished valance. Cut interlining and fabric to same shape, leaving 1-inch seam allowance on each edge. Cut lining, leaving ¼-inch seam allowance.

Baste interlining to wrong side of fabric. Then place interlining against buckram. Turn 1-inch seam allowance over buckram. Clip and notch edges as required for curves. Catch-stitch raw edges to buckram. Pin lining to back of buckram, turning raw edges under ½ inch. Slip-stitch to turned edge of drapery fabric and interlining. Sew hooks or loops to the back of the finished valance, about 1½ inches down from the top edge. Hang on curtain rod.

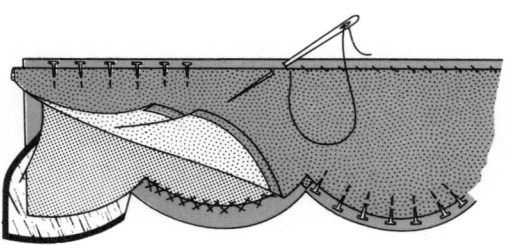

Many variations are possible through use of different shapes on top and bottom edges and through the use of decorative braids and trims.

Soft Valances

Soft valances are shortened versions of the curtains and draperies which they resemble. They may be unlined, lined or interlined, depending upon the weight of the fabric used.

First, determine the length desired. Add 2 inches for the hem and the amount necessary for the heading. Any type of heading may be used. Figure the fullness and construct, following directions for the corresponding type of curtain or drapery. The only difference is in the length and in the depth of the bottom hem.

BEDSPREADS

Bedspreads are fun to make. Begin with a few rules and then let your imagination run free. Directions for basic types of spreads are given here. Combine them and trim them; the variations are endless.

Important Measurements

Begin by taking measurements when the bed is made up with blankets and sheets in place, since these will increase the size of the bed. Measure top length, top width, side overhang, foot overhang, head overhang, depth of top mattress, top of box spring to floor and "returns" at head overhang. With these measurements, it is possible to make any type of spread.

The term "return at head overhang" is one used in discussing beds with headboards. It is an extension of the side treatment at the head end. It rounds the corners and runs 6 to 10 inches in along the headboard, holding the side overhang in place. The return is also used on beds without headboards, when the head end is against the wall.

To the measurements, add ½ inch for each seam allowance and 2 inches for hems. The bottom hem should clear the floor by ½ to 1 inch. If the pillow is to be covered by the spread, add 30 inches to the top length measurement to allow for pillow covering and tuck-in. In planning the yardage requirements, the full width of the fabric is always placed down the center of the bed. Any piecing necessary is done on either side. This may increase the yardage required.

All bedspreads described here are for beds with headboards only. If your bed has a footboard, do not add foot overhang. Allow only for tuck-in at foot. If you do not have a headboard, add head overhang.

Draped or Throw Spread

To determine size, use this formula:

Total length = Top length + foot overhang + head tuck-in + hems (2).

Total width = Top width + side overhang (2) + seam allowance (4) + hems (2).

Cut one length of fabric and place it, full width, down the center top of the bed. Join side sections of equal length to center section. Cording can be inserted in the seams, or braid and fabric bands added for decorative effect.

Corners may hang in points or be rounded. Finish edges with hem, cording or a novelty trim.

Three-Section Tailored Spread

To determine size, use this formula:

Top section:

Length = Top length + foot overhang + head tuck-in + hems (2).

Width = Top width + ½-inch seam allowance on each side (+ 2 seam allowances if top piecing is required).

Side sections:

Length = Top length + head tuck-in + hems (2).

Height = Side overhang + hem (1) + seam allowance (1″).

Place center section down top of bed. Piece side to cover top section, if necessary. Leave ½-inch seam allowances at side edges of top.

Hem side overhang sections at bottom and at foot end. Join side overhangs to top section, starting at the head end with plain seam. Foot overhang and side sections will just meet at the foot corners of the bed. Hem side and bottom edges of foot overhang. Hem edge at head of bed.

These spreads are generally lined, because the underside shows at the open corners.

Fitted Spread with Box-Pleated Corners

To determine size of top section:

Length = Top length + seam allowances (2).

Width = Top width + side seam allowances (2) + seam allowances for piecing, if necessary (4).

Place full width of fabric down center of bed. Piece sides, if necessary. Cut off excess at side edges, leaving ½-inch seam allowance. If lining is used, cut to exactly the same measurements as the fabric sections. Cord edges around sides of top section, if desired.

To determine size of overhang section:

Sides: (Cut 2, on lengthwise grain).

Width = Top length + 3 inches for pleats (2) + seam allowance (2).

Height = Side overhang + seam allowance (1) + hem (1).

End, or Foot Overhang: (Cut 1, on crosswise grain).

Width = Top width + 9 inches for pleat (2) + seam allowance (2).

Height = Foot overhang + seam allowance (1) + hem (1).

Front Returns: (Cut 2, on crosswise grain).

Width = 12″ for return + 9″ for pleat (1) + seam allowance (1) + side hem (1).

Height = Head overhang + seam allowance (1) + hem (1).

If overhang sections are to be lined, cut height of lining 1½ inches shorter than bedspread fabric.

Join side sections to end section with ½-inch seams. Press open. Lay out joined sections on a flat surface.

From seam, measure 3 inches into side section and mark. Pin a fold on this line. Measure into end section from seam, 3 inches and 9 inches. Mark each point. Pin a fold on the 9-inch mark. Bring pinned folds together to meet on the 3-inch line on the end section. This is your box pleat. The seam is at the inside turn of the pleat. Repeat on other seam. Press pleats.

Hem inside edges of front returns and join returns to side sections. Make pleats as before, measuring 3 inches into the side overhang, 3 inches and 9 inches into the front returns. Finish hem on overhang and join overhang to top section.

Fitted Spread with Mock Pleats at Corners

Cut spread as for spread with box-pleated corners, except, do *not* add pleat allowance. Instead, add 4 inches to end overhang, 4 inches to each side overhang, and 2 inches to each front return section. Turn

back a 2-inch fold to the wrong side on each side end. Turn in raw edges and hem. Hem bottom edges of all overhang sections.

Cut four strips for backing pieces, 7 inches wide and the height of the overhang sections. On each piece, make ½-inch side hems and 2-inch bottom hem. Make center fold down each backing piece.

Place one side edge of end-overhang section on top of the backing, against the center fold, matching bottom hems. On the other side of the center fold, place the adjacent edge of the side overhang, matching bottom hems. Overhang sections should meet exactly, and completely cover the backing piece. Stitch overhang pieces to backing, a scant ½ inch from the top edge. Repeat for other side and end corner, then for sides and front returns. Join overhang to top section.

A decorative touch may be added by using a different fabric for the backing pieces.

Other Fitted Spreads

Overhang sections for fitted spreads may be varied in many ways: they may be pleated all around, made with spaced pleats, gathered, gathered with ruffles, etc.

Boxed Spread with Dust Ruffle Attached

Make top of spread, as in fitted spread. Cord edges. Make boxing:

Height = Depth of top mattress + seam allowances (2).

Side lengths (2) = Top length + seam allowances (2).

Head and foot lengths = Top widths + seam allowances (2).

Join all corner seams. Apply cording to lower edge of boxing.

Make dust ruffle:

Height = Distance from top of box spring to floor + seam allowance (1) + hem (1).

Length = Twice the distance to be covered by the dust ruffle.

Join lengths together with ½-inch seam allowances and press seams open. Hem bottom edge and inside edges of returns. Gather along top edge. Join skirt to lower edge of boxing. Join top edge of boxing to top section of spread.

The attached flounce may also be made with inverted box pleats at the corners, with pleats all the way around, or with grouped pleats.

Ruffles may be added to gathered skirt and to lower edge of boxing.

Separate Dust Ruffle Covering for Box Springs

This type of covering is placed between mattress and springs.

For the strip which covers side of box springs, cut strips 5 inches wide. The length will follow this formula: Top lengths (2) + top width (1) + 8 inch return (2) + seam allowances for joining seams.

Join strips together. Place around top edges of the box spring, wrong side up. Outer edge should extend ½ inch beyond the edge of the box spring. Miter corners. Press seams.

For the center piece, cut muslin to fit across the top of the box spring, inside the fabric strips. Allow ½-inch seam allowance on all sides.

Pin muslin to facing strips, starting at the foot edge and working to the head on each side. Hem muslin across head edge, between front returns. Stitch muslin to facing strips with ½-inch seam. Press seam open.

Replace muslin and facing on top of box spring, right side up.

For dust ruffle: Cut strips for flounce.

Height = Distance from top of box spring to floor + hem (1) + seam allowance (1).

Length will be determined by the type of flounce.

Dust ruffle may be pleated or gathered, in any variation desired. First, hem bottom edge. Gather or pin pleats in skirt, and stitch across top of skirt to hold fullness in place. Pin, then stitch dust ruffle to top section covering box spring.

The dust ruffle may be attached in other ways. A pleated flounce may be applied to box spring with twill tape. Allow 2½ inches extra on the height of the flounce. Stitch pleats into place both at the top edge and 2 inches down from the top. Stitch twill tape along pleated top edge. Pin flounce to box spring, gathering in fullness of tape at the corners. With strong thread and curved needle, whip tape to box spring.

Gripper tape provides a flounce that will detach easily for washing. Sew socket edge to box spring 2½ inches in from the edge. Stitch ball side to wrong side of flounce at the top edge of 2½-inch allowance. Snap flounce into place.

Coverlet

To determine size, use this formula:

Length = Top length + depth of top mattress (2) + hems (2) + overlap (2 to 3 inches on each end).

Width = Top width + depth of top mattress (2) + hems (2) + overlap (2 to 3 inches on each side) + seam allowances, if piecing is necessary.

Lining: Cut to same measurements as fabric.

Place full width of fabric down center top of bed. Join side sections to achieve required width. Edges will extend 4 to 5 inches below top of box spring on all sides (overlap + hem allowances). If cording, fringe, or other edging is to be used, stitch to right side of fabric.

Pin lining to coverlet, right sides together. Match side piecing seams of lining to corresponding seams in fabric. Stitch around sides and foot of coverlet. Turn coverlet right side out. Press. At head, turn in raw edges and slip-stitch together.

Other Spreads to Use with Dust Ruffle

The coverlet is actually a shortened version of the draped spread. You may make any type of top spread desired, following directions given for the full-length spread. Change only the height of the overhang. For the top spread, the overhang equals the depth of the top mattress plus 2-to-3 inch overlap over the box-spring. Allow 2 inches for hems. If scalloped or other shaped patterns are made on the edge of the overhang, a stiffening fabric and lining should be used.

PILLOW COVERS

Pillow Sham

Measure length and width of pillow over the fullest parts. Add 1 inch to both measurements.

For top pillow section cut to measured length and width. Stitch trimming, if any, around edge of top section, right sides together. For bottom section cut to measured width. To length, add 3½ inches. Fold section in half lengthwise. Cut on fold. Make 1-inch hem

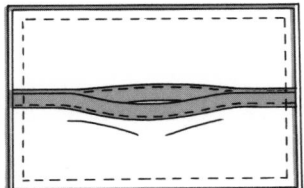

on both cut edges. Overlap hems 1½ inches. Pin overlap together on wrong side.

Pin top and bottom sections together, right sides facing. Stitch around edges. Take pins from overlapped hems at center of bottom section. Turn sham

right side out. If desired, snaps may be sewn on overlapped opening, but it is not necessary.

Decorative edge trimmings such as ruffles, fringe, cording, fabric bands, lace, eyelet can be used.

Separate Pillow Throw, Sewn to Spread

The width of the pillow throw is the same as the width of the spread. Seams are placed to match seams in spread. Side edges are finished in the same manner as on the spread. The pillow throw is lined if the spread is lined.

The pillow throw must be long enough to go over the pillow, to tuck in under the pillow and to tuck in at the headboard. To this length, add 3 inches for hem and seam. Make 2-inch hem at top edge of pillow throw. Finish side edges.

With right sides together, pin bottom edge of pillow throw to spread, about 12 inches from the head edge of the bed. Stitch on pinned line, across entire width. Turn under raw edge of pillow throw, and stitch again.

Place pillow over seam line. When pillow throw is drawn up over pillow, it appears to be tucked in underneath.

Bolster Roll

To determine size of inner form, cut a rectangular piece of heavy muslin or sailcloth, four times the desired height of the pillow, by top width of bed plus 8 inches.

Stitch long edges together. Gather around the edge of one end, and pull gathering up tight to close the end. Fasten securely. Turn tube right side out. Pack tightly and evenly with stuffing material. Close open end same as the first end.

For the cover, measure inner form for correct length and circumference. Allow ½ inch for seams. Join long edges. Cut two fabric circles to fit over end sections, adding ½-inch seam allowance all around.

Stitch one end section to tube section. Turn right side out. Insert inner form. Stitch other end section to tubing by hand.

Bolster covers may be made in any shape in this same manner. The tubing, cut to the correct circumference, will take the shape of any inner form. Only the end pieces are changed. Their shapes are determined by pinfitting the fabric to the inner form.

SLIPCOVERS

If you have time and enjoy precision work, making slipcovers will give you a great deal of satisfaction. It is always fun to see a "new chair" take shape.

Fabric Required

The following chart shows the amount of fabric needed for various types of slipcovers. Remember these are *average* measurements, for *average*-size chairs and *average*-size prints.

In measuring, figure the yardage required for each section of the chair. Ample allowance must be made for centering the decorative motif on each section. With 54-inch fabric, reduce yardage five per cent.

Begin by pinning the fabric to each section of the chair. Place the fabric right side up if there is a pattern or design to be matched. Solid-colored fabrics can be placed wrong side up on the chair. This eliminates the step of having to unpin and turn the seams for stitching after slipcover is fitted.

Place the design so it blends to best advantage with the pattern on surrounding pieces. Be sure the grain line is straight.

Pin the fabric to each section of the chair, beginning at the center of the section, then pinning out toward the seam lines. The fabric should fit smoothly and snugly at every point. As you fit each section according to the following instructions, mark the seam lines,

YARDAGE CHART FOR SLIPCOVERS

Type	No. of Cushions	Yardage				Cording or Trimming
		48″ Wide Plain - Pattern		36″ Wide Plain - Pattern		
Armchair (Club, Lounge & Cogswell)	1	7½	8½	11½	12½	18
Wing Chair (Fanback & Barrel)	1	8	8½	12	13½	18
Ottoman	0	2	2½	3	3½	6
Sofa (6–7′)	2–3	14	15½	21	23	36
	1	13½	15	20½	22½	33
Sofa Bed	2	14½	16	20	21	40
Cushion	1	1¼	1¾	2	2¼	5

following the construction lines of the chair. Cut away the excess fabric, leaving 1-inch seam allowances.

Pin-Fitting and Cutting Slipcovers

INSIDE BACK. Remove chair cushion. Place fabric right side out on the inside back section. Center design, then pin from center out to seam lines. At top seam, make a 2-inch fold. Pin. Then, pin fabric back across top boxing. Allow 1 inch seam allowance beyond back seam. Cut off excess. Cut through center of 2-inch fold.

At the crevice at the bottom of the inside back, allow 5 inches for tuck-in allowance. Cut off excess. At the side seams, allow 1-inch seam allowance. Where inside back is joined to curved section of arm, shape around top of arm, clipping seam allowances where necessary. Mark seam line. Where chair back and arm are separated, allow 5-inch tuck-in.

SEAT. Smooth fabric over seat. Pin from center out. Allow 5 inches for tuck-in at back and side edges of seat.

At seat front, bring fabric down over the spring-edge and pin down the front of the chair. Cut off excess fabric at bottom edge, 2 inches below the skirt line.

OUTSIDE BACK. Center design on chair back with straight of goods running up and down. Pin from center out. At top edge, pin seam line to top boxing. Leave 1-inch seam allowance. At side seams, leave 1-inch seam allowance, and cut away excess. At bottom edge, leave 2-inch allowance.

SIDE BACK (above arms). Grain line runs from top to bottom. Center the design, then pin from center out. Mark seam lines. Pin to top boxing, inside and outside back pieces. Allow 1-inch seam allowance.

FRONT ARM SECTIONS. Place design on front arm section. Grain line should run up and down. Pin from center out. Mark seam lines. Allow 1-inch seam allowance. Remove from chair.

Front arm sections must match perfectly. Lay cut piece, right side down, on right side of fabric. Match design and cut second piece, using the first as a pattern. Trace seam line to second part.

INSIDE TOP ARMS. Grain line should run from front to back. Center design on top of arm. Pin from center out. Mark front seam. Allow 1-inch seam allowance. Mark back seam. Allow 1-inch seam allowance where arm and chair back are joined. Allow 5-inch tuck-in where arm and chair back are separated.

At bottom of inside arm, allow 5-inch tuck-in at seat crevice. Cut away excess and remove piece from chair. Cut second inside top arm section, by matching cut piece to design on fabric and tracing seam lines, as for arm fronts.

Pin both arm pieces to chair. Make sure that design is centered evenly, matching on both sides. Pin from center out. Check marked seam lines.

Sewing Slipcovers

On each section of the slipcover, you will stitch the inside (plain) seams first, then the corded seams.

  a) To make self-covered bias cording, see page 233

  b) To apply cording to the slipcover:

The cording is applied to the right side of the fabric. The raw edges of the cording are placed toward the raw edge of the fabric piece. Stitch cording to the marked seam line of one piece of the fabric, using a cording foot on your machine. Place the second piece of fabric over the piece with the cording, right sides together, and pin the seam. Place the piece with the cording uppermost on the machine and stitch just inside your first row of stitching. The two rows of stitching strengthen the seam and prevent the cording from slipping as it may if you try to stitch cording and seam all at once.

OUTSIDE ARMS. Straight of grain should run up and down, along front edge. Pin from center out. Smooth fabric under curve of arm top. Mark seam line. At bottom edge, cut away excess 2 inches below the skirt line.

All pieces should now be pinned together, except at tuck-ins. Check to see that grain line runs straight on all sections, and that all pinned seams are tight-fitting and as straight as possible. If slight changes must be made, you have ½ inch extra in each seam allowance with which to make changes. Then, trim seam allowance to ½ inch on all seams except zipper seam.

MARKING. On the chair, spread seams open, one at a time. Make chalk marks between layers along pinned lines. Marks will be on the wrong side of the fabric.

At 2- to 3-inch intervals, make straight lines across seams. On curved areas, make cross lines 1 inch apart. These "notch" marks will help in matching seams together again.

BACK SECTIONS. Remove only the pins joining arm sections to inside, outside and side back sections. Remove back from chair, pins still in place. Straighten seams along pinned lines and correct markings. Remove pins.

Matching seam lines and notches, stitch top boxing to top of side back, with plain seam. Press seam open. Put section on chair. Check seam placement.

INSIDE BACK. Stay-stitch top edge and upper corners, and curved lines where inside back meets arm of chair. Stitch cording along seams which join inside back to side back and top boxing. Pin corded edge to top boxing and side backs on marked seam lines, matching notches. Use machine-stitching on cording for stitching guide lines.

OUTSIDE BACK. Stay-stitch across top and upper corners. Attach cording (see page 293) around side and top seams. Pin outside back to top boxing and side back, matching seam lines and notches. Stitch one side and top edge. On other side, where zipper will be inserted, stitch from upper corner down to top of

placket opening, depending on length of zipper to be used.

Return whole back section to chair. Check for fitting on all seams and adjust where necessary.

ARM SECTIONS. Remove arm sections, still pinned, from the chair. Check and straighten seams. Remove pins. Stay-stitch back of inside top arm section (where seams join to back section). Join inside top and outside arm sections with plain seam. Press seam open.

Stay-stitch around edges of front arm section. Stitch cording to side and top edges. Baste front arm section to outside and inside top arm sections. Check fitting on chair. Stitch on basting line. Put arm section back on chair, and check fitting again.

Join arm to back sections. On zipper side, remove arm and back sections from chair. Pin top arm to side back on marked seam line, matching notches. Stitch.

Pin inside top arm to inside back on marked seam lines, to area where tuck-in allowance begins. Stitch, running seam down to edge of tuck-in allowance. Join edges of tuck-in allowance.

INSERTING ZIPPER. Be sure to use a slipcover zipper with wider tape. Trim the corded seam allowance to ½ inch along placket opening. Place the open zipper face down with top end of zipper at lower edge of slip cover. (If you are putting a skirt on your slipcover, the top end of zipper should be 1 inch from floor. Insert zipper after skirt has been attached.)

Match edge of tape to edge of corded seam allowance. Attach zipper foot and adjust to right-hand side of needle. Stitch close to zipper teeth. Turn in seam allowance on other side of placket opening and press. Turn slipcover to outside and close zipper. Lap folded edge of placket opening over zipper teeth to corded seam line. Stitch across the end and down the side of the zipper to give the appearance of a lapped application.

Now, join the other arm sections to the inside and side back. Then, join outside arm to outside back section.

SEAT SECTION. With plain seams, join front arm sections to spring edge section of seat. Join tuck-in allowance on the sides of the seat section to tuck-in allowance at bottom of arm section. Stitch side edge of tuck-in allowances up to the end of the seam, joining front arm and spring edge. Join tuck-in allowance on back of seat to tuck-in allowance at inside back. Place cover back on chair. If you have checked every section as it was finished, your slipcover should fit perfectly.

Bottom-Edge Finishes

TUCK-UNDER FINISH WITHOUT SKIRT. A snugly fitted slipcover with this finish at the lower edge is difficult to tell from upholstery. Gripper snap tape attached to bottom of slipcover and chair hold the cover firmly in place.

Tack one half of gripper tape to inside edge of chair frame between legs on bottom of chair. Put slipcover on chair and pull down firmly on all sides.

You have left 2 inches of fabric below the lower edge of the chair frame on every side. Mark the bottom edge of the chair on the fabric with chalk. This is the line where fabric will be tucked under. Extend line around chair legs.

At chair legs, cut fabric away ½ inch from chalk line. Apply facing of 1½-inch bias strip to right side of slip cover around leg marking. Stitch on chalk line. Clip seam allowance and turn facing to underside. Fold under edges of slipcover at bottom of chair and turn in raw edges in line with gripper tape tacked to chair frame. Pin other half of gripper tape to this edge. Stitch all edges of tape securely in place. Tape makes it possible to remove cover easily for cleaning.

SKIRT (tailored with 4-inch inverted pleat at each corner). Turn up bottom of chair cover at skirt line. Determine finished height of skirt from cover to floor. Add ½ inch for seam and 1¼ inches for hem.

Cut four strips to this depth, on the crosswise grain of the fabric. Pin one strip to front of chair, centering design. Mark corner edges. Take off chair. Add 8½ inches from each corner marking. Cut away excess. Repeat for sides and back.

Leave zipper corner open. Join strips for skirt at other three corners, with plain ½-inch seams. Press seams open. Hem bottom of strip (1-inch hem and ¼-inch turn-under). Press.

At each joining seam, measure 8 inches away from the seam in both directions. Mark. Bring markings to meet at seam, on right side, forming pleats. Baste folds of pleat together. Press.

At edges left open for zipper, mark ½-inch seam allowance. Measure 8 inches in from seam allowance and mark. Bring markings to seam allowance. Baste and press.

Stay-stitch around top of skirt, through pleats, ½ inch from top edge. Stitch cording to right side of skirt on stay-stitching line. Pin skirt to chair cover. Match

corners and centers on each side first. Pin into place. Skirt is attached to cover by stitching to cording. Begin and end stitching at zipper opening.

Many variations are possible on the skirt section. Continuous box- or knife-pleated, group-pleated, or gathered skirts may be used. They are applied to the chair cover in the same manner as described above.

To hold cover firmly at bottom edge, attach a piece of cotton twill tape to the corner seams of chair cover, just above each chair leg. Place free ends of tape around leg. Draw tapes tightly to inside edge of chair leg. Tie, or fasten with heavy-duty snaps.

Upholstery finish may also be used on cover with skirt. Allow 1-inch seam allowance on seam joining slip cover to skirt. Stitch one side of gripper tape to wide seam allowance and tack other side of gripper tape to chair frame as described on page 295. Snap slipcover to chair frame to hold cover securely in place.

Seat Cushion Cover

Place cushion on chair. Place fabric on cushion, centering design to produce best effect in relation to chair back. Pin from center out to sides. Mark seam lines on outer edges of cushion.

Remove fabric from cushion. Cut away excess, leaving ½-inch seam allowance. Place cut section on fabric, right sides facing. Match design. Using cut piece as a pattern, cut the bottom of the chair cushion.

Place cording on right sides of both sections. Stitch ½ inch from edge. Cording should join on one side of the cushion, about 3 inches from the back corner.

BOXING:

Front. Measure depth of cushion. Add 1 inch for seam allowances (½ inch for each seam). Cut crosswise strip this depth, from selvage to selvage. Center design on front of cushion. Pin across front, around corners and halfway back on each side.

Back. Cut another crosswise piece, the cushion depth, plus 3 inches (2 inches for zipper and ½ inch for each seam), and same length as front.

ZIPPER. The placket opening is in the middle of the back boxing. It must extend around at least one corner for the widest possible opening.

Fold back boxing strip in half lengthwise, and press. Cut on fold entire length. Place strips with right sides facing and stitch together with 1-inch seam. Stitch 1½ inches with regular stitch and back-stitch. Then use machine-basting stitch for length of zipper, returning to regular stitch for balance of strip. Press seam open. Use lapped seam application for inserting zipper. Press the application and remove basting. Front and back sections are now the same width.

Pin back boxing to cushion back, meeting front boxing at center of cushion sides. Mark seam lines. Remove from cushion. Stitch side seams of boxing with ½-inch seams. Press seams open.

Attach top and bottom to boxing. Pin top cover to boxing with right sides together and stitch on cording line. Open zipper. Pin bottom cover to boxing, right sides together, and stitch on cording line. Turn cover right side out through zipper opening and place on cushion.

INDEX

INDEX